Contents

iv

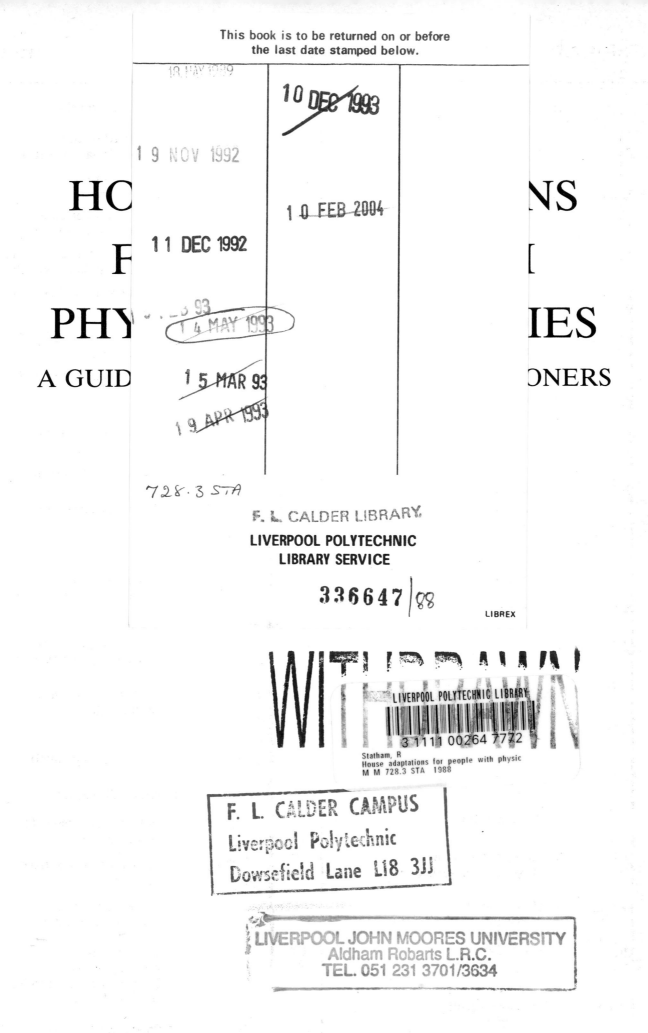

HO...NS
F...
PHY...IES
A GUID...ONERS

HER MAJESTY'S STATIONERY OFFICE

ISBN 0 11 751759 3

Supplementary Technical Reports

Preface

The purpose of this publication is to guide practitioners in the undertaking of house adaptations for disabled people. It is the report of a study commissioned by the Department of the Environment from Home Assessment and Advisory Services for Disabled People; the views expressed are those of the authors, or in respect of individual case studies the reported views of clients or members of project teams, and should not be held to represent the views of the Department.

The major part of the report comprises a series of 22 individual case studies. To protect confidentiality the clients concerned were offered the option of a pseudonym and in the presentation of the reports there is no identification of those clients who elected instead to retain their real names.

In the case studies the products of particular manufacturers are identified where in the authors' judgement there was a likelihood that a reader (for example a practitioner dealing with a case involving similar circumstances on which guidance was being sought) might for assessment purposes need to know the precise product concerned. The Department of the Environment emphasises that it is not being suggested that the product identified should be preferred where a comparable product by another manufacturer might serve equally well for the purpose, nor is it implied that the quality of the product identified is assured.

Each case study is in three parts: the history and circumstances that prompted the undertaking of the adaptation; a record of the adaptation works and an evaluation of the outcome. The central section has subject headings reporting the features incorporated, why they were specified and how they are used. Cross references are made to comparable or alternative provision reported in other case studies. The fold of the end cover of the book has a scale that can be cut out to check measures on plan drawings. A key to symbols and abbreviations used on the drawings is on the inside front cover.

As noted in the introduction, the 22 case studies reported were selected by the authors as representative of successful major house adaptations for the purpose of presenting informative practical guidance. They are not typical of house adaptations generally, and nor should it be assumed that the management procedures reported (and in particular funding procedures) are ones which local authorities may as a matter of course wish to adopt or be expected be adopt. A cautionary note is warranted in respect of the employment of improvement grants, which played a prominent part in the cases reported. The assistance that can be offered by the grant system is limited. Improvement grants (as distinct from intermediate grants) are discretionary and on this account local authorities must, if they are to ensure that grant funding is allocated where it is most needed, balance all circumstances relevant to an application from a disabled person against other applications. Where grant aid is not available other means of raising funds for a house adaptation will need to be explored, for example the possibility of a new or additional mortgage.

The authors and the Department will be pleased to receive comments from practitioners on the guidance presented in this report. Correspondence should be addressed to the Architectural Policy Division, Department of the Environment, 2 Marsham Street, London SW1P 3EB.

Acknowledgements

As readers of this book will clearly appreciate our paramount indebtedness is to the disabled people and their families whose home adaptations are recorded. Their cooperation with us was unlimited in its generosity. They welcomed us into their homes, some of them many times over. They dealt patiently and with great good humour with all our probing and questioning on sensitive issues. They recalled memories that were painful. Their comments on the adaptation work that had been undertaken were invariably thoughtful and informative. Their wish was that the recounting of their experiences should be of benefit to others; the use of this book will, we hope, confirm that their trust is rewarded.

Our own wish would have been for each of them to be personally acknowledged. Most of them elected, however, to have pseudonyms for their reports and there cannot therefore be any names. However, they will know that without their collaboration this book could not have been produced and that our debt to them is sincere and immense.

Among those who assisted and who can be named, there are too many for all to be recorded. There is special gratitude to members of project teams who helped us; notwithstanding their frequently pressurised work schedules they unstintingly gave their time, they tolerated our awkward questions, they readily embraced constructive criticism and they shared with us their wealth of experience.

We record our gratitude to:
Mrs P Abbott, Enterprise 5 Housing Association.
Mr C Altoft, Environmental Health Officer, Enfield Borough Council.
Mrs A Askew, Occupational Therapist, Dudley Social Services Department.
Mr L Atkinson, Architect, The Napper Collerton Partnership.
Mr R Axtel, Surveyor, formerly with Three Rivers District Council.
Mr I Balmer, Administrator, Clinical Services, St Thomas' Hospital.
Mrs W Blanchard, Occupational Therapist, Nottinghamshire Social Services Department.
Mr B Breakwell, Environmental Health Officer, Stroud District Council.
Mr D Capon, S M L Medical Limited.
Mrs C Chenery, Occupational Therapist, formerly with Gloucestershire Social Services Department.
Mr J Coleman, Home Dialysis Administrator, St Thomas' Hospital.
Mr G Collett, Collett Brothers Builders.
Mr M E Davis, Architectural Assistant, Tewkesbury Borough Council.
Ms R Dodd, Project Co ordinator, Horticultural Therapy.
Mr C Edgell, Stannah Lifts Limited.
Mr A Evans, Structural Engineer, London Borough of Harrow Engineering Department.
Mrs J Freeman, Occupational Therapist, Wiltshire Social Services Department.
Mr M J Firmedow, Andrisa Design and Construction.
Mrs M Ford, BBC In Touch programme.

Mrs L Gilland, Occupational Therapist, formerly with Gloucestershire Social Services Department.
Ms J Hammond, Director, Alternative Housing (Walbrook) Limited.
Miss M A Hawkins, Architectural Consultant.
Mrs P Healey, Occupational Therapist, Nottinghamshire Social Services Department.
Mr A Hill, Municipal Building Surveyor.
Mr P Jenner, Architect, formerly with Tewkesbury Borough Council.
Miss L Jones, Abucon.
Mrs R Jones, Occupational Therapist, Mid Glamorgan Social Services Department.
Miss J Kent, Principal Rehabilitation Officer, London Borough of Southwark Social Services Department.
Mrs P Kershaw, Occupational Therapist, Leicestershire Social Services Department.
Mrs S Killick, Occupational Therapist, Hertfordshire Social Services Department.
Mrs L Lee, Occupational Therapist, Cambridgeshire Social Services Department.
Miss E Lundin, Disabled Living Adviser, London Borough of Harrow Social Services Department.
Mrs I Mearns, Principal Occupational Therapist, London Borough of Barnet Social Services.
Mr A Morris, Architect, Shaftesbury Housing Association.
Mr R Newton, Building Surveyor, London Borough of Harrow Architects Department.
Mr L Pescodd, ex Home Dialysis Administrator, St Thomas' Hospital.
Mr P Pickering, Occupational Therapist, Birmingham Social Services Department.
Mrs J Raper, Occupational Therapist, Gloucestershire Social Services Department.
Mrs S Rawlings, Occupational Therapist, Nottinghamshire Social Services Department.
Mr A J Reid, Architect, The Napper Collerton Partnership.
Mr D Richards, Principal Housing Management Officer, Tewkesbury Borough Council.
Mr W J N Ross, Building Surveyor, Welsh Office.
Mrs K Skilling, Occupational Therapist, Newcastle Social Services Department.
Mrs D Sweitzer, Occupational Therapist, Mid Glamorgan Social Services Department.
Miss K Snow, Occupational Therapist, formerly with London Borough of Enfield Social Services Department.
Mr R J Steer, Building Surveyor.
Mr R Stone, Senior Housing Officer, Three Rivers District Council.
Mr J Tarry, Building Surveyor, Nottingham.
Mr T Thornton, Urban Renewal Officer, Kirklees Metropolitan Council.
Mr B G Tibbetts, Architect.
Mrs J Tuckwell, Occupational Therapist, Disability Advisory Service, London Borough of Tower Hamlets Social Services Department.
Mr K Wainwright, Keith Wainwright Development and Planning Consultants Limited.
Mr R Watson, Architect.
Mr R H Warwick Smith, Wessex Medical Equipment Limited.
Mr E G Wilkinson, Director, Hill Brothers of Nottingham Limited.

Mr J White, J and T Builders Limited.
Mrs M Worthington, Occupational Therapist, Cheshire
County Council Social Services Department.

For professional support and for practical guidance on the
organisation of the project we are indebted to Rosemary
Bowden who was Occupational Therapy Officer at the
Department of Health and Social Security during the early
stages of the project and is now District Occupational
Therapist with Oxfordshire Health Authority. Our thanks
are also extended to Stephen Thorpe for his advice and
practical help in site surveys, case study content, drawings,
presentation and an experienced overview of our work.
Our particular thanks, too, to those who have worked
tirelessly towards the final production of the project—
Adrian Shannon for his help and advice in printing the
photographs, Pauline Crowley for collation of photographic
material, Linda Di Mizio for production of sample layouts
and our secretary, Sheila Farley, for handling the enormous
correspondence, collation of information, processing of
reports and preparation of early and final drafts. That all
was achieved with such unfailing goodwill is of merit to
their dedication and belief in the importance of the subject
matter.

The introductory commentary and the section on legislation
and regulations were drafted by Selwyn Goldsmith, the
Department of the Environment's professional adviser on
housing services for disabled people. Our most important
indebtedness is to him; he conceived, devised and
administered the project, supported us throughout and
aided us with his wealth of knowledge and experience in
the field of designing for disabled people.

Rosemary Statham
DipCOT, MBAOT, SROT

Jean Korczak
DipCOT, MBAOT, SROT

Philip Monaghan
BA(Hons), DipArch

Home Assessment and Advisory Services for Disabled
People
Woodcock Hill
Durrants Lane
Berkhamstead
Herts HP4 3TR

Introduction

The background

People who are severely disabled may, on account of their own problems or the effects that their disablement has on those who are caring for them, have special housing needs. But only rarely will they have a requirement for new special housing that has been purpose-designed; their more likely need (taking account perhaps of the support they obtain from relatives, friends, neighbours and local services) will be for suitable modifications to the existing family home, or a move to a nearby house that can be conveniently adapted.

In tackling the housing needs of disabled people, local housing authorities have in recent years been encouraged by government policy and associated legislation and regulations to work in tandem with social services authorities on house adaptations. The principal instrument that has increasingly been used is home improvement grants for disabled people, whose scope under the Housing Act of 1974 was extended in the early 1980s. The growth there has been in recent years in the number of dwellings adapted for disabled people with the help of grants is recorded in table 1.

The essence of successful house adaptations for disabled people is collaboration, between housing and social services authorities, within authorities among the different departments involved, and on the ground among members of the project team. Local authority procedures for organising house adaptations, examining in particular the response to official advice issued in 1978[1], were the subject of the 1982 report "Organising house adaptations for disabled people"; this found that, while social services departments were frequently handicapped by not being able to recruit as many occupational therapists as they needed, cooperation was generally good[2].

Such documentation as is currently available on the practicalities of undertaking house adaptations for disabled people is variable in character and limited in scope[3]. To fill the gap and to provide a substantial practical guidance manual, Home Assessment and Advisory Services for Disabled People (HAAS) was commissioned by the Department of Environment. The manual is aimed primarily at occupational therapists, architects, building surveyors, technicians, environmental health officers and housing and social services administrators, but it will, it is hoped, be of value also to contractors engaged on house adaptation work for disabled people, and disabled people considering adaptations to their home and looking for guidance.

The Case Studies

The brief to HAAS was that the material for the proposed publication would be drawn entirely from individual case studies, the intention being that the cases reported would demonstrate good practice and would collectively represent successful major house adaptations for disabled people; it was on this basis that cases for inclusion were selected by the authors. Initial checks were made through professional

Table 1   **Grants paid to private owners and tenants for disabled persons dwellings,** England 1976–1986

Number of dwellings/£ thousand

	Improvement[1]		Intermediate[2]		All	
	dwellings	amount	dwellings	amount	dwellings	amount
1975[3]	50	..	75	..	125	..
1976	221	160	341	69	562	229
1977	306	259	445	100	751	359
1978	631	576	508	156	1,139	731
1979	1,064	1,052	640	205	1,704	1,257
1980	1,726	1,990	789	283	2,515	2,272
1981	2,449	3,183	954	484	3,403	3,666
1982	4,955	8,991	1,261	927	6,216	9,918
1983	9,969	22,328	1,966	1,851	11,935	24,179
1984	12,597	33,164	2,629	2,533	15,226	35,717
1985	13,271	33,929	2,404	2,196	15,675	36,125
1986P	17,201	36,749	2,036	1,724	19,237	38,474

P Provisional.

[1] Conversion or improvement grants to make dwelling suitable for the accommodation, welfare or employment of disabled persons.

[2] Provision of standard amenities where existing standard amenities are not readily accessible to disabled occupants by reason of their disabilities.

[3] July to December only.

Source: Housing and Construction Statistics. DOE.

contacts (principally architects and occupational therapists) and voluntary organisations, and a notice in the British Journal of Occupational Therapy yielded an encouraging response. Of the some 250 cases brought to the author's attention, about a hundred were considered. Visits were made to the 50 or so that seemed most promising, from which the 22 schemes reported were selected.

A primary consideration was the reporting of a wide range of typical house adaptation features, such as ramped entrances, thresholds, kitchen modifications, roll-in showers, stairlifts and through-floor lifts, and the contents list cataloguing the provision incorporated in each of the case studies confirms the scope of the coverage. In the course of the inquiry examples of distinctive or good alternative solutions to particular problems were obtained from schemes that did not warrant full case study treatment, these being documented in supplementary technical reports.

For each case study the principal source of information was the disabled client and members of the household, along with the evidence of the adapted dwelling at the time of the visit. To corroborate the client's account, checks were made where possible with all members of the team engaged on the project. The authors' decision was that the case study reports must be individual snapshots taken at the time of visiting, and the text was not amended for those cases where subsequent reports indicated that circumstances had changed. The studies do not, for example, report readaptations that were prompted by the probings of the authors when they visited.

Aside from technical provision, a range of variables relating to the characteristics of the disabled clients and their dwellings was considered, and an analysis of these is in table 2. Table 3 summarises for each of the 22 cases the problem that was presented and the means by which it was tackled. Invoking the concept of therapeutic intervention, the definition of the role of a house adaptation on which table 3 is based is:

> Where a disabled client or the members of his family are handicapped by the existing home environment, where the handicap is affected by the disability of the client, and where the handicap can be alleviated by a therapeutic intervention in the form of a house adaptation, either to the existing home of the client or to a house elsewhere.

Of the 18 house adaptations for physically disabled people reported in the case studies, 16 were assisted by public funding. Table 4 summarising how funding was obtained needs to be interpreted with caution; in some instances it was difficult for the authors to obtain reliable and comprehensive information, there were often uncertainties about who paid for what and when, and how much of the cost was carried by the client or his family.

Improvement grants were the principal means of funding, employed in 12 of the 16 cases. In two cases the social services authority made a substantial contribution; elsewhere only some 3 per cent of the cost of all the work was found from social services department votes. The two mobile homes (not included in table 4) were funded by social services, there not being eligibility for an improvement grant. One public sector case was funded wholly by the housing authority.

Table 2. **The 20 disability adaptations: Characteristics of disabled clients and dwellings**

Tenure

*	local authority tenancy	Ali, Chandler, the Patels, French, Watts, Stokes
*	housing association tenancy	Beagle, Henry
*	owner-occupation	Brown, Watson, the Musgraves, Neale, Fletcher, Johnson, the Kidsleys, Collins, Hurrell, Thomas
*	mobile homes	Thorpe, Chamberlain

Household composition

*	client living alone	Beagle, Brown, French, Henry
*	husband and wife both disabled	the Musgraves, the Kidsleys
*	client with spouse	Neale, Fletcher, Watts, Thorpe, Chamberlain
*	client with spouse and children	Ali, Chandler, Watson
*	caring parents with child client	Johnson, Hurrell
*	caring parents with adult child client	Stokes, Thomas
*	parents having disability or handicap	Johnson, the Patels, Thomas
*	siblings with disabilities	the Patels

Cultural diversity

*	disabled client from ethnic minority background	Ali, the Patels

Communication

*	non-English speaking	the Patels
*	speech impairment	Johnson, Henry, Thorpe
*	visual handicap	Brown, the Patels, Johnson

Mobility

*	wheelchair dependent, not independently mobile	Johnson, Hurrell, Thorpe, Chamberlain
*	wheelchair dependent, independently mobile inside the home with electric wheelchair	Beagle, Mr Musgrave
*	wheelchair dependent, independently mobile inside the home with manual wheelchair	Ali, Chandler, the Kidsleys, Henry
*	part wheelchair dependent, part push around on floor	the Patels

*	part wheelchair dependent, part ambulant	Watson, Mrs Musgrave, Fletcher, French, Watts, Stokes, Thomas
*	ambulant	Brown, Collins

Dwelling type

*	bungalow	Watson, the Musgraves
*	chalet bungalow	Thomas
*	terraced house	Fletcher, the Patels
*	semi-detached house	Ali, Neale, Johnson, Watts, the Kidsleys, Stokes, Hurrell
*	detached 2-storey house	Brown
*	ground floor flat	Beagle, Chandler, French, Henry
*	first floor flat	Collins
*	mobile home	Thorpe
*	caravan	Chamberlain

Location

*	north of England	Fletcher, Henry
*	midlands	the Musgraves, the Patels, Johnson, the Kidsleys, Thorpe, Chamberlain
*	south-east	Ali, French, Collins
*	south-west	Brown, Neale, Watts, Stokes
*	London	Beagle, Chandler, Watson, Hurrell
*	Wales	Thomas

Table 3 **The handicaps and therapeutic interventions of the 22 adaptations**

Name	The handicap	The therapeutic intervention
Ali	Existing local authority house unmanageable for chairbound man and family.	Move to adapted 2-storey house.
Beagle	Chairbound woman living in residential home, autonomy precluded.	Move to adapted ground floor flat.
Chandler	Existing wheelchair flat delimiting potential of chairbound man and adversely affecting family relationships.	Adaptation of existing flat.
Brown	Existing home and environment socially isolating and unsupportive for recently widowed visually handicapped woman.	Move to adapted cottage alongside supportive family.
Watson	Woman disabled from childhood, becoming more wheelchair-dependent, existing dwelling not facilitating independent management or family supervision.	Adaptation of existing bungalow.
Musgraves	Couple both chairbound, living in local authority prefab scheduled for demolition.	Move to adapted owner-occupied bungalow.
Neale	House with facilities inadequate and not accessible to man with hemiplegia.	Existing house adapted with through-floor lift.
Fletcher	House not manageable for client with deteriorating disability condition.	Adaptation to ground floor of existing house.
Patels	Local authority house not manageable for 3 siblings with severe disabilities.	Move to adapted 2-storey house.
French	Stresses in family home, independence and autonomy of disabled young woman precluded.	Move to local authority ground floor flat.
Johnson	Family home inconvenient and hazardous for mother with disability caring for severely handicapped son.	Existing house adapted to permit caring in ground floor rooms.
Watts	House with upstairs facilities inaccessible to disabled man.	Existing house adapted with stairlift installation.
Kidsleys	Couple both chairbound, potential for developing quality of life constrained by rented wheelchair flat.	Move to adapted owner-occupied 2-storey house.
Collins	Aged widow unable to manage own home, insecure.	Daughter and son-in-law's house adapted to give self-contained flat.
Henry	Man with hemiplegia in residential home, autonomy precluded.	Move to adapted housing association ground floor flat.
Stokes	Rented cottage not manageable for parents and divorced wheelchair-dependent son.	Move to local authority house adapted to give two self-contained flats.
Hurrell	2-storey house increasingly unmanageable for family with severely handicapped son, becoming progressively more disabled.	Existing house adapted for care in ground floor rooms.
Thomas	Chairbound woman living with mother and disabled stepfather, chalet bungalow precluding convenient management.	Ground floor of existing chalet bungalow adapted and extended.
Thorpe	Existing 3-bedroom house unmanageable for man with hemiplegia and caring wife.	Move to adapted mobile home.
Chamberlain	Caravan home unmanageable and hazardous for elderly husband caring for disabled wife.	Caravan adapted.

| Smith | Renal failure, hospital treatment stressful, inconvenient and uneconomic. | Existing home adapted to provide dialysis treatment room. | Dudley | Renal failure, hospital treatment stressful, inconvenient and uneconomic. | Existing home adapted to provide dialysis treatment room. |

Table 4 **The 16 subsidised disability house adaptations: Summary of costs (£1000s)**

Local authority property		total cost	improve-ment grant	social services dept funding	housing dept funding	other sources
Ali	1984	23.6	7.7	—	15.9	—
Chandler	1978–84	11.2	4.0	0.1	7.1	—
the Patels	1983	7.3	3.8	—	3.5	—
French	1982	(1)	—	—	(1)	—
Watts	1981–3	1.7(2)	—	(3)	0.1	1.5(4)
Stokes	1983–4	29.5	—	—	29.5	—

Housing association property		total cost	improve-ment grant	social services dept funding	housing assoc grant	other sources
Beagle	1980–84	7.8	1.8	1.0	4.1	0.9(5)
Henry	1983	(6)	—	1.2	1.2(7)	—

Owner-occupied property		total cost	improve-ment grant	social services dept funding	client contri-bution	other sources
Watson	1984	9.1	5.7	—	1.4	2.0(8)
the Musgraves	1984	30.5	9.2	10.0	1.8	7.5(9) 2.0(10)
Neale	1984	7.2	5.4	—	1.7	0.1(11)
Fletcher	1983	10.9	6.4	1.3	3.2	—
Johnson	1984	10.2	9.0	0.2	—	1.0(9)
the Kidsleys	1982	(12)	6.4	7.0	(12)	(13)
Hurrell	1984	17.1	10.3	0.5	6.3	—
Thomas	1984	8.8	4.9	0.5	3.4	—

(1) costs not ascertainable

(2) plus costs not recorded, principally client funded

(3) small contribution, not recorded

(4) charitable trust

(5) voluntary organisation

(6) total cost not ascertainable

(7) plus substantial costs not ascertainable

(8) local authority loan

(9) interest-free local authority loan

(10) disturbance allowance

(11) loft insulation grant

(12) total cost and client contribution not ascertainable

(13) A housing association grant of £7,500 for improving the property for sale was part of the package but was not disability-related.

Measures of success

Since each house adaptation case is ad hoc, individual, peculiar and unique it is predictable, as the evidence of the case studies confirms, that there cannot be formula prescriptions for assuring a successful outcome. Although the occupational therapist, the architect and the contractor will each have their own stringent professional standards, the crucial assessment will come from the client, with customer contentment being a valid measure of success. In all the 22 cases reported the disabled clients and their families were pleased with the eventual outcome, notwithstanding the irritations, misunderstandings, delays and shortcomings in execution that invariably accompany any major house adaptation operation. In the majority of cases there was immense satisfaction, with only one where the realisation did not fully match expectations. That there was this degree of customer contentment does not, however, mean that all the cases demonstrate good practice. For the sake of representativeness two mobile homes were, for example, among the cases reported and the proposition that living in a caravan constitutes good practice for a severely disabled person is questionably supportable. But for both customers concerned the accommodation was what they wanted, and their satisfaction cannot be disregarded. Elsewhere in the case studies other examples of unorthodox practice can be found, engineered in the cause of achieving successful solutions.

While the aim of this publication is to guide practitioners by reporting successful adaptations, it happens in practice that many house adaptation schemes on which practitioners embark are ultimately not successful. The cause may be events that cannot be controlled. It may happen that the client dies or becomes permanently hospitalised. Family relationships may already be under stress and the client's marriage may break down while work is in progress. Or despite much preliminary work having been done and the harmful effects there may be on himself and his family, the client may convince himself there will be a miracle cure and put a halt to the operation.

There can be other obstacles for the project team. The client's medical prognosis may be unreliable or unpredictable, and adaptation works undertaken to deal with immediate problems may not anticipate future needs. There may be uncertainty about how positively the client might respond to an environment to promote his independence. Or it could happen that the changed circumstances of the client indicate that the proposed works should be abandoned and an alternative solution developed.

There is acknowledgement therefore that on account of their success the cases reported in this book are not typical of all major house adaptations. That does not, however, prevent lessons being drawn from them. As has been noted, there can be no formula prescriptions for the realisation of good practice or success, and general recommendations cannot therefore be derived from the evidence. Thus the summarised findings are presented simply as guidelines—for the assessment of need, for management and for designers.

Guidelines for the assessment of need

* For the occupational therapists and other professionals in social services departments whose duty it is to consider competing client claims, determine priorities and allocate financial resources equitably (or advise housing authorities on allocation resource) assessments will need to be made with impartiality and sensitivity. In particular there may be a need to examine carefully the claims for priority treatment of articulate and determined clients. The merit of vigorous client advocates is that they know what they want and what might be available, they understand the system and their assessment of their needs may well be in agreement with that of the professionals. They may also have the capability to instruct the architect and the contractor on the work to be done. If the go-ahead is given the prospects for a successful adaptation may well be encouraging. The claims of a client of this kind will, however, need to be balanced against those of others who are not so advantaged, but whose needs may be equally or more compelling. Cases which may warrant special attention and persistency are those where:

  ● the client is inarticulate;

  ● the need is to relieve the burden on a carer (for example of a mentally handicapped child) who may be diffident about seeking help, uncomplaining about difficulties and anxious not to be demanding;

  ● there is more than one person in the household with a disability and needs may conflict;

  ● family relationships are stressful and there is uncertainty whether a house adaptation will alleviate or exacerbate the stress;

  ● the client cannot speak English and has to communicate through an interpreter;

  ● clients are from non-English cultural backgrounds and may have distinct perspectives, for example on the merits of independence and the role and status of women in the household.

Guidelines for management

* Management of a major house adaptation scheme will be better exercised where there is a project team comprising all those who have a direct interest. For the preliminary work this will usually mean (i) the client, (ii) the occupational therapist, (iii) the architect or building surveyor, and (iv) the local authority grants officer where the scheme is grant-aided, or the housing administrator in the case of a public sector property. The contractor will join the project team when the building stage is reached.

* Where the disabled person is being treated in hospital preparatory to his return home, co-operation between hospital and local authority professionals will be essential, with a view to anticipating needs and avoiding delays.

* For clients from non-English cultural backgrounds an awareness of cultural differences will be needed by professionals and the contractor if misunderstandings and frustrations are to be avoided.

* Where a major adaptation to the dwelling in which the client is already living and will continue to live is undertaken, it will help if the client and his family can arrange to live elsewhere while the building work is in progress; should they remain in their home with work going on around them the disturbance and inconvenience with which they will contend may well be troublesome

and disrupting. Where it is proposed that the client is to move from his existing accommodation the element of choice may be introduced into the search for a dwelling suitable for adaptation.

Guidelines for designers

* In all major house adaptations for disabled people attention to detail can be critical. Instructions to the contractor will need to be clear and precise and the contractor will need to check carefully with the client and professionals where there are uncertainties.

* Where a bungalow or ground floor flat having tight circulation is adapted for a wheelchair user, the alternative to extensive reconstruction may be limited modifications only, with wheelchair manoeuvrability problems not being fully resolved.

* A bungalow having a frontage on the building line will more easily be extendable at the rear where bedrooms are at the front and living room and kitchen at the rear.

* Ground floor flats in houses built in the latter part of the 19th century or the early years of the 20th century may be more spacious than flats built since 1920, and potentially more suitable for adaptation for wheelchair living.

* Where for a proposed new adaptation potentially suitable ground floor or bungalow options are not available, consideration may be given to the adaptation of a two-storey house with the incorporation of a through-floor lift.

* Where a family has a public sector tenancy, the search for a two-storey house that can be suitably adapted may well be extended. Post-war public sector houses do not customarily have spaces that can conveniently be adapted for wheelchair use; the small upstairs bathroom will commonly present adaptation problems.

* For private sector clients considering a new adaptation, the two-storey house option may be more practicable, since the search can be among older properties with sufficient space for convenient wheelchair management. It may also be practicable with such properties for the downstairs accommodation to be adapted for wheelchair use, with the upper storey being used by other members of the family.

* Where a through-floor lift is installed, its accessibility and precise location can be of critical importance; the contractor will need to check the installation with care. In a two-storey semi-detached house a lift installation should preferably not be on a party wall where the noise and vibration may irritate the neighbours.

* For personal washing the disabled client may prefer a shower to a bath. A shower installation requires more space for approach, manoeuvre and the actual washing process than does a bath, and when the modification of an existing bathroom is proposed careful consideration will need to be given to space requirements.

* A satisfactory shower installation may be difficult to achieve by adapting an existing bathroom; at ground floor level the floor structure and drainage infrastructure can be constraining, and at first-floor level timber joist construction can present difficulties.

* For wheelchair management in a dwelling where space is restricted it can be helpful for there to be no lobby between a living room or bedroom and the wc. For private dwellings the 1976 Building Regulations did not permit direct access between habitable rooms and wcs, other than for a second wc approached from a bedroom. The 1985 Building Regulations have limited the restriction to rooms where food is prepared or stored.

* Consideration should be given to storage space needed by disabled clients, in particular those with more than one wheelchair; it may be sensible not to lose storage space in favour of living or circulation space.

* Where the possibility of adapting a mobile home for a wheelchair client is proposed, three constraints will warrant consideration. The first is that the floor will be some 700m above ground level, meaning that a long approach ramp has to be constructed, with perhaps a platform lift being needed as well. The second, in part because of the air space below the floor, is thermal insulation. The third is that the layout and planning of the dwelling, determined by dimensional limits associated with transportation, mean that room spaces can be confined and relatively unamenable to adaptation.

Summary

Three principal themes emerge from this brief commentary on the evidence of the case studies. First, that tackling house adaptations for disabled people requires collaboration, co-operation and co-ordination among the range of agencies and individuals involved. Second, that on the practicalities of provision there are no formula prescriptions that can be generally applied. Third, that however diligent professionals and administrators may be, success can be elusive.

In all the 22 adaptation cases reported there was client satisfaction with the outcome, notwithstanding the obstacles, irritations and troubles that were encountered along the way. There are lessons to be drawn from the case studies which follow; they are accounts of achievement that speak for themselves.

[1] "Adaptations of housing for people who are physically handicapped". Joint Circular (DOE 59/78; DHSS LAC (78) 14; Welsh Office 104/78), HMSO, 1978.

[2] DOE, DHSS, Welsh Office. "Organising house adaptations for disabled people", Patricia Prescott-Clarke (Social and Community Planning Research), HMSO, 1982.

[3] For example (1) "Made to measure", Cheshire County Architect's Department, 1980 (2) "Housing adaptations for disabled people". Terence Lockhart. Architectural Press for the Disabled Living Foundation, 1981.

MR OZDEMIR ALI

Aged 32. C6 lesion tetraplegia.

Married with a daughter aged 5 and a son aged 3.

Living in district council property.

Adaptation of a two storey house.

In 1982, eight months after being made redundant from his job as an amusement arcade manager, Mr Ali took his wife and two children on holiday to his native Cyprus. The trip was intended to help lift his depression at being unemployed and to give relatives the opportunity of seeing his children. Whilst spending a day on the beach, he had a diving accident, suffering a complete spinal lesion at the level of C6. Immediate treatment was given at the local hospital and transfer made to a spinal unit in southern England within forty eight hours. It was thirteen months before he was able to return permanently to his suburban home.

Immediate problems related to Mr Ali's poor health, urinary and respiratory conditions, as well as the family's shock at witnessing the accident, and subsequent demands on Mrs Ali to take on a new and demanding role in the family. The hospital social work department informed the house owning local authority and social services of the admission and warned of the need to identify and organise suitable accommodation. In practice, little more could be done at that time than to acknowledge that Mr Ali's house was not suitable for a wheelchair user, and that there was no specifically designed housing in the area for a family of this size and special needs.

Precise assessment details proved difficult to acquire as only a limited report on functional performance was forthcoming from the hospital, not helped by Mr Ali being frequently very unwell and exhibiting a total disinterest in a future that would not include his walking. Mrs Ali could not be easily available to either hospital or community staff as her time was taken up with the children's basic needs, preparing food to replace that rejected by her husband at the hospital and undergoing a long daily journey on public transport to reach him.

The case was allocated to a social services occupational therapist, who worked closely with the housing authority in determining the family's possible needs and the relationship of this to housing stock available. Options considered for the existing home were to install a through ceiling lift to give access to the upper floor or to adapt the house to wheelchair standard by structural alteration/extension. The former was rejected on the grounds that the rooms were already small and a lift installation would have reduced space beyond that of viable wheelchair circulation in the living area and the main bedroom above. In addition, considerable work would still have been required on the ground floor to give access to a bathroom and adequate use of the kitchen. It was felt that the layout and size of the rooms had nothing to commend them for wheelchair use and that even with a purpose built extension, many fundamental problems would have remained and resulted in Mr Ali having only partial use of his home.

The family were already on the list for transfer to be near Mrs Ali's family on an estate owned by the same authority some miles away, and the girl was not felt to be particularly well settled at school. There were only a few contacts in the immediate area, with the family's life tending to gravitate towards the relatives. Experience proved that there was limited practical support on an ad hoc basis in the vicinity and a view was formed that there were no grounds to make exceptional efforts to keep the family in the existing accommodation.

The occupational therapist and the senior housing officer visited Mr Ali in hospital in an attempt to gauge levels of functional ability to enable temporary arrangements to be made for his return home and to plan facilities required for any new accommodation. While there was no discharge date on the horizon and nobody could be sure when Mr Ali's poor health would improve, it was obvious from the lack of suitable housing stock that he was unlikely to be discharged directly to convenient accommodation.

Information was gleaned and formed the basis upon which special facilities were planned:

Mobility. Mr Ali used an Everest and Jennings self propelling wheelchair with an overall seat height of 570mm including a gel cushion, width 660mm and depth 1090mm. He was able to propel the chair for short distances and on gradients not greater than 1 in 20. This markedly deteriorated with fatigue. He was able to independently transfer sideways to equable seat heights. Standing was to be done daily with a specially constructed frame with a base of 900 x 700mm. It was hoped that at some stage Mr Ali would have an outdoor electric wheelchair.

Personal care. He could be independent in washing and hair care, using tenodesis grasp with the assistance of limited hand and arm movements, and provided the washbasin was of a height to allow him to support his forearms on the sides. A beard eliminated the need for daily shaving.

Wc. Catheterized. Assistance was required for bag emptying. Independent bowel evacuation was achieved following suppositories, although this could take some hours. Unable to clean self.

Dressing. Independent for upper half in casual clothes that were most usually worn. Problems of spasm, however, meant that he required assistance with the lower half.

Bed. Able to transfer to and from a Kings Fund bed of overall length 2130mm and width 1020mm. A ripple mattress was used and he required assistance in turning once during the night.

Bathing. Maximum help required. Independent use of an electric hoist was not possible.

Eating and drinking. Independent, except for cutting meat.

Domestic tasks. He was able to make a hot drink and snack, if necessary, but was not keen on developing these skills for use on a regular basis seeing responsibility for domestic chores as erosion of his masculine role in the family.

Hobbies and interests. Mr Ali enjoyed watching television, reading the newspaper, photography and being with his family.

1

The occupational therapist and the district council senior housing officer worked together with the aim of finding three bedroomed accommodation that could be suitably adapted, was vacant and in the area of Mrs Ali's family where support was readily available. Housing stock was looked at in general with the principle that the house for conversion should have large rooms, be on a level site and not too far from shops and other facilities.

The combination of a terraced house which had a mobility standard bungalow attached was considered, but discounted as it would have tended to isolate Mr Ali from the rest of the family, even after adaptation to an integral unit, as not all of the accommodation would have been accessible to him. Two units of this arrangement were also thought most unlikely to become vacant simultaneously. Additionally, all the houses of the type initially thought to be most suitable were found to have been sold under the Right to Buy scheme.

From the time that Mr Ali's health became stable enough to make his return home look likely, it ultimately took three months to find a house that was suitable for adaptation and acceptable to Mrs Ali, who visited the property. A further six months was used to design the specific work of adaptation and refurbishment required and to obtain planning and building regulations approval and to assure funding. Building work and tenancy arrangements took three months more, meaning that the family did not move house until twenty two months after the accident.

In the meantime, little notice was given of Mr Ali's impending return home for trial weekends and the first ones were spent without some of the necessary equipment. However, portable ramps were used to give wheelchair access to and from the house via the front step, and a single bed was brought downstairs to the sitting room. A ripple mattress was supplied by the local health department. Mrs Ali slept on the settee and was required to turn her husband each night.

Mr Ali's independent personal care was achieved with a bowl of water placed on his wheelchair tray and his wife gave blanket baths and manual evacuations. He was unable to gain access to the bathroom owing to the obstruction of the door opening against the washbasin, and there was no easy solution of widening the opening because of the position of the stairs and an under stairs cupboard. Even had this not been so, the bathroom was too small with the position of the bath and wc precluding transfer, and the width of the open door impeding access to the washbasin.

Mr Ali spent most of his time in the sitting room as, while he could gain access to part of the kitchen, he found the turns required by the narrow corridor very difficult to manage. By the time that Mr Ali was finally discharged from hospital, the Kings Fund bed had been supplied but, while this improved problems of disturbed nights, its size further dominated the small sitting room and, in practice, designated the room as no longer being a family one.

Mr Ali's muscle power and motivation diminished with lack of opportunity for basic exercise. He was unable to consolidate skills acquired in hospital as only temporary solutions could be employed and most of the house remained inaccessible to him. Tensions rose in the family, which could be anticipated in a situation where sleeping, nursing and personal care arrangements were carried out in the main living area. The children learned to avoid father's discipline by escaping to the upper storey and all difficulties came to be attributed to inappropriate housing.

In consequence, many emotions became focused on the projected move and delays caused further depression and frustration. Increasing involvement from the general practitioner, health visitor, community nurse, occupational therapist and housing welfare officer became necessary to help support the family during the nine months until the move was achieved. The family and the members of the support team all saw the social services occupational therapist as the key worker, both in her involvement with problem solving in both houses and in her wider responsibility of encouraging realistic planning of a future beyond that of purely housing requirements.

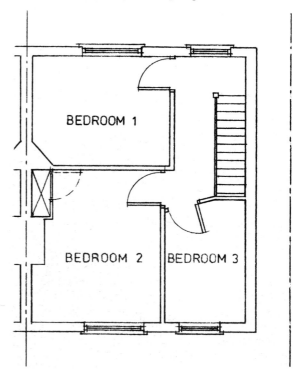

Ground floor plan of original house. 1:100

First floor plan of original house. 1:100

Attempts were made by the occupational therapist to help Mr Ali maintain functional levels by attendance at a rehabilitation centre and/or day centre. Unfortunately, limited staffing levels at night meant that he could not be accommodated on a residential course, and he lived just outside the boundary for daily transport. He declined attendance at a day centre after a few visits as he found it depressing to have to mix with elderly people. The pressure, therefore, remained intense to effect the move as quickly as possible, both in terms of halting further physical and motivational deterioration in Mr Ali and in averting breakdown in family relationships.

Front view of the property

Rear view of the property

THE PROJECT TEAM

County council social services occupational therapist.
District council senior housing officer.
District council surveyor.

THE AIMS

To allow access to all parts of the house, the garden and the road in a wheelchair.
To give optimum circulation space.
To facilitate environmental control from a wheelchair.
To provide facilities for Mr Ali's special needs in terms of a wc, shower and bedroom.
To promote maximum independence, with the flexibility necessary to cope with changing circumstances created by growing children, potential development of work and hobbies and possible fluctuations in Mr Ali's medical condition.

THE PROPERTY

* A three bedroomed semi detached house built in 1955.

* Gross internal floor area 102.4m² before and 104.3m² after adaptation.

The house was situated on an estate on the outskirts of a large town, close to relatives of Mrs Ali. There was a sloping garden to the rear, but the rest of the site was level. When the property became available, it was in need of a substantial amount of refurbishment, even to bring it up to the standard of reletting as ordinary council accommodation. It was thought that it would be less expensive, ultimately, to incorporate the special provisions in a house needing repair, rather than to disrupt something that was already in good condition. This also gave the design team greater scope in tailoring the work to Mr Ali's particular needs.

THE ADAPTATION

* Lift shaft constructed against rear of house to connect dining area to main bedroom and top part of chimney rebuilt.

* Approximately one third of rear garden lowered and patio constructed, giving effect of terracing rest of garden.

Access from ramped patio doors affords the opportunity for raised bed gardening at the rear of the house, but Mr Ali would have preferred a greater sense of freedom had a ramped pathway been extended to the rear of the garden. However, this was not carried out as, in order to get the required gradient, the pathway would have had to curve and double back on itself, thereby taking up much of the space being reached.

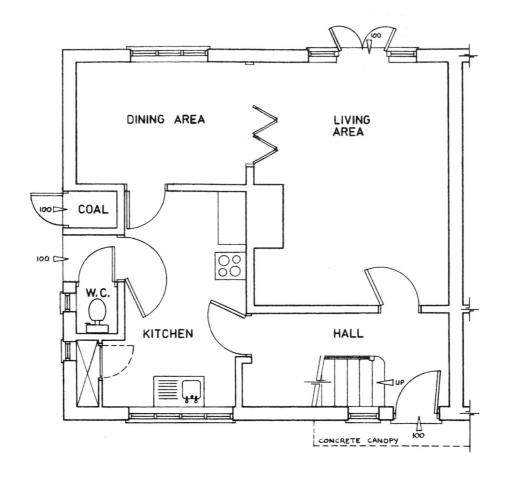

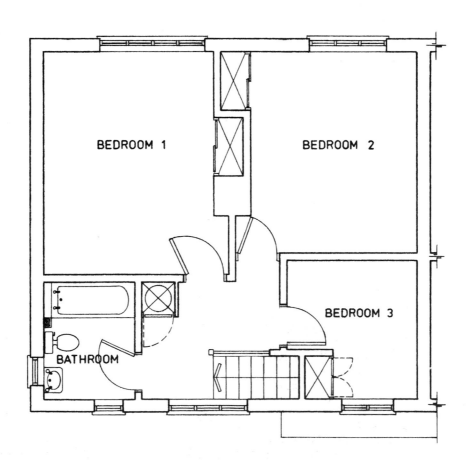

Ground and first floor plans before adaptation. 1:75
MR ALI'S HOUSE

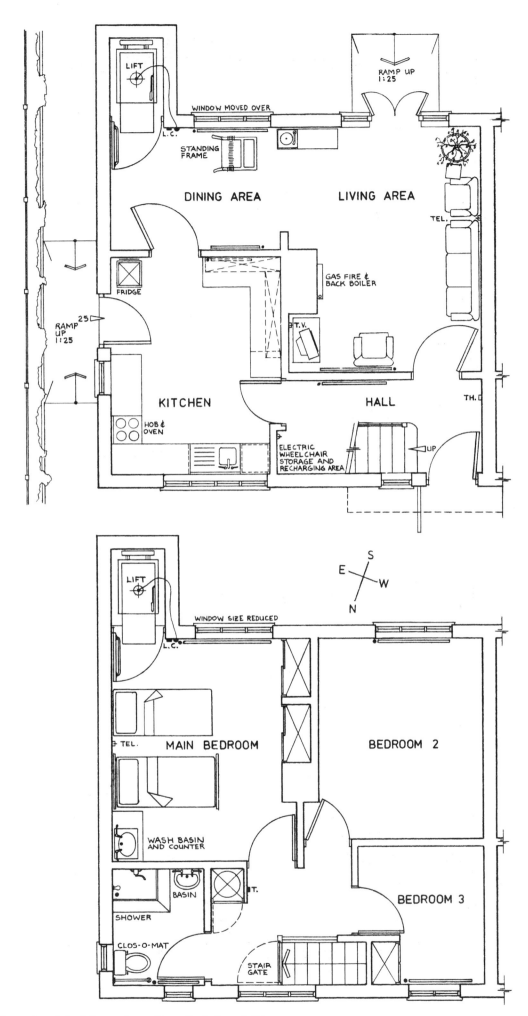

LIFT

L.C.

WINDOW MOVED OVER

STANDING FRAME

RAMP UP 1:25

TEL.

DINING AREA

LIVING AREA

FRIDGE

GAS FIRE & BACK BOILER

RAMP UP 1:25

T.V.

KITCHEN

HALL

TH.

HOB & OVEN

ELECTRIC WHEEL CHAIR STORAGE AND RECHARGING AREA

UP

LIFT

L.C.

WINDOW SIZE REDUCED

S
E   W
N

MAIN BEDROOM

TEL.

BEDROOM 2

WASH BASIN AND COUNTER

BASIN

T.

BEDROOM 3

SHOWER

CLOS-O-MAT

STAIR GATE

Ground and first floor plans after adaptation. 1:75
MR ALI'S HOUSE

5

EXTERNAL DOORS AND PATHWAYS

* Front and side doors replaced, giving new door leaf size of 910mm.

* French doors at rear of lounge replaced with outward opening, double glazed aluminium doors with high security locking system.

* Extruded aluminium Sealmaster thresholds, with flexible rubber seals installed to all external door openings.

* 920mm wide path to front door raised to come flush with front door threshold.

* 110mm wide path at side of house given two 1 in 25 ramps rising to platform outside kitchen door. Platform finished 25mm below threshold and sloped slightly away from door.

* 1 in 25 ramp constructed from french doors to patio.

* Temporary lean to structure outside kitchen door removed.

The front door and pathway give good access to the pavement, and the sheltered aspect prevents rain penetration across the flush threshold detail. The increased risk of rain penetration at the less sheltered side door prompted the designer to incorporate an external lip, and a slight slope on the ramp platform to carry water away. Mr Ali finds it difficult to negotiate the lip in the wheelchair, especially when he is tired, and the platform slope propels him towards the boundary in an already confined space.[1] He tends, therefore, not to use this doorway and gains main access to the house at the front door, and to the garden via the patio doors.

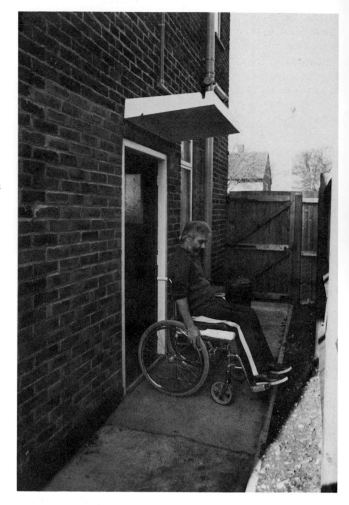

The side doorway, platform and ramps

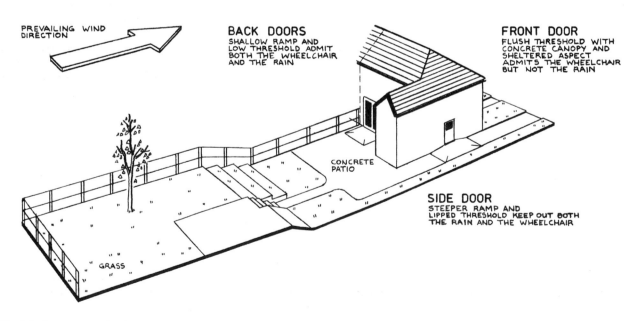

Wheelchair access and rain penetration

[1] See Musgrave outer bedroom door threshold, page 56.

6

Mr Ali has no difficulty in negotiating the flush threshold at the patio doors. However, rain penetrates the threshold, especially when driven by the prevailing wind. Water leaks in across the central bolt plate which interrupts the rubber threshold seal, and the run off moulding is too short and too high to afford any protection.

Front door threshold

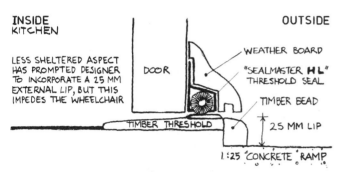

Side door threshold

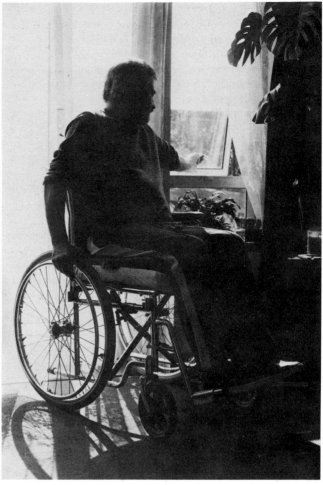

Mr Ali has difficulty opening the windows very far

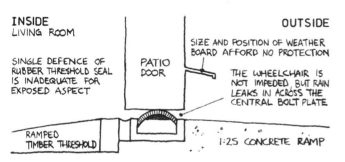

Patio door threshold

WINDOWS

* Window opening to dining area moved closer to patio doors to make room for new lift shaft.

* Window opening to main bedroom reduced to accommodate lift shaft, and aligned with new opening below.

* Two small windows that served wc and larder replaced with one new window closer to new external kitchen door.

* All windows replaced with double glazed aluminium units on mahogany subframes. Top hung casements, opened by lever handles, supported on cantilevered parallelogram stays to hold window out at base.

The family is pleased with the comfort afforded by the new windows and with their appearance. However, Mr Ali finds it difficult to push the windows open because of the friction in the stays, that are designed to keep the window at any chosen degree of opening, and because he can only reach a short distance from his chair.

ELECTRICAL WORK

* House rewired with power socket outlets at 550mm and light switches at 1350mm above floor.

* Additional socket under stairs for recharging electric wheelchair.

Light switches and power points are all easily usable. The fuse box in the hall is also accessible from a wheelchair, although Mr Ali does not have sufficient strength and dexterity to actually change a fuse.

HEATING

* New gas fired central heating system installed, driven from back boiler in chimney of lounge.

* Gas fire with top control fitted in place of old fireplace.

* Central heating controls set at 1330mm above floor outside main bedroom.

The gas fire was chosen for its ease of operation and slim line in terms of protecting circulation space, and Mr Ali has no problem using this or the central heating.

INTERNAL DOORS
* Doors and frames enlarged to 910mm and all internal thresholds removed.

* Doors hung to open against walls and lever handle furniture used throughout.

The extra wide doorways allow Mr Ali to approach from an angle without the need for careful alignment and he is especially pleased that the children's rooms were included, so that he may enter to bid them goodnight. He had not thought this particular feature to be important at the time of planning.

The internal doors were specially made and attention was given to making them as light weight as possible. Kick panels were not thought or proved necessary owing to easy operation of the doors and the amount of circulation space.

HALLWAY, LANDING AND STAIRS
* Self closing half door at head of stairs.

The stairgate removes the risk of the wheelchair falling down the stairs, as turns are made to and from the shower room

The team had hoped to remove the hot water tank and airing cupboard from the landing to improve access to and from the bathroom and to allow installation of a sliding door. However, no alternative site could be found that did not create greater problems. In practice however, the use of the stair gate, on a self closing spring, allows a greater turning circle in manoeuvering the wheelchair to and from the bathroom in safety.

The space under the stairs was conceptually reserved for storage and recharging of an electric wheelchair, but is used as a general storage area for the household. If the wheelchair is supplied, a different storage arrangement will become necessary, which it is hoped will not need to interfere with circulation space.

LIFT
* Home elevator by AMP Engineers Limited installed in purpose built lift shaft at back of house.

* Lift doors to dining room and bedroom, with internal horizontal grab rail and external D handle.

* Lighting in shaft controlled by switch at each door.

The lift at the upper storey

Mr Ali has some criticism of the lift as its internal depth of 1170mm means that the ramp, which folds as a gate, closes against the toes of his shoes. Very precise alignment for entry is required owing to the limitations of width, which is further reduced by the ramp raising control arm. On the ground floor, the ramp is a little steep for him to manage when he is tired and the design team acknowledge that the floor of the lift shaft should have been lowered by 40mm so that the necessary clearance of the bottom of the lift would have allowed it to rest level with the dining room floor. He considers the need to hook a walking stick through a grab rail on the door to close it to be incompatible with the sophistication of the rest of the work, although he cannot deny the efficiency of the solution.

LIVING AREA

* Lounge and dining area made open plan by removal of concertina partition.

There is good circulation space, but to ensure easy access to the lift and to the kitchen, there would only be sufficient space for a small table close to the wall in the dining area. This part of the room is not used as an eating area and the amount of space in the kitchen becomes, therefore, of additional importance. Mr and Mrs Ali elect to keep the standing frame in the area by the lift, notwithstanding its use of circulation space, as it is immediately accessible for use and has a reasonably interesting and unisolated environment for the daily standing task.

KITCHEN

* Kitchen enlarged by demolition of internal toilet, coal store and larder walls.

* External door to coal store bricked up.

* Kitchen refitted using Nicholls and Clarke Phlexiplan system of sink, kitchen units and fitments.

* Breakfast bar and plumbing for automatic washing machine.

The choice of one three tray unit, one corner unit with swivel trays, plus the sink, were based on the assumption that Mr Ali should be able to make a hot drink and snack when on his own, but that further facilities for food preparation and domestic tasks were not appropriate for him. The sink allows clearance of 760mm under, as required by Mr Ali, but could be adjusted for another wheelchair user. The breakfast bar was designed specifically in the belief that limitations of space in the dining area would probably mean that the kitchen was used as the day to day dining area.

The family is pleased with the kitchen and welcomes the space that allows them to meet there all together. However, Mr Ali is unable to get his feet into the 240mm space allowed under the kitchen units which limits his use of the kitchen and access to certain cupboards. In these circumstances, Mrs Ali feels that space could have been utilized as extra storage for her use. They would have liked a built in broom cupboard to have been included as the vacuum cleaner, ironing board and brush are currently housed under the stairs.

The team deliberated at some length about the removal of the ground floor wc as, while additional space was needed in the kitchen, a second wc was envisaged as being useful as Mr Ali can take some time in the bathroom.

BATHROOM

* Existing wc, washbasin and bath removed.

* Clos o mat Samoa automatic wc and bidet unit, set on plinth to give seat height of 530mm, corresponding to wheelchair and individually tailored self propelling shower chair.

* Washbasin with lever action pillar taps and knee clearance of 760mm, installed 80mm from adjacent wall.

* Invadex Opendeck shower base.

* Mira 722 thermostatically controlled lever action mixer with sliding rail attached, adjustable and removable shower head.

* Altro safety flooring.

* Wall and floor mounted horizontal rail by wc at height 615mm above floor.

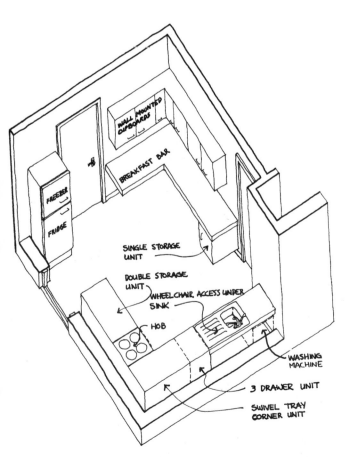

The kitchen layout

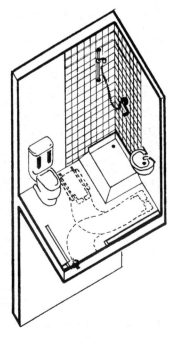

The bathroom layout

Mr Ali goes forwards into the bathroom, turning inside the room to position himself in the space of 780mm allowed between the shower base and the Clos o mat, for transfer to the wc to the right. He finds the Clos o mat a very significant feature of his independence although, as was envisaged, the children have some difficulty with the increased seat height and need to use a mounting block until they are taller. The family acknowledge that it would have been ideal to have had a second wc, especially when the children are home from school all day and there is more pressure on the bathroom.

The position of the washbasin so close to the adjacent wall means that Mr Ali cannot centre himself well at the basin and he catches his hands on the wall in making a direct approach.

He is unable to use the shower independently as the gradient of the sides of the base is too steep for him and the large size of the control knob and lever over the small base impedes access. In order to avoid the possibility of increased spasm causing injury to his feet against the tiling, he would need to enter the shower backwards. However, the position of the shower head on the adjacent wall to the control means that either the spray or the mixer would always be behind him.

The required solution of a custom built flush shower base was rejected by the surveyor for two reasons. Firstly, the wedge that would have been removed from the top of the floor joists to achieve the necessary fall, was considered to weaken the joists to a point where additional structural

support underneath would have been necessary. Secondly, such a shower base would have meant some protrusion of the shower trap below the level of the kitchen ceiling and this was considered to be aesthetically unacceptable. In the event, with the solution used, water did penetrate the ceiling below as the flooring had been mistakenly cut around the edge of the base rather than extended underneath.[2]

BEDROOM

* Built in wardrobe in second bedroom annexed by repositioning of part of wall between two rooms.

* Inset washbasin with lever action pillar taps in 900mm width surround with clearance of 760mm under.

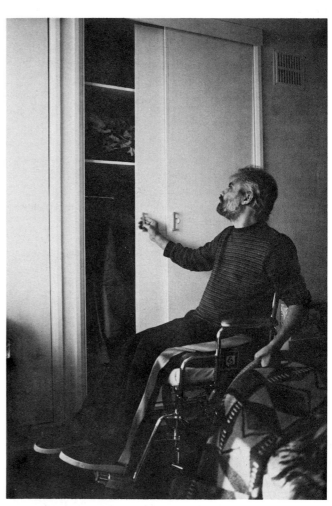

Mr Ali cannot reach the cupboard shelves.

When the house was first identified, a factor in its choice was the reasonably large size of the main bedroom in relation to many council houses. Notwithstanding, it is only just large enough and meant that the adjoining wall to the bathroom could not be moved to enlarge the bathroom, as had been considered at one stage. The annexing of the cupboard from the adjacent bedroom gave Mr Ali sufficient storage space without reducing or disrupting circulation space available in their bedroom. Built in cupboards saved space and were in response to the realization that there could be no additional furniture to that of the Kings Fund bed and Mrs Ali's divan, if circulation space to and from

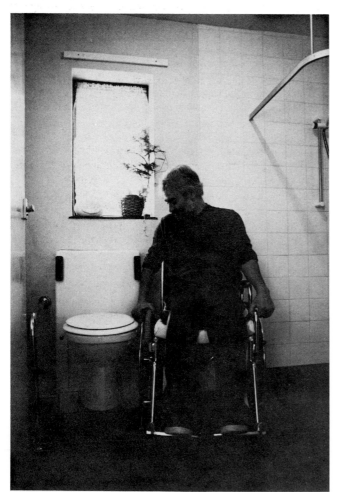

Preparing to transfer to the Clos o mat.

[2] See First floor roll in shower, page 212; Kidsley first floor shower, page 123.

the lift was to be preserved. The cupboards have accessible hanging space, but no shelves or drawers that can be reached from a wheelchair.[3]

The washbasin, while taking valuable space, was considered vital for Mr Ali's personal and, if necessary, nursing care. The washbasin in the bedroom is particularly useful as it allows Mr Ali the time he needs in personal care, without pressure from the rest of the family for access to the bathroom.

COSTING

1984		
Repairs and refurbishment		£6,542.00
Windows		3,230.80
Doors		1,136.00
Ramps		169.00
External work		1,251.00
AMP Lift		2,954.00
Lift Shaft		5,603.00
Bathroom		843.00
Clos o mat		900.00
Phlexiplan kitchen		968.00
	Total	£23,596.00

FUNDING

District council maintenance budget		£5,005.00
Improvement grant, 75% of £10,200 maximum		7,650.00
District council housing budget allocation for the disabled		10,941.00
	Total	£23,596.00

* The district council acted as agent for Mr Ali and an improvement grant of 75 per cent was made on the grounds of the house being council property and not on the client's dependence upon state benefits as could have attracted a 90 per cent grant.

* Additional funding was transferred to the budget allocation for disabled people, after application to the housing committee, to ensure that the entire remainder of the budget for the year was not swallowed up on this one project.

CONTRACTUAL PROCEDURE

The contract drawings, together with the full specification of the works, were prepared and sent from the district council to three individual building contractors for tender. A local builder was nominated and the contract made with the district council. Subcontractors were AMP Engineering Limited for the lift installation and Weatherman Limited for the double glazed aluminium windows, french doors and locking system.

[3] See Musgrave bedroom cupboards, page 61.

EVALUATION

The special needs and difficulties of Mr Ali and his family, the onset of severe traumatic disability, hospitalization and then inaccessibility of amenities at home have all the features of a family in crisis. The housing adaptation discussed is part of this total picture, albeit an important one when family life became so disrupted by the difficult living conditions in the original home.

Supporting the family and confronting practical problems cannot have been straightforward, affected as it was initially by geographically separated agencies with time lost in transmission of information. That Mr Ali returned home without some of the necessary equipment did not assist a difficult transition or inspire confidence in him that his physical care would be properly maintained.

Theoretically, the practical needs could have been met by provision of three bedroomed accommodation designed to DOE wheelchair standard. Such a dwelling would have needed to have been in the specific area required and conveniently vacant. The urgent need to rehouse this family could not have encouraged ideas on the lengthy process of purpose building, even had a suitable site been available. The only realistic course was to consider adaptation of existing property and even this proved problematical, as the most straightforward type was found to have been sold.

The property chosen for adaptation was built in the 1950s when amenity standards were poor, but space generous. The overall area is some 105m^2, compared with Parker Morris standard for a five person house including storage of 86m^2, but layout still caused some constraints particularly in respect of the bathroom and lift installation. Some limitations can be seen to be resolved by removal of the coal store and larder from the kitchen and by positioning the lift in its own shaft at the rear of the house. The bathroom could not, however, be enlarged without taking essential space from the bedroom.

Beyond the originally identified limitations of the property for conversion, additional technical problems emerged and centred mainly upon the **bathroom**. The original plan proposed with the family was for Mr Ali to aim for as much independence in personal care as possible and this would include use of a shower, rather than a bath for which he would need a lot of help. However, concern about structural problems in reducing joist thickness came to overrule the possibility that a flush shower base could be installed. Similar limitations to independence, as rejected in association with bathing, therefore became a real possibility with choice of a base over which he could not propel himself in the shower chair. In addition, the use of such a large shower control knob and lever, with its extension over the shower base by 220mm, makes an impossible obstacle to access in an already confined space.
It is apparent in practice that the washbasin in the bathroom could have been better positioned 100mm out from the rear wall to allow the wheelchair to go farther underneath and thus to remove the risk of Mr Ali falling when pulling himself forward in the chair to use it. The right hand edge could also have been sited a further 150mm, 230mm overall, from the adjacent wall as this would have allowed better centering of the chair and free arm movement.

The Clos o mat is very successful for Mr Ali and the rest of the family are coping with difficulties caused by the increased seat height. The fact that this is the only wc in the house and that Mr Ali can take a long time in using it does not seem to be a great problem. In fact, Mr and Mrs Ali are adamant that the decision to remove the ground floor wc in favour of increasing kitchen size is still the one they would make. However, it must be said that for most spine injured people a second wc would be considered essential and would certainly have been desirable in this instance.

The **kitchen** is large, allows easy wheelchair manoeuvre and is used extensively. The extra space freed by the removal of the original wc allows multiple use of the kitchen and the room has become a focus of much of the family's daily activities. The ability to use the kitchen in this way is important to the Alis and explains why they did not wish to see its space reduced in order to provide a second wc in the house.

The washbasin in the **bedroom** is useful as it allows Mr Ali the time he needs in personal care. The surround could have been some 250mm smaller in width, while still allowing space for objects being used, and this would have allowed the bed to have been placed nearer to the wall giving consequent additional turning space at the lift. A shaver socket and mirror might also have been included.

Problems of **storage** exist throughout the house as exemplified by use of the understairs area for a purpose for which it was not intended. In addition, Mr Ali is not able to use all of the cupboards provided; as seen in the kitchen and in the lack of pull out drawers in the bedroom.

The installation of a **lift** was essential to enable Mr Ali to use the house fully. By siting it in a specially constructed shaft at the rear and by positioning it at the detached corner of the house, a significant number of advantages were gained in that no space was lost from either the dining area or the main bedroom and the special shaft meant that the lift was fully enclosed, giving a degree of privacy to the two rooms, which could not have been achieved with a through ceiling installation. This is particularly important if Mr Ali is unwell and in bed, as family life can continue without the need for undue quiet. It also affords greater control of heating and ventilation and any noise from the lift is away from the main living area and the party wall. The shaft is visually discreet and, with its pitched roof, could be considered to improve the outside of the house.

Wheelchair accessibility to the **exterior** is very successful at the front and patio doors with the special thresholds and gentle ramps whose gradients were not affected by limitations of space. Rainwater does, however, penetrate the patio door threshold with its single line of defence, afforded by the rubber seal set into the threshold and which is interrupted by the bolt plate. The lack of water penetration problems at the front door are directly attributable to the three tier system of protection afforded by the concrete canopy and its sheltered orientation, the large traditional run off which protects the third defence of the proprietary threshold seal.

Greater mobility around the property has resulted in an improvement in Mr Ali's ability to propel his wheelchair and gradients are not the problem they once were for him. As illustrated in this instance, therefore, there seems to be a good case for planning ramps for manual wheelchair use, wherever possible, unless an electric wheelchair is definitely to be supplied to cope with steeper gradients.

The expectation that purpose built accommodation can be automatically available is erroneous and early **planning** for rehousing or adaptation is largely dependent on detailed information being available from the hospital. The need for good communication links, close cooperation between agencies and maximum involvement of the person for whom the work is intended is emphasised as being of paramount importance by all concerned.

The family were fortunate that there was determination and enthusiasm in the occupational therapist, a generous funding authority, a vacant house for adaptation in the area required and a builder who completed the work without delay. All the work has been finished to a high standard, giving the impression of a spacious and comfortable home that is not overdominated by Mr Ali's special needs. The overall result is enhanced independence and improved family life which has justified the upheaval of a move to a new area.

Important lessons can be drawn for local authorities who may be faced with a comparable situation, inevitably unexpectedly, in that the only housing solution may be a major and costly adaptation to existing property. Notwithstanding, there may also be the need to acknowledge that some aspects of the work will be a compromise between the special needs of the disabled person and the able bodied family members within the technical constraints and organization of a dwelling that was not designed for its new task.

MISS ANN BEAGLE

Aged 28. Poliomyelitis.

Adaptation of a new ground floor flat in a warden assisted housing association scheme.

Miss Beagle was three and a half years old when she contracted poliomyelitis in 1955. A long period of hospital treatment followed before she was well enough to return home to the flat over the public house of which her parents were tenants. She attended a local day school for physically handicapped children to the age of sixteen, when a place was gained at a residential assessment and work training college. She advanced well in the clerical and academic subjects of the eighteen month course, but made little progress in her ability to transfer herself from a wheelchair or to dress independently.

On qualifying she returned home to unemployment and dependence upon her parents for help with toileting, dressing and lifting up the stairs. The brewery that owned the property refused application to install lifting equipment and there was concern about the adverse effects that lifting was having on her father's already poor health.

After a year of searching she was successful in gaining employment as a receptionist to a charitable organization and this gave her financial independence. It did not, however, eliminate the fundamental problems at home and in 1973 she successfully applied to the local social services department for sponsorship to a residential home for independent disabled people over a long stay hospital. A powered hoist and an electric wheelchair gave her a degree of freedom, socially and at work, that she had not previously known and she remained a resident of the unit for six years.

Thoughts of greater independence though, than were allowed in a unit entered via long stay wards with little privacy led her to approach the sponsoring authority again about a move, this time into the community. With the right equipment and some help with dressing, shopping and domestic tasks she felt confident she could live alone in a suitably planned flat.

Social services were sympathetic but could not offer more than a home help service and equipment loan. Help with personal care could only be offered on an emergency basis, whereas she needed daily help with dressing her lower half, and at a specific time if she was to hold down her job. She had heard of a housing association that provided purpose built accommodation for the elderly and disabled and, at the same time as a friend from the unit, applied for a ground floor flat in the London area. She was visited by the management officer of the association and additional notes on health, housing needs and personal circumstances were recorded in addition to the application. It was suggested that the core problem with morning dressing might be overcome if the warden of the block of sheltered housing concerned were to agree to assist.

When a wheelchair accessible ground floor flat in a block, newly built by the housing association a few miles from her parents home, was offered seven months later and the warden found to be agreeable to the special tasks, Miss Beagle's dream of an independent life in the community started to become a reality.

A local authority occupational therapist was allocated to the project and made the functional assessment on which adaptation decisions were made.

Mobility. Miss Beagle was wheelchair dependent with no active movement in her lower limbs and required help in transferring to and from her indoor and outdoor electric and manual wheelchairs. The left hip and shoulder were dislocated and there was flexion contracture of the left knee. A combination of trick movements enabled her to compensate for there being no active movement in the left shoulder and little power in the full range movement of her elbows. Her restricted growth had limited her length of reach and while both hands were capable of weak gross grip, opposition of the left thumb was lost and she was only able to lift weight to a maximum of 2lbs with the stronger right arm. There had been surgery to correct spinal curvature and a tendon transplant from the right middle finger had given useful opposition to the thumb. She had chosen, however, not to repeat this operation on her left hand preferring to retain the active finger flexion and extension vital to her typing skills.

Dressing. She could manage all clothes except getting pants and tights over her hips in the morning.

Wc and bathing. She could be independent in transfer, cleaning and management of clothes using an overhead tracked hoist and two piece sling.

Personal care. She required an accessible level surface on which to support her elbows to bring her hands into a functional position for face and hair care.

Eating and drinking. Increased power and coordination was achieved by supporting her forearms on the table for cutting and locating food on a plate.

Domestic tasks. She required help with laundry, shopping and most cleaning tasks. She could, however, cook her own meals with the use of some specialized and well positioned equipment.

Hobbies and interests. She enjoyed sewing, knitting, stamp collecting, evening classes and committee work.

A surveyor from the housing association worked closely with Miss Beagle and the occupational therapist. Opportunities were given for Miss Beagle to test ideas in the flat before final adjustments were made and she was actively involved in the project from its inception. The structural work required took five months to plan and execute and Miss Beagle moved in January 1980; her friend from the unit was, coincidentally, housed in the same block a little ahead of her.

Unfortunately, she was only able to continue her job for a few more months as the taxi driver, who had helped in her transport needs for eleven years, left his job. Replacement drivers were not always keen or able to do the lifting required and sometimes hurt her in the process. In addition, alterations to the lavatories at work meant that, instead of there being space for the help of two female colleagues, only one person could lift her and this had to be a man. As a result, she began to avoid the need to use the wc with consequent kidney infection and stones.

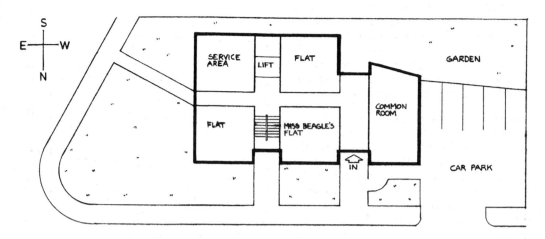

The site plan

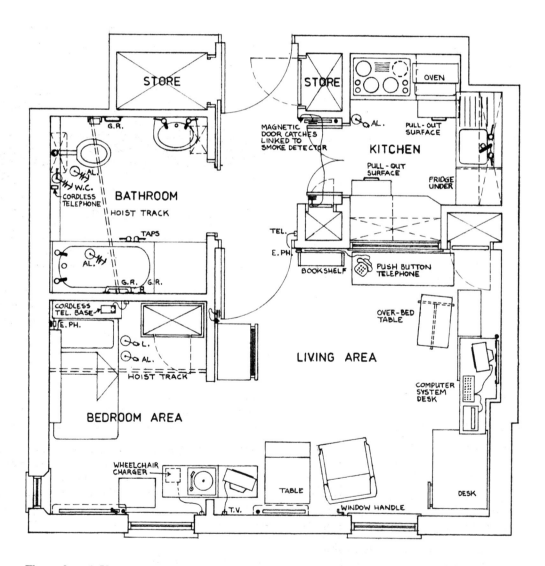

Floor plan. 1:50
MISS BEAGLE'S FLAT

After leaving work she bought herself an Elswick Envoy car through the Motability scheme and is presently saving up for the mechanism that will allow her to operate the side hung door behind her. The limitations of this lack of independence are overcome either by forewarning assistance of her time of arrival or by use of a cordless telephone with a range of 200 metres, from the reception unit in her flat, to the warden's flat on her return.

The advent of the car has meant changes in wheelchairs used, of which she currently has four. Within the flat she uses a DHSS issue indoor electric wheelchair. In case of a breakdown or battery recharging and going out in someone else's car she has a folding manual chair, with large self propelling wheels at the front which she can manage on level surfaces. The car demands its own chairs for attachment to the securing brackets, with the electric chair used when she knows that the heavy chair will not need to be carried over steps, otherwise the manual chair is employed.

THE PROJECT TEAM

London borough council social services occupational therapist.
Housing association surveyor.
Architect.

THE AIMS

To promote maximum independence in all activities of daily living in a setting where help could be available if required.
To provide facilities compatible with an active and varied lifestyle of work, hobbies and interests.
To meet the fine tolerances imposed by short stature, limited reach and dependence on specialized equipment.

THE PROPERTY

A ground floor flat in a four storey block of sheltered accommodation built in 1979.

* Gross internal floor area 35.1m², unchanged.

The site forms the corner of a road, some half a mile from a busy suburban shopping centre. To the side of the four storey block there is a small car park for residents and visitors and the rear is laid to garden with raised flower beds, paved areas and seating.

THE ADAPTATION

Modification of a wheelchair standard flat.

EXTERNAL DOORWAYS AND PATHWAYS

* Clear plastic kick panels and additional pull handles to main door of block and to all ground floor doors in communal areas, specifically for Miss Beagle's use.

* Latch lock to front door of flat replaced by mortice lock and latch, operated by lever handles on either side, and a mortice lock, operated by key outside and lever inside.

* 1450mm wide external brick pathway widened and ramped to give wheelchair access to car park.

The original pull handles to the doors in the communal areas were not moved as Miss Beagle's short stature and limited reach requires a level that is too low for most ambulant users. The lift controls proved to be too high, but were not altered as operational difficulties are overcome by

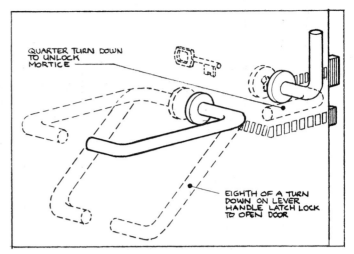

The front door locking system

use of a long handled reaching aid. She finds her front door locks easy to use, although the design has meant that it cannot be linked to an electronic door intercom, as is used for the main entrance. In consequence, if the mortice lock has been engaged, she needs to call the warden to open the door if a visitor arrives at a time when she is otherwise occupied.

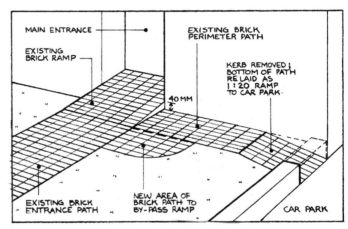

The perimeter path was widened at one end and ramped at the other to give direct access to the car park

The steps in the external pathway presented no problem to the kerb climbing chair that Miss Beagle used at the time of the move, but had to be altered when she purchased the car as the securing clamps could not accommodate such a model.

WINDOWS

* Tall windows with low cills, horizontal operational bars and 910mm height winding handles to operate top ventilators installed in wheelchair standard flats.

In theory, Miss Beagle has no problems in operating the windows or the pull cord curtains system her mother had fitted, although the placement of necessary furniture on the very limited wall space available has meant that the windows have become less accessible. The low cill heights give good visibility from a wheelchair and the flat a sense of space.

ELECTRICAL WORK

* Power points set at 965mm and light switches at 760mm throughout flat.

* Two banks of switches to operate extractor fan, hob, oven and kettle set at 760mm in addition to existing switched sockets at back of kitchen work surface.

* Power point, light switch and emergency bell reset button in hallway resited to allow installation of sliding door to bathroom.

* Emergency lighting system connected to existing circuit for corridors.

* Extractor fan linked to light switch in bathroom.

* Extra electrical circuits provided for overhead tracked hoists in bathroom and bedroom.

* Bell push switches on long cords sited by bedroom hoist and in kitchen, pull cords over bath and wc. All linked to warden call system.

* Door entryphone to main door added in bedroom to that already sited in living area.

Switches to the kitchen power points were repositioned as Miss Beagle was not able to reach the ones at the back of the work surfaces. If power failure occurs when using or needing to use the hoist, she can summon assistance quickly, with sufficient light from emergency lighting to locate the call bell. All pull cords are extra long and arranged for easy access in the event of accident or hoist failure.

Miss Beagle's father fitted a bedside lamp, with the switch on a long flex, to a shelf by the bed as the two way lighting system switch on the bedroom wall could only be reached when sitting up in bed.

HEATING

* Radiators in living area, bedroom, and hall fed from gas fired boiler serving block.

* Small radiator in kitchen removed to allow repositioning of switches.

The kitchen is warm and the loss of the radiator from the most accessible wall for power switches is of no consequence. Miss Beagle is unable to turn the radiator control valves and, in conjuction with her difficulties in getting close to the windows, has little command over the temperature in her flat. In addition, the heating pipes run under the floor of the main room and, in all but the coldest weather, she finds the room too hot for comfort.

HALLWAY AND DOORS

* Outward opening kitchen door replaced with two half width side hung doors.

* Kitchen doors and side hung living room door held open on electromagnetic catches linked to smoke detectors.

* Outward opening bathroom door converted to suspended sliding door. Throw over action bolt incorporating coin operated lock, for emergency use, fitted outside and lever handle inside.

* Non slip thermoplastic tiles laid to hall floor and extended into kitchen and bathroom.

Miss Beagle uses the raised plates of the locking device to push the sliding door, which she finds easy to operate. The other doors are held open all the time for ease of

circulation and there is no necessity for closing to increase warmth in the rooms.

It was necessary to alter the kitchen and bathroom doors as their opening into the hallway eliminated wheelchair circulation space. It was not possible to use a sliding door to the kitchen because of the lack of wall space. However, the magnetic catches on the half doors allow them to remain open, and their linking to smoke and heat detectors means that the catches are automatically deactivated and the doors closed, in the event of fire. The hallway, while being large enough for Miss Beagle's small chair, presents problems in turning into rooms for friends who use chairs with extended footplates.

She is not able to gain access to the main storeroom as the doorless opening is not wide enough for her chair. The room is not large enough for all her needs; her mobile hoist and three of her four wheelchairs are stored in an outside cupboard for communal use or in the corridor.

LIVING AREA

* Varnished pine board flooring.

* 745mm high, 730mm depth worktop installed by a friend to one wall after contract completion.

The smooth surface of the floor presents minimal friction to a wheelchair, but the soft wood has meant that marks have been left by castors in the movement of furniture, which Miss Beagle finds unsightly. She has considered cushion flooring as an alternative, but the need for sheet hardboard under this has increased the price beyond her means.

The living room is bright and modern in its fittings and furnishings, reflecting Miss Beagle's busy daily life. The worktop provides an ideal site for operation of her home computer, printer and monitor, all used in her work as treasurer for a transport scheme as well as other projects in which she is actively involved.

KITCHEN

* Shallow sink and draining board at 835mm with 685mm clearance under.

* Lever taps resited from front edge of unit to conventional position at back of sink.

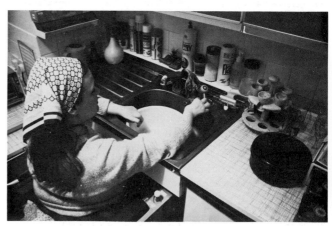

Knee space under allows Miss Beagle to get close to the sink, and the taps can be easily reached across the small bowl

* Two sets of drawers with pull out work surfaces above sited under 695mm high worktops.

* Wall cabinets with autolatch catches fitted to two walls.

* Two ring electric hob replaced with three solid ring one, set into 670mm high worktop.

* Refrigerator mounted on large wall brackets to bring door opening forward to edge of work surface and to allow footplate clearance of 300mm under.

Miss Beagle uses the deep drawers to store saucepans and large cooking utensils and the shallower ones for food packets and tins. The pull out worktops are used as a a a surface for eating and for ironing, as well as for food preparation. Envisaging this, she resisted the idea of holes being cut to stabilize bowls, and instead uses non slip rubber pads or mixes in lightweight plastic bowls in her lap. She can only reach the base shelf of the wall cabinets with

Storage drawers are easily reached from work areas

her reaching aid, which she also uses to push release the autolatches. These cupboards are, however, very useful extra storage space for bulky items and replacement groceries, which are transferred to the drawers below by the home help.

The worktops, organized to give work areas on three sides of the small room, are too deep for Miss Beagle to reach. She has devized a system of storage trays kept on the worktops, which allow working space in front of them, but which can be pulled easily forward when required. Items kept on each tray are organized for specific tasks, which

promotes efficiency in time and effort. Additional labour saving items used and stored on the worktops are an electric can opener and a three in one slow cooker.

A three ring only hob could be used because of the limitations of the 13amp power socket which had been judged sufficient for the likely cooking requirements of residents using a surface mounted cooker.

The small drop down oven door, used in conjunction with a pull out work surface, allows Miss Beagle to rest her forearms without risk of burning herself

Miss Beagle changed the oven for one at which she could rest her forearms on the worktop to position her hands without needing to lean on the hot interior of the door to take pans out of the oven. The Proctor Silex model purchased by Miss Beagle can be used as a grill, toaster or oven, and has a drop down door of only 120mm height. She uses waterless saucepans which, although rather heavy, eliminate risk of boiling water being spilled in the draining of food.

The taps were transferred back to a more conventional siting as Miss Beagle found that her body tended to get caught up on the levers as she approached the sink and that the arms of the wheelchair could inadvertently operate the taps. She finds the new positioning satisfactory with the levers being large and far enough forward for her to reach. There is sufficient knee clearance for easy access to the sink and for heat not to be transferred through the stainless steel base to her knees.

Miss Beagle's small wheelchair can circulate in the kitchen more easily than a larger model, although careful alignment is still required. The room would be considerably more difficult to use if extended foot plates to the wheelchair were required

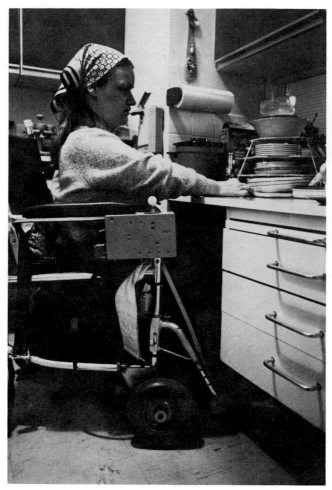

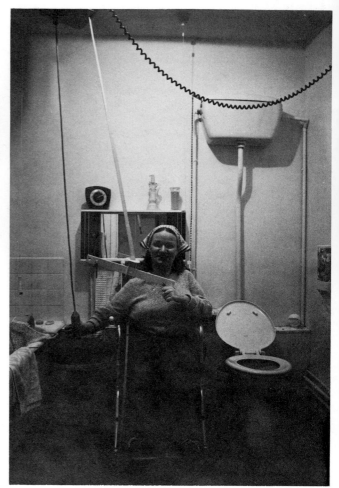

Trays are used to bring stored items forward on the deep work surfaces

The space between the bath and the wc is used for transferring to the hoist

A home help does her laundry, some weekly shopping and most of the cleaning. The controls in the communal laundry room are inaccessible to Miss Beagle and problems of shopping for clothes are overcome by mail ordering, for which she is an agent.

BATHROOM

* Low level cistern wc replaced by high level cistern type, with right handed use chain and large round ball pull.

* Wc turned by 90° from its original position and set 350mm out from the wall; pan height of 405mm.

* Diagonal tracking for Wessex hoist mounted on wall with steel angle brackets to give traversion over bath and wc.

* Lever taps mounted on side of bath.

* 820 x 120mm area cut out of base of bath panelling.

* Wall mounted washbasin with lever taps, 660mm knee clearance under and mirror fronted bathroom cabinet alongside.

* 10mm diameter horizontal grab rail at height 940mm next to wc, in addition to vertical and horizontal 305mm grab rails that were standard features by baths throughout the block.

The wc was moved and a high level cistern installed to achieve optimum positioning when using the hoist and to

allow Miss Beagle to lean back into the position that is most functional for her. It enables her to pivot sufficiently to manage her clothes independently, and she uses the edge of the pan or rim of the lid as hooks for her fingers or elbows to gain leverage or stabilization in doing so.

With the hoist she uses two narrow slings, which she can manage easily without the need to sit on them all the time, and steadies herself on the arm of her chair, the grab rail and the toilet roll holder for positioning over the wc. She likes the fast operation of the hoist mechanism as toileting

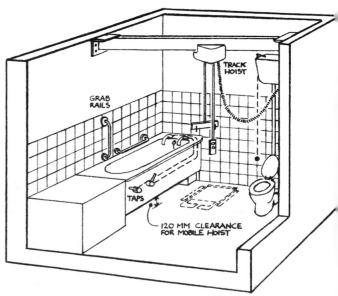

The bathroom layout

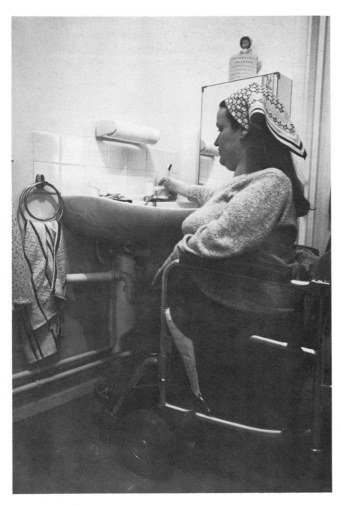

Access to the washbasin is good, and its height and design allows Miss Beagle the essential capability of resting her forearms to perform tasks

The hoist had to be installed across the room

can now be a speedy operation in which she is totally independent. The joint features of the hoist and a very precisely positioned wc have given her the final degree of independence in dressing and personal care which is so important.

Miss Beagle has no problem in using the bath, finding the positioning of the taps on the side panel useful both from the bath and the chair. The vertical handrail is not used but the horizontal one acts as a pivot point for her left elbow in positioning. The use of a foam pad on the base of the bath alleviates pressure problems caused by her dislocated hip. The cut out in the base of the panelling allows use of an attendant operated mobile hoist, which is stored in a cupboard in the block, for times of power cut or electrical hoist breakdown.

BEDROOM

* Wall mounted overhead tracked hoist installed across width of room on special spreader plates.

* Narrow shelving on wrought iron brackets fitted by bed.

The shelving beside the bed is useful for essential items and does not take up circulation space from the small room as a freestanding bedside cabinet would. In addition, the hooks on the sturdy wrought iron brackets have proved useful as grab handles to assist in sitting up in bed. Clothes are stored in a free standing child's size wardrobe with an easily opened magnetic catch. Recharging the batteries of

her indoor and outdoor wheelchairs is also done in this room and, while this is contrary to advice on the risk of fumes, there is no alternative site by a hoist and a power point in the flat.

Additional problems to those of the bathroom installation existed here, as mounting the hoist track 330mm from the edge of the wall was necessary because the only other site for correct positioning over a bed would have involved the window. There is only space enough for one wheelchair

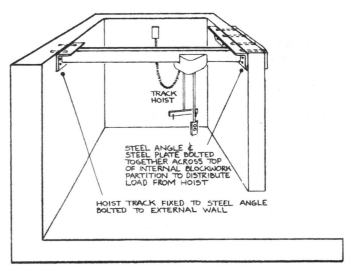

TRACK HOIST

STEEL ANGLE & STEEL PLATE BOLTED TOGETHER ACROSS TOP OF INTERNAL BLOCKWORK PARTITION TO DISTRIBUTE LOAD FROM HOIST

HOIST TRACK FIXED TO STEEL ANGLE BOLTED TO EXTERNAL WALL

The hoist had to be fixed to the walls, as the hollow pot floor above was considered to be structurally unsuitable

C

next to the bed, meaning that this hoist cannot be used for transferring to a second chair without assistance as would have been permitted had the tracking run the length of the room.

COSTING

1980		
Electrical work		£1350.00
Hoist installation		190.00
Doors		590.00
Kitchen		1490.00
Bathroom		892.00
Extras and delays on day work items		996.00
Fees		1059.00
	Total	6567.00

1984	
External ramp	1230.00

FUNDING

Grant from sponsoring social services	£1000.00
Improvement grant from local borough council	800.00
Polio Fellowship for electro magnetic door catches and emergency lighting	904.00
Housing association special fund	2863.00
Housing corporation for ramp	1230.00

CONTRACTUAL PROCEDURE

As builders were already on site, completing the general work on the block, they were invited to do the adaptation work during the defects liability period as a variation to the main contract. Wessex Medical Equipment were contracted to install the hoists, with the electrical supply and track fixing plates being completed in advance by the contracted builder.

EVALUATION

Three major factors governed Miss Beagle's move from residential care into the community: she required wheelchair accessibility to the property, the feasibility of adaptation to her own very special needs and the goodwill of a warden to help her with her initial dressing problems. That these were all met with a vacancy so quickly after her first application is of merit to the housing association and staff employed. It was additionally providential that the flat was in the area of family contacts and friends, which all helped to ease the transition.

Miss Beagle's dependence on very specialized, mostly electrical equipment and trick movements required fine planning and attention to every detail. The close working of the project team and the opportunity for Miss Beagle to try out ideas before final adaptation and moving in was, therefore, of paramount importance.

The layout of the site and the communal areas present no real problem to Miss Beagle and she finds the **ramp** and access to the car park very easy. The designer's intention was that wheelchair access to the block would be from the pavement at the front or via the rear door from the garden. This meant a more circuitous journey from the parking area than is now given for Miss Beagle and other wheelchair users visiting in cars.

The flat is small which is of no problem to Miss Beagle, other than perhaps in the kitchen, as she has a small wheelchair. It does, however, present problems to other wheelchair users as is seen particularly in turning from the hallway. The need for so much equipment to be kept elsewhere in the block is also an indication of insufficient **storage** provision. If supplementary space had not been possible, three wheelchairs in addition to the one being used, plus a mobile hoist, would have made circulation in the flat impossible. The flats were originally designed in 1976 to standards that have since been updated and, if designed now, would probably be 7m² to 8m² larger.

The limitations of wall space against which to place furniture in a room with three windows and two doorways has caused items to impede access to the **windows** in the **living area**. The choice of furniture on castors for movement according to the needs of the room has gone some way to overcoming the problems, but has caused unsightly marking of the softwood floor. The difficulties in operating the **heating** and the windows cause Miss Beagle some discomfort which might have been overcome by thermostatic heat control or alternative radiator valves.

The elimination of **doors** opening into the hall was essential for Miss Beagle's own use, especially as the bathroom door opened across that of the living area. The linking of the magnetic door catches to smoke detectors has proved valuable as it enables her to leave doors open for ease of movement, yet also meets the fire precautions used in the rest of the block of flats.

The drawers in the **kitchen** are particularly successful with items easily reached. While not all the wall cabinet space is accessible to Miss Beagle, it is nevertheless needed as back up in a small room, where knee clearance under work surfaces must be preserved at the expense of storage cupboards. The work surfaces were too deep for Miss Beagle to reach over to use the power points, but the two new banks of sockets and switches on accessible wall space work very well. The problems of depth are largely overcome with the ingenious use of trays and, in fact, the space proves useful in placement of the labour saving pieces of equipment needed and which would be too heavy to store other than at their site of operation.

The presumption that a two ring hob and small oven would be sufficient proved erroneous, as Miss Beagle likes to entertain friends and family for meals. The new oven works very well for her needs and allows versatility in one piece of equipment, rather than many, which would further reduce working space.

While the siting of the sink taps on the front of the worksurface would have seemed an ideal solution to Miss Beagle's problems in limitation of reach, in practice they proved both an irritation and a hazard. Siting the taps at the back of a small sink has not created difficulty as long as reach is not required.

The use of the hoist in conjunction with the highly successful resiting of the **wc** means that Miss Beagle can now be totally independent when dressing. She has devized her own methods of positioning and management of clothes with determination and in a series of trick movements, which are possible when she can lean well back.

The space in the **bath** panelling to enable use of a mobile hoist is a wise precaution against power cut or hoist breakdown and is something that might have been easily overlooked. For those as dependent on sophisticated electrical equipment, but living outside a sheltered environment, arrangements would need to be made for an emergency back up such as the warden service here.

The space in the bathroom and lower siting means that the bath taps do not create the same problems as existed in the kitchen and are, in practice easily used from the wheelchair and the bath. In a ground floor wheelchair standard flat, it was unfortunate that no provision was made in the floor structure above for load bearing of hoist tracking. While technical problems have been overcome by wall mounting, it has meant the tracking could only go across the narrow width of the **bedroom**, if mounting on the window was to be avoided. There is, therefore, insufficient space for chairs to be placed side by side for transfer and she has to arrange for assistance both for recharging and for collecting a second chair from elsewhere in the block for alternative use. The need to recharge her electric wheelchair in the bedroom is a major drawback, but is unavoidable as it is the only site by both a hoist and a power point.

The project was comparatively unusual in that the architect and builder were asked to do some major adaptation work to their new building before it was finally completed. The architect worked quickly to produce a draft plan and was assisted in this by the detailed briefing of a surveyor experienced in the housing needs of the physically handicapped. Advantage was taken in using the contractor that was already on site, although there was some cost increase in delays for workers awaiting necessary materials that had not been ordered in time.

Miss Beagle's flat caters well for her confident independence and active life in the community. Her determination to succeed has enabled her to devize new methods to increase independence based on some sound planning and detailed work at the beginning of the project. She has the support of a warden when required and a sense of security that living in such a scheme can give. She is able, however, to pursue her own lifestyle and interests well beyond that which would ever have been possible in the residential setting that she once knew.

MR LESLIE CHANDLER

Aged 40. C5/6 lesion tetraplegia.

Married with a stepdaughter aged 10.

Adaptation of a local authority ground floor flat.

In 1967, at the age of 23, Mr Chandler suddenly felt very unwell one day at work in his job as an electrical engineer. Despite the pain in his back, he decided to drive himself to hospital; on arrival his eyes were bloodshot and spasm in his legs so intense that he could barely walk. He was not admitted and was referred to his general practitioner.He felt so ill, however, that he went on to another hospital where he was admitted. Within two hours, he developed paralysis in all four limbs and was transferred to a London teaching hospital.

Weeks of bedrest, passive physiotherapy to maintain joint range and tests to determine diagnosis followed, before identification of a C5/6 incomplete lesion, caused by haemorrhage, was established. Not having been treated for spinal injury from the start was compounded by no bed being available in a specialist unit, with transfer only effected six months from the date of onset of the condition. Prolonged bedrest had resulted in flexion contractures of the elbows and most joints of both hands.

Mr Chandler spent nine months in the spinal injuries unit before transferring for further rehabilitation and residential care to an assessment and training centre. He was unable to return to living with his parents in their unadapted bungalow which, although all on one level, was not designed for wheelchair use, and its isolated rural position further added to problems. While the district council would consider buying the property and rehousing the family, his parents did not really want to move or he accept that he would always live with them.

In 1969 Mr Chandler married a member of staff he met at the rehabilitation centre and moved to London to a ground floor flat in an Edwardian house owned by a friend. The couple approached social services for assistance in adapting the property to overcome problems of split floor levels and an outside wc, but, after years of making no headway, their friend decided to sell and in 1975 the couple were rendered homeless.

The borough council housed them in the only ground floor accommodation available, which meant that Mr Chandler's entire life and personal care was transacted in the living room until structural alterations could be effected to give access to other rooms. On top of the history of accommodation difficulties, this put a great strain on the marriage and, six months after the move, he and his wife separated.

As his wife had played the vital role in his care, he could not continue in the flat and was admitted to a residential establishment which, as there was no unit for the young chronically sick in the area, meant an old peoples' home. His daily management became the responsibility of the district nursing service until, some months later, a place was found in a new unit for young disabled people in a hospital close by.

Mr Chandler remained in the unit for three years until he met and married a voluntary worker at the hospital and looked around for a flat for them and her daughter from her previous marriage. He had heard that new building for disabled people had been undertaken by his old housing authority, and successfully applied to them to go on the housing list. He was given medical priority when one of the flats became available, and the family moved in 1977.

The block, consisting of two ground floor flats and four maisonettes, was situated on a level site close to a shopping centre. While it had been built to general wheelchair standards, further adaptation was necessary to provide features for additional special needs, and this work was effected over a period of time as new solutions became available or needs changed. Throughout the process, Mr Chandler was most active in researching and organising the work, based on his own knowledge of his condition and its limitations:

Mobility. He had no power in his lower limbs and although sensation was present, it was not intact. He had flexion contractures of the elbows and no active movement in his hands with finger flexion powered by wrist extension. Trunk and shoulder girdle strength was reduced and he was unable to take weight on his arms. He could propel his wheelchair, using the tread of the tyres for a better grip than afforded by the rims, that had been removed to reduce the width of the chair. He required help with all transfers.

Dressing. Dependent on assistant.

Wc. Although he had full sensation and knew when he needed to pass urine, he chose to use a penile sheath and drainage bag as this allowed him longer periods without the need for a carer to be present to take him to the toilet. Independent bowel evacuation could take up to one hour following laxatives administered the night before and a suppository in the morning.

Bath/Shower. Could not hold soap, wash or bath himself.

Bed. He required help with transfers. Full length sheepskin used for pressure relief.

Personal care. He could use an unadapted toothbrush, electric razor and a hairbrush with a handle that curved over the hand.

Eating and drinking. He relied on finger flexion mechanism and contractures in the little and ring fingers to hold standard cutlery. A cup was held with both hands, but he could not cut up meat.

Hobbies and interests. These were many and varied and included telephone market research, teaching at adult literacy classes, an Open University course on disabled people, correspondence courses in law and medieval history, typing regular bulletins and switchboard work for an organization for people with spinal injuries.

THE PROJECT TEAM
London borough council housing manager.
London borough council technical services officer.
London borough council social services occupational therapist.
London borough council environmental health officer.

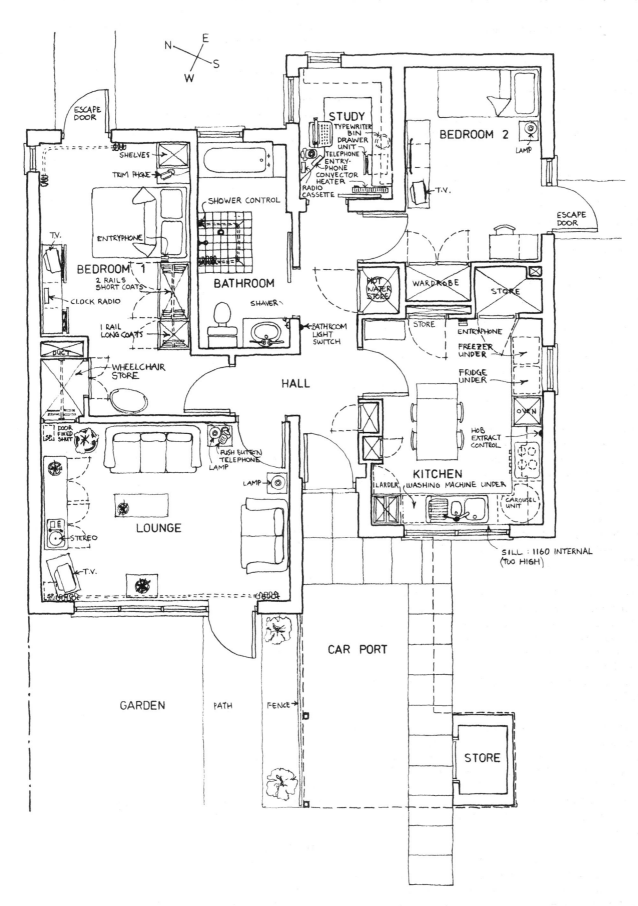

N E S W

ESCAPE DOOR

SHELVES

TRIM PHONE

ENTRYPHONE

T.V.

BEDROOM 1

2 RAILS SHORT COATS

CLOCK RADIO

1 RAIL LONG COATS

DUCT

WHEELCHAIR STORE

DOOR FIXED SHUT

SP.

STEREO

E

LOUNGE

T.V.

SP.

SHOWER CONTROL

BATHROOM

SHAVER

BATHROOM LIGHT SWITCH

PUSH BUTTON TELEPHONE LAMP

LAMP

HALL

STUDY

TYPEWRITER
BIN
DRAWER UNIT
TELEPHONE
ENTRY-PHONE
CONVECTOR HEATER
RADIO CASSETTE

BEDROOM 2

LAMP

T.V.

ESCAPE DOOR

HOT WATER STORE

WARDROBE

STORE

STORE

ENTRYPHONE

FREEZER UNDER

FRIDGE UNDER

OVEN

HOB EXTRACT CONTROL

KITCHEN

LARDER

WASHING MACHINE UNDER

CAROUSEL UNIT

SILL : 1160 INTERNAL (TOO HIGH)

CAR PORT

GARDEN

PATH

FENCE

STORE

Floor plan. 1:75.
MR CHANDLER'S FLAT

THE AIMS

To provide facilities exactly tailored to special needs in the most attractive and unobtrusive manner.

To maximize independence or ease of care in all aspects of daily life, work and hobbies.

To promote the needs of all the family without over dominance of wheelchair use.

To provide as normal an environment as possible in which to bring up a child .

THE PROPERTY

A ground floor unit in a block built in 1976.

* Gross internal floor area 82.4m² before and 88.6m² after adaptation.

The three storey building consists of two ground floor flats and four maisonettes above. A carport covering the front curtilage, including the front door, had been provided for the flat. A small grassed area and stocked borders alongside were made by Mrs Chandler.

Mr Chandler does not do any gardening himself, although he hopes to develop an interest in bonsai culture and intends to have a shelf installed on the fence for this. He has good wheelchair access around the site and appreciates being able to reach and transfer to the car in a dry and sheltered place.

THE ADAPTATION

Modification of a wheelchair standard flat.

Front view of the block of flats

EXTERNAL DOORS AND PATHWAYS

* Standard latch lock fitted to main door.

* Panic bolts replaced by Briton push release ones on external glazed fire escape doors from bedrooms.

* Duraflex rubber seal threshold installed to 970mm opening main door.

Level access is afforded to the front door from the garaging space under the carport and from the road via a pavement crossover. Mr Chandler has difficulty in operating the latch lock, but is reluctant to change it because of local break ins, where a coathanger has been passed through a letterbox and hooked onto the slide lever type to open the door. He has no problems with the threshold of this door either in wheelchair use or with rain penetration at the entrance protected by the carport canopy.

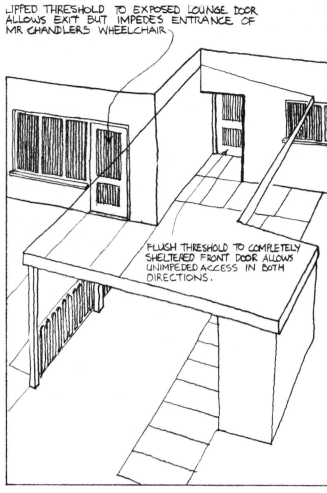

The car port gives sheltered access to the front door

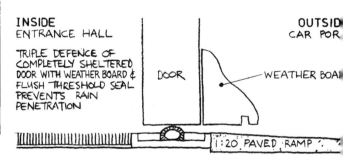

Front door threshold

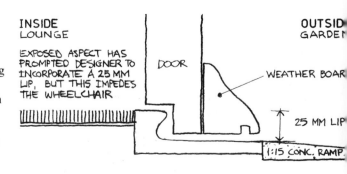

Lounge door threshold

The external door from the living room also serves as access to the front garden, but while Mr Chandler can get over the stepped threshold, he is unable to regain entry independently. The cill, however, forms an effective weathertight threshold for this exposed door.

WINDOWS

Horizontal central pivot windows with low level lever handles replaced by horizontal sliding sashes.

* Secondary double glazing fitted.

The window over the sink is inaccessible and, with its cill height of 1160m, affords no useful visibility from a wheelchair. The side window cill of 1010mm is more useful but, as it looks over a public footpath, it creates privacy problems. Cill heights of 680mm in the living and bedroom areas allow good sight lines.

The original windows were in a poor condition; it was not possible to secure them all and the Chandlers complained of difficulties with the curtains catching on the central pivot type of window. Subsequent to their move, the family had the windows replaced with sliding sashes to allow installation of secondary glazing units. While Mr Chandler cannot operate these, he feels he has lost little because of the problems that existed before. He can operate the external living room door independently, and uses this for additional ventilation if necessary.

ELECTRICAL WORK

* Sockets set at approximately 920mm throughout bedrooms and living area.

* Light switches at 1300mm from floor.

* Power sockets repositioned 115mm over new work surfaces in kitchen.

* Door entryphone receiving sets, operating front door, sited beside bed, in kitchen and study.

* Power socket positioned externally by front door for recharging electric wheelchair or car.

The 920mm high sockets are easily accessible to Mr Chandler. Although he does not use an electric wheelchair, the family have found the protected outdoor power source invaluable for charging the car battery and as a work area for using power tools. Mr Chandler arranged for installation of the door entryphone system himself and then applied successfully to social services to fund the provision.

HEATING

* Electric ceiling heating installed throughout.

* Gas fire in living area.

* Radiant heater over wc.

* Thermostats set in each of main rooms at height of 1500mm, recommended as optimal for best functioning of this method of heating.

The Chandlers found that the need to keep the temperature at around 22ºC with single glazing and no insulation produced very high fuel bills. Mr Chandler successfully applied to the council for cavity wall insulation which was supplemented by secondary glazing units. The effects were a reduction in fuel bills by 50 per cent, the ability to leave doors open and the removal of the gas fire, which was no longer necessary in the even and comfortable level of heating throughout the flat. He is not able to reach the high thermostat controls in each room, but this is less significant now that the temperature is better regulated.

HALLWAYS AND DOORS

* 1200mm wide central corridor. 910mm wide doors with lever handles.

* Doors to bathroom removed, one opening blocked up, and sliding door fitted to other.

The wide passageway allows ample space for turning into rooms with kick panels neither used nor needed. Doors to all rooms are usually left open, apart from the bathroom door which is easy to operate with its inset handle and light weight.

LIVING AREA

No adaption was made to the ample sized room, other than to remove the gas fire when heating problems were overcome.

KITCHEN

* Sink unit, wall cabinets and small corner worktop that constituted original kitchen removed and replaced with full set of Beckerman units with 160mm plinths.

* Single sink, drainer bowl and board, incorporating toggle tap and waste disposal unit with double doors under.

* Full height larder unit with vertically sub divided lightweight wire racks.

* Floor units incorporating drawers, cupboards and corner

* carousel with worktops at height 860mm over.

* Bosch ceramic hob recessed with flat sealing strip into worktop with extractor hood over.

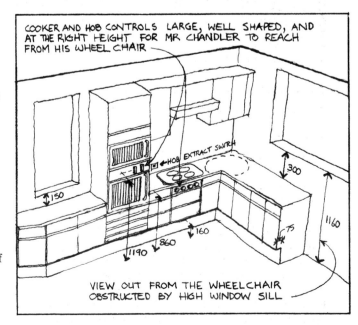

Heights of window cills, cooker and hob switches, worktop and plinth

* Full height unit housing Gaggenau 580 double oven.

* Floor covered in carpet tiles.

* Table with sliding extension flap placed in room as the only dining area in flat.

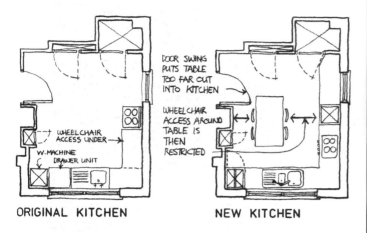

ORIGINAL KITCHEN   NEW KITCHEN

Kitchen alterations

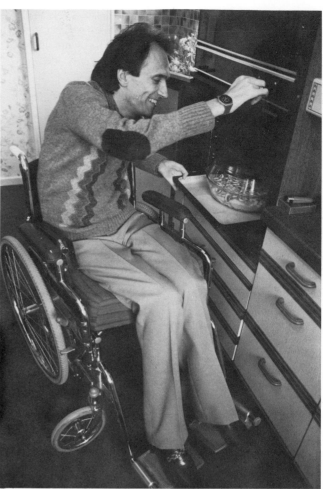

Mr Chandler is only able to reach the lower oven with ease; as it is also a grill it is sufficient for most of the day to day needs and the flip lever switches are easily turned between his fingers

All doors and drawers are easily operated with pull handles, spring loading and touch control. The plinths are large enough to allow easy footplate clearance and the worktop is of a height useful to Mr Chandler and not prohibitive for an ambulant user.

The oven was the only one they found to have the necessary wheelchair access of 180° door opening with control knobs at a suitable height between the ovens. He has difficulty reaching the cooker hood controls but can use the main power switch sited just above the worktop.

The hob has a warming area, touch controls, a residual heat warning light and is operated by large knob controls mounted on the front panel. Pans can be moved on a level surface owing to the flat hob, which is also used as an additional work surface. There is no knee room under the hob as Mr Chandler prefers to sit sideways to work; this enables him to use his stronger arm more effectively and reduces the risk of him spilling hot liquids into his lap.

The fitments and units are attractive. Mr Chandler finds the D handles ideal for partially flexed fingers and the spring loading highly efficient. Layout and storage design allow commonly used items to be stored close to their point of use. The waste disposal unit proves a useful addition although, initially, it was incorrectly adjoined to the washing machine plumbing outlet and caused refuse to appear in the washing machine if both were used at the same time.

The free standing table has a sliding flap which gives wheelchair access to a dining surface. The swing of the kitchen door means, however, that the table is so far set out that it restricts wheelchair access to the units. The carpet tiles have started to move out of position owing to the friction of the chair when negotiating tight corners.[1]

[1] See Spaceaider table, page 210

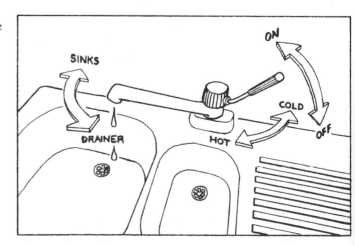

The toggle tap gives ease of operation with its one touch on/off, hot/cold selection and facility for extending the mixer over the drainer

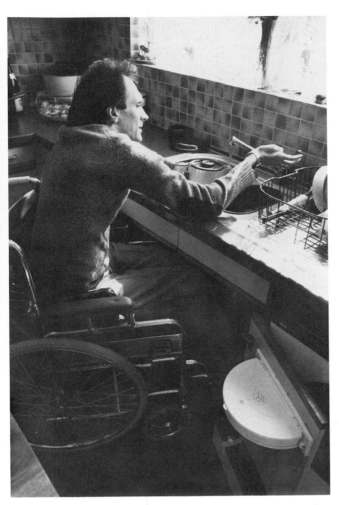

The sink becomes accessible to a wheelchair user on opening the unit doors, with plinths attached, to reveal level access and knee space underneath

The vertically divided multiple storage system of the larder unit gives access to provisions, but Mr Chandler is only able to reach the lower baskets and so ensures that commonly used provisions are stored there

The occupational therapist had reservations in recommending the kitchen plan, as she saw it as an opportunity to bring facilities up to a standard for any wheelchair user rather than just for Mr Chandler's needs and preferences. In particular, she was concerned about the position of the table and that there was no knee room under the hob. She did not agree with the housing authority's assessment, however, that the original kitchen in the purpose built flat was suitable for a wheelchair user and endorsed Mr Chandler's application for a new kitchen in general terms.

The family and the occupational therapist looked at various alternative kitchens, but could not find anything at that time that catered for Mr Chandler's special needs and was cheaper than those selected. He was able to prove that a less expensive range would have needed so much further adaptation as to make it ultimately a more costly solution than the custom designed one used. A kitchen specialist was helpful with suggestions on layout and design practicalities. A ten day installation period was identified but, in practice, it took four months, which was very distressing and disturbing to the family.

BATHROOM

* Bath, washbasin and wc were removed and replaced by coloured suite.

* Bath sited against end wall instead of previous position extending into room.

* Low level flush wc positioned out from wall with cistern supported on 220mm spacer box.

* 200mm deep washbasin with lever taps set in formica topped vanitory unit with shaver socket and mirror over.

* Level access shower, enclosed on two sides by timber frame and breeze block partitions, built against wall in centre of room with non slip ceramic floor tiles.

* Shower enclosure later removed and tiled area extended to 1200 x 1050mm floor area falling 25mm to offset drainage point.

* Outlet linked to bath waste pipe and covered with removable grating.

* Intentionally overlong shower curtains suspended from three sided rail to fall one tile in from edge.

* Supermix shower with adjustable head installed on wall and the large controls just within curtain fall.

* Remainder of floor laid to carpet tiles.

The installation of coloured bathroom suites was contrary to usual council practice, but as the family were able to find one that was less expensive than the white one proposed

Central positioning and flush floor finishes give good access to the shower

The washbasin surround gives useful storage space and arm support

and felt very strongly that the room should not look clinical, the policy was relaxed.

The resiting of the bath and washbasin allowed space for shower installation and retention of a bath in the large room. The siting and height of the wc enables Mr Chandler to be pushed over the pan in his commode/shower chair with sufficient room for assistance by the forward siting of the unit.

The worktop surround to the washbasin is useful for storage of commonly used items and as a base for forearm support when carrying out personal care. The edge of the worktop aids security as it stops Mr Chandler toppling sideways when using the wc. The basin is, however, too deep to allow knee room for optimum use and the high rim impedes straightforward access to taps.

It proved difficult to give Mr Chandler the assistance he needed in the shower cubicle because of the restrictive walls, which also blocked all natural light to the wc and washbasin area. Within months, the timber framing began to warp, tiles to fall away and the floor to overflow when the shower was in use. No provision had been made for access to clean the blocked waste outlet which was, subsequently, found to contain a substantial amount of tile grouting cement. After inspection by the council, discussion and the alternative design idea offered by Mr Chandler, the cubicle was removed and repair made to the drain to allow

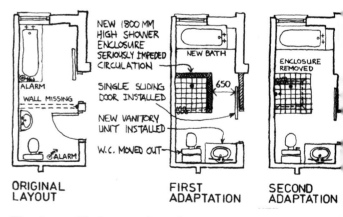

The stages of bathroom adaptation

installation of the replacement shower. The position of the shower controls allows regulation from outside and the operator need not get wet as well, although, in practice Mrs Chandler often showers herself at the same time. The curtains contain splash and their length eliminates seepage with the result that, in fifteen months of use, there has been no problem of water damage to the surrounding carpet. The removable grating allows hand cleaning of the gulley.

Textured tiles were avoided as Mr Chandler has problems of hypersensitivity of the soles of his feet and also found heavily textured surfaces to be difficult to clean.

28

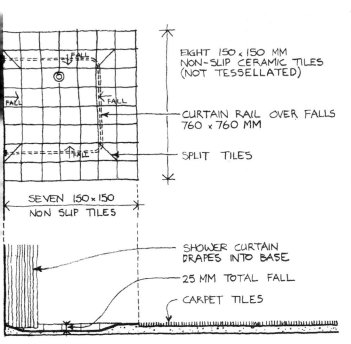

EIGHT 150 x 150 MM NON-SLIP CERAMIC TILES (NOT TESSELLATED)

CURTAIN RAIL OVER FALLS 760 x 760 MM

SPLIT TILES

SEVEN 150 x 150 NON SLIP TILES

SHOWER CURTAIN DRAPES INTO BASE

25 MM TOTAL FALL

CARPET TILES

Shower details

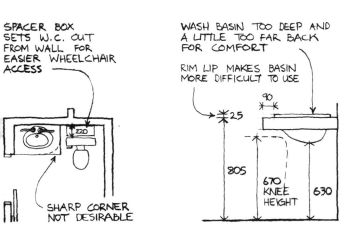

SPACER BOX SETS W.C. OUT FROM WALL FOR EASIER WHEELCHAIR ACCESS

220

SHARP CORNER NOT DESIRABLE

WASH BASIN TOO DEEP AND A LITTLE TOO FAR BACK FOR COMFORT

RIM LIP MAKES BASIN MORE DIFFICULT TO USE

90

25

805

670 KNEE HEIGHT

630

Dimensions of the washbasin and wc are critical to access, and safety would be improved by removal of the sharp corner of the washbasin surround

BEDROOM

* Additional doors to cupboard abutting service duct installed to give access from bedroom to that already possible from living area.

* Free standing dressing table and wardrobes opened by suspended loop handles.

* Hanging rail in one half of wardrobe lowered to 1170mm.

* Telephone point sited by bed.

The built in cupboard provides useful storage for a second wheelchair. The plinth of the free standing units prevents level access and Mr Chandler, therefore, sits sideways to use the open shelving and successful height rail. He is able to hook his fingers easily into the handles to operate the doors, which was the main feature in the family's choice of this range of furniture.

The less than ideal positioning of the bed and cupboards was unavoidable as it was determined by the need for access to the fire escape door, the position of the service duct, the windows and the shape of the room.

STUDY

* Dustbin housing area outside flat annexed to give additional room to flat.

* Opening made at end of hallway and sliding door fitted.

* Two windows made in room.

* Floor screeded to level with rest of floor area and interior brought up to standard.

As wheelchair circulation space had to be preserved in the main bedroom, part of Mr Chandler's stepdaughter's room became used as his office and study area. Tensions built up within the family with this increasing invasion of her domain and the need to leave papers and equipment out for easy access and use. Mr Chandler approached other residents for their views on moving the dustbin store; they were in favour as the area had been persistently used by glue sniffers and was not the most easily accessible place for refuse disposal.

The room is successfully used for Mr Chandler's various commitments and interests, many of which generate a lot of papers which can be left out in an easily accessible place without inconvenience to the rest of the family.

The U shaped Study layout gives good access to equipment

COSTING

1978
Door entryphone   £78.00
1979
Bathroom and first shower   3500.00
1981
Office   1800.00
1983
Kitchen   5250.00
1984
Second shower   600.00

FUNDING

Social services for door intercom   £78.00
Improvement grant, 90% of £4459.00 eligible
expense for the kitchen   4014.00
Housing department 10% top up   445.00
The costs of the bathroom, shower, study, windows and
double glazing were met from the borough council housing
and maintenance budgets.

The cost of the work to create the study was considered for
an improvement grant on the grounds of it being an
employment facility but, in the event, the cost was met
from the housing maintenance budget as sufficient funds
were found to be available at the end of the financial year.

As the housing department considered the flat to be
already adapted, they could not agree a fully fitted
wheelchair accessible kitchen and the family applied for an
improvement grant with full information on plans, costing
and installation. The environmental health officer
concerned was unsure of the interpretation of Circular
59/78 in terms of a male housewife and applied to the
Department of the Environment for advice; they agreed the
principle and recommended the involvement of an
occupational therapist, if this had not already been
arranged.

For the kitchen a full eligible grant was given on all
fitments except the wall cabinets, which were inaccessible
from a wheelchair. Payment was made to Mr Chandler,
who witheld 10 per cent of the final payment to the
supplier for correction of the washing machine and waste
disposal plumbing problems. The housing authority initially
saw the 10 per cent top up to the improvement grant as the
responsibility of social services, who had been instrumental
in seeking a new kitchen for the family. Social services
could not agree that the original and purpose built kitchen
was to wheelchair standard. Convinced that it had been
brought up to such a standard and increased in value by the
new work, the housing authority met the final outstanding
sum.

CONTRACTUAL PROCEDURE

For the initial adaptation to the bathroom and the
replacement windows, the council's direct labour
organization was used. For construction of the study and
work on the second shower, the housing department placed
the contract with a local builder and with a specialist firm
for the double glazing. The contract for the kitchen was
between Mr Chandler and a firm of kitchen specialists.

EVALUATION

The size of the flat, being some 90m^2 is generous and
allows ease of circulation and a sense of spaciousness. This
has proved very important to Mr Chandler, whose earlier
life had a history of overcrowding and accommodation
difficulties, and to his stepdaughter who once felt a loss of
privacy when her bedroom was used as an office. The
layout of the flat has not, however, allowed the best use of
the space; in the **bedroom** the need to preserve access to
the fire door and to arrange furniture around the service
ducting has created further problems of wheelchair
circulation in the already narrow room.

A considerable amount of work was done in the kitchen,
bathroom and study of a flat that was already designated,
by the housing department, as being suitable for use from a
wheelchair. The social services occupational therapist had
some difficulty in persuading the housing department that
the flat they considered to be already suitably adapted was
nearer to DOE mobility standard than to the wheelchair
one and that, therefore, further adaptations would be
required.

No small instrument in making the changes was Mr
Chandler's personality and desire to organize his own life.
Each problem was approached in a knowledgeable and
determined way with some definite and well researched
ideas on the solutions to be employed. He was able to
persuade the housing and grant giving departments of his
special needs and was not willing to settle for anything less
than the best. He persisted with his concept of the correct
design of **shower** for him and, despite the radical idea of a
roll in shower extending into a carpeted room, has been
proved right. He was also able to persuade changes in
policy, as seen in the choice of the coloured bathroom
suite, in order to allow the flat to look as attractive as
possible. As with this, his argument in favour of an
expensive custom built kitchen was on the grounds of a
saving in projected finance, as would appeal to an authority
needing to justify every expenditure.

The precise knowledge of his condition, abilities and
limitations, with which he has lived for many years, has
made Mr Chandler impatient at times of personnel who do
not always agree with his assessment of the problem or
with the projected solution. Early experiences which could
not produce the house adaptations he so badly needed,
might also be said to contribute to this attitude. His
dependence on full time support from a carer has also been
consistently reinforced by experience that the loss of a live
in carer means transfer to a residential establishment and it
seems regrettable that he has never been assessed in using
such equipment as an electric hoist, although he cannot
envisage it being any help to him.

The features not aiding independence for a wheelchair user
are only in areas that are unimportant to Mr Chandler or
fulfil some other priority in the family. There is limited use
of the external openings with panic bolts that are
inoperable in conjunction with the stiff **doors**, and there is
a threshold over which he cannot gain access to the flat.
His difficulty with the front door lock is less important to
him than ensuring security and he has little confidence in
other systems which he might use more easily, as he
considers them be more vulnerable to intruders. The
internal doors, other than the kitchen one in relation to the
table, present no problems and, as a result of the work to
improve heating, can be left open without adverse effects
on temperature.

The fact that Mr Chandler can no longer operate the **windows** independently has been entirely his own decision and greater emphasis on countering heat loss. The central pivot windows were, anyway, in poor condition and created problems in trapping curtains which was a source of irritation.

The **kitchen** is appreciated by all the family with units that are very easy to use, attractive and well finished. The handles into which Mr Chandler can hook his fingers, in conjunction with the touch control, allows a far higher degree of independence and responsibility for domestic tasks than was possible in the previous layout. The design of the sink unit affords unobtrusive provision of knee space when not in use and ample cabinets elsewhere make up for this loss of storage space. The corner carousel unit is particularly easy to use, as is the toggle tap with its adjustable mixer and programme of uses.

The position of the table is regrettable as it considerably hinders circulation in a well designed layout of fixtures, and rehanging of the door would allow little more useful space. However, while there is sufficient space in the living area for its repositioning, the greater distance from the kitchen would cause Mr Chandler difficulties in serving that he does not presently have. The funding for the work was agreed on the grounds that he was required to take on a domestic role, and his wife the breadwinning one.

The size of the **bathroom** and its original layout with two doors presumably allowed the possibility of dividing the wc area from that of the bath, if required. To the Chandler family it meant the possibility of reorganization and sufficient space for retention of a bath with installation of a shower in addition.

The positioning of the **washbasin** in its surround is not ideal and could have been improved by the use of a basin at least 50mm less deep. In addition, the provision of a washbasin with a flush rim lip might have alleviated the problems created for Mr Chandler. The edge beside the wc is useful but he would have preferred the front corner to have been rounded off as he can catch himself on this sharp edge when gaining access to the wc.

The level access **shower** works very well, despite some fears that siting it in the middle of a carpeted floor would cause problems of water damage. The overall effect of the room is of warmth and luxury with features which meet the varying needs and preferences of all the family members.

The **study** proved to be invaluable both to Mr Chandler and to his stepdaughter whose bedroom he had previously used as an office. It would be difficult and exhausting for him to set up everything he uses on a daily basis in an area of general use, and relationships within the family might have been permanently soured by inability to meet the needs of his stepdaughter in a property so much organized to his special needs.

The ideas Mr Chandler so usefully applies in his flat are examples of his thoughtful approach to problems and painstaking research prior to application for installation. The background work, which incorporated study on exact solutions, identification of the most appropriate agency and the correct legislation to invoke has made him a powerful, articulate and knowledgeable advocate of his own needs and those of other disabled people. His home, its comfort and style coupled with attention to functional requirements is the epitome of this and his approach to life.

MRS VIOLET BROWN

Aged 79. Bilateral cataracts, glaucoma and mild osteoarthritis.

Widowed and living alone.

Reconstruction of a barn into a cottage.

In her early seventies Mrs Brown became increasingly aware that her sight was deteriorating. Her mother had been visually handicapped for the last twenty years of life and there were practical lessons of this experience to be used. With the support of her husband, she set about organising her home to make the best use of natural and artificial light, to identify useful and invariable positions for essential equipment and to eliminate potential hazards.

Mrs Brown was treated for glaucoma and in 1978 underwent surgery for removal of a cataract. Unfortunately, there was no improvement and, while she had light and shape perception and could sometimes find a clear patch of vision, her sight generally was very misted. She developed an interest in reading and writing braille, enjoyed the talking book service and also kept up her correspondence, although she could not read her own writing. She had a little domestic help with cleaning but otherwise continued responsibility for running the home.

Shortly after Mrs Brown's return from hospital her husband died and she was left to face life alone in her large isolated farmhouse. Her family were worried about her living on her own, but she was reluctant to consider alternatives as she did not want to leave the home she had shared with her husband for nearly fifty years, and her circle of friends. The house, though large, was entirely familiar to her and a move to new surroundings with failing sight was thought to be a difficult proposition. A network of support was set up which included a daily set time telephone call to a relative which would have triggered a check visit if it had not come, regular visits from her son who lived ten miles away and from her daughter who lived two hundred miles away. Friends, neighbours, nephews and neices all visited from time to time as well as tradesmen who delivered her weekly provisions.

Discussions about a move continued however, especially when the rather isolated position of the house started to outweigh its advantages to Mrs Brown. Options considered were that she continue to live alone with support, move in with her daughter or seek suitably adapted accommodation close to a family member. She was strongly opposed to the mixing of generations and to relinquishing independent living, although she recognised that some assistance was becoming necessary.

Eventually a property was sought in the village where her daughter lived, in the south west of England. Nothing was immediately available and, as it was a small village it was thought that it could be some time before a suitable property was offered for sale. It was then that her daughter had the idea of approaching her neighbour who owned the house and farmyard immediately adjacent to their own property and who had planning permission for conversion of a haybarn to a two storey dwelling.

The neighbour and Mrs Brown agreed to this mutually beneficial idea of building a new house and, while the shell was defined, the family were left to organise the rest of the property to suit their own particular needs. They firstly assessed Mrs Brown's requirements on the detailed information that they had, which was that she could see, as if in twilight; she was able to recognise colour contrast; she had a good sense of touch and smell and only minimal hearing loss; she was of small stature and had restricted use of her right shoulder. She was otherwise fully mobile, clear thinking and able to anticipate practical problems. Areas of potential difficulty were identified from the assessment, and planning was based on the principles of utilizing other senses to compensate for visual handicap, that dependence on residual sight should not be allowed to become a crucial factor and limitations of mobility, associated with old age should also be considered.

An architect had already drawn up plans for the reconstruction of the barn into a cottage, which the neighbour had started to build himself. The new project was more urgent, and a local builder was appointed to the task. Mrs Brown's daughter and son in law, Dr and Mrs Thurston, worked closely with the builder in planning the layout of rooms and the details. It was decided to annexe part of the cow pen adjoining the barn to form a second reception room/bedroom and a cloakroom so that Mrs Brown could remain on the ground floor if necessary. An additional external door at the side of the house was proposed to allow the most simple traffic between the two properties. Mrs Thurston contacted national organizations dealing with sensory handicap and was given some general pointers on design.

Planning and preparation for the move was given maximum attention as building work commenced in late 1979. Dr Thurston made a wooden scale model of each floor to window cill height which allowed Mrs Brown to familiarize herself with the size and layout of the rooms. Using small pieces of cardboard cut to scale, she was able to plan the arrangement of her furniture in order to assess suitability, positioning and preservation of circulation space. Lists and discussions were recorded on cassette tapes, to which she could refer.

The building was in a worse state of repair than had first been realized. Whereas the original plans called for bricking up the central opening in the front wall and the insertion of four new windows, the wall itself was found to be bowed and had to be removed. The 355mm thick wall was taken down, and bricks retained for the reconstruction. At this point the building inspector decided that the foundations also needed attention and were to be replaced in concrete. The front wall was rebuilt with a load bearing blockwork inner skin and an outer skin of old bricks. Originally the floor level in the annexe was to have been lower than that of the main building, but the family insisted that an internal step would not be desirable and a new flush concrete floor was laid throughout. The raised level of the floor combined with the eaves of the cow pen resulted in a reduced head height for the main entrance door, which the builder set as high as possible, and the building inspector accepted.

When the first floor was erected at the minimum height of 2300mm above the raised floor, there was no longer sufficient headroom below the level of the existing roof trusses for the first floor rooms and, as the feet of the rafters were badly rotted, it was decided to raise and renew the entire roof structure. The raised roof line required more planning permission and it was agreed on site that it could be submitted as an amendment to the original permission given, which the builder filed himself.

On completion of the building, new carpets with textural and tonal changes to delineate rooms were fitted and it was with these and just the empty shell that Mrs Brown first experienced her new home. She moved from the farmhouse in October 1980 and spent the first two weeks with her daughter, taking time to learn about the new property and to organise her furniture which arrived a few days later.

Everyone had been apprehensive about the first weeks when Mrs Brown would be at her most vulnerable and problems at their most acute. It was felt that the long term success of the project would be jeopardised if difficulties and failings in the cottage contributed further to the trauma of the move. In the event, the transition was smooth and Mrs Brown took to her new home immediately, eased by diligent preparation work with the scale model and tapes, good planning and a positive approach from all concerned.

Mrs Brown was able to learn the layout of her new cottage from the scale model

THE PROJECT TEAM
Dr and Mrs Thurston.
A local builder.

THE AIMS
To preserve an independent lifestyle in close proximity to family support.
To promote safety in the home by careful planning and, where possible, to eliminate hazard.
To utilize residual sight without dependence on it.
To allow flexibility for possible changes in circumstances associated with increasing age and limitations of mobility.

THE PROPERTY
* A two storey cottage.

* Gross internal floor area 82m².

The cottage was formed from a barn which backed onto the boundary wall of Dr and Mrs Thurston's house. Part of an adjoining cow pen was annexed and rebuilt to form a single storey extension of entrance hall, cloakroom and reception room/bedroom. Internal walls were organised to give an L

shaped lounge/dining area and a kitchen on the ground floor with two bedrooms and a bathroom above.

A small garden bed was formed at the side of the house and the entire front area was laid to gravel. The garden was planted with fragrant shrubs, bright flowers and contrasting foliage supplemented by the use of plants in easily tended concrete tubs.

Mrs Brown finds the garden's size and design easy to cope with and gains pleasure from being able to continue a life long interest in a manageable setting. The choice of plants was influenced by colour contrast, light reflection and fragrance.

THE ADAPTATION
Reconstruction of a barn to form a purpose built home for a partially sighted person.

EXTERNAL DOORS AND PATHWAYS
* Single glazed panelled external doors with latch locks and lever handles.

* 170mm threshold step at front entrance and 120mm at side.

* Concrete path constructed from side door to the Thurston's house via gateway made in boundary wall.

* White guide rope suspended on poles at height 840mm at edge of the path.

It had been hoped to avoid steps altogether, but in a straight choice between threshold steps used infrequently and an internal difference in floor levels, the former was accepted as preferable. In the event, Mrs Brown safely negotiates each of the steps knowing them to be potential hazards that can be avoided by care and attention. The steps prevent rain penetration to the unsheltered external doors. The glazed doors help to increase light in the house and the side door, the pathway and safety rope afford easy access between the houses. The sound of footsteps on the gravel gives Mrs Brown early warning of an approach and the pale colour of the stones increases the amount of light admitted to the house.

WINDOWS
* Large casement windows with single glazed panels and large lever furniture installed in front wall of house.

* Small high level window sited at back of house to give light to stairway.

* Skylight to ground floor cloakroom.

* Casement window to bathroom on side wall.

There are no trees or other obstructions in front of the south facing windows and winter sunshine penetrates deep into the house. The property does not however, become overly hot in the summer as the area of glazing has been kept down to 10 per cent. This and the use of thermally lined curtains means that heat loss through the single glazing is minimal. The layout of the house is organized so that the larger spaces of the lounge, kitchen and bedrooms

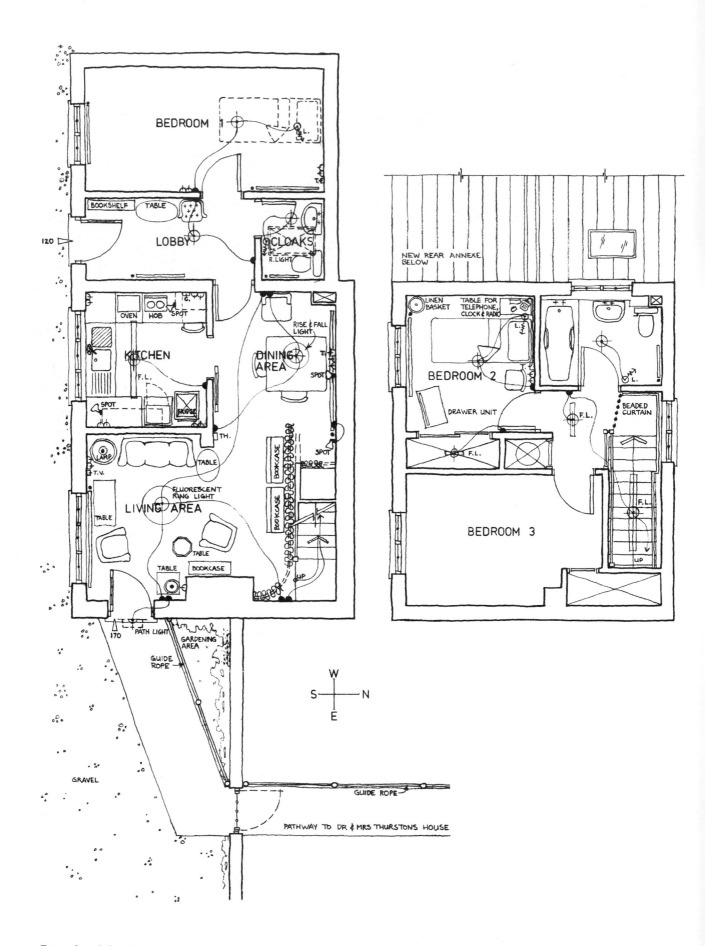

Ground and first floor plans. 1:75

MRS BROWN'S COTTAGE

The reconstructed barn and annexed cow pen. The path on the right leads through a gateway in the wall to her daughter's house

receive the strong sunlight, and the smaller and more easily identified ones, a darker backdrop. In practice the house is divided into a light and bright half at the front and a darker area at the back, both of which are used to good effect in allocation of space to specific tasks.

There does not seem to be any problem of heat loss in relation to the single glazing but the use of curtains with thermal linings at windows and doors is an additional feature that helps at night.

ELECTRICAL WORK

* Power points set at 400mm and light switches at 1300mm above floor level and marked with fluorescent coloured tape.

* Four double switched power points at worktop height in kitchen.

* Two way system operated lighting for stairs and main rooms.

* Pull cord light switches in bedrooms and bathroom.

An ample number of sockets allows the use of supplementary spot lighting if necessary in all of the main rooms. Mrs Brown finds the bright tape[1] helpful for location of outlets on the pale, light reflecting walls; she would have liked them to have been sited higher on the wall to obviate the need to bend or reach around furniture. A sufficient number of power points allow appliances to be kept at their centre of use without the need to interchange

plugs in the sockets. Their positions on the rear walls and in corners eliminate the risk of trailing flexes, but she has difficulty in reaching to operate them because of shoulder joint stiffness. The two way switching system of lighting in the main rooms and between the stairway and landing means that Mrs Brown can assure light ahead of her and switch off behind her. Pull cord switches to good lighting eliminates the need for freestanding bedside lamps, which could be knocked over.

HEATING

Spare capacity in the Thurstons' boiler permitted linking the oil fired system to give radiators in all rooms of the cottage and control on an individual basis.

In practice, Mrs Brown leaves all management of the heating to her daughter and there has been no need to adapt controls to overcome problems of visual handicap. The ample provision of radiators allows the house to be kept at an even and warm temperature, as required by Mrs Brown's sedentary lifestyle.

INTERNAL DOORS

* Half glazed sliding door installed to kitchen.

* All other doors made to open against walls and lever handles used throughout.

* Half glazed door between dining area and hall.

[1] Brightly coloured electrical plugs and socket plates are now widely available.

D

* Locks, opened with a coin from the outside in an emergency, fitted to bathroom and cloakroom doors.

The choice of a sliding door means that space is not restricted in the kitchen or circulation impeded by an outward opening door across the area of movement from the lounge to the dining room/hallway. The well constructed and easily moved door means that Mrs Brown can operate it at a touch to the edge, from the dining room, and to the recess of the glass panel from the kitchen. She finds these methods easy and there has been no need for door furniture. Doors opening against walls reduce the risk of them being left half open and in a position into which she might walk.

HALLWAY, LANDING AND STAIRS

* Broad hallway formed to link front door with second reception room/bedroom, cloakroom and rest of house.

* Bannister with intermediate rail installed to give protection to open side of stairway.

* Stout timber rail mounted on wall at 780mm above pitch line to give continuous support up to top and around small level landing area to bathroom door opening.

* Bead curtain hung across landing.

As there was no immediate need to eliminate use of the stairs, the single storey extension incorporating features essential to ground floor living could be separated off initially in terms of heating and daily living. In fact, Mrs Brown currently uses the additional room as a store which has proved useful in the retention of possessions from a large house. However, the provision of a pull cord light, telephone point, heating and the adjacent cloakroom means that it could be easily converted to a bedroom if necessary.

The use of the bead curtain at the top of the stairs was first identified by Mrs Thurston who was concerned that her mother might make a wrong turning out of the bathroom, perhaps in the night, and be at the top of the stairs thinking it was the bedroom door.

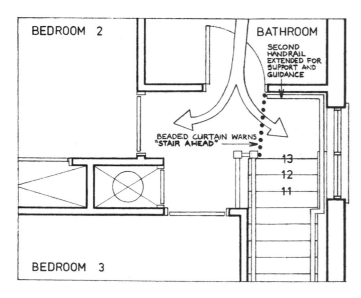

The sound of the bead curtain immediately warns Mrs Brown that she is nearing the stairs

A cuckoo clock on the wall of the stairs relentlessly keeps Mrs Brown aware of time throughout the house and is easily wound with chain pulleys.

LIVING AREA

* Shallow shelves formed in understairs space in dining area.

* Rise and fall light with telescopic flex fitted over proposed position of the dining table.

* Telephone point installed as close to anticipated position of telephone as possible to avoid trailing flex.

* Curtain rail and pulley fitted to room side of staircase.

* Walls painted milk white with brilliant white colour used for woodwork and ceilings.

Mrs Brown uses the dining table as a work area with equipment such as a talking book machine and brailler conveniently stored on the nearby shelves. The lamp can be easily pulled down or retracted to get the best degree of lighting from the 60 watt bulb and she finds the comparative darkness around useful in giving a contrast and complete focus to the type of task she undertakes here. The table and shelves are organised to give each item its own invariable place and the position of the dining area and table close to the kitchen door is helpful when entertaining, as she is able to move in a straight line between the two rooms for serving.

Mrs Brown can reach through the edge of the bead curtain with her left hand to have continuous bannister support to the foot of the stairway

Cord operated, oatmeal coloured curtains were installed to divide the stairway from the living room and to decrease heat loss. However, in practice, they have also helped in identifying the side of the stairway making it more clearly visible to Mrs Brown than the more difficult shapes of the ballustrade. The milk white walls give good light reflection and cause furniture to be shown in stark contrast.

KITCHEN

* Floor covered in dark red, short pile, washable carpeting.

The food preparation and cooking area of the kitchen

* Work surfaces installed at height 770mm and covered in dark edged bright white melamine.

* Worktop under small surface mounted oven lowered by 50mm to allow door to drop down to height equal to that of adjacent work top.

* Double sink and single drainer sited under window and large handled mixer taps fitted in uniform order of hot on left as used throughout the house.

* Standard flat pack undersink cupboard, with outward opening doors and integral rubbish bin that opened automatically with door on a pull cord.

* Upward opening top box wall cabinets fitted at height 1390mm from floor.

* Three deep shelves made under work surface and set of drawers and larder unit brought from Mrs Brown's old house.

* Fluorescent light strip supplemented by individual spot lamps clamped to wall cupboards.

The sink and tea making area of the kitchen

* Tea caddy with automatic measuring mounted on wall under one of top cupboards.

Mrs Brown has organized her kitchen into three maintask orientated areas of cooking, washing and tea making. The cooking area consists of the oven and hob and adjacent work surface. Heat control knobs are marked in fluorescent tape and temperature is judged by degree of turning. Ingredients are stored in the wall cupboard above and saucepans on the shelves below. A spotlight operated from its own push button switch can be easily adjusted to direct light either onto the work surface or hobs. Immediately adjacent to this there is knee hole space at which she sits on a kitchen chair to eat when on her own. The washing and soap storage area is between the oven and the sink and does not adjoin a worksurface where items could be confused with food packets. The sink divides this from the tea making area, which also has its own spotlight. Mrs Brown uses a short spout upright kettle which can boil just one cup of water at a time and pours with the cup on a tray to give easy cleaning of any spillages. Crockery is kept on foam lining to the drawers, which helps to stop them sliding when the drawer is opened, and cups are stored upside down to reduce risk of breakages as she touches to locate them.

The bright work surfaces with their delineated edges give a good contrast to dark coloured utensils. Their depth of 580mm gives sufficient working space but is difficult for Mrs Brown to reach over in order to operate the corner electric socket outlets. In the same way, the shelves are nearly as deep and are therefore difficult to reach into and cause stored items to get easily lost.

The opening of the top box doors, which will only lock open in the maximum upward position, eliminate the hazard of walking into a half open door. The undersink cupboard doors have their firm snap closing on magnetic catches to help reduce the hazard of them being left open in the mid position. The silver coloured bars which act as handles on the cupboard doors and drawers tend to catch the light and help Mrs Brown to locate them.

The positioning of the tall fridge freezer by the door does not allow its height to interrupt working levels. There is sufficient space for storage of an ironing board between the freezer and the wall, which not only makes it easy to retrieve but prevents it from being knocked over as might happen in a cupboard or in a more open space. The automatic opening of the rubbish bin lid is helpful as it allows Mrs Brown a free hand to check the location of the rim of the bin. The floor carpet is easily cleaned and contrasts well with the white units. The window blind eliminates the risk of swishing curtains knocking anything over, although Mrs Brown is too well organized to allow items to be left in this way.

The second sink is kept permanently covered and is used as an additional work surface. This unit was one of the few requirements made by the leaseholding neighbour and has been easily adapted to Mrs Brown's needs.

Mrs Brown's kitchen plan 1:50. The U shaped organization gives access to maximum area of work surface from minimum area of floor

BATHROOM

* Pastel coloured suite of bath with integral grab rails, wc and washbasin installed in first floor bathroom.

* Black seat given to wc and black panelling to bath.

* Large adjustable mirror sited on wall immediately adjacent to window.

The colour contrast used here and in the ground floor cloakroom is helpful and the position of the mirror allows adjustment to catch the best possible light from the window. The bath grab rails are some help in enabling Mrs Brown to get out of the bath safely, but she acknowledges that she may soon need a rail higher on the wall than at bath rim level.

BEDROOM

* Built in cupboard with hanging space, shelves and sliding doors.

* Telephone point sited by proposed position of bed.

The doors on the cupboard are easy to operate and Mrs Brown keeps a small number of easily recognised clothes in this wardrobe. Her daughter helps her to organize this and the cupboard in the spare bedroom is used as the back up store.

COSTING

1980		
The building		£32000.00
Top box kitchen cupboards - approximately		33.00 each
Rise and fall lamp - approximately		17.00
Spot lamps - approximately		7.00 each
Bead curtain - approximately		8.00

FUNDING:

Improvement grant given on the grounds of bringing a building up to standard and not on disability £2800.00

CONTRACTUAL PROCEDURE

A contract was made between the site owning neighbour and a local builder, although much of the administration of the project was undertaken by the Thurston family.

EVALUATION

Moving two hundred miles from such a long term home and the many friends and contacts must have seemed a daunting proposition to Mrs Brown. That the move and the building project proved so successful is the merit of three people's single minded tackling of the problems involved, with original plans from an architect and support from a committed and interested builder. The family's previous experience of visual handicap, along with Dr and Mrs Thurston's own medical backgrounds, helped generate a capable team.

The success or failure, however, rested with Mrs Brown who, having acknowledged the need to move to her daughter's village, committed herself to thoughtful and painstaking preparation. She was able to learn constructively from her own mother's experience of blindness and could adapt positively to moving without passive reliance upon her daughter.

The result is that the occupants of the two houses lead their own lives but can share interests and gain support at will. Mrs Brown enjoys being able to do her own things in her own time and appreciates that this is at no expense to anxiety of her family. She has made new friends in the village and keeps in close touch with news, family and friends in the area of her old home.

The family were fortunate that such a convenient site existed, that planning permission had been given and that the neighbour was willing to comply so readily. Had a site been found elsewhere in the village, it is doubtful whether it could have had equal advantages and certainly could not have allowed such frequent and easy traffic between the houses. Equally, the fact that Mrs Brown could fund the new home, before a move from the old, gave time for comprehensive planning.

The shell of the building was predetermined by the existing hay barn and the site. This presented no constraints in meeting Mrs Brown's particular needs other than the creation of door steps which, while they might ideally have been avoided, do give protection from water penetration at the exposed external **doors**. The position of the cottage against the Thurston's boundary wall meant that any **windows** on the back wall would have overlooked their property, and while this has resulted in nearly all windows being sited in the front wall, it has also had the effect of giving useful light changes within the house. The use of glazed doors has also assisted and the general impression is of a light and airy home.

The fluorescent tabs marking **switches** and carpet colour and texture changes between rooms were also helpful in the first few weeks when the house was unfamiliar. They became less critical however, once room layout was well known, which proved fortuitous as Mrs Brown's sight has subsequently deteriorated.

The **kitchen** is well designed, work areas being reached easily with a U shape promoting efficiency with the maximum number of units accessible from the minimum of floor space. A double sink is beyond the likely needs of a person living on her own and in this instance would have increased problems of possible confusion between the sinks being used, had one not been covered. The top boxes, though low, are ideal for Mrs Brown's small stature in terms of reach and head clearance. Sound ideas are utilized in layout, in choice of contrasting utensils, white plates with dark rims, scissors where possible instead of kitchen knives and in scrupulous attention to methods of storage and lighting. All items are standard equipment and inexpensive. However, some time and effort was required to find things that were exactly right and the builder created or adapted certain features, such as the easily managed sliding door, worktops and built in cupboards.

A gross internal floor area of 82m² would seem more than adequate for a person living on her own. However, Mrs Brown was used to a very much larger home and the ability to bring as much of her own furniture as possible was important in easing the transition. The use of familiar things contributed to the process of settling in the new house and Mrs Brown commented that the sitting room soon felt just like her old one.

While some general advice was available from relevant organizations, the family was not directed towards any literature or specialist in the field of design and adaptation for the visually handicapped.[2] The family, therefore, had to develop their own ideas as seen in the use of the preparatory model, the bead curtain, colour contrasts, kitchen methods and principles of layout and light. The result is a product of thoughtful planning, hard work, good communication and understanding of the problems of visual handicap.

[2] The Disabled Living Foundation has recently opened a demonstration kitchen. See page 211.

MRS JANET WATSON

Aged 35. Poliomyelitis.

Married with a daughter aged 5.

Adaptation of an owner occupied bungalow.

Mrs Watson contracted poliomyelitis at the age of two and a half and underwent medical treatment and surgery in following years. Her family were determined that she should lead an ordinary life and gave her every encouragement to overcome physical limitations and attain full independence. She attended local primary and secondary schools, going on to secretarial training at the age of eighteen. Qualifications achieved were put to good use in full time employment with various commercial firms in the following years and she maintained an active social and sporting life.

When, in 1975, she became engaged to be married, she and her fiance looked around for suitable accommodation in outer London that would meet her special needs within reasonable travelling distance of work and families. Finance available to first time buyers directed them towards flats and maisonettes which, with their often insufficient parking space, could not guarantee the necessary short distance for getting from her ministry tricycle to the door. In addition, many blocks seemed to be in hilly areas with difficult access and steep steps compensating for sloping sites.

Mrs Watson's degree of handicap was considerably reduced by the use of trick movements and her expectation was that she should be independent in her role as career woman and housewife. Nevertheless, certain features were required in the home to assist her and were planned on her knowledge of her own strengths and limitations:

Mobility. Her right leg had little strength and required the use of a full length cosmetic caliper with a hinged knee. The left leg was stronger, but the foot dropped and everted. The left shoulder was arthrodesed and there was no active movement in the upper right arm. Tendon shortening surgery had been successful in giving opposition of the thumbs and in allowing the left elbow to compensate for lack of strength in the arm muscles. By placing her left hand and arm into a functional position, with her right, she could use her shoulder girdle to achieve movement. She could walk short distances with concentration on balance and walking and used an outdoor electric wheelchair and a ministry tricycle for longer distances.

Dressing. Mrs Watson was independent with careful choice of clothes.

Wc. An increased seat height and support rails were necessary to remove the risk of her falling backwards onto the wc and to assist in rising.

Bathing. She could not get onto or off the base of the bath or negotiate the rim without considerable help and support.

Bed and chair. She was independent, providing seat heights were not too low.

Domestic tasks. She enjoyed cooking and was a firm believer in healthy eating and the rejection of convenience foods. Some labour saving equipment was necessary to assist with food preparation, washing and cleaning if her limited energy was to be conserved. She could hang out washing providing items were not very big or the line too high.

Hobbies and interests. Mrs Watson was involved in secretarial work for a voluntary organization and enjoyed gardening, sewing and sporting activities.

Eventually Mrs Watson and her fiance found a suitable bungalow in a level area adjacent to a large park and completed the purchase four months before their marriage in 1976. The fact that such a property came into their price range was explained by its very poor state of repair and, as a result, Mr Watson spent the months before the move doing the essential work of bringing the bathroom up to standard and raising the front pathway and garden to reduce the steep steps at the main entrance.

Mr and Mrs Watson gradually incorporated special features in their new home as they improved and enlarged the bungalow in the following years. Mr Watson did the general work, such as rewiring, plumbing, replacement of ceilings and repairs himself, and the first major project of extending the living area was completed with the help of a builder in 1977.

When in 1979 their daughter was born, new difficulties arose in mangement of a baby that Mrs Watson could not carry and whose every need was her sole responsibility during the day. An occupational therapist visited and discussed practical ways of managing and a home help assisted with some of the domestic tasks.

A perspex box replaced a cot and was fitted to the wall at a suitable height, allowing Mrs Watson easy access and the baby the possibility of seeing around, in compensation for not being carried from place to place. Reinforcement of the base of a playpen, with fitment of a gate and castors, allowed it to be moved around and be strong enough to support Mrs Watson's weight, as she got into it with the baby for feeding, playing and changing.

A ramp and platform was suggested for the side door into the carport but, although the steps were difficult, she felt able to cope with the support of a handrail and grab bar. She gave up her tricycle for a car with automatic transmission, so that she could take the child out with her and, in later years, a wendy house in the garden gave their daughter a playroom, in order that toys were not kept in the small bungalow where they could be a hazard to Mrs Watson's safe mobility.

Work continued on the bungalow and included upgrading of the kitchen to include some special features for her use and, on completion, she applied for an improvement grant which she hoped would be paid retrospectively. Shortly after making this request in 1983, she badly sprained her ankle when she fell down the side steps and had to be dependent on a wheelchair in the house for the first time.

It was then that the general limitations of size and layout, particularly in the kitchen, became forcefully apparent in her loss of independence. Help was sought from the occupational therapist, who provided a castor wheelchair and suggested a shower, and sliding doors to the living room and second bedroom. Neither the visiting environmental health officer nor the occupational therapist could agree that the kitchen was suitable and Mrs Watson had to acknowledge that it was small and had areas that were inaccessible to her.

Consequently, the retrospective grant was refused, with payment agreed for a suggested extension to enlarge the kitchen to the line of the lounge extension and to incorporate some features of the old kitchen to reduce costs and, thereby make a contribution towards the expense that Mr and Mrs Watson had already incurred. In addition, a new layout and fitments would improve the use of the room and promote maximum independence in activities that Mrs Watson enjoyed.

THE PROJECT TEAM

Mr and Mrs Watson.
London borough council social services occupational therapist.
London borough council environmental health officer.
Builder.

THE AIMS

To bring the property up to a good structural and decorative standard, incorporating features for special needs and maximum independence.
To promote the needs of family life in provision of a comfortable home and environment in which to bring up a child.
To allow a traditional role of housewife and mother.

THE PROPERTY

* A two bedroomed bungalow built in 1935.

* Gross internal floor area 47.0m². 56.3m² and 64.2² following two extensions.

The bungalow was situated on a slight slope within a generally flat area close to a small shopping centre. A carport with outward opening doors adjoined the property to the side and allowed space for storage and car parking. To the rear a garden was laid mainly to lawn with the addition of two garden sheds.

Front view of the property

Modifications gradually made over the years produced an extension to the lounge and kitchen and, in the garden, raised borders supported by 400mm retaining walls, terracing, additional paving and sitting out areas. A wendy house was sited close to the bungalow and the paved area.

Mrs Watson has no problem in driving up to the car port over the pavement crossover or in parking her car, as there is sufficient room for car doors to be opened to the

maximum angle for ease of getting in and out. She enjoys gardening as a hobby and finds that she can tend plants easily from a seated position on the retaining walls.

Their daughter enjoys the wendy house which not only successfully performs its function of keeping large toys out of the house, but also is a great attraction to her friends. While Mr and Mrs Watson were keen to ensure that their child should not have a home dominated by special equipment and obtrusive adaptation that would make it different from that of her friends, they have increased her stature among peers who would also like such a playroom.

THE ADAPTATION

Extension and alteration of a two bedroomed bungalow.

EXTERNAL DOORS AND PATHWAYS

* Patio doors relocated from side wall at time of kitchen extension.

* Security lock to patio doors set at height 1100mm from floor in addition to standard floor level fitment.

* Latch lock on front door converted to slide operation.

* Lever extension fitted to garage latch lock to allow operation of the double doors.

* 940mm long 1 in 9 ramp formed to patio doors.

* Front garden and pathway raised to leave two 50mm steps at front door.

* Handrail and grab rail installed to the two 100mm side entrance steps.

* Small patio formed against lounge extension.

Raising the front pathway was a first priority as the original steep steps were too great for Mrs Watson to manage in order to reach the main door and operate her key. The two shallow steps prove to be no problem to her and their retention avoided the work and expense of raising the ground to the maximum in order to eliminate them completely.

The 1 in 9 ramp at the patio doors is steep for Mrs Watson, but she finds this inconvenience preferable to the ramp's extension over valuable patio space and the possibility of trip hazard. With the support of a grab rail on the external wall, she is able to get a trolley over the ramp and the raised threshold of the sliding doors, in order to serve food outside, which the family enjoy in summer. The ramped pathway into the rear garden gives her access to the drying area, with laundry transported in a wheelchair that she had as a child. Paved areas and pathways allow her access to all parts of the garden in safety on a hard, non slip surface.

Mrs Watson can operate the lock to the front door and also that of the patio doors, where the pull handle was chosen as being most suitable for her grasp. The additional push button security lock is set at a convenient height and overrides the standard floor one, which is less accessible and rather stiff to operate. The lever handle and mortice lock on the side door were not altered.

The kitchen and dining room extension to the rear

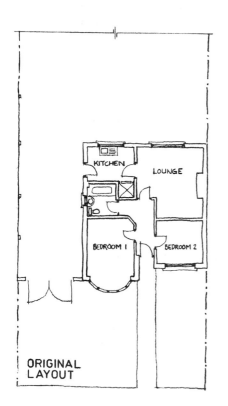
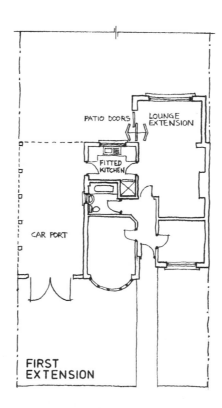
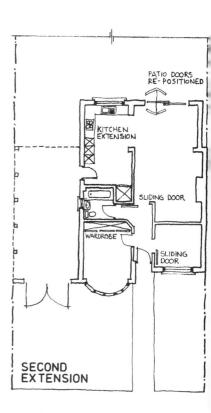

ORIGINAL LAYOUT

KITCHEN

LOUNGE

BEDROOM 1

BEDROOM 2

FIRST EXTENSION

PATIO DOORS

LOUNGE EXTENSION

FITTED KITCHEN

CAR PORT

SECOND EXTENSION

PATIO DOORS RE-POSITIONED

KITCHEN EXTENSION

SLIDING DOOR

WARDROBE

SLIDING DOOR

Major adapation to the bungalow was in two stages

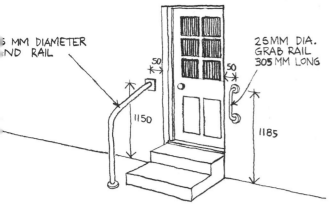

5 MM DIAMETER
ND RAIL

25MM DIA.
GRAB RAIL
305 MM LONG

50   50

1150   1185

With the support of the handrails, Mrs Watson is able to negotiate the side doorway with comparative ease

WINDOWS

* Original windows replaced with double glazed units set in aluminium frames of a type with no opening other than louvre ventilators.

* Top hung window opening, with low level catch for kitchen extension.

Mrs Watson is able to reach the high louvre windows by rotating her shoulder girdle and throwing her hand up to catch onto the lever. She can reach over the sink to the base catches on the kitchen windows and to push the window outwards. She cannot however, reach to close them and goes outside to do this if she has opened them more than a small degree.

ELECTRICAL WORK

* House rewired and light switches set at 1300mm, and most power points at 710mm.

* Double sockets for appliances mounted at 230mm above work surfaces in kitchen.

* Power supply to shower, activated by pull cord in bathroom.

* Power point in carport for recharging of electric wheelchair.

All points and switches are easily accessible with heights adjusted to allow Mrs Watson to get her weight behind her arm in pushing plugs into sockets over the work surfaces. While she can easily reach the socket in the carport, she cannot recharge the batteries on her chair as she cannot reach the connection point on the chair.

HEATING

* Gas fired central heating from back boiler sited in lounge installed to feed radiators in every room.

* Gas fire with top control in lounge.

* Pull cord wall heater and heated towel rail in bathroom.

Mrs Watson can operate the central heating clock in its easily accessible position at height 1270mm in the airing cupboard in the lounge. She finds the overall level of heating, in conjunction with the double glazing, to be efficient and economical. The position of the gas fire, set into a stone fire surround, necessitated the removal of a

Mrs Watson can reach the top hung window over the sink, but cannot push it open very far

small piece of the stone to allow her flexed fingers to clear the stone when operating the top control. The large radiator in the kitchen reduced the amount of wall space where storage units could be placed, but is a valuable source of heat in the open plan area.

HALLWAYS AND DOORS

* Archway entrance made from lounge to kitchen extension.

* Kitchen door from lounge blocked off.

* 760mm wide sliding doors with finger panels installed to lounge and second bedroom.

* Existing 710mm doors with clear opening widths of 650mm to bedroom and bathroom reatined.

The 1040mm wide hallway to the front door and 970mm passageway to the bathroom door present no problem to Mrs Watson, although access to the bathroom proved very difficult during the time she was dependent on a wheelchair, and continues to be so for non ambulant friends who visit her.

LIVING AREA

* Small living area increased by approximately 9m² by extension of room to rear.

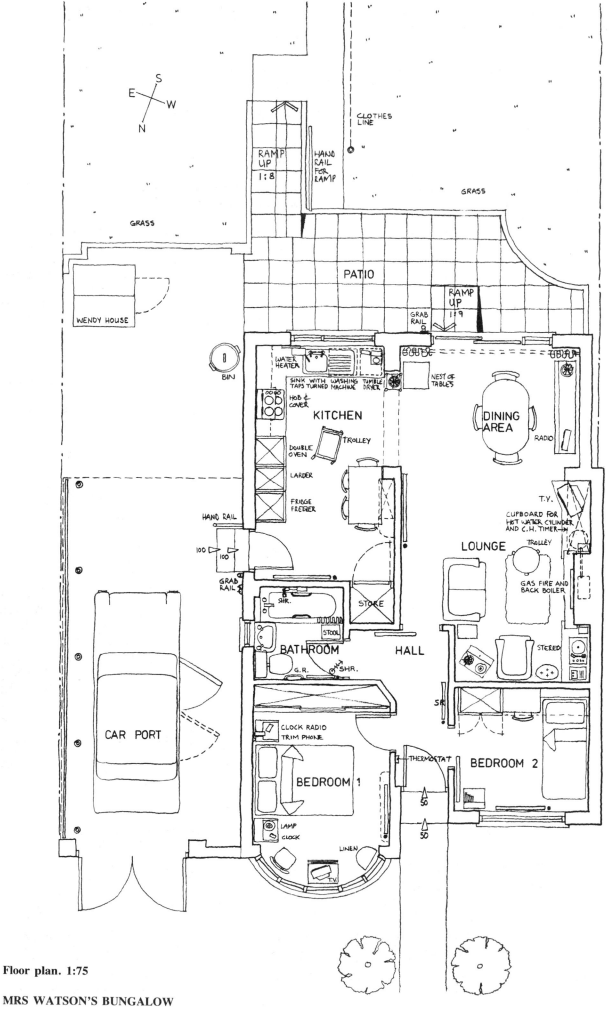

Floor plan. 1:75

MRS WATSON'S BUNGALOW

44

* Hot water tank and airing cupboard with shelves starting at height 1120mm installed to chimney alcove.

The archway between the living and kitchen areas has proved invâluable to Mrs Watson as it allows her to keep an eye on her daughter without having to have her in the kitchen at the same time. It also means that she is not cut off from the rest of the family when involved in domestic tasks which may take some time to complete.

Mrs Watson acknowledges that limitations of space still remain, particularly as there is no space for an activity area for such interests as sewing and the typing that she does, from time to time, for a voluntary organization. A sewing machine or typewriter cannot be left permanently in an operable position and she is unable to set these up for herself. Mr and Mrs Watson envisage, however, being able to convert part of the carport to form an additional room some time in the future, as funding and time permit.

KITCHEN

* Kitchen extended to boundary line of lounge extension.

* Beckerman Capri units on 190mm plinths, incorporating single sink and drainer, full height larder unit, floor and wall cabinets, varying depth drawers, shelves, corner carousel, double oven and refrigerator/freezer.

* Moben electric hob with side controls resited from old kitchen into 900mm high continuous work surface, with extractor hood 600mm above.

* Small unit of perspex storage drawers mounted on underside of wall cabinet.

* Lever taps, with reverse operation, to sink.

* Instant water heater mounted on wall. Attached with flexible hosing to cold tap.

* Washing machine and tumble drier set on plinths under work surface adjacent to sink.

Mrs Watson is very pleased with her kitchen and its efficient and easily maintained layout, which was chosen after extensive consideration of types, designs and manufacturers available. Where possible, she chose internal division of units to reduce the weight she would have to pull out. She uses the low deep drawers to store bottles and tall jars and the shallower ones and corner carousel for tins, crockery and saucepans.

She finds the handles on the units ideal as they permit her to hook her flexed fingers over them for ease of operation in conjunction with the spring loading of the catches. The wall cabinets were set at 360mm above the work surface,

Using shoulder rotation and trick movements, Mrs Watson is able to use the top box wall cabinets

The corner carousel utilizes corner space and the lightweight, spring loaded operation gives easy access to pans stored there

which was assessed as the optimum height that would allow her to reach up to the handles and into the cupboards, and this has proved to work well. The perspex drawers, mounted under a wall cabinet, are used to store dry ingredients and are easily accessible over a work surface close to their point of use. This idea is her own and proves very useful in that commonly used items do not need to take up working space.

A small table placed against the wall of the archway is used as additional working space or for informal meals, where its proximity to the cooking area facilitates serving. The lower oven is used on a daily basis, with its drop down door allowing Mrs Watson to support pans for transfer to the trolley she uses to transport items. The larger oven is used for batch baking less frequently as she needs help in transferring heavier items from the higher shelves. The hob is sited below an easily raised stainless steel cover, which closes flush to give additional working space when the hob is not in use. The extractor hood was set at the lowest height possible for efficiency and she is just able to reach the operating switch.

The taps were reversed in order that the levers could meet in the centre in the off position as this is more accessible and allows Mrs Watson better control of water flow. The water heater replaces a kettle that Mrs Watson has difficulty in using and permits pans to rest on the work surface for filling. She can easily attach the hosing to the tap as necessary, but acknowledges that it would have been ideal to plumb the heater to a direct water supply. However, owing to the position of the window, there was no wall space on which to mount it that would allow the spout to spill over a sink in case of leakage.

Various labour saving appliances are used and stored on the work surfaces, including a food processor and an electric can opener. The front loading washing machine is set at a useful height but, at the time of purchase some years ago, she was not able to find one with a control that she could manage. The problem has been overcome by the use of a specially constructed wooden lever turner. Mrs Watson is able to hang out small items on the line, one length of which was lowered to 1500mm as the height she requires. Larger items are done by the home help or the tumble drier is brought into use.

Mrs Watson would have liked to incorporate a dishwasher in the overall plan, but there was no wall space. She does not regret the omission of a sink refuse disposal unit and finds the bin sited on the sink unit door, which opens automatically, quite sufficient and small enough for her to empty into the dustbin in the carport.

A firm of kitchen planners provided detailed layouts catering for each facility identified by Mrs Watson and the occupational therapist. The builder completed the work comparatively quickly and kept prices down by relocation of features, rather than new provision, where possible.

BATHROOM
* Old and badly worn items replaced by coloured suite of bath, pedestal washbasin and wc.

* Wc set on shaped wooden plinth to give seat height of 480mm.

* 305mm grab rail set on wall by wc at 21° rising starting at 260mm above seat height.

* Taps with large acrylic heads installed to washbasin.

* Dolphin preset shower, with pillar attached flexible head, set over bath.

Mrs Watson transfers over the bath rim from a stool onto a board over the bath. Her husband assists in raising her legs, but she is otherwise independent in showering herself. She can manage the large water flow controls andthe push button temperature setting with ease, and the curtain along the inner edge of the bath contains water splash without problem.

The grab rail is suitably placed to assist her in lowering and rising from the wc and she has no difficulty in using the washbasin. The design of the taps does not create the problems that would exist with such a provision in the kitchen. The small washbasin allows Mrs Watson to lean over to attain the best functional position for her to turn the taps, which is not possible at the deeper sink unit in the kitchen.

The Watsons chose to have a bath installed as this was considered by them to be conventional and preferable in its use to that of a shower cubicle only.

BEDROOMS
* Full height unit of shelves and hanging space, with suspended sliding doors, built entire length of one wall in master bedroom.

* Rail for hanging clothes in one cupboard lowered to 1300mm for Mrs Watson's use.

* 1140mm high shelf with mirrored cabinet above set on wall opposite bed.

* Free standing units of dressing table and wardrobe, with similar handles to those of kitchen units, used in second bedroom.

* Additional storage achieved by drawers under bed.

The large sliding doors to the master bedroom cupboards are lightweight and very easy for Mrs Watson to operate. She finds this large area of storage useful for linen and other household items as well as for clothes, which she can hang easily in her part of the cupboard. She is able to manage the doors and drawers to the units in her daughter's bedroom; the horizontal and vertical D handle design was chosen specifically as most suiting her grip. The shelf in the master bedroom acts as a dressing table at a height upon which she can rest her forearms for support in applying make up and in hair care.

COSTING
1984

Extension to kitchen	£5879.00
Kitchen units and fitments	2654.00
Shower and sliding doors	540.00
Total	9073.00

FUNDING

Improvement grant, 75% of £7642.00 eligible
expense   £5731.00
Local Authority loan   1951.00
Client contribution   1391.00
                                    Total   9073.00

Mrs Watson became very concerned about funding arrangments as some considerable expense had been incurred in the first kitchen adaptation, and in the car that she needed in order to transport her daughter with her. Mr and Mrs Watson felt that they could not make a large committment and social services agreed a loan to meet the 25% over the improvement grant. The borough council valuation department placed a charge of £1375.00 to be repayment of the loan on the sale of the property.

CONTRACTUAL PROCEDURE

Mr and Mrs Watson commissioned an architectural design consultant to make the necessary drawings and the building work was put out to tender with the sum and contractor selected approved by the grant authority. The specialist firm responsible for installation of the kitchen chosen were contracted by Mr and Mrs Watson.

EVALUATION

Mrs Watson's emphasis on achievement is exemplified in the way she has approached an active and full life, firstly as a career woman and then as a housewife and mother. Her full range of trick movements allow her to undertake most tasks in the home, apart from very few limitations associated with weight and balance. On her own admission she is grateful to her parents, who made little of disability and focused upon encouragement to overcome physical limitations as a natural course of events.

This legacy from her family is shown in the manner in which she competed for and was successful in attaining jobs in the open market and in the way she and her fiance set about planning their future. Finding the right property required patience and determination as they had strict limitations on area, access and financing. They considered themselves very fortunate to find a bungalow that met the most important requirements, albeit that the property was small and in a poor condition. It was, however, an advantage that special features for Mrs Watson could be included in the major work of repair and refurbishment. Mr Watson's ability and inclination to do much of the work himself allowed their budget to go further and to include an extension of living space as an early priority.

The small size of the home has advantages in that it is easy to manage with facilities in close proximity, which promotes efficiency. Mr and Mrs Watson have assured ample **storage** space with the full length wardrobes in their bedroom, the unobtrusive airing cupboard in the lounge, supplementary units in their daughter's room, as well as the substantial number of units in the kitchen. The lack of a play area has been imaginatively overcome by the use of the wendy house, with the additional advantage of their daughter gaining, rather than losing, by any physical limitations of her mother. The size of the bungalow did, however, become crucial when Mrs Watson had to temporarily resort to using a wheelchair indoors. This possibility does not seem to have entered greatly into their planning of the home, although Mrs Watson had used a wheelchair inside, prior to the move, when particularly tired or unwell. Had resources permitted, access to the bathroom and bedroom could have been restructured, and a suitable shower incorporated.

Space problems have been sucessfully overcome by the **kitchen** extension and design which promotes efficiency of use, as well as allowing room for easy access and movement. The cost of the kitchen would seem high, but may be justified by the detailed work and design essential to meet Mrs Watson's precise requirements of utilising trick movements in her role of a busy housewife and cook, needing to spend a lot of time in her kitchen. A high degree of independence is achieved in use of the units, work surfaces, hob and oven.

A dishwasher might have been considered a necessity, rather than a luxury, as handling soapy crockery is difficult and the operation of washing up both tiring and time consuming. However, siting under a work surface was not possible and a position elsewhere in the room would have hindered the good circulation space. The need to attach the rubber hose to the tap to fill the water heater is an incompatible feature in such a successful and sophisticated kitchen.

The small **bathroom** could not accommodate a shower area in addition to the bath, which was generally preferred. The over bath shower that was chosen does not allow Mrs Watson complete independence as she still needs to have her legs lifted over the side. For her, this is preferable to the removal of a bath, which she considers to be the standard fitment a family should expect. The operation of the shower is ideal to her needs, with easily used temperature setting and a large control knob. The increase in wc seat height and angle of the grab rail meet her needs, without creating difficulty for the rest of the family.

Lever taps might have been considered for the washbasin as being easier to use, although Mrs Watson does not have the same difficulty here as she would at the less accessible and more frequently used kitchen sink.

The type of **windows** chosen in the main part of the bungalow are in keeping with the type of property but, with no low level facility for opening, are not the most suitable for her. This was recognized in the choice of window in the kitchen, although its position over the sink limits the possibility of opening it very far.

Adaptation to the property in any way to meet Mrs Watson's special needs tended only to be contemplated as a last resort, as seen in the kitchen extension at the time of her sprained ankle, and in the original move with priority given to the front **ramp** when it was found that she could not reach the keyhole from the deep steps. The work done here is attractive and forms a useful frontage which gives no indication of special provision. The ramp at the patio doors is rather steep and, although it was deliberately made so by shortening to reduce the trip hazard, its extension over some of the transverse traffic route could present a danger to the inattentive. The design of the rear **garden**, with raised borders and paved areas, is very attractive and allows Mrs Watson to pursue a keen interest in gardening.

Factors governing the choice of installation were those of using standard features wherever possible, attractiveness and economy. Avoiding obtrusive special provision is typical of Mrs Watson's upbringing and a determination that family life should not be dominated by the physical disability of one member. Imagination has been used in overcoming problems and in converting features and equipment to meet Mrs Watson's special needs as is seen in storage, baby equipment, reversal of the kitchen taps, the wendy house and the turner for the washing machine. To this has been added advice from professionals in the field of designing for the needs of the physically handicapped, the overall result being an attractive and efficient home which meets Mrs Watson's needs and those of the rest of the family.

MR RICHARD MUSGRAVE

Aged 33. Myositis ossificans progressiva.

MRS DOREEN MUSGRAVE

Aged 29. Cerebral palsy

Purchase and adaptation of a bungalow.

There were signs of deviated and shortened toes at birth, but the diagnosis and full implications of Mr Musgrave's medical condition were not made apparent to his family until 1955 when he was six years old. Following attendance at hospital for treatment of a greenstick fracture of his right arm, there were tests and a bone biopsy was sent to America for confirmation of the diagnosis of myositis ossificans progressiva. His family were told that he was unlikely to live long into his teens and that multiple treatment processes should be expected.

Mr Musgrave continued his education at a local day school with frequent interruptions for hospital admissions and surgery, which was ultimately found to aggravate rather than help his condition. Attendance at school had to cease abruptly at the age of eleven, when deterioration in his right hip joint rendered it unable to take his weight and he had to depend on crutches for mobility. Three hours of tuition per week at home was organized by the education department and this continued until he could be accepted at a specialist training unit at the age of fifteen. He felt isolated, however, as the youngest resident by some considerable margin, and was unable to settle.

Failure at the unit and return home made him determined to take responsibility for his own education, and he arranged correspondence courses for subjects in the general certificate of education. The local authority acknowledged this endeavour and, in the light of improved medical knowledge that did not put a limit on his lifespan, offered intensive home tuition to help achieve the results he sought. Although he worked hard, to his great disappointment he was unable to sit the examinations, further joint deterioration requiring a long period of hospitalization two months prior to the target dates.

Despite having no formal qualifications, Mr Musgrave was able to gain a place at a further education college via interview, and the course chosen initially went very well. The amount of travelling that was required, the change of classroom from ground to first floor and the use of a distant annexe, however, took its toll on his health during the following months and he had to give up attendance. He did not give up studying and read avidly, developing interests in many and varied subjects, although it transpired that he was never able to take the examinations he had planned.

Mr Musgrave continued to live at home and to study until, at the age of thirty, his left hip suddenly and markedly deteriorated, requiring another hospital admission and the confirmation that permanent use of a wheelchair for mobility was a necessity. This proved devastating to him in

his thoughts for his future and his self image. From his hospital bed he decided that he could not face the physical difficulties of wheelchair living at home or the effect this might have on his ageing parents, who, he felt, should have a life of their own. A hospital social worker was able to secure a place in a local social services hostel for the younger physically handicapped; during the two months before the place became available, he returned home to a life that, more or less, confirmed his worst fears.

Mr Musgrave saw the move to the hostel as the best option available to him, although it was not one he relished as he came up against the regime and rules of institutional living for the first time. The freedom he had known at home was not the norm in the new setting, and he came to resent the staffing levels that could not allow much individual attention and which turned personal and intimate care into a regimented and somewhat public affair.

He developed ideas, fostering them among the other residents, of the rights of disabled people to determine their own lifestyle, and was concerned to learn how limited were their expectations. His views on the subject came to focus particularly on a female resident whom he saw as a victim of the system he rejected, and beneath whose anti social behaviour he could see frustration and a desire for greater fulfilment. They had a common interest in music and their relationship flourished to the point where they considered marriage.

Mr Musgrave had always considered that he neither would nor should expect to marry, and he found himself overwhelmed and fearful of the responsibility that such a relationship would bring. He thought about leaving the hostel to the point where a place in alternative residential care was found. However, after much consideration, the couple decided to go ahead; they were married in 1979 and retained their places in the hostel, the only change being to convert Mr Musgrave's room into a double one.

Mrs Musgrave's background had been very different to that of her husband. She was diagnosed as quadraplegic athetoid cerebral palsy soon after birth, and most of her life had been spent at special schools and units with little interest in education or academic attainment. The expectation that she should remain at home permanently from the age of sixteen proved very difficult for her to accept and problems were further exacerbated by unsuitable housing for her partial dependency on a wheelchair.

Behavioural problems, that had manifested themselves from time to time, increased and required periodic admissions to hosital for psychiatric care. After some eighteen months at home she, her family and her social worker considered that she might be better suited by moving to a hostel where she could be with those of a similar age and physical problems and, although she was not very happy in residential care, she became more settled after the move. She did not like some aspects of the care received, but was used to the arrangements by the time Mr Musgrave became a resident, and did not share his reservations about marriage, having always viewed marriage and having her own home as an uncomplicated ideal.

Although they were the second residents to marry at the hostel, little was made in the way of adjustments to their new situation by the establishment. In deference to other residents, they were not treated any differently and became angry to find that this involved not being able to lock their door, because of fire regulations, and that there were instances of staff entering their room without knocking.

Shortly after their marriage, they attended a short course run by the Spastics Society aimed at maximizing potential for independent living and this opened doors to ideas previously unimagined by Mr Musgrave and only superficially perceived by his wife. The social worker for the course did not automatically assume, as they did, that they needed total care, and did not discount Mrs Musgrave's idea of having her own home. He encouraged personal endeavour, where, if necessary, flooding the bathroom was acceptable if independence in personal care was achieved.

On their return to the hostel, they made tentative approaches to social services and to a voluntary organisation for sheltered housing, but were warned that waiting lists meant that they could not be considered for several years. Conversation about independent living with a local authority councillor in Mr Musgrave's parents' area led to application being made to the city council housing department, and they were accepted onto the priority housing list. Social services were informed, and an occupational therapist visited to ascertain their particular needs and possible difficulties in order that suitable housing could be identified:

Mobility. Mr Musgrave was dependent on a DHSS issued semi reclining electric wheelchair with an extended back. He also had a small self propelling chair which he could manage with difficulty indoors when the battery of the other chair was being charged. He needed to sit on a Roho cushion during the day, which increased his height and footplate clearance in the chair. He could take his weight when standing, but needed help to rise and pivot to transfer. He had little use of his right arm and could not lift his left arm above shoulder level.
Mrs Musgrave used an indoor electric wheelchair, a self propelling chair or a castor wheelchair. She was able to walk very short distances with the help of a wheeled frame or could move around the floor on her bottom. She could transfer independently and help her husband with some aspects of his care.

Dressing. Mr Musgrave needed help, particularly with his lower half. Mrs Musgrave could be independent providing there were no difficult fastenings.

Wc. Mr Musgrave needed help with transfer to the wc but could use a urine bottle independently. A Clos o mat had been suggested on medical grounds for Mrs Musgrave in management of a gynaecological problem.

Bathing. Both needed help with bathing.

Bed. They could use an adjustable height and position bed, to which Mr Musgrave needed help to transfer and operate the adjustment mechanism. Mrs Musgrave could independently transfer using it at its lowest setting.

Eating and drinking. Mr Musgrave was independent. Mrs Musgrave's constant involuntary movements made eating and drinking difficult. She could be independent using a straw, plate guard and enlarged cutlery, if attention was given to optimal positioning.

Domestic tasks. They were both interested in cooking and responsibility for domestic tasks, but needed help with shopping and heavier housework.

Hobbies and interests. They both enjoyed music and the television. Mr Musgrave had developed interests in the rights of disabled people, magazine compilation and word processing on a computer, in addition to those of long standing in poetry reading and writing. Mrs Musgrave enjoyed some gardening and craftwork, developed during attendance at a day centre.

The occupational therapist looked at accommodation to be offered ahead of the Musgraves, and turned down one suggestion before agreeing with the city council that a prefabricated bungalow on an estate built in 1947 could be suitably adapted. She organized the work with the council that she considered essential to enable wheelchair use in the accommodation and the Musgraves set about organizing fixtures and fittings that would be required in addition to the limited possessions they had needed in residential care. Two sets of deep steps at the external doors were replaced with ramps, the kitchen was fitted with a rise and fall sink and a breakfast bar, and a standard mixer shower in a cubicle with stepover base replaced the bath. Improved circulation space in the kitchen was achieved by repositioning the power meters, and the property was rewired with socket outlets set at useful heights.

The Musgraves were delighted to have a home of their own, and moved in 1980 with the support of regular community nursing and home help services. While the property did not prove to be well designed for wheelchair use, they coped and were content with a situation in which they could largely control and organize their lives. With the financial help of a local trust, they made useful changes and additions to deal with some of the difficulties encountered. The two way opening door to the bathroom, which would swing back and catch them on the back of the head when they passed through it, was replaced by a sliding one. The wc with a high level cistern that Mrs Musgrave could not reach to operate was substituted by a low level type, and the small corner washbasin was changed for a larger one. They bought additional heaters since the prefabricated type of construction made the property very cold in winter. The hinged wooden slatted seat provided for the shower proved uncomfortable, especially for Mr Musgrave who had difficulty in transferring and sitting comfortably because of limited hip flexion resulting from ossification of muscle tissue around the joint. He applied to social services for an upholstered Pressalit shower seat, that he considered would be most suitable for him, and asked the hospital consultant to endorse his request. Such sophisticated and expensive equipment was not usually issued by the social services department and the occupational therapist instead arranged for the local group of REMAP to develop a suitable alternative.

By early 1982 Mr and Mrs Musgrave felt that, although the shower problems were not resolved, they had a comfortable and attractive home of which they could be proud. Although they had known that the bungalows were to be modernized at some stage in the future, they were disquieted when rumours began to circulate that the scheme was to be brought forward, and were concerned about whether their special needs would be met. The housing authority confirmed the rumour and informed them that the scheme was to demolish all the bungalows down to their concrete bases, upon which new prefabricated accommodation would be set. Tenants were to be rehoused on a temporary basis, but no definite time schedule could be given. They were assured, however, that every consideration would be given to their particular case.

Mr and Mrs Musgrave felt unable to passively accept this prospect and decided to research appropriate alternatives open to them. Discussion with their occupational therapist ascertained that she was unable to identify any suitable housing in the area, as had previously occurred with the choice of the prefabricated bungalow which, while not ideal, was the best that was available in terms of layout and size. She discussed the situation with the housing department, who came up with the plan of leaving the couple in their bungalow as the properties around them were worked upon, and to adapt an adjacent site for them to move into, upon completion. It was assessed that there would only be one week of major upheaval for Mr and Mrs Musgrave, during which time they might consider going away for a holiday.

The occupational therapist took the idea and the plans of the new bungalows to Mr and Mrs Musgrave for their opinions and some indication of the features they would wish to see incorporated. Upon consideration, however, the couple felt that there could not be sufficient circulation space for a wheelchair with extended footplates, as Mr Musgrave could forsee he might need at some stage in the future, and there could be no provision for a live in carer. He, therefore, set about making contact with national and local specialist organizations and people with knowledge of the housing needs and rights of disabled people, in order to find alternative housing.

Three housing associations with property in the area were approached, but could only offer placement on lengthy waiting lists or had a primary interest in the elderly. In reply to their request for a loan to adapt a new home or to allow private purchase under the Local Government Act 1972, the housing authority suggested that implications should be considered nearer the time of the modernization scheme for their present accommodation. Their social worker introduced them to a couple who had overcome some considerable housing difficulties by buying into the private sector, and Mr Musgrave studiously followed up any reasonable idea put to him.

The occupational therapist introduced them to a local building society who agreed the principle of a 100 per cent mortgage based on their combined incomes from state benefits. This allowed application to estate agents for details of potentially suitable properties for sale. It was acknowledged that purpose built housing would not be available and, therefore, that adaptation would be required. No limitation was put on the type of property, other than a price range that would allow DHSS supplementary benefit to make the interest repayments on the mortgage and their own state benefits to meet the capital repayments. To evaluate the information sent to them about properties, the couple made assessments of their physical strengths and limitations, their long term needs and, from experience gained in their first home, the precise type of adaptation needed.

In the meantime, problems continued with their shower as the new REMAP seat did not meet Mr Musgrave's requirements to the level he could envisage with the Pressalit seat. A second opinion was requested and a senior occupational therapist visited. She suggested removal of the cubicle, a new floor that would allow a dipped area and a mobile chair. However, technical services were not keen to do major work on a property that only had a limited life, and opted for removal of the cubicle and use of a flat base. The chair proved too large for the base, with the result that a lot of water splashed onto the bathroom floor. The base did not drain well and because of frequent flooding, the fibreboard walls started to rot, and tiles fell off revealing holes behind. Vermin were found in the bathroom, but little more was done than to board up the holes. The shower unit burnt out and six weeks elapsed before replacement parts were received; when it still did not work after this, Mr Musgrave's mother gave them a new type with preset temperature regulation which was better suited to their needs. Mr and Mrs Musgrave resolved to obtain greater control of their housing situation, and to ensure that the limitations of their present accommodation were not repeated.

They had in mind a relatively inexpensive, perhaps prewar, bungalow which they could convert for their purposes. They were attracted to a small market town, some fifteen miles from the city, in which Mr Musgrave's family had lived and he had spent his childhhod. They found the kind of house they were looking for in a street of small detached bungalows on the outskirts of the town. It had small rooms and a narrow hallway but, they considered, it could be suitably adapted.

They enquired about local facilities, receiving good reports of health care and domiciliary services, gaining the impression that the caring attitude of a small community was more supportive than that of the large city. They approached the local district council and learned that they could be considered for an improvement grant for the adaptation work and, in early 1983, made an offer for the property which was accepted at £24,495. The building society surveyor's valuation covered the full purchase price and the society agreed a 100 per cent mortgage providing written confirmation was received from DHSS that they would meet the interest payments and that the Musgraves had sufficient benefits to meet their part.

At about the same time, notice was given that work was to commence in January 1984 on the part of the estate in which they lived. People on the estate began to feel very unsettled, morale dropped and properties visibly started to deteriorate. The Musgraves felt glad that their chosen housing option meant that they would be able to leave earlier than forced and would not have to see the decline through to its conclusion.

However, despite their planning and preliminary enquiries things did not go as smoothly as anticipated. DHSS refused to give written confirmation of their status for the building society; they were not prepared to consider mortgage interest repayments on a property that was not owned and lived in by the applicants. In addition, they advised that the Musgraves had security of tenure as council tenants and that rehousing responsibility was that of the housing authority.

Realizing his dependence on a firm commitment from DHSS, Mr Musgrave responded by trying to bring pressure to bear directly on the local supplementary benefits office, through his member of parliament, the media and the regional social security officer of DHSS. He requested written agreement that they would pay if he moved into the property; this was again refused on the grounds that

E

hypothetical situations were not assessed by the department. The benefits officer volunteered that, if payment was agreed in principle, there was unlikely to be a restriction in the amount as the property was not considered to be excessively expensive. This proved sufficient for the building society and the sale was allowed to proceed, with completion at the end of September 1983.

The Musgraves now felt able to apply themselves wholeheartedly to the adaptation work that would be required. Mr Musgrave acted as his own architect, although he had no building experience aside from the understanding he had obtained from the adaptation work to the prefabricated bungalow. He relied on reference books, in particular Selwyn Goldsmith's Designing for the Disabled, and visits to aids centres and exhibitions. Exact planning resulted in a long and detailed schedule of work, which he sent to several builders. Response from them was mixed, but a firm of builders they already knew tendered a provisional sum of £20,000 to £24,000 for the radical reorganization of the layout of the property and the incorporation of sophisticated features that Mr Musgrave identified as necessary to the couple's independence.

An occupational therapist and a surveyor used by social services in the new area visited the bungalow and suggested work they deemed to be essential. This included removing a corridor wall; incorporating the garage with the second bedroom to form the lounge; increasing the size of the bathroom and installing a shower. The cost was suggested to be in the region of £6,000 and, of this, the occupational therapist identified that 75 per cent might be expected from an improvement grant, and a payment of up to £1,600 from social services. Mr Musgrave could not agree with the limitations of an assessment that allowed for little of the major structural work that he envisaged, left some of the original passageway and had the main bedroom at the front. He felt that many features of both an essential and desirable nature had not been contemplated and that he and social services were not in accord on the type of home needed.

Mr Musgrave resolved to proceed with his original ideas and, on the recommendation of the builder, employed a building surveyor to draw up plans for submission to building control. The project gained approval, but social services asked for changes: to give greater space for a possible live in carer; an extension to the lounge to allow another entrance to the bedroom, in addition to the only one planned via the bathroom, as the occupational therapist was concerned about privacy in the use of the room. The fire officer suggested the use of fire resistant doors. Costs increased by £6,000 in order to meet these modifications. A second set of plans was submitted and agreed by the building control officer, with the only change being made to marginally increase the space for the carer, as Mr Musgrave tried to keep some limit on cost of the project.

Mr Musgrave now set about researching ways of financing the work and approached the city housing authority for payment for disturbance and loss of housing under the Land Compensation Act 1973, as was applicable to all householders who had to be rehoused on account of the modernization scheme. He was informed that they were not entitled to this as they had bought alternative accommodation ahead of a compulsory move. The housing committee did, however, agree an ex gratia payment but

were unable to indicate the sum until an assessment had been made by the technical services department immediately prior to modernization work the following year. At the same time the Musgraves applied to the district council for an improvement grant and were dismayed to learn that an embargo had been put on discretionary grants until the next financial year, when applications would be considered in strict date rotation. They warned the city housing authority that this would delay their projected move and tried to put pressure on the grant authority, to no avail.

As Mr and Mrs Musgrave were still paying rent on the council property they were living in, and were additionally faced with capital and interest repayments on their mortgage, they obtained a bank loan to help meet payments. They approached the building society for a second mortgage for the adaptation work, but the society could not agree to a total commitment of £48,000 on a property that had been valued at half that sum. To allow essential works to enable the couple to move in, however, a loan of £5,000 was offered, on condition that a firm committment be made by DHSS, but the offer was withdrawn when this was not forthcoming.

The couple became desperate about their financial situation; they were paying on two properties, neither of which in their state at the time had any long term use to them. It seemed likely that they would be obliged to sell and take whatever local authority housing was allocated, or return to residential care. Their solicitor supported them in their endeavours to fund the project and worked without the prospect of reimbursement until legal aid was assured. In order to limit the debts being incurred, they asked the city council to allow a reduced rent and the building society to allow reduced payments; the latter was agreed on a temporary basis. They applied to DHSS for the payment of one month's overlap of housing costs for bridging a transfer between properties, but they were not eligible as they had not yet moved.

By the beginning of 1984 large areas of the city council estate had been vacated or were being utilized only as temporary accommodation for tenants whose homes were to be modernized, and work on demolition began. The technical services department made the assessment for the disturbance and home loss payment to Mr and Mrs Musgrave; this was set at £2,000, and based upon the adaptations of doorways, electrical work and a shower that were required in the new property. No features could be considered that were not in the existing home as the legislation only allowed for replacement and not for material betterment. Mr Musgrave asked the builder to start work to the limit of £2,000, but social services warned that commencement could subsequently jeopardize entitlement to an improvement grant. The district council grant officer advised that they would have given informal agreement in the previous year to any work agreed by the occupational therapist, provided it was finished before the new financial year. This assurance was sufficient for Mr Musgrave, and he instructed the builder to commence to the limit of the combined improvement grant and disturbance allowance sums. However, the builder was by then committed to other projects and could only offer a starting date in April. He also warned that changes in VAT relating to home improvements and a wage claim would increase the price of the work if it were allowed to run into June.

In April 1984, the work commenced with the builder paying close attention to every detail to ensure that each feature was exactly right for the needs identified. Mr and Mrs Musgrave needed to get on site to assess and experiment with the provision being made. Tail lift transport was arranged on one occasion, but did not return for some hours. As the plumbing work had not been completed, the workmen found themselves having to rig up temporary toilet facilities, which became embarrassing for all concerned. The builder subsequently organized transport himself or visited them when possible.

As Mr and Mrs Musgrave were unable to vacate the prefabricated bungalow on schedule, demolition at this site could not be commenced and four other families were unable to vacate their homes as a result. There was tension between them and the Musgraves, who were blamed for causing them to continue to live in an area that was a massive building site. Vandalism was rife and the Musgraves suffered abuse from builders who saw their bonuses being affected and from neighbours who were angry about the press sympathy being given to the couple, when no mention was made of the effect the delay was having on them.

With their health suffering and Mrs Musgrave needing temporary admission to psychiatric care, Mr Musgrave's brother, a nurse, moved in and took over his brother's care. In June, function in Mr Musgrave's left arm became so severely affected that much of his independence in personal care was permanently lost and he now required help with feeding. It was acknowledged that some features, particularly in the kitchen, would no longer be needed; this had the effect of reducing costs, with the greater dependence put on a carer.

No date could be fixed for Mr and Mrs Musgrave's move as they had still not financed the whole project and mortgage repayments they had planned would be met by DHSS were threatening the limit of their bank loan. Mr Musgrave realized that their very unhappy position was also creating financial difficulty for the city council, whose modernization scheme was being delayed and was incurring penalties. He wrote to the city council requesting a payment of £15,000, which he calculated as the amount he still required to complete work on the new accommodation and so achieve the move. The council would not agree the full sum, but offered an interest free loan repayable on the sale of the new property. Mr Musgrave again approached social services and was able to invoke the principle of giving major grants to do a few highly effective projects, rather than numerous minor ones. The sum allowed as a result enabled the full building work to be undertaken and completed in August 1984.

The move was made at the end of the month, with the builders volunteering help for installation of domestic appliances, picture hanging and reorganization of furniture. An exceptional needs payment was made by DHSS to cover some essential household items. Social services arranged for a family aide for the Musgraves for the first ten weeks until a more permanent pattern of support could be established, as they were still adjusting to the recent deterioration in Mr Musgrave's condition and Mrs Musgrave was convalescing from a hysterectomy operation.

The programme of care resolved into two family aides being employed by social services to give six and a half hours per day assistance with personal care and domestic support, supplemented by visits from the community nursing service to assist Mr Musgrave in getting up and going to bed. In addition, occasional outings were offered by a local women's club and Mrs Musgrave commenced attendance at a social services day centre.

The mortgage payments, anticipated to be met by DHSS from the start, the requirement to pay rent at the same time, the builder's accrued interest charges, and the costs of household fittings for the new bungalow, resulted in a debt of £5,000 to the bank for the Musgraves, and on which they continue to pay interest.

THE PROJECT TEAM

Mr and Mrs Musgrave.
Builder.
Electrician.
Building surveyor.

THE AIMS

To provide suitably spacious accommodation for two wheelchair users.
To permit privacy and independence and yet allow a pleasant and efficient environment for a carer.
To allow flexibility in use, as might be associated with changes in functional levels, and to permit live in help if required.
To ensure a high standard of fitments and finishing in a home in which a lot of time was to be spent.
To allow visiting and use of facilities by disabled and able bodied friends.

THE PROPERTY

* A two bedroomed bungalow built in 1960.

* Gross internal floor area 67.7m² before and 85.0m² after adaptation.

The bungalow was built on a level site in a quiet residential road approximately half a mile from the centre of a market town and near to a local shop. The front garden had been surfaced in tarmacadam and the rear laid to grass with a small pathway.

The property was chosen for its level site, garden, proximity to neighbours and shops and potential for adaptation to meet special needs. The internal layout, however, needed reorganization.

THE ADAPTATION

* Reorganization of the internal structure and layout of a bungalow.

* Rear door and frame removed and opening bricked up in matching facing brickwork and blockwork, with gas and electric meter housing boxes built in new wall.

* Chimney breast and stack removed and roof timbers and tiling made good.

* Front door and frame, up and over garage door and frame removed and flat roof supported to allow

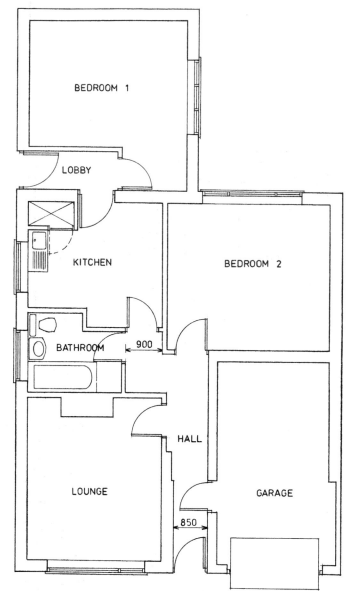

Floor plan before adaptation 1:100

Front view of the bungalow after adaptation

An aviary was converted to a summerhouse

construction of new front wall incorporating external door frame and window.

* Felt roof to garage and all guttering renewed.

* New porch made of 250mm reinforced concrete raft with facing brick walls and concrete ramp.

* Rolled steel joist inserted to allow removal of wall between second bedroom and garage.

* Partition wall and doorway forming rear entrance lobby demolished.

* Hall/garage wall demolished and all wall and ceiling surrounds made good.

* Foundation to external garage wall widened and new 100mm thermal block wall with insulation to cavity built up to ceiling level and finished to form new lounge.

* Door and frame, larder walls and sink unit removed from kitchen.

* 100mm blockwork wall constructed directly off thickened concrete base to form straight wall for bathroom.

* Corridor wall, door and frame to bathroom demolished.

* Bath, washbasin and wc disconnected and drain connections sealed.

* Tank, cylinder, airing cupboard and wall tiles stripped out.

* Rolled steel joist inserted and boxed in plasterboard to allow removal of old lounge/bathroom partition wall.

* New concrete foundations built by breaking through lounge floor for construction of 100mm blockwork wall to form new second bedroom and larger new kitchen.

* Wall extended in stud partition plasterboard part way across new lounge to form entrance area.

* Floor screed renewed.

EXTERNAL DOORS AND PATHWAYS
* Rear window frame to new lounge removed and brickwork cut down to floor level for installation of thermal break aluminium double glazed patio door.

* Night vent and external cylinder lock fitted to mahogany sub frame.

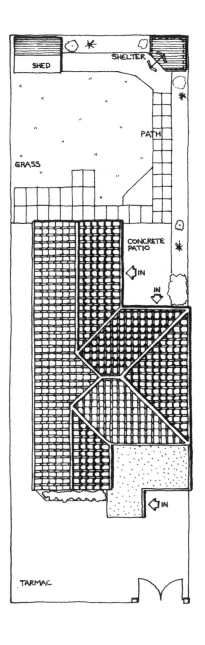

Site plan. 1:100

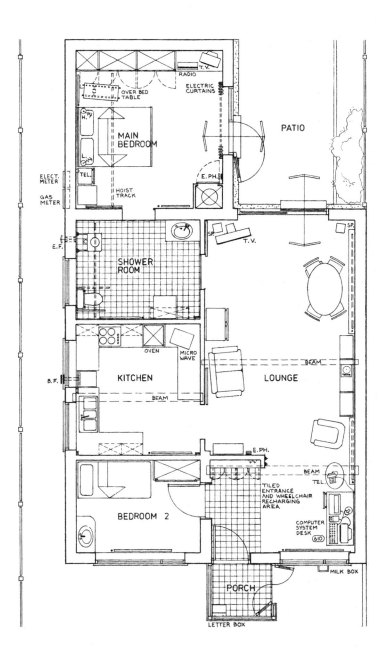

Floor plan after adaptation. 1:75
MR AND MRS MUSGRAVE'S BUNGALOW

* Window frame and brickwork below removed from main bedroom external wall and replaced by sidelights and outward opening double glazed doors, fitted with Briton panic bars and mortice lock.

* Both rear thresholds fitted with small external mahogany ramp bridges, set against 20mm high metal cill of sliding door and slight rise of hardwood cill of casement doors.

* Half glazed front door with lever handles and latch lock to 910mm wide door leaf.

* Opposite opening half doors with mortice lock, letter plate with internal mail box and parcel shelf made to porch.

* Splayed corner doors to aviary in rear garden removed to form an open summer house.

* Hinged wooden bench and front concrete apron formed.

* Paving slabs taken up and reused to form pathway to summer house.

* New 900 x 600mm slabs laid to connect side pathway to patio. Additional slabs bedded in concrete to form turning areas.

* Patio in 100mm concrete made to rear right corner of property flush with slab path.

* Upstand curb formed to boundary side and aggregate filled drainage channel made adjacent to bungalow.

* Wire mesh fencing replaced with wooden interlapped type to height of 1800mm and new garden shed provided.

The external porch door was a problem. Outward opening was across the living room window and inward opening took up space that was vital for wheelchair turning to the main door. The half doors which part in opposite directions go some way to resolving the situation, but are not very easy to operate from a wheelchair.

The patio doors glide easily and there is no problem in negotiating the small bridging ramps and the slightly raised cills in the electric wheelchairs. The opening side of the lounge patio door was handed to keep passage away from the bedroom opening and so remove the risk of collision if both doors were used at once. However, this on site decision was made after electrical work had been completed, with the result that the television needed to be moved from its proposed position, which would have impeded access to the new opening. Instead it now blocks access to the power points and the switch to the external light.

There is level access on hard surfaces to all parts of the site, with easy access to the summer house and garden shed. The pathways are sufficiently wide to allow some deviation in the route of Mrs Musgrave's chair, caused sometimes by involuntary movement affecting control of a direct line in the electric wheelchair. The Musgraves enjoy their garden and sitting out on the sheltered patio which, along with the external bedroom door, is afforded privacy by the solid wooden fencing. The summer house provides some shelter and shade with provision made for visitors to use the fold away bench. This does not take away space necessary for the two wheelchairs when Mr and Mrs Musgrave wish to seek shelter internally when on their own.

WINDOWS
* Half height glazing to porch on two sides.

* Window frame of original kitchen removed and resited in new kitchen as second window.

* Wall bricked up from old cill height and 1200mm wide x 340mm deep double glazed high level window fitted to new bathroom.

* Window frame, lower casement and cill removed from old lounge and replaced by 2400mm wide window with casement opening and higher cill.

* 1800mm wide x 1200mm double glazed window made to front of new lounge with cill height of 800mm.

* Cord operated curtain tracks fitted to all windows, with electrically operated ones to each of full length glazed doors.

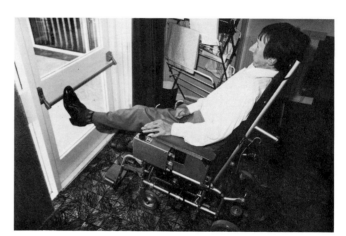

The panic latch on the bedroom external door presents no resistance to hand operation by Mrs Musgrave or to Mr Musgrave, who kicks it open with his foot

Mrs Musgrave is able to reach the openable window in the second bedroom, but not the high opening ventilators to the kitchen. Long pull cord blinds that have been fitted to the kitchen windows can be managed by Mrs Musgrave if cords are left to trail over the work surfaces for easy reach.

Main ventilation to the bungalow is achieved by extractor fans in the bathroom and kitchen and with the two external doors at the rear of the property which also give good light to the rooms they serve.

ELECTRICAL WORK
* All power points set at 530mm and rocker light switches at 840mm above floor level.

* Eight power points, television and FM sockets allocated to living area.

* Two double power points to battery charging cupboard in lounge.

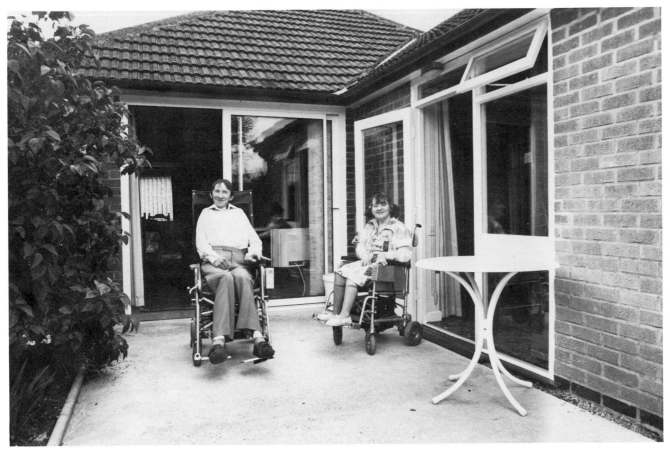

The patio at the rear of the bungalow is accessed via the sliding door from the living area and the casement door from the bedroom

* Four power points, immersion heater point, hoist, television and FM aerial points to main bedroom.

* Step down transformers for hoists sited in main bedroom cupboards.

* Fuse box mounted in corner of bedroom to abut ceiling.

* Two power points and television socket to second bedroom.

* Electrical provision made for wall heater, shower, shaver, extractor fan, hoist, Clos o mat and washing machine in bathroom.

* Eight power points, cooker outlet, extractor fan connection and waste disposal outlet to kitche

* Watertight external power outlet at rear patio.

* Fluorescent strip lighting to bathroom and two pendant lights each to kitchen and bedroom.

* Wall lights with dimmers to living area.

* Provision made for Silent Gliss electrically operated curtains to both sets of patio doors, and to divide living area in line with small partition wall at a later date.

The banks of switches are sited in easily accessible places, except for the switch for the rear external light and the television, now sited behind the patio door. Mr Musgrave is able to support his left hand on the arm of his wheelchair and so raise his fingers to operate the light switches, and uses a reaching aid to operate the curtains.

The Crabtree Corinthian rocker type switches do not require fine precision to operate and are sited to allow switching between the lounge, bathroom and bedroom as being rooms most used. The curtains to the bedroom can be operated both in that room and from the lounge. This allows them to change into night clothes in the bathroom before entering the privacy of the remotely curtained bedroom. The division of the lounge from the entrance area by curtaining is planned, as finances will allow, to help conserve heat in the winter and to give greater privacy to the rest of the room from the front of the property and from the area designated for a live in helper.

A television point was considered important in the bedroom as Mrs Musgrave likes to retire early, finding the change of position from sitting all day to be essential to her physical well being. There are sufficient power points throughout the property for the various electrical appliances used and the extractor fan controls are easily used from their positions at height 875mm above the floor. The extractor fan for the kitchen was sited in a window as the only other vacant space on an external wall was directly over the boiler.

Pendant lighting was suggested for the kitchen; a flourescent strip would not have given a good light from a central position on the downstand beam and the use of two pendant lights would ensure some light on the failure of a bulb. The meter box was set high on the wall where it would not interfere with circulation space as the Musgraves did not envisage that they could use it.

The bathroom hoist main is operated by a pull cord at the bathroom/lounge door; the pull cord for the bedroom hoist main is by the bed. The whole system can be shut down at

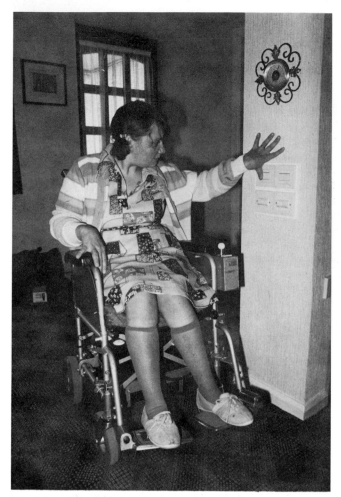

Mrs Musgrave supports the base of her hand on the wall to reach the large rocker switches with her fingers

night, but is easily reactivated without the need to move from the bed. The Musgraves rejected the idea of using a complete environmental control system, preferring direct control of power sources and equipment from their electric wheelchairs.

HEATING AND WATER

* 100mm fibreglass quilt laid to loft.

* Balanced flue boiler installed in kitchen to serve seven radiators with individual thermostatic controls.

* Warm air blower mounted on bathroom wall.
* Platform constructed in loft to take new cold water storage tank.

* Domestic hot and cold water supplies renewed.

* Airing cupboard containing new hot water cylinder built in main bedroom.

* New manhole and connections made to existing drains.

A warm even temperature is easily maintained throughout and a boost given in the bathroom with the warm air heater.

The boiler was set on a 40mm insulation plinth over the floor, causing the top to rise above the level of the adjacent work surfaces. This was contrary to original planning, but has not been changed as it is not a crucial factor to those now using the kitchen most.

HALLWAY AND DOORS

* Raised thresholds eliminated internally.

* 965mm flush plywood doors, hung on Henderson ball race sliding door gear and covered with hardwood pelmets, installed to new openings at bedroom, bathroom and kitchen.

* Finger panels at height 770mm fitted to doors and aluminium buffer strips to height 860mm, bent to profile on door jambs.

* Plastic beading to divide decorations in reveals.

* 20mm high shotgun flexible rubber strips by Tennant Rubber Company set to bathroom door thresholds.

The sliding doors are easy to operate and the finger panels are accessible to both Mr and Mrs Musgrave. The depth of the finger panels was chosen for ease of use in conjunction with a long handled reaching aid as used by Mr Musgrave. Additional beading was later fixed to the edge of the bathroom door reveals, when it was found that a mirror reflected the bathroom through a gap between the door and frame and privacy was lost.

The rubber thresholds contain water well within the bathroom and protect the carpeting in each of the rooms beyond. The highly durable yet flexible material allows it to flatten forward as the wheelchair crosses and to then spring back.

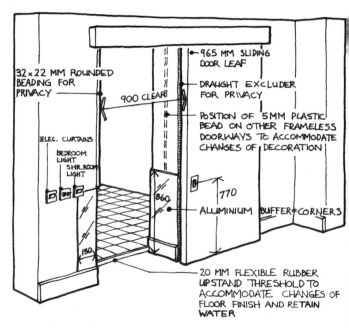

The sliding door to the shower room from the bedroom

THE LIVING AREA

* Floor of area between front door and small partition wall surfaced in 150 x 150mm tiles.

* Remainder of floor finished in carpeting.1315mm wide x 760mm high x 220mm deep cupboard with one shelf built against partition wall for battery recharging.

* Full width mirror fitted above cupboard; telephone point installed on other side of room.

The 1320 x 2250mm tiled area allows for cleaning of wheelchairs on coming in from outdoors and provides a suitable surface for wheelchair battery recharging. The partition helps to divide the entrance area from the rest of the room and gives privacy to the second bedroom doorway.

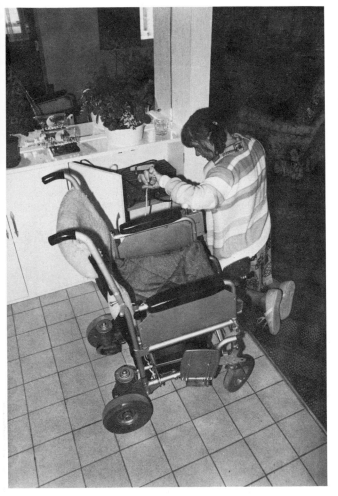

Mrs Musgrave sets up the battery recharging operation with power sources at a convenient height for her

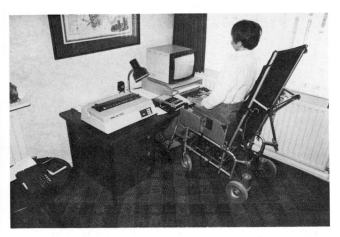

A lowered desk housing a computer and visual display unit is easily accessible in the living area

The room is sufficiently large to allow easy passage of two wheelchairs around the room. Furniture, including a dining table and chairs, settee, fireside chair, television and bookcases is positioned to maintain access to the five doors which open from the room.

KITCHEN

Shallow stainless steel inset sink, single drainer, Franke Kuglette 2000 mono block mixer tap and soap dispenser.

* Floor units of drawers, cupboards, and worktops.

* Wall cabinets.

* Inset electric hob with side controls, microwave oven, large refrigerator and freezer installed to new kitchen.

The washerless ceramic disc operated tap is easy for Mrs Musgrave to use by hand and for Mr Musgrave to catch with the reaching aid. A high outlet tap was chosen to assist in filling tall items over the shallow sink; this is particularly helpful to Mrs Musgrave. The drawer units are light and allow touch control, with the lip on the edge of the units being useful for operating doors and drawers with the reaching aid. The large freezer allows for bulk buying and the use of foods most suitable to a microwave oven.

Mr and Mrs Musgrave do not use the kitchen much, with all food preparation and cooking being done by the family aides. The kitchen provides an attractive and efficient centre for domestic tasks and allows sufficient space for two wheelchairs so that the Musgraves can supervise.

Original planning had allowed for a rise and fall sink, low level worktops and wall units organized precisely to Mr and Mrs Musgraves' own individual needs. These would be supplemented by a hob, microwave and food processor. The electrician worked on devising a 45° angled control board with a ring main circuit to be sited under the worktops to serve the domestic appliances. The hob chosen was to be set flush with the worksurface with front or separate control as would prove most useful in practice. A large number of sockets was planned to reduce the need for trailing flex and the protruding trap to the waste disposal unit was to be moved to the exterior to conserve knee room under the sink.

Work study principles were applied to layout so that collision potential could be reduced in a room which had circulation space considerably reduced by diagonally placed work areas across corners for maximum accessibility. Exact heights were gauged to allow easy use of storage and appliances and space for hand operation of electric wheelchair control boxes under surfaces. Strips placed on the outer edges of work surfaces would allow a manual chair to be pulled in by hooking fingers onto them.

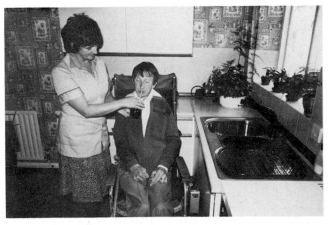

Mr Musgrave and a Family Aide in the kitchen

As Mr Musgrave's health deteriorated and costs escalated, however, he decided to plan the kitchen as a centre for a carer's use, rather than for wheelchair management.

BATHROOM

* New bathroom fitted with inset washbasin, Franke Kuglette 2000 mono block tap and pop up waste in 920 x 540mm vanitory surround at 710mm above floor.

* Tiled splashback, full width mirror, towel rail to side and shaver socket at height 900mm.

* Clos o mat Samoa with 430mm seat height.

* Linido drop down rail to height 710mm and Intrad Grab 27 at height 860mm on either side of wc.

* Pressalit adjustable height shower seat.

* Mira 722EU shower unit with control at 940mm from floor and flexible hose head with two varying height sliding rail mountings.

* Wall cabinet, washing machine/tumble drier, soap dish at height 790mm and urine bottle holder at 360mm next to wc.

* Entire floor dished to give 1 in 50 fall to corner outlet.

* Floor covered in non slip tiles to 1220 x 1220mm tesselated tiled shower area. Ceiling joists reinforced and spreader plates used for installation of Wessex travelmaster hoist with overhead tracking in straight run between wc and shower seat.

Mr Musgrave uses the shower seat at height 420mm and Mrs Musgrave at 360mm or, alternatively, she squats on the floor using the shower head by hand. Water that sometimes splashes around the room caused by involuntary

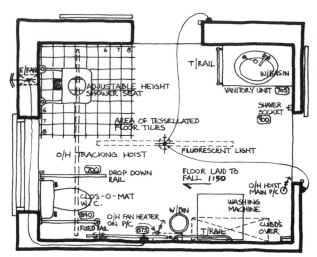

Layout of shower room. 1:50

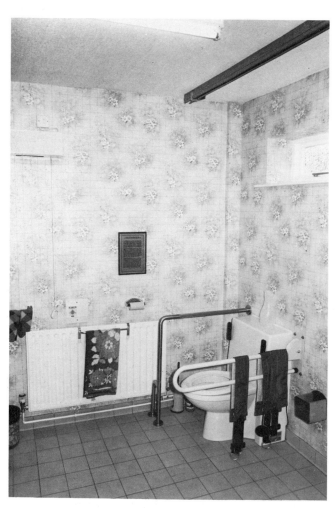

Wc area

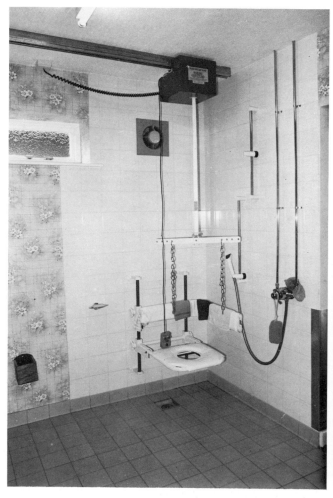

The shower area

movement, is well contained within the floor area of the room by the rubber strip thresholds. The two height shower rail allows for flexibility in use by visitors or a live in helper.

Mrs Musgrave uses the shower, Clos o mat and washbasin independently and finds the rails helpful, although the operational pad for the Clos o mat tends to get in the way of transfer. Mr Musgrave uses the hoist for transfer to the Clos o mat and shower as the two piece, sheepskin lined slings allow for better positioning and support than can be achieved by forward transfer with the help of the nurse or family aide.

They find it useful to have the washing machine in the bathroom as this is the place where clothes are changed and, therefore, do not have to be carried far.

The drop down rail allows for sideways transfer for visiting guests and use of the hoist, although Mr Musgrave finds that he is able to clear the rail in the downward position. The wall cabinet houses soap for the machine as well as other frequently used items that might impede easy use of the vanitory unit if they had to be stored there. The high outlet tap gives sufficient space over the washbasin for rinsing of a urine bottle which is neatly stored and easily reached in a holder on the wall next to the wc.

The hollow beam floor had to be taken out as it was not possible to obtain the required fall to the shower area in surface screed.

BEDROOMS

* Fitted wardrobes incorporating drawers, shelves, hanging space and pull out baskets built to one wall of main bedroom.

Mrs Musgrave can select clothes from the low level baskets when moving around on the floor, which is her most useful method of mobility after getting out of bed

The washbasin and vanitory unit

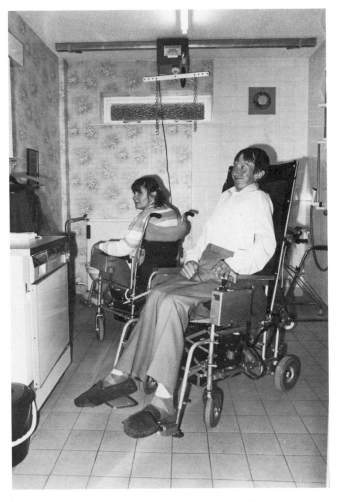

There is sufficient space in the bathroom to allow the passage of two wheelchairs simultaneously

* Large shelf allowed for video recorder and tactile radio and angle wall bracket made for television.

* Wessex Travelmaster hoist installed over adjustable bed.

Mrs Musgrave can operate the air switch of the adjustable bed for her independent use and to assist her husband, although he needs additional help in positioning the two piece sling and in hoisting.

A washbasin, vanitory unit, telephone and television points were fitted in the second bedroom for ease of conversion to a bedsitting room if required. However, at present it is useful space that is more easily accessible than the alternative of the garden shed as storage for the castor wheelchair and wheeled walking frame.

COSTING
1984

Structural work	£17,253.00
Electrical work	2,113.00
Central heating	1,950.00
Bathroom vanitory unit, basin and fitting	205.00
Shower and fittings	144.00
Clos o mat Samoa	1,089.00
Pressalit shower seat	421.00
Bedroom wardrobes	450.00
Wessex Travelmaster hoists	683.00
Kitchen units	740.00
Waste disposal unit	140.00
Sink and fitments	362.00
Lounge patio doors	967.00
Electric curtain tracks	1,431.00
Internal and external decorations	1,967.00
Fees	630.00
Total ex. VAT	£30,545.00

FUNDING

City council interest free loan	£7,500.00
Disturbance allowance	2,000.00
Improvement grant, 90% of the maximum	9,180.00
Social services grant, adaptations budget	10,000.00
Client contribution	1,865.00
Total	£30,545.00

* VAT was zero rated on hoists, internal and external doors, conversion of bathroom and all fitments, floors, ramps, garden paving, electrical work and garage conversion totalling £12,273.00 of the costs.

CONTRACTUAL PROCEDURE

Mr Musgrave contracted the surveyor and builder and employed an independent surveyor to advise and check on aspects of the work, such as costs and essential repairs. The surveyor was not involved beyond the stage of agreement to final plans, with all changes and additions to specifications decided on site between the builder and the Musgraves.

EVALUATION

Mr Musgrave had a very clear idea of what he required, having meticulously studied every aspect of his and his wife's daily life and the physical limitations imposed on it by the poorly designed prefabricated bungalow. The building specification that he composed was exhaustive, with every detail entirely researched and justified by him for the home in which he expected to spend some considerable time and for which there would be little opportunity for change, once the initial work had been completed and funded.

Choice of equipment was made by Mr and Mrs Musgrave following use of reference books, visits to a rehabilitation centre and to specialist organizations that could demonstrate aids available. It was not by the social services occupational therapist, whose remit was to meet essential needs of many clients and who was not in agreement with the extravagance of the work contemplated. There were additional problems in liaison, however, as the occupational therapist who knew the couple best could not be easily available in the new area, which was some distance away from her own territory.

The builder was tireless in his efforts to meet exact requirements, not always resting at identifying the best product available, but being prepared to adapt if necessary. His contribution, along with that of his team, was exceptional; he saw the project as a challenge and spent time and energy in research work and in getting the Musgraves to the site to examine and test features prior to permanent installation. The engagement of this builder proved to be the crucially important factor in the whole venture. The relationship was harmonious; he understood what the Musgraves needed and had confidence in them, and they had confidence in him. The contract relied more on good faith, it would seem, than a guarantee that the funding needed would be found.

The Musgraves have an extremely well designed, comfortable and useful home. Changes in Mr Musgrave's functional levels, which he acknowledges may mean use of an extended leg support wheelchair and total dependence on help for all activities of daily living, have been confronted and catered for in the expectation that special needs do not allow casual changing of accommodation as new problems arise. Mrs Musgrave's levels of independence are allowed to be maintained and have, in practice, been heightened as the use of tailor made facilities and responsibility for her own home has increased confidence.

Reorganization of the **layout** of rooms and incorporation of the garage has allowed spaciousness that can comfortably accommodate two wheelchairs. Despite the need to maintain uninterrupted access to the many doors leading from the living area, there is still sufficient space for furniture used by the Musgraves and visitors. Equipment for work and leisure can be easily reached without the need to involve others in setting it up. Storage space is ample, with built in units throughout and a discreetly housed wheelchair battery charging area in a cupboard over suitable flooring.

The internal **doors** are well designed and easy to operate, as are the patio and casement external doors. The opposite opening doors in the porch are more successful than a casement door, but are not the easiest to operate.

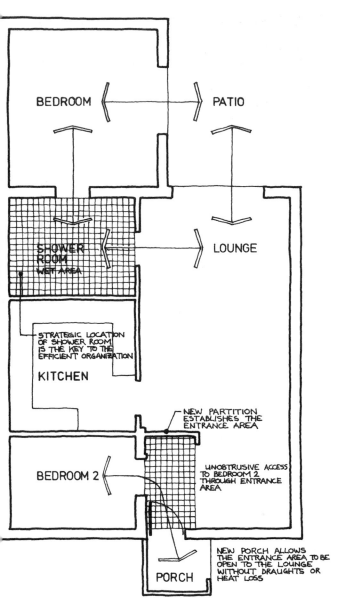

BEDROOM   PATIO

SHOWER ROOM WET AREA   LOUNGE

STRATEGIC LOCATION OF SHOWER ROOM IS THE KEY TO THE EFFICIENT ORGANIZATION

KITCHEN

NEW PARTITION ESTABLISHES THE ENTRANCE AREA

BEDROOM 2

UNOBTRUSIVE ACCESS TO BEDROOM 2 THROUGH ENTRANCE AREA

NEW PORCH ALLOWS THE ENTRANCE AREA TO BE OPEN TO THE LOUNGE WITHOUT DRAUGHTS OR HEAT LOSS

PORCH

Strategic organization plan 1:100

There is insufficient space for a sliding door and resiting of the opening to the front would mean that it was on the more exposed side of the house and would require a less direct route of access to and from the gate.

The agreement by building control to waive the regulation for a lobby to the **bathroom** from the living area was vital. The bathroom is easily accessible from the lounge and the bedroom and is maintained as a large space for the dual purpose of circulation within the room and passage through it. It is possible for two wheelchairs and an assistant to move freely within the bathroom, allowing Mr and Mrs Musgrave to help each other and permitting the most efficient use of nursing time when they are attended to simultaneously. The lack of alternative internal access, however, imposes limitations both on privacy and on free movement between the bedroom and lounge, if the bathroom is in use. The problem would be increased with the addition to the household of a live in carer needing to use the bathroom.

Facilities in the bathroom have proved with use to be entirely suitable. High quality equipment and finishing has been used throughout with a consequent good record of reliability and low maintenance costs. The whole room can be a wet area, if necessary, and allows Mrs Musgrave the freedom to use the **shower** independently, and in the manner she wishes, with any excess water well contained within the rubber strip thresholds. The vanitory unit was designed particularly for her use and allows everything she needs to be easily to hand, although a rounding of the outer corner might have assisted an approach line to the bedroom door. There could have been one hoist on a long track to serve the wc, shower and bed which are positioned in a direct line to one another. This would not however, have allowed use of a hoist to facilities simultaneously in the bathroom and bedroom by Mr and Mrs Musgrave, which is required on occasions.

The total expenditure on buying the property and then adapting it, was substantially more than any mortgage valuation of the adapted property might be. It could have been that the Musgraves had they looked further, might have found a more suitable bungalow to adapt. However, narrow corridors are the norm in bungalows of this kind, and there was in this case the advantage of a flat site.

Despite the information from the preliminary enquiries, the community of the small market town has not been as supportive as anticipated. Other residents of the road in which the Musgraves live tend to lead insular and self absorbed lives, with little contact among each other as residents of long standing, let alone with newcomers. House extension and refurbishment is a source of competition and envy. While there is a local shop, the round trip to the town centre is beyond the range of electric wheelchairs and the Musgraves are dependent on others for transport, which is not forthcoming from the local community. Support systems from social services are more difficult and expensive to organize as they are not part of a large and coordinated network of staff, as in the city.

The Musgraves were fortunate to be able to turn the city council modernization scheme to their advantage in funding the large adaptation project. In addition, the approach to social services for financial help coincided with a policy that saw the total needs of a few disabled people as a preferable target to be met, rather than limited service to all. This policy was never adopted on a permanent basis and the use of such a large proportion of the annual budget to one scheme has had long term effects on a department that quickly reverted to committment to all disabled people according to assessment of need.

Mr Musgrave gained people's interest, using various agencies and the media to achieve his aims. He spent considerable time gathering information on legislation and how it could be applied to their particular situation. His solicitor proved a staunch ally and helped to bring the pressure to bear that was to ensure the purchase of the property and the considerable funding needed to follow it. A determination to succeed and an ability to overcome difficulties have helped Mr Musgrave to develop his own resources. He was able to sustain his belief in the right to own their home against odds that would have daunted many people, enabling him to take responsibility for his wife and his home in the setting he planned.

MR PERCY NEALE

Aged 69. Left hemiplegia.

Living with wife.

Adaptation of an owner occupied semi detached house.

Four years after his retirement from the engineering firm with whom he had worked for forty two years, Mr Neale had a severe cerebral haemorrhage resulting in a dense left hemiplegia. Onset first became apparent when, on Christmas eve 1982, he realised that he felt too unwell to walk the steep road leading directly to his house from the town centre and that he must take the longer but more gently graded alternative route. On his return, he went to bed and the following day felt well enough to enjoy Christmas celebrations with his wife and to visit his sister who lived nearby. The next day he could not stand and had no power or sensation in his left arm and leg. Having seen similar symptoms in his mother, he knew that he had had a stroke and the emergency duty general practitioner was called. Bedrest was recommended and daily visits set up from his own doctor. Three days later, when no improvement had been made, he was admitted to an acute medical ward of the nearest general hospital.

He had six weeks of treatment there before an assessment visit home could be considered. The hospital occupational therapist contacted her counterpart in the area social services and a joint visit was arranged which would, if successful, develop into a trial weekend at home for Mr Neale. Both he and his wife felt apprehensive about how they would cope and the observations made during the day visit were used to identify the support needed:

Mobility. Mr Neale was unable to walk, but could propel himself independently in a single hand operated wheelchair. He needed considerable help in transferring, could not negotiate steps or stairs and could not stand unaided.

Dressing. Maximum help was required.

Wc. The ground floor wc was inaccessible in a wheelchair owing to differences in floor levels.

Bathing. He required maximum help in hospital and the bath on the ground floor at home could not be reached because of the inadequate width of the door to the room and the differences in floor levels.

Chair. He required considerable help to transfer which was not eased by the low seat height of his armchair and awkward access to it in relation to other furniture.

Bed. Mrs Neale had arranged for their double bed to be brought downstairs to the lounge and, as the height of the bed was equal to that of the wheelchair, transfer was easier than to the armchair.

Eating and drinking. He could manage food if it was cut up for him.

Personal care. He could be independent in shaving and washing from a seated position, but had to have a bowl of water brought to him as there was no accessible washbasin.

Domestic tasks. Much of the responsibility, except for shopping, had always been left to his wife.

Hobbies and interests. Mr Neale enjoyed home activities of gardening, decorating, reading, painting and doing crosswords.

An immediate trial weekend was agreed; a commode being supplied by the local health clinic and chair raising blocks by social services. The social services occupational therapist ordered a self propelling wheelchair for his permanent use and discussed purchase of a more suitable armchair, which the family actually bought during the weekend. Additional support to Mrs Neale in caring for her husband was given by Mr Neale's sister and two further successful trial weekends were organised before Mr Neale was discharged home permanently. Out patient physiotherapy was arranged, with a programme of exercises at home to supplement treatment sessions. The hospital technician was asked to supply a wooden ramp at the side door, but this plan was dropped in favour of a more permanent arrangement.

In accordance with the agreed policy between social services and the district council, the occupational therapist contacted the environmental health officer with a view to arranging an early meeting at the Neale's house, to discuss adaptations required and methods of financing them. The main problems identified were that Mr Neale had no access to a suitable bathroom and the living area was being used as a bedroom, while the upper floor remained unused. It was accepted that major adaptation to the property could not be achieved within a time that was reasonable to help Mr Neale with his immediate problems and it was agreed that the first aim should be to give level access to the existing wc. The low cost project of raising the level of the concrete floor in the conservatory between the dining area, side and wc doors was identified to eliminate the uneven surface and the steps at the doors.

The subject of a longer term plan to adapt and improve the whole house was broached with the family, who agreed to give careful consideration to such a scheme in the light of Mr Neale's medical progress and experience of the improved access to the existing wc.

The estimated cost of the work on the conservatory floor was found to be over the social services department budget limit of £100 and the environmental health officer was again approached about funding via an improvement grant. He agreed to consider this in the grant application for the major work that was likely to follow, and the work was completed within two weeks of Mr Neale's discharge from hospital.

Reasonable access to the ground floor wc did not resolve all the difficulties, however, as Mrs Neale had problems in assisting her husband to transfer in the confined space of the room. Although the occupational therapist was able to demonstrate a successful method of management, Mrs Neale lacked confidence about using the manoeuvre herself when Mr Neale was tired or stiff, as was the case in the mornings. To assist, a castor wheel commode chair for use over the wc was ordered and a raised toilet seat and a grab rail were supplied by social services and installed by the Neales' son in law.

In the next weeks, Mr Neale's mobility improved with physiotherapy to the point where he could walk short distances with a tripod and it was felt that the longer term issues could be reviewed. Options considered were that Mr and Mrs Neale should move to more suitable accommodation or major adaptations and improvements be made to their present home. They were reluctant to think of moving from the home they had shared for thirty six years and the area in which they were well known. In addition, they relied on help from Mr Neale's sister who, as she lived in the same road, could easily visit. The poor state of the roof and rear extension of the house would not allow a high enough price on the sale of the property for a bungalow to be bought, and there were no ground floor flats in the town that were suitable for wheelchair use. The family had reflected upon the idea of wholesale adaptation of the property, as mentioned in the first meeting with the occupational therapist and the environmental health officer, and resolved that this would best meet their needs.

Mr Neale arranged for the services of an architectural consultant, through the builder he wished to use, to investigate how the house might be adapted, and to produce some alternatives for consideration by the occupational therapist and environmental health officer. The option of extending the house at ground floor level was discarded as it would still not have given Mr Neale full use of his house despite considerable expense. The design of the staircase prevented stairlift installation, and it was resolved that access to the first floor could best be achieved with a through ceiling lift. The walk in larder with the third bedroom above was nominated as the site for the lift. The balance of space in the bedroom was to be made into a bathroom and enlarged landing. Final plans were drawn up and applications made for building regulations approval and an improvement grant.

The occupational therapist warned of the likely upheaval of the building work and a social work student worked with the family to find alternative care for Mr Neale for the two weeks of the more major construction, which would include excavation to renew and level the kitchen and dining room floors, denying access to the wc and kitchen facilities. The Neales' daughter was keen to help, but had a house that was not large enough or suitable for a wheelchair and it was suggested that he spend two weeks in a nearby residential home for the elderly that was suitable for a wheelchair user. The builder could not guarantee an exact starting date, so a month had to be booked to ensure coverage of the appropriate time. The family were concerned that the work was to be done in the winter, but a short stay was more readily available at a time of year when there was little competition for holiday placements.

Mr Neale enjoyed his stay in residential care, finding the longer distances he needed to cover to reach facilities improved his walking. The close proximity of the home enabled his wife to visit often and to take an active part in his daily routine. In two weeks he was able to return home and together they coped with the ensuing building work. The main structural work took a month and a further two months elapsed before all installations were complete.

The front of the house. The sloping side pathway and steep road are difficult for a wheelchair user

The rear of the house, showing the conservatory that gives covered access to the ground floor wc

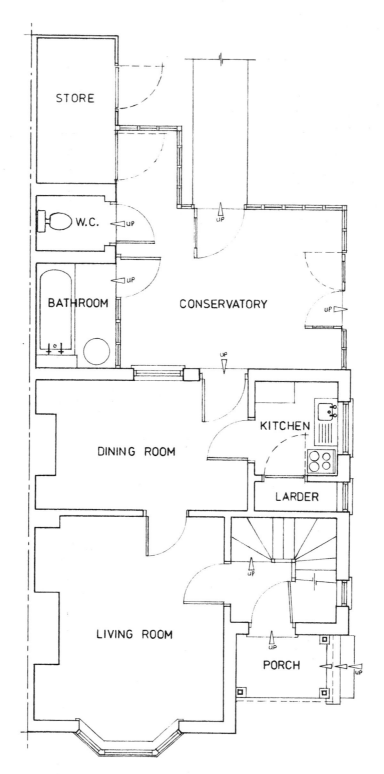

Ground floor plan before adaptation. 1:75
MR NEALE'S HOUSE

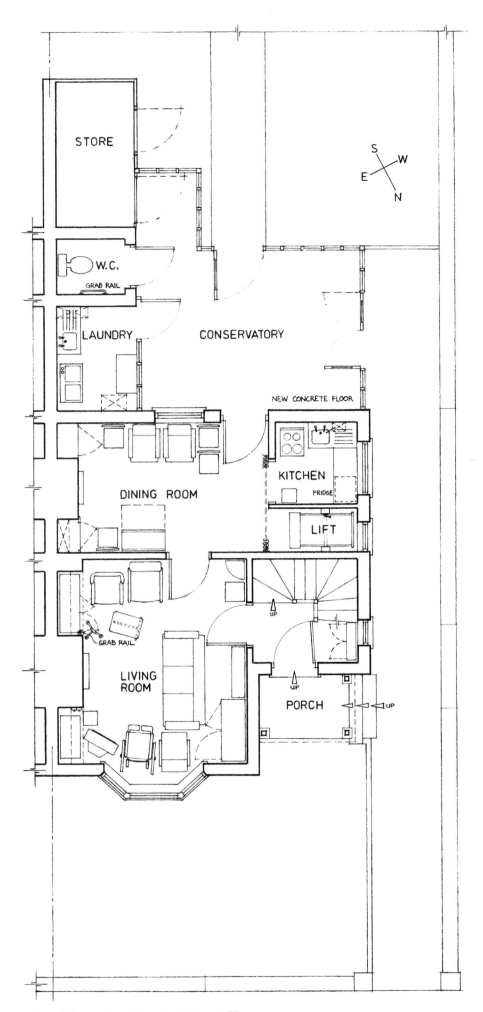

STORE

S
W
E
N

W.C.
GRAB RAIL

LAUNDRY   CONSERVATORY

NEW CONCRETE FLOOR

KITCHEN
FRIDGE

DINING ROOM

LIFT

GRAB RAIL

UP

LIVING
ROOM

UP

PORCH   UP

Ground floor plan after adaptation. 1:75
MR NEALE'S HOUSE

F

THE PROJECT TEAM

County council social services occupational therapist.
District council environmental health officer.
Architectural consultant.

THE AIMS

To give wheelchair access to all parts of the house.
To promote independence and ease of care.
To provide an internal bathroom and wc.
To bring the house up to a good standard of repair.

THE PROPERTY

* A three bedroomed, semi detached house built in 1897.

* Gross internal floor area 72.3m² unchanged.

The house was situated on the hilly outskirts of a small west country market town with a small garden to the front and a longer area to the rear. Outdoor access to the single storey wc and bathroom extension of the original building had been enclosed by a conservatory across the remaining width of the house. Adaptations made for Mr Neale focused on the kitchen, conservatory and third bedroom.

THE ADAPTATION

* Conversion of a three bedroomed house.

* Walls between landing and third bedroom, and between larder and kitchen demolished.

* Opening of 1220 x 840mm cut in joists over larder and divided from adjacent rooms on each floor by stud partition wall to form lift shaft.

* New stud partition wall erected to form bathroom off enlarged landing.

* Roof repaired and retiled, loft insulated and conservatory rendered watertight.

EXTERNAL DOORS AND PATHWAYS

* Floor of conservatory raised in concrete by approximately 100mm.

The front door, with steep steps that preclude wheelchair access, is kept locked and the side door is used as the main entrance to the house. The new floor eliminated the uneven surface of steps from the dining, bathroom, wc, garden and side doors allows wheelchair access to all parts of the ground floor, the rear garden and side pathway.

External door leaf sizes of 850mm permit easy passage of the chair, which is used for the longer distance to the garden or the sloping side pathway and road. However, Mr Neale rarely goes out as the hill on which they live is steep to manage in his wheelchair, and he is prone to travel sickness when riding in a car.

WINDOWS

No adaptation was made to the secondary glazed main windows and small casements above.

Mr Neale can reach the openable windows, but does not usually do so as he is rarely on his own for long enough to need to be responsible for controlling ventilation.

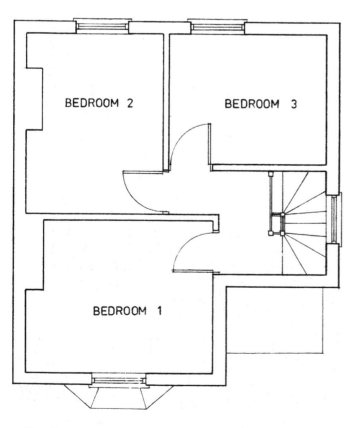

First floor plan before adaptation. 1:75

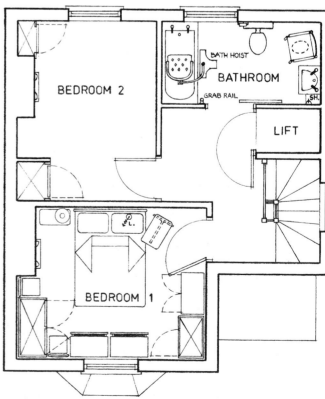

First floor plan after adaptation. 1:75

ELECTRICAL WORK

The house had been rewired ten years earlier, and a double set of power points raised to 960mm on the side of chimmney breast in living area.

No further adaptations were made, and Mr Neale is unable to reach any of the skirting board level power points from standing, although he is able to reach down sideways from the wheelchair. It is not essential for him to use electrical appliances independently, except for the television which is controlled remotely. He is able to operate the light switches at their general height of 1400mm.

HEATING

* Hot water tank and immersion heater resited from ground floor bathroom to second bedroom.

* New water storage tank mounted in loft.

The occupational therapist discussed the provision of additional heating with Mr and Mrs Neale, having discovered that the couple usually converted the lounge to a bedroom for warmth in the winter and that the the upper floor would only be partially used by Mr Neale at that time. The decision was made, however, not to incur any additional expenditure for the couple and the occupational therapist contacted the architectural consultant who undertook to ensure the optimum level of insulation in the new roof.

An electric fire sited in the chimmney breast in the living area, and electric wall heaters in the bathroom and bedroom are the only heating appliances used in house. However, the loft insulation, in conjunction with increased use of existing appliances, has meant that a higher temperature can be maintained with the Neales keeping their upper floor bedroom throughout the year.

INTERNAL DOORS

* 790mm opening made to new bathroom and sliding door with D handle fitted. Half door with magnetic closing catches made to lift shaft at upper storey and later replaced by full length one.

All doors, except to the old ground floor bathroom, permit wheelchair passage and Mr Neale has no difficulty with the sliding door to the new bathroom. The half door to the lift shaft was replaced to reduce draught and to prevent their young grandchildren climbing onto the low door and falling into the shaft. The magnetic catches, which cannot be opened unless the lift is at the floor, are standard provision with the lift chosen and give confidence that the shaft can be safely closed off on the first floor when not in use.

HALLWAY, LANDING AND STAIRS

* Upper landing increased in width by 1020mm on repositioning of wall to third bedroom.

* Second loft access point cut above landing.

The additional space on the landing allows easy access to and from the lift and for turning to the bathroom or main bedroom.

The new water storage tank could not be passed through the small opening to the loft in the third bedroom and necessitated a new opening.

THE LIFT

* Terry manually powered home elevator installed in shaft with standard features of key operation, pull cord release to floor locking bolts, handle movement initiation and individual weight setting.

Mr Neale has no problem with the lift, finding its operation simple and reliable. He enters the confined space of the lift forwards and reverses out into the larger spaces of the landing or the dining area. Since he only has the use of one hand, he is unable to hold down the pull cord bolt release and simultaneously operate the turning handle as is required for the lift to move. He has, therefore, tied a hook to the cord which he fits over the lift's safety bar to hold it taut and which he releases when he finishes turning the handle on arrival at the required floor. He finds the gradient of the tailgate/ramp simple to negotiate and its raising and lowering lever easily accessible to his right hand. However, he would have liked the lift to be a little wider for the precise alignment required to mount the platform.

LIVING AND DINING AREAS

* Grab rail installed on side of chimmney breast in lounge.

* Uneven flagstones in dining area lifted, concrete floor installed and finished in vinyl tiles.

Mr Neale spends much of his day in his armchair in the lounge, at which he also eats and pursues hobbies at a cantilever table. The floor in the dining area provides a

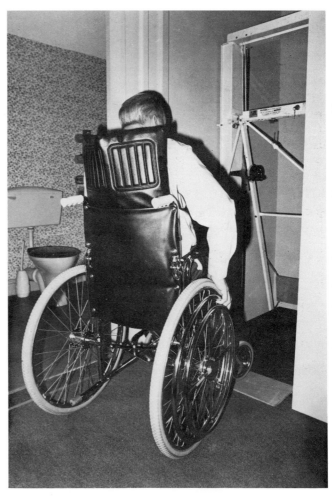

The position of the lift gives good access to the bathroom and bedroom on the first floor

The grab rail helps Mr Neale to rise from his armchair

The kitchen and lift shaft can be closed off by the curtains which help reduce draught from the shaft and prevent cooking odours dispersing through the house

smooth surface that gives no friction to the wheelchair. Care has to be taken, however, to avoid spillages, which render the floor very slippery.

KITCHEN AND UTILITY ROOM

* Bath removed from ground floor bathroom for conversion of room to utility area.

* Sink unit, wall cabinet and washing machine sited in utility room from kitchen.

* New and smaller sink unit with single drainer and cupboards under, work surface and matching drawer unit fitted to kitchen.

* Shelves built over units in kitchen.

* Electric cooker resited from position next to larder wall to opposite wall.

* Matching curtains installed to doorway of kitchen and adjacent lift shaft.

* New refrigerator to fit under work surface bought by Neales.

While Mrs Neale regrets the loss of the storage space she had with the walk in pantry, the impact of the reduction in size of the kitchen has been reduced with the creation of a utility room for laundry and storage in place of the old bathroom. As Mr Neale prefers to take his meals at a cantilever table in the lounge, the dining area is rarely used as such and doubles as extra kitchen space.

BATHROOM AND WC

* Suite of bath, pedestal washbasin and low level cistern wc installed to new first floor bathroom.

* Autolift bath hoist mounted on floor next to bath.

* Floor finished in vinyl tiles.

* Grab rail fitted at height 860mm and angled up by 40° in ground floor wc.

Mr Neale uses his castor wheel commode chair over the upper floor wc and at the washbasin, to which he is pushed by his wife. The pedestal of the washbasin does not permit optimal positioning forward to the basin, although its knee clearance height of 760mm suits Mr Neale.

Mrs Neale helps him transfer to the Autolift, steadies the seat and lifts his legs over the side of the bath. He can turn the handle to lower the chair, but Mrs Neale again finds

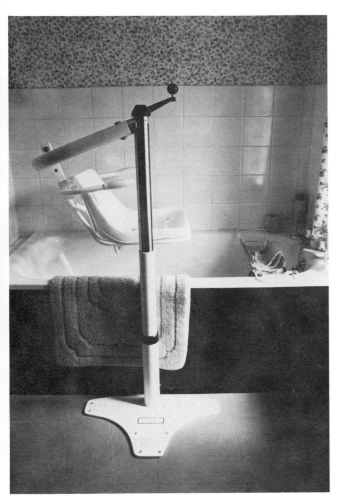

The position of the bath hoist close to the taps restricts independence

she must hold the seat, if the impetus of his turning the handle is not to cause him to bump against the side of the bath. The Autolift was positioned at the mid point along the bath for easiest fixing of the baseplate to the floor joists, but leaves insufficient room to avoid the wall and taps for Mr Neale to use the technique of supporting his left leg with his straight right to negotiate the bath rim. The seat of the lift clears the rear wall by 140mm, which creates a very confined space in which Mrs Neale must guide her husband's legs. They have cut additional drainage holes in the back of the seat as water previously tended to collect there and spill onto the floor as he got out, thus rendering the vinyl tiles very slippery. There is space for Mr Neale to reach the taps, but his wife fills the bath for him, as he anyway needs help in the bathroom.[1]

Morning stiffness means that Mr Neale cannot walk to the bathroom from the bedroom, although he can walk with a tripod to this room from the lift at other times of the day. He usually walks to the ground floor wc during the day, considering this good exercise. He is independent in the use of the wc, with the support of the grab rail and raised toilet seat which gives an overall height of 510mm, although his wife needs to help with management of clothes.
Rather than having a raised seat, the occupational therapist considered having the new wc in the bathroom raised on a 100mm plinth, but discounted this as Mrs Neale's small stature meant that she would have had difficulty with the

[1] An Autolift locking device is available, but is not a standard feature.

increased height. In practice, it proved more beneficial to use the castor wheel commode chair over this wc, one transfer only being required, in the bedroom, in the mornings. At this time, Mr Neale is at his most stiff and transfer most difficult, so the support of a chair with arms is helpful for use over the wc and at the washbasin.

BEDROOM

* Airing cupboard with shelves and hanging space built around new position of hot water tank in second bedroom.

No adaptation was made to the main bedroom which has sufficient space to allow wheelchair access to the side of the bed through the sufficiently wide doorway. Mr Neale does not have access to the wardrobe but relies on his wife to organize his clothes when dressing him.

COSTING

1984	
Terry lift	£1558.00
Shaft	500.00
Kitchen floor, damp proofing and fitting	1333.00
Bathroom and hot water system	1876.00
Fees, conservatory floor and decorations	1887.00
Total	7154.00

FUNDING

Improvement grant, 75% of eligible expense	£5365.00
Loft insulation grant	69.00
Client's contribution	1720.00
Total	7154.00

* Autolift supplied from social services stock.

* Mr Neale paid initially for the raising of the floor in the conservatory, which was agreed to be included retrospectively in the improvement grant paid to him for the major adaptation.

CONTRACTUAL PROCEDURE

Mr Neale selected the builder he wished to use and he, in turn, suggested the architectural consultant who drew up the plans, as was the reverse of the usual and preferred order by the environmental health department. The plans and tender sum were accepted by the grant authority and the work was contracted to the builder by Mr Neale. The Autolift was installed by the builder for social services and the lift was delivered and installed by Terry Lifts Limited.

EVALUATION

A family history of cerebrovascular accident and the immediate awareness of the cause of the paralysis did nothing to lessen the shock for the couple when the symptoms became apparent in Mr Neale. Concern for his life, the need for Mrs Neale to lift her tall husband and the unsuitable layout of the house made the early stages after discharge from hospital very difficult. The comparatively small adaptation of raising the floor to give access to the ground floor wc took away some of the pressure and allowed time for precise and long term requirements to become apparent.

That this stage of the urgently required work was completed quickly is of merit to good working relationships between staff. The environmental health officer applied Section 57(5) of the 1974 housing act as he was satisfied that there were good reasons for beginning the work before application was approved.

The later and more major work gave Mr Neale use of all of his house and also raised the general standard of facilities. The structure and condition of the extension to the rear was of a type that would have necessitated demolition, rather than adaptation, and access to it across the conservatory would have been cold in winter. The size and layout of the house was one that lent itself well to reduction in the number of bedrooms.

The **lift** has been successful for Mr Neale and he has ingeniously overcome his difficulties with the bilateral operating method, although it eliminates one of the lift's safety features. The counterbalancing that was set to match his individual weight has meant that he must always use his wheelchair for travelling in the lift, despite his progress in walking. However, he is most likely to use the lift in the mornings and evenings which are times when walking is most difficult for him because of tiredness or stiffness. The use of a curtain to divide the shaft off on the ground floor and the original half door to the landing seem inadequate to avoid draught and heat loss, although to some extent this has been overcome by the installation of a full door on the upper floor.

The space in the **bathroom** is ample for movement of the castor wheelchair which is used in this room and for transport to and from the bedroom. Use of a wall mounted washbasin, however, would have allowed Mr Neale to sit farther under the bowl, without catching his knees. The need for a short bath limited the options available for siting the **Autolift**, but the precise requirements for optimal use were not adhered to and the most straightforward position, technically, took precedence over alternatives. The result is that Mr Neale cannot use the bath independently and Mrs Neale has great difficulty in giving him the help he requires in the confined space.

While outings have been severely curtailed for Mr Neale by the hilly nature of the area in which he lives and by his inability to travel in comfort in a car, his interests, which always focused on the home, have not entirely changed. He greatly regrets, however, no longer being able to manage the garden, and worries about its unkempt nature compared to the very high standards applied previously, or to do small jobs around the house and to help his wife.

Mr and Mrs Neale do not regret, however, their decision not to move to more suitable accommodation, even if a property had been available to them. They are well supported in a community that has known them for many years and they have the vital additional help of Mr Neale's sister who lives close by. Their very supportive family see continuation of tradition in the home of their youth and that of previous generations of the family. Overemphasis is not given to change brought about by an alteration in the health of a family member and Mr Neale can look forward to a future in a refurbished and warmer house.

MRS OLIVE FLETCHER

Aged 59. Multiple sclerosis.

Married.

Adaptation of the ground floor of an owner occupied mid terraced house.

Extreme fatigue, altered vision and a foot that tended to drag were attributed to multiple sclerosis when Mrs Fletcher was twenty six years old. Her view of the condition and its outcome was limited to her experience as a tax officer when claims were made for relief by the carers of highly dependent people. She was unable to discuss her prognosis or gain further information from her hospital consultant or general practitioner, and feared the most severe and rapid deterioration.

She had a series of relapses and remissions, but was well able to hold down her job, leaving five years later in 1956 to have a baby. She brought up her family and managed to successfully run their mid terraced house without any great problem until 1973. At this time she realized that the gradual deterioration in her mobility had began to exclude her from family walks, outings and shopping expeditions. She was given a wheelchair for her forty eighth birthday from her father in law and enjoyed the lease it gave her family life. The chair chosen was self propelling and she began to find it useful indoors at times of tiredness or on particularly bad days. She asked her general practitioner for a DHSS model for indoor use and looked for other equipment that might help her maintain her role at home.

As secretary of the local multiple sclerosis society, she was in contact with people with similar problems and tapped this source of information and experience. No specialist advice was available from social services as there was no occupational therapist in post, although the department provided a chemical wc for use on the ground floor when requested. This was placed in the kitchen, so as not to impose its presence on either of the reception rooms, and helped overcome problems of frequency and urgency of urine. Mr Fletcher emptied the unit on a weekly basis for eight years until they discovered that this service was available to them from the local council. On several occasions Mrs Fletcher visited a hospital aids demonstration centre in a nearby city, and tried out equipment that might be helpful to her.

During these years, she needed to use the wheelchair increasingly, but the effects of the insidious change came to a head on bad days for her, when she could not walk to the chemical wc or get the wheelchair through the narrow kitchen doorway to reach it, and incontinence became a reality. She decided that the time had come for a major change.

The family were not keen to consider a move from the area where they were well known and had friends. They found that bungalows were a rarity and that the sites were anyway unlikely to be suitable in the hilly surrounding area. They could not afford to buy into this sector or to find a property that was as convenient as their own in terms of Mr Fletcher's requirement for easy transport to work.

They resolved to adapt their present accommodation and once again Mrs Fletcher asked social services for advice. Again, there was no occupational therapist in post, but home help support for two hours per week was agreed to assist with the domestic tasks that she found most difficult. The home help organizer suggested that Mrs Fletcher might contact a hospital based occupational therapist, who in September 1981 visited and discussed possible adaptations to the house. These included a stairlift, addition of ground floor wc facilities and kitchen enlargement. Her knowledge and practical experience of major structural alterations was limited, but she was able to supply some out of date Equipment for the Disabled books and to request social services to supply a walking frame and castor wheelchair.

Armed with the books, more visits to the demonstration centre, advice from the home economics adviser of the local electricity board and greater knowledge of the likely course of her condition, Mrs Fletcher set about planning structural changes to the house. It became clear to her that, as she had tried to use professional advice and found it unavailable, she was in the next best position to organize the work with her own knowledge of her requirements and functional limitations.

Mobility. Indoors Mrs Fletcher could walk with the support of two sticks or one stick and leaning on the furniture, but invariably used a wheelchair outdoors. Her legs were weak, her gait unsteady and she found that she had a very low tolerance to fatigue. She used a self propelling wheelchair, without footplates, for up to half a day in the house and avoided risk of falling out by using a long handled aid to reach items not immediately accessible. She could manage the stairs, with considerable difficulty, and considered the exercise to be vital to her continuing health.

Dressing. She could not bend down safely or raise her legs sufficiently to put clothes on her lower half and her husband helped her with this. Some weakness and lack of coordination in the left hand made small buttons and fastenings difficult.

Bed. At a height of 550mm, the bed was of the most useful height for her to rise to stand independently. She usually needed support in getting up because of increased stiffness and spasm. Help was usually needed at night to lift her legs into bed, to turn over or to get up to reach the commode.

Wc. She only used the first floor wc first thing in the morning and last thing at night, with a commode by the bed used if necessary, during the night. A toilet frame issued by social services gave useful support on rising from the first floor wc and a chemical wc was used on the ground floor.

Bathing. A bath seat and board had proved helpful for several years in allowing her to use the bath. However, pushing up from the seat became too difficult and she had resorted to using the board only, although she felt very nervous of toppling from this. It was also becoming a greater strain for her husband to lift her legs over the side of the bath.

Eating and drinking. Weakness in her left hand could sometimes cause problems.

Domestic tasks. Mr Fletcher organized the shopping around his work schedule and a home help assisted with heavier domestic tasks. Mrs Fletcher did all the cooking, having changed from a gas oven to a microwave. The self igniting rings of the gas stove presented no problem to her, although she tended to use only the front ones unless help could be given. She did her own ironing if the board was set up for her, but found the kitchen inaccessible to her wheelchair and thus limited in its use to times when she was mobile with sticks.

Hobbies and interests. She greatly enjoyed study and had spent eight years doing various courses and attaining a degree with the Open University, whose facilities and attitudes to disabled people she commended. She and her husband had been active for a long period in the local multiple sclerosis group. She was also interested in music, tapestry, reading and attended a local social club for disabled people.

In February 1982 she felt confident enough to brief a building design consultant whom she selected on hearing that he was interested in designing for disabled people. Various options were considered, such as incorporating a small wc within the existing ground floor and using a stairlift to the first floor. The structure of the stairway, with a right angled bend at the top of the main flight, would have needed the lift to rest level with the top step and a platform to be used to bridge the gap. This would not be practicable if she ever needed help to transfer to a wheelchair, as there would be insufficient space. In addition, the restricted area of the landing, bathroom and wc could not accommodate a self propelling wheelchair. The small size of the bathroom precluded a hoist installation and the presence of any helper or wheelchair. The decision was to discount the upper floor and plan to convert a ground floor reception room to a bedroom, if necessary. Sketches were made and proposals agreed that would allow total elimination of the use of the stairs.

At the beginning of March 1982, Mrs Fletcher's building design consultant contacted the urban renewal section of the borough council directorate of health and housing to apply for an improvement grant for the work. In accordance with departmental policy to process grants for disabled people as a priority, the officer immediately sought confirmation of Mrs Fletcher's registrability under the Chronically Sick and Disabled Persons' Act 1970 and requested observations and recommendations from social services on the proposed adaptations to provide a wheelchair accessible ground floor bathroom and kitchen.

The building design consultant submitted the plans for building control approval. While the site was in a conservation area, it was determined that planning permission was not required, although the exterior of the extension was finished in local stone to match the existing house in accordance with the town planning officer's suggestion. Building control approval was achieved in seven weeks with an agreed relaxation that would allow them to dispense with the second door from the lobby into the bathroom, on the grounds of the special needs of a disabled person.

In June 1982, after consultation with the hospital occupational therapist, social services responded positively to the proposals. The case was referred to the council's improvement grant panel, but a decision was deferred for further information as to why a vertical lift was not being used. Explanation of the difficulties of using a wheelchair on the first floor, however, obtained grant approval in principle for the proposed work a month later.

The building design consultant obtained estimates for the work and in September made formal application for final approval showing the actual sum. Subject to minor amendments to the door at the head of the cellar and ventilation to the bathroom lobby, required by the improvement grants panel, approval for a 75 per cent grant of the maximum eligible expense of £8,500 out of a total estimated cost of £11,500 was recommended and subsequently confirmed by the housing committee chairman.

When the Fletchers discovered how much their contribution would be, they decided to make savings by substituting a shower tray for the level access shower, so obviating major structural work to the bathroom floor. The revised plans were submitted for the grant, but the new proposal proved unacceptable to the health and housing department, who advised social services of their objections.

The divisional social services officer visited the couple, and the Fletchers were reluctantly persuaded to be means tested for a financial contribution from social services adaptations budget. In March 1983, they were granted the sum of the shortfall in the approved cost of the work.

Work commenced on the project in mid May. All structural work was completed in nine weeks, although it was October before all fitments were installed. Difficulties in finding a private position for the chemical wc were encountered with builders at both the front and back of the house and some features were incorrectly installed while the couple were on holiday.

The health authority community occupational therapist visited and advised on the positioning of rails, that were

The front view of the house

fitted by the builder, and later approved the work on completion of the project.

THE PROJECT TEAM

Mr and Mrs Fletcher.
Building Design Consultant.
Borough council urban renewal officer.

THE AIMS

To provide wheelchair accessible bathroom facilities on the ground floor and to avoid the need to use stairs.
To enable wheelchair access to and from the property.
To plan a new kitchen that could be useful to ambulant and wheelchair users and allow continuance of domestic roles.

THE PROPERTY

* A mid terraced house built in 1890 and situated in a conservation area.

* Gross internal floor area 102.3m² before and 108.8m² after adaptation.

The site for the house, as typical of those in the area on the outskirts of a town set in hills, sloped steeply away to the rear of the plot. A block of garages for the terraced houses was some distance away and parking therefore tended to be in the street at the front.

THE ADAPTATION

Conversion of a ground floor kitchen to a bathroom and provision of wheelchair accessible kitchen facilities.

* Extension constructed from 150mm secondhand stone to match existing, with 75mm cavity, 110mm thermal blocks and

* 10mm plasterwork built alongside kitchen extension to rear of property to include cellars and ground floor.

* 100 x 100mm structural timber post installed to form outer corner linking windows.

* Soil and rainwater pipes relocated.

The slope of the land away from the house meant that walls had to be built up from well below ground floor level. Additional major excavation and construction work proved necessary and escalated the total cost, as the new building crossed the line of the main drains for four houses in the terrace and an accessible inspection chamber had to be provided.

EXTERNAL DOORS AND PATHWAYS

* 760mm wide external door with lever handle, mortice lock and central glazed panel installed to new kitchen.

* Front and back door thresholds fitted with cushion strips.

* Gate hung to open opposite side.

* Three 180mm deep stone steps at front resited forward and separated from front door by 1750 x 1200mm wide level platform.

* 1200mm wide ramp made from platform to run across front of house, 480mm forward of house wall.

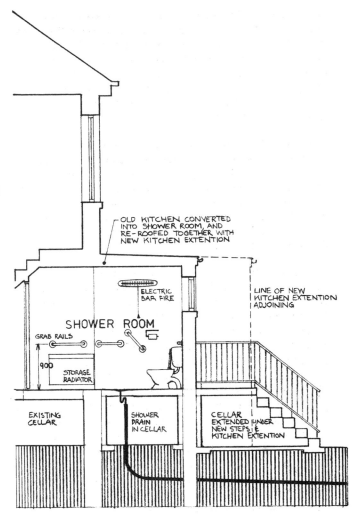

Rear adaptations. 1:75

* 180° level turning platform made 3050 x 1200mm onto second ramp to level area of 1300 x 1200mm at gate.

* 920mm high metal handrail installed to steps.

* 480mm high double board decorative fencing constructed at exposed edges of ramp and central platform.

* Central vacant portion of garden planted with tall flowering shrubs.

* 1975 x 1100mm balcony constructed at rear of property, with flight of stone steps to garden.

* 900mm high metal handrail and balustrade to enclose balcony, with gated access and handrails to steps.

* New surfaces finished in 100mm thick tamped concrete.

Mrs Fletcher uses the central platform of the front ramping as a sitting out area when the sun is on that side of the house. She is a little nervous of going the full length of the ramp when she is alone, in case she tires too much to get back to the top.

Turning from the kitchen through the back door to the balcony involves a tight right angled turn and requires careful alignment to avoid catching her knuckles. The threshold strips present no problem to independent access and, as the back door is at right angles to the exposed rear aspect, there are no problems of rain penetration. She is

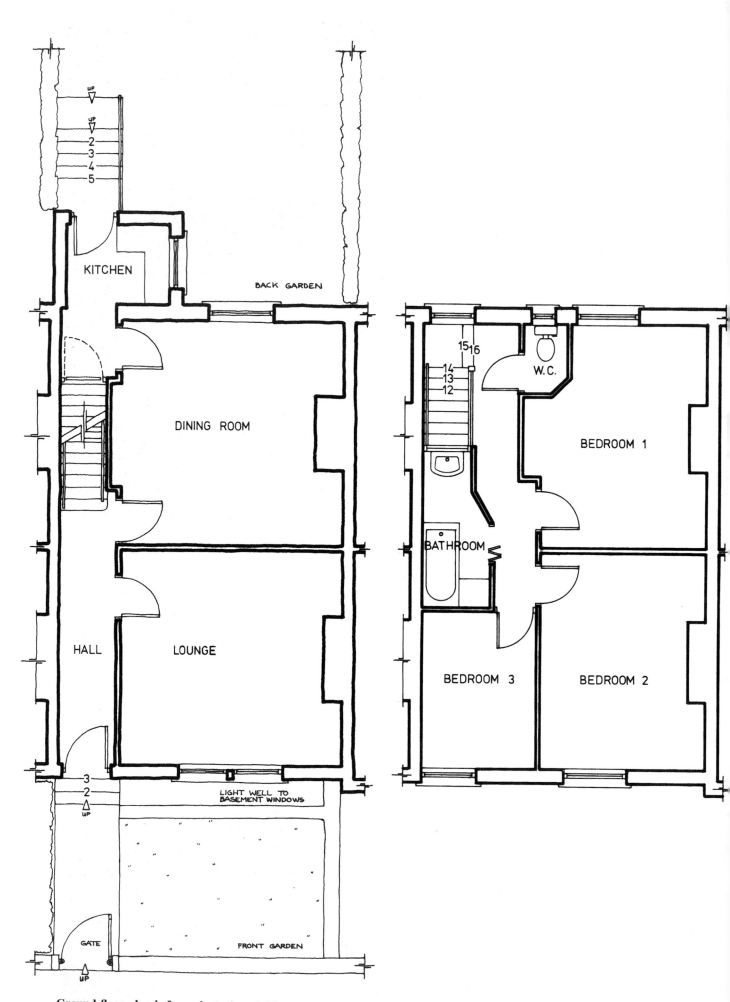

KITCHEN

BACK GARDEN

UP
UP
2
3
4
5

DINING ROOM

15 16
14
13
12
W.C.

BEDROOM 1

BATHROOM

HALL

LOUNGE

BEDROOM 3

BEDROOM 2

3
2
UP

LIGHT WELL TO
BASEMENT WINDOWS

GATE

FRONT GARDEN

UP

Ground floor plan before adaptation. 1:75

First floor plan unaltered after adaptation. 1:75
MRS FLETCHER'S HOUSE

76

The rear view of the property showing the new extension

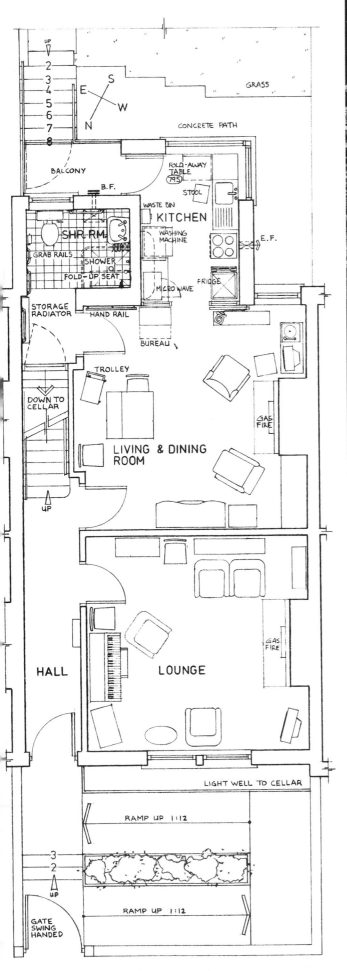

Ground floor plan after adaptation. 1:75

able to turn independently in the limited space on the balcony and enjoys sitting out there in a position that commands excellent views and maximum sunshine. Gardening had always been her husband's interest and responsibility and it is of no regret to her that she is unable to reach the back garden she can best enjoy viewed from the balcony. A washing line hooked to the railings allows her to put out a small amount of washing with ease.

The fencing and shrub beds are attractive. Planners had suggested kerbed edges and a metal handrail but agreed to Mrs Fletcher's idea which is equally functional, and visually more pleasing. Original planning had also allowed for the ramp to be built against the front house wall and for

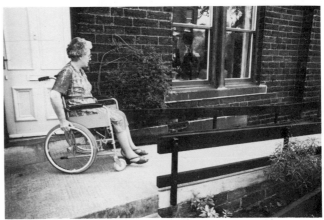

The ramps give easy access to and from the house

ventilation shafts beneath the ramp to maintain air circulation to the cellars. However, Mr Fletcher wanted to retain the front basement window which provided the only source of natural light to an area he used as a workshop. The platform at the front door was therefore extended so that the ramp starting point could be set sufficiently far forward of the front wall for the window to remain useful.

WINDOWS

* Original window to living area removed to make way for kitchen extension.

* Single glazed raised head sash window with cill height of 900mm to match others in the terrace, formed in rear wall next to position of extension.

* Original end kitchen door partially blocked up to allow small high level opening window over proposed position of wc.

* Side facing kitchen window removed and aperture blocked up and made good.

* Large single glazed windows, one with small top opening operated by pull cord ratchet system, made to side and rear walls of new kitchen.

Mrs Fletcher can operate the pull cord window opening system in the kitchen and the long pull cord arrangement for both blinds and curtains. Secondary double glazing, being gradually installed to the sash windows as finances permit, helps considerably in maintaining the warm temperature she needs but means she cannot open the window in the living area. However, she is able to get sufficient ventilation through open doors and windows to the kitchen. The bathroom window is inaccessible to her.

Although cill heights are rather high in the kitchen as governed by sink and work top heights, the sloping site means that the view would only be of tall trees anyway. This factor was used to gain planning permission to install the side window which ostensibly overlooks a window of the neighbouring property, but in fact only gives a sight line into their house from the farthest and most inaccessible part of the room. As there was only sufficient space for a window to the lounge to allow the minimum of 10 per cent for floor area required, it was desirable to create the opportunity for borrowed light from elsewhere. The provision of two windows and a half glazed door to the kitchen allow the room to flood with light and, in conjunction with the south facing aspect, successfully allows additional light to the room behind.

ELECTRICAL WORK

* House rewired and power sockets in living area set at height 840mm.

* One double and three single power points in kitchen at heights 1110mm and 900mm respectively.

* Light switches set at 1370mm above floor, in keeping with rest of house.

* Power provided to extractor fan in kitchen.

Power socket outlets have proved adequate in number and easily accessible to Mrs Fletcher.

HEATING

* Wall mounted radiant electric bar heaters fitted in kitchen and bathroom; later supplemented by night storage heater in bathroom lobby.

* Multipoint water heater mounted on bathroom wall to serve kitchen and bathroom.

The bathroom heater proved insufficient for the cold bathroom. While the additional night storage heater has improved the temperature, the tiled walls and floor surfaces are still cold to the touch.

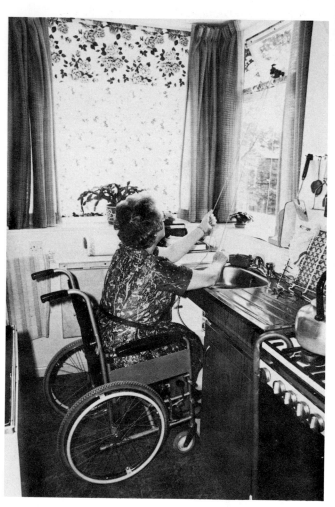

Mrs Fletcher can get close to the sink in her wheelchair, using the knee space underneath, and finds the pull cord window opening easy to use

HALLWAYS AND DOORS

Sliding door with upper half of obscured glass installed to 735mm wide opening from living area to new kitchen extension.

Door clearance is satisfactory for Mrs Fletcher providing she has straight access. Turns, however, are particularly tight from the rear reception room to the hall, where the position of the bottom stair and wall reduces the clear space to 650mm, and at the back door to the kitchen.

Mr Fletcher fitted a coat hook above the pull handle on the door from the dining room to the bathroom lobby, which Mrs Fletcher finds easy to catch with her walking stick and so avoids moving the wheelchair back and forth to open the door. A 45mm diameter mopstick rail fitted by Mr Fletcher in addition to the bannister on the other wall gives his wife sufficient support for her to manage the stairs and is an exercise she considers to be vitally important to her continuing health. Space is very limited on the 810mm wide first floor landing with the wc door opening onto the top of the stairs. Replacement of the inward opening bathroom door by a concertina type, undertaken prior to the major adaptation, allows just enough space for a castor wheelchair when required.Building regulations were relaxed for the ground floor bathroom, allowing access from the living area with no enclosed lobby.

LIVING AREAS

No additional structural work was done to the two reception rooms other than in connection with windows and doors. A previously installed horizontal handrail at height 920mm gives support for walking from the kitchen door to the bathroom.

The rear room is used as the day to day living area, while the front room is kept as a more formal sitting room. Mrs Fletcher transfers into an armchair with seat height of 450mm, to match that of her wheelchair when wishing to spend time in the living area. Despite the limited space for manoeuvering her wheelchair, she has no problems in using these rooms and finds the short pile carpet suitable for walking.

KITCHEN

* Galley style arrangement of double cupboard floor unit with 890mm high worktop and shallow wall cabinets with top shelf height of 1650mm.

* Small drop down table, supported on integral bracket hinged to wall beneath rear window to form 800mm high work surface.

* Custom made floor unit, housing 130mm deep sink with dome headed taps, single drainer and cupboards below, set on return wall.

* Base plinth to sink unit set at height 85mm and shelving cut back to give knee room under.

* Floor finished in short pile washable carpeting.

* Loose laid melamine topped work surface set on top of front loading washing machine to overlap adjacent unit with microwave oven mounted above.

* Wall mounted refuse bin positioned above storage place of perching stool next to rear door.

* Upright gas cooker and refrigerator/freezer installed adjacent to draining board.

The custom made sink unit allows Mrs Fletcher to rest her feet on the 85mm base plinth and to have knee clearance above of 640mm. The large dome headed taps were chosen by the builder and fitted in the Fletcher's absence. The original request for conventional screw down taps would have allowed for planned use of extended lever tap turners if needed at a later date. The shallow shelf allowed here is useful for storage of cleaning materials and pans, but does not affect the space required for sitting at the sink, which she does either in her wheelchair or on her 620mm height perching stool. The wall unit shelves are only accessible

when Mrs Fletcher stands to work at the 930mm high surface over the washing machine; this provides a more comfortable height for other members of the family to work on and a resting surface for dishes taken from the microwave oven.

Mrs Fletcher only uses the top rings of the gas cooker. She is able to slide pans onto the draining board to avoid lifting, but cannot manage the oven or grill. Her main cooking appliance is the microwave oven which she likes but regrets that there is no alternative place to put it in the room, where space could be allowed in front of it to rest items being moved in and out. Having to lift dishes out and immediately move them to a worktop to the side is not always easy for her, especially as she needs to approach sideways to the unit in her wheelchair.

The lift up table and the unit adjacent to the sink provide a useful working area and the table does not impinge upon circulation space in the small kitchen when it is not in use

Mrs Fletcher uses a small lightweight tea trolley for transporting things from the kitchen to the living area, pushing it either from her wheelchair or when walking. She finds the carpeting practical for cleaning and the surface warm and easy to walk on. The waste bin is of sufficient size for daily domestic requirements and is emptied into the dustbin in the back garden by her husband when necessary.

The size of the kitchen was determined by the limitations on the rear projection to the building line and, while small, it is larger than the old kitchen and Mrs Fletcher finds it efficient and well suited to her needs.

BATHROOM

* Stone slab floor of old kitchen, suspended 1500mm above ground level over garden store, removed.

* Reinforced concrete suspended floor constructed to be continuous with that of new extension.

* Floor area for shower dished giving fall of 30mm to central trap, and waste projected into void below floor slab.

* Floor surface of room finished in lightly textured non slip ceramic tiles; wall surfaces of shower area finished in contrasting coloured wall tiles.

* Mira 722 thermostatically controlled mixer installed with fixed position shower head mounted at 1070mm on adjacent wall.

* 330mm deep x 770mm wide drop down hardwood shower seat, supported on legs cantilevered from bottom of wall, finished in high gloss varnish and hinged to wall to give seat height of 450mm.

* Large brass hook fitted to hold folded seat when not in use.

* Low level wc with seat height of 410mm set 300mm from adjacent wall.

* Washbasin with conventional screw down taps mounted on wall to allow 600mm knee clearance.

* 620mm long grab rails sited horizontally at height 900mm from floor in lobby and between wc and washbasin.

* Two 460mm grab rails sited between lobby and wc at height 900mm above floor.

* 460mm rail mounted next to wc starting level with front edge of pan at height of 760mm from floor rising 48°.

* 620mm rail installed vertically next to shower head starting at 870mm from floor.

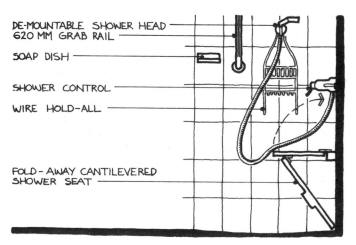

DE-MOUNTABLE SHOWER HEAD
620 MM GRAB RAIL
SOAP DISH
SHOWER CONTROL
WIRE HOLD-ALL
FOLD-AWAY CANTILEVERED SHOWER SEAT

Shower area. 1:20

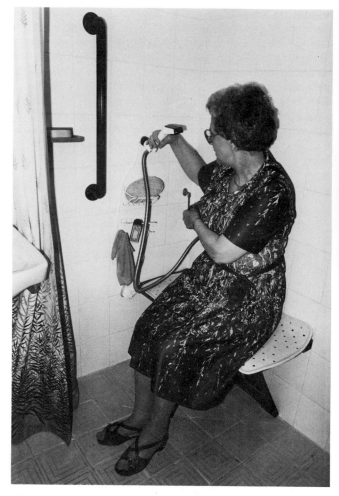

The shower mixer close to and on the same wall as the shower seat, makes it awkward to reach from a sitting position and the long lever controls are essential

Mrs Fletcher finds the controls on the shower mixer easy to operate, using the twin lever system for temperature and volume of water. Although she manages to operate the shower unit, she acknowledges that it would have been better sited on the same wall as the head. The height of the shower head was specified by her as being easiest for her to reach and hand hold the spray unit, and although quite low it is possible to sit under for hair washing. She finds the high gloss of the seat extremely slippery when wet and so uses a non slip bath mat on this and wears cotton slipperettes on her feet for showering to combat the cold she feels from the floor. The water drains away quickly and easily to the centre trap and she has no problems of access and transfer to this area. She feels confident about walking through the lobby and around the bathroom as she can use rails for support at each point.

BEDROOM

No change was made to the room other than by Mr Fletcher who fitted a double handrail to the foot of bed.

The top rail is used as support in walking and the lower as a bed cradle to remove weight from Mrs Fletcher's legs of the heavier duvet used in winter.

COSTING

1983

Building work, fees, fixtures and fittings	£10,925.00

FUNDING

Improvement grant 75% of £8,500 maximum	£6,375.00
Social services adaptations budget	1,287.00
Client contribution	3,263.00
Total	£10,925.00

CONTRACTUAL PROCEDURE

Contract for the building work was made between Mr and Mrs Fletcher and the builder, with the building design consultant acting as agent and supervisor of the work throughout.

EVALUATION

Despite efforts to involve specialists from statutory authorities, Mrs Fletcher was unsuccessful in obtaining the advice she sought and was left to rely on her own resources. She had a building design consultant who was interested in designing for disabled people and who was prepared to take on the responsibility of arrangements for which Mrs Fletcher lacked confidence, prior to building commencement. The adaptation was thoughtfully and carefully researched. The stringent limitations imposed by the site were well tackled with the resources the Fletchers had available to them.

The **ramp** and platforms allow Mrs Fletcher to get out in good weather at the front of the house, as well as giving good wheelchair access to and from the house generally. The provision of a small **balcony** was also very important to Mrs Fletcher, who had no alternative means of being outdoors at the back of the house owing to difficulties in reaching the steeply sloping garden.

It was fortunate that the long term investment value of injecting a sum from the social services adaptations budget was realized in time, so that the original plan for a level access **shower** could be preserved, thus ensuring continued use if a wheeled shower chair is needed. The bathroom is successful for Mrs Fletcher at present, despite the less than ideal arrangement of the shower unit, head and seat. The shower seat is a faithful reproduction of one shown in the out of date reference book and, had Mrs Fletcher had access to an occupational therapist, choice could have been made from a wider range of seats that are now available.

The **kitchen** is small, although slightly larger than the one Mrs Fletcher previously was used to. Problems of space still exist however, in terms of the lack of working space around the microwave oven, although the use of the hinged table goes some way to allowing sufficient worktop space elsewhere in the room. The room is light and airy and proves to be a pleasant place in which Mrs Fletcher may spend some considerable part of the day. She does much of the day to day cooking and sees scope for other minor modifications if necessary, which she can approach with confidence after organizing a major project. Owing to the site limitations, it would not have been possible to incorporate all the facilities and space needed if insistence

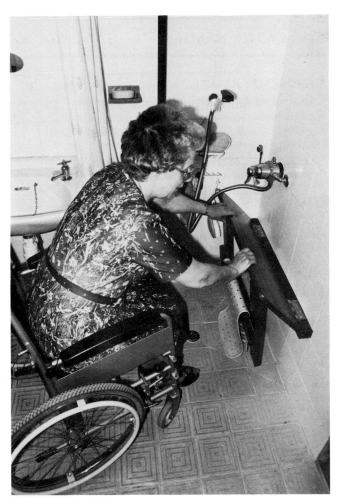

Operation of the shower seat

on a closed lobby to the bathroom had been made by the building control department, as it would not have been possible for Mrs Fletcher to negotiate the already tight turns if space had been further reduced by door swings. In this way, the Fletchers were fortunate to have a building control surveyor who was experienced in the needs of disabled people and so saw the essential nature of relaxing the regulation concerned.

The Fletchers do not regret their decision not to move house and consider that they have overcome most of the difficulties that were encountered by the increasing need to use a wheelchair indoors. Either of the reception rooms could readily be converted to a bedroom and entire living on the ground floor be achieved, although, at present Mrs Fletcher prefers to continue using the stairs for as long as possible. The ground floor alterations were considered to be a more economical alternative to a lift, that would still have necessitated major adaptation to the ground floor kitchen and to the bathroom and wc on the upper floor. The arrangement used leaves the house entirely in keeping with the rest of the terrace and the area. There is still scope for minor modifications and the family remain in an area in which they are well known and which is convenient to the needs of all family members.

THE PATEL FAMILY

MR AND MRS PATEL.
KANU. Aged 45. Spinal muscular atrophy and retinitis pigmentosa.
CHANDU. Aged 39. Spinal muscular atrophy and retinitis pigmentosa.
SAVITA. Aged 28. Spinal muscular atrophy, bilateral cataracts and retinitis pigmentosa.

Living in a three bedroomed city council house.

Move to and adaptation of a four bedroomed terraced house.

As Ugandan Asians, and hence in disfavour with Idi Amin, the Patel family were expelled from Uganda in 1972. The family had had successful business interests including supermarkets and a haulage company. They owned large properties and had several servants to run their house and care for the special needs of the three of their six children, who were born with leg and trunk paralysis and eye disorders. All family members were attended according to their needs and wishes, and there was no expectation that any of them would develop independence skills.

One daughter had already left home, so along with Mr Patel's mother, Mr and Mrs Patel and their five other children fled to England with only the £50 they were allowed to bring with them. They were housed at a reception centre in the south of the country for six months until a three bedroomed council house was allocated in a new town development area in the east of England. The house had a ground floor wc which was useful to the disabled children and their grandmother, who all slept in the living area as none could climb stairs.

The three elder members of the household could not speak any English; Mr Patel had difficulty accepting that he had lost everything and could not return to Uganda, and the climate aggravated asthmatic and arthritic conditions causing persistent respiratory problems and joint stiffness. Mrs Patel, with cataracts and arthritis herself, had to attempt to make a life for her family, a function to which she was not accustomed. Mrs Patel senior developed senile dementia and became prone to falls, wandering and incontinence to the point where she finally became bedridden in the lounge. In the following months, the second daughter moved out to marry and live in the Midlands.

The youngest daughter, aged sixteen, and now the only member of the household who was not disabled, proved the most adaptable, learned English well and became the spokesperson for the family. She contacted social services who introduced a social worker and an occupational therapist. The social worker offered support and assistance when problems arose with there being no washing machine, a need for a television to help the rest of the family learn English, lack of adequate heating and carpeting for the disabled members who pulled themselves around on the floor, and high electricity bills. With them she went to a community relations tribunal, the ophthalmologist and doctor, and assisted in disputes with a neighbour, applications to the Ugandan Asian relief trust and in arranging a holiday. The occupational therapist supplied grab rails and a toilet frame to help management of the ground floor wc.

In mid 1977 the family were moved to another property in the same road, while their house was refurbished under a modernization scheme. This house had a bathroom, as well as a wc on the ground floor and the reception room was again used as a bedroom. They accepted the offer of returning to their modernized house on the understanding that the ground floor wc and fuel store would be converted into a shower room with wc and accessible washbasin, as recommended by the occupational therapist. The work was completed and carpets supplied through a DHSS special needs payment, allowing the family to move back in October. They were disappointed, however, with the results as the roof leaked, the sash windows remained draughty and there was not the central heating that had been promised.

On the grounds of health and special needs, the Patels applied to the housing department for transfer to something more suitable for such a large family, the majority of whom could not use the upper half of the house. Several properties were offered in the ensuing months, but as they only had two or three bedrooms, the family saw no improvement and turned them down.

In 1975 Mrs Patel senior died and in the same year the youngest daughter moved out to follow her career. The family felt isolated without their spokesperson and Mrs Patel regretted the loss of the help at home she had been accustomed to. Social services were asked to give help with housework and get the handicapped family members out of the home to give everyone a break. A home help was organized, but only lasted for one day, as conflict arose between the worker as a social services' employee and the family who were used to organizing servants in their own home. Twice weekly attendance at a day centre for the elderly was, however, successfully instigated for Kanu, Chandu and Savita.

The occupational therapist was asked to advise on improved mobility in the existing home. It transpired that the shower had never been successful, since the water heater could not be regulated and there was a risk of scalding. The shower was therefore used as a washing area with water in a bucket. Chandu's response to this unsatisfactory situation was to drag himself upstairs to the bath; when he had a bad fall there, the family urged him to make contact with social services as the new spokesperson with the best command of English.

The occupational therapist arranged installation of a stairlift with a hinged seat, removable arms and a safety harness. Mrs Patel was to supervise and help those using the stairlift, although Chandu was able to climb onto the seat and operate the lift independently. The process was, however, difficult for the others and it is believed that Savita took to riding on the footplate, because she could not get onto the seat, and contributed to its many breakdowns.

Although the stairlift permitted an increased use of the accommodation, there was still not the central heating that Mr Patel, in particular, felt was essential. He continued to press for alternative housing through their Asian councillor, who also dealt with their neighbourhood disputes.

In June 1983 the family accepted a four bedroomed city council house on an estate adjacent to the city centre, near the home of the youngest daughter. The housing welfare officer contacted social services for advice on adaptations that would be required. The occupational therapist who had been involved previously had left and her successor visited and completed a functional assessment.

MR PATEL suffered from arthritis and asthma. Joint stiffness and pain affected walking and climbing stairs, and he had been hospitalized on several occasions with pneumonia. He was not expected to contribute to the running of the household or to help in the care of its members, and considered it a personal dishonour that his only sons were handicapped.

MRS PATEL also suffered from arthritis which, combined with obesity, made walking difficult without the frame that she depended on. Her vision was limited by cataracts and she rarely went out of doors.

KANU PATEL was registered as partially sighted and had not progressed in his understanding or communication in English.
Mobility. He was unable to bear weight through his legs and pulled himself around on his hands. He had little trunk control and no active hip flexion, but his arms and shoulders were strong. He could pull himself up from the floor to chairs and to his self propelling wheelchair in which he was taken out.
Dressing. He was independent.
Wc. Independent with rails and a toilet frame with which he supported himself in pulling up.
Bathing. He used the bucket technique over the shower base.
Bed. He rolled out onto the floor and could pull himself onto the 500mm height without difficulty.

CHANDU PATEL was registered as partially sighted, had a good command of English and was vociferous in his demands and complaints of the treatment the family had received in Uganda and England.
Mobility. He was unable to weight bear through his legs, but could flex his hips and sit back on his feet. He had good trunk control and strong arms, using these and weight bearing through his knees to get around on the floor. He also had a self propelling wheelchair, which he could get himself in and out of, and in which he was taken out.
Dressing. He was independent.
Wc. He was able to pull himself up onto a standard height wc with the support of rails.
Bathing. He preferred to use the bath to the irregular temperature shower, hauling himself onto the rim and then dropping down onto the base on his knees.
Eating and Drinking. Chandu had no problems with eating and drinking, did not attempt any domestic tasks, did some craftwork at the day centres and enjoyed watching television at home.

SAVITA PATEL was registered as partially sighted and was the most handicapped member of the family.
Mobility. She had complete lower limb paralysis, weak trunk control and arms, although she was just able to drag herself around on the floor if necessary. She was usually transported around the ground floor in a self propelling wheelchair and in a castor wheelchair on the first floor. She needed to be lifted into the wheelchairs and was dependent on the community nurse's twice daily visits to get her in and out of the chair.
Dressing. She needed help because of poor sitting balance.
Wc. She had to be lifted on and off.
Bathing. Once lifted to floor level, she could crawl to the shower base and wash using the bucket method, providing the water was drawn for her.
Eating and drinking. She used a spoon in her slightly stronger right hand.
Domestic Tasks. She was not able to participate, although she would sometimes be placed in the kitchen when meals were prepared.
Hobbies and Interests. The social worker for the visually handicapped had noted that Savita had become isolated and depressed at the day centre when deterioration in her vision made joining in with activities difficult. Surgery for removal of bilateral cataracts had helped in that she regained colour and shape perception in close proximity to her. Her wheelchair position in the living area was farthest from the television, but as she could hear what was said she had built up some command of English. Her quiet personality meant that her role was a retiring one and her status, as female and handicapped, was the lowest in the family.

The occupational therapist arranged to visit the new house with Chandu, being the most mobile and articulate in English, and the city council housing welfare officer who had been trying to find suitable accommodation for the family over the years. It was agreed that the focus of adaptations should be on the stairs, wc and bath. The occupational therapist recommended that the bath be retained and a hoist installed but the welfare officer advocated a shower. The decision was made to opt for a shower rather than a bath, and rested finally with the financing authority who took the opinion of their own housing welfare officer who had known the family longer than had the occupational therapist. In view of the constant breakdown problems there had been with a stairlift, it was resolved to install a through ceiling lift, and the agreement of the city council environmental health officer was secured for an improvement grant.

The work was completed and the family moved to their new accommodation in late 1984. Although they could see some improvement in their living arrangements, they were by no means satisfied with the work done or the amount of support available. The timing of the nurse's daily morning visit to get Savita up and ready was dependent on other commitments in the nurse's round and Savita was, therefore, not always ready for the day centre transport. A Crossroads care attendant was introduced, but the family preferred to use her time for meal preparation and Savita's situation largely remained unchanged. Home helps were reintroduced and, although the service has persisted, the priorities in tasks requested by Mrs Patel are not those of the service. Any shortage in staffing means, therefore, that the family is one of the first to lose sessions.

The relationship between the housing welfare officer and occupational therapist deteriorated, with disagreements over the shower versus bath installations and siting of the lift aperture and the ground floor wc. Workmen on the site felt abused by the family's dissatisfaction with their work and, therefore, were disinclined to do more than the bare essentials. Because of the costs already incurred, the council were not prepared to extend the stair rail or remove the blockwork wall that later impeded access to the reinstated bath.

G

At the day centre, the staff had difficulty lifting Savita in and out of her wheelchair to the wc, as did the nurse in the confined space at home. As a result, Savita decided to limit her intake of food and liquids on her day centre days and use the ground floor wc, that she could manage independently, before the nurse arrived. It was discovered, however, that she was refusing all food and liquid on the days she did not attend the centre, as there was no day time help available at home and she could not get to the wc unless she remained on the floor all day and dragged herself to the ground floor one.

The Patel family and the occupational therapist

THE PROJECT TEAM

County council social services occupational therapist.
City council housing welfare officer.
City council housing department coordinator of adaptations for the handicapped.
City council environmental health officer.

THE AIMS

To achieve maximum levels of independence in personal care for three severely handicapped people within the limits of functional levels, background and cultural demands.
To compensate for limitations in help available from outside and within the family for the most severely handicapped member.
To improve wheelchair access to and within the house.

THE PROPERTY

An end terrace, city council house built in 1978.

Gross internal floor area 112.0m² unaltered.

The entire front area of the terraced block was laid to lawn, with a narrow pathway to the front doors and a small garden to the rear of each house. Access to the back door of the property was reached via a pathway and side gate to the street.

The front area was designed for ease of maintenance and to promote neighbourliness among residents. Mr Patel does not tend his rear garden and the front lawn is mown by the council. The occupational therapist recommended covering the rear area with a patio; this is to be done by the community service scheme for offenders, financed by the family and social services jointly.

THE ADAPTATION

* Conversion of a four bedroomed house for use by a family with multiple and varied handicaps.

* Ground floor storeroom partitioned to permit installation of vertical lift to fourth bedroom.

* Ground floor wc adapted to meet cultural requirements.

* Adaptations to first floor bathroom.

Front view of the house

EXTERNAL DOORS AND PATHWAYS

* 900 x 900mm timber platform and 3000mm long ramp made to 250mm high back door threshold.

* 65mm upstand kerb and 880mm high handrail made to ramp and platform.

* Vertical grab rail fitted to wall beside front door, starting 1300mm from ground level.

The front curtilage had to be maintained as an open area and it was not possible to ramp the front pathway to give wheelchair access to the front door over the 245mm high threshold. While turns are required to the path and gateway to the rear, there is no problem with this or the internal rise of the back door threshold, since able bodied assistants always push the wheelchairs. Mr Patel is able to manage the front door step with the support of the grab rail.

WINDOWS

No adaptation was made to the single glazed full length windows in the dining and living areas or to the horizontally sliding sashes in other rooms.

The windows are not usually open, since the family prefer to open back and front doors to create ventilation. Mr Patel finds the draughts from the ill fitting windows particularly irksome and, for this reason, large furniture is placed against the windows in the living area and the curtains kept half closed in winter.

ELECTRICAL WORK

* Light switches lowered to 1100mm and power sockets retained at 430mm from floor level.

The light switches are accessible for Chandu, but are usually operated by the more mobile family members or are not switched on at all. Long pull cord light switches in the bathroom and ground floor wc are easily reached from floor level.

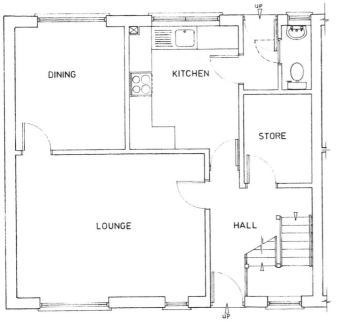

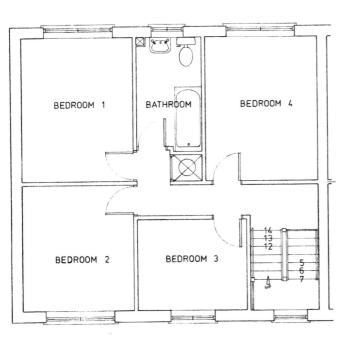

Ground and first floor plans before adaptation. 1:100

HEATING

No addition was made to the gas central heating and boiler, sited in kitchen, or to thermostatic controls set to top of radiators in every room at height 700mm from floor.

Heating levels are generally kept high to relieve discomfort felt by Mr Patel. Savita has her legs covered for warmth and modesty, but her brothers use short trousers, to save wear and tear as they move around the floor. Mr Patel controls temperature levels and does not need to bend down to reach the thermostatic valves.

HALLWAYS AND DOORS

* Outward opening door to ground floor wc replaced by sliding door, giving clear width of 730mm.

* New doorway formed to partitioned fourth bedroom to match all other internal doors with clear width of 670mm.

* Half hour fire resistant door with spring closure built to top of lift shaft.

* Half height door later installed to ground floor shaft area.

The sliding door to the cloakroom gives easier access and allows privacy for the user of the room. Wheelchair access is difficult, especially as Savita needs to be lifted from the chair and there is insufficient space for a helper in the confined space. The additional door to the ground floor was fitted to prevent Mr and Mrs Patel's grandchildren from playing with the lift controls when they visited.

The narrow hallway and landing widths cause particular difficulty in turning Savita's wheelchair from the kitchen to the cloakroom, from the living room to the kitchen, from the area of the lift shaft to the first floor landing and into the bedroom she shares with her mother.

The open area under the stairs provides a useful space for storage of wheelchairs when not in use. The mopstick handrail installed to only the first flight of stairs is not long enough to give Mr Patel the support he needs using the stairs. The housing authority does not see this work as a priority in a house that already has a lift, although the work will be done eventually.

THE LIFT

* Stannah Homelift installed in shaft from ground floor store to partitioned fourth bedroom.

* External master controls set at height 1270mm on ground floor and at 1360mm on first floor.

* Controls for lift set at height 855mm internally.

* Hinged seat installed to rear wall of lift at height 480mm.

Mr and Mrs Patel and Chandu use the lift independently and find the seat and access to the controls quite easy. Kanu and Savita cannot reach the lift controls and ride on the floor accompanied by their mother. Savita is transported in a wheeled carrying chair in the lift when being assisted by the nurse. For Kanu, Chandu and Savita the 85mm raised metal runner for the bottom of the lift door is uncomfortable to negotiate when they crawl into the lift. The hinged seat, even in the upward position, reduces space for alignment of the carrying chair.

The lift had to be mounted on a load bearing wall; this created problems in that the space available in the ground floor store allowed only a 570mm clearance between the open half door and the lift shaft. The outer shaft door at the first floor station closes on a strong spring, as is required to engage the door with the frame and allow the motor to operate, presenting a further impediment to those crawling across the floor or using the carrying chair. A slide bolt was mounted on the floor to hold the lift door open; it can be released by the foot of a standing passenger while

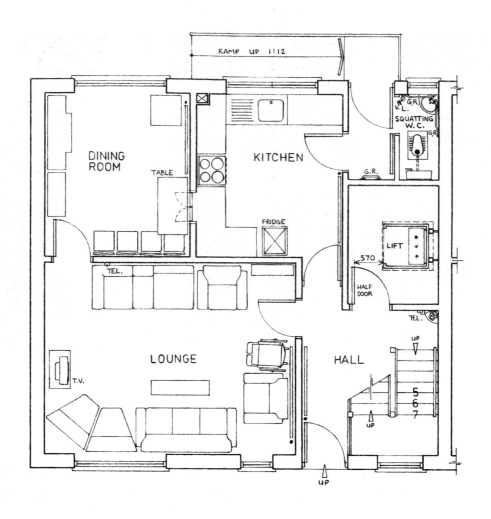

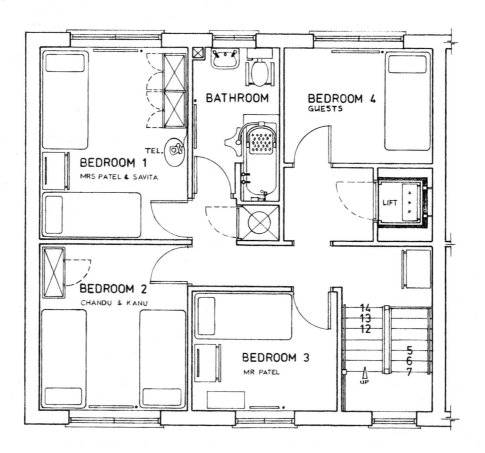

Ground and first floor plans after adaptation. 1:75
THE PATELS' HOUSE

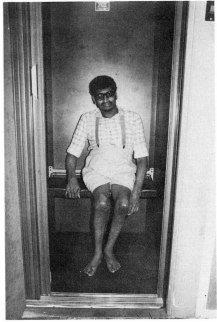

Chandu using the lift to descend from the first floor

holding the door open by hand, but cannot be operated by Kanu or Chandu, who crawl into the lift and must leave the door free to close behind them, the result is that the heavy door on its strong spring bounces against their legs as they crawl into the lift.

When the lift was first installed, Savita was pushed into it in her castor wheelchair. However, the chair was difficult to align in the lift and the door closing locator was frequently dislodged as a result of the manoeuvres and the lift put out of action. A small carrying chair was used instead, and the locator was moved to the top of the door edge out of the way. The occupational therapist asked for a rail to be installed inside the lift to enable Kanu to pull up to reach the seat and the controls. This was not done, the lift manufacturer advising against it because of the limitations of the lift wall material.

Negotiations between the housing department and the lift company had already commenced by the time the occupational therapist became involved and, in the absence of an alternative solution to offer, she went along with the plan. She requested that a more open plan arrangement be made by removal of walls on the ground floor to improve access to the lift. Despite demonstation of the lift cut out to Mr and Mrs Patel, they remained convinced that their grandchildren were in danger of being squashed under the lift and insisted that the area be enclosed.

When the lift was chosen and ordered, dimensions for the floor aperture were supplied by the manufacturer, in order that the builder could do the preparatory work prior to installation by the specialist company. The work was not, however, carried out in accordance with the instructions and, when the engineers came to install the lift, the aperture was found to be 50mm too far from the structural wall that was to bear the lift. They had to wait a day for the work to be corrected, so increasing the cost of the project.

Soon after installation, the adjoining neighbours complained of the sound of the lift being used, often into the early hours of the morning. The environmental health officer approached the lift manufacturer and it was ascertained that the sound was being transmitted from the motor through a cross member beam through the party wall, despite anti vibration mountings on the motor. To have installed sound insulation would have been expensive; the matter was dropped with explanations and requests for consideration to both parties being made and accepted.

LIVING AREA
No adaptation was made to this room.

The size of the room allows for ample seating and wheelchair manoeuvre, although Savita is rarely pushed into the room and watches television from a position by the doorway. The dining area is used for storage, along with the remainder of the storeroom from the lift shaft, to house bulk purchased non perishable goods.

KITCHEN
No adaptation was made to this room.

The thermoplastic floor tiles provide a surface on which Savita can more easily crawl and slide across to cloakroom.

CLOAKROOM
* Washbasin and wc removed.

* Squatting wc installed in floor; cistern with flushing handle mounted on wall at height 1170mm.

* Hot and cold water taps mounted on wall to right of cistern at height 660mm from floor.

* Washbasin mounted in opposite corner of room with rim height of 430mm.

* Two grab rails mounted vertically at height 945mm on walls above washbasin and a third mounted diagonally, starting at height 420mm on wall beside wc.

* Walls covered in ceramic tiles to height 900mm.

* Thermoplastic floor tiles installed up to front edge of wc.and family fitted linoleum to rest of floor.

The occupational therapist misunderstood Mr Patel's explanation as to how the wc was to be used and the taps were installed in the incorrect belief that there would be no turning round to use the wc as there is in western culture. The taps were, therefore, put at a height and position to be in front of the disabled members of the household, but even for this method, they were on the wrong side as they should have been sited on the left of the cistern to allow cleansing of the body with the left hand only; the right hand being reserved for use when eating. It was decided, however, not to change the positioning once the error had been identified, as the washbasin at a low level faced the wc and could be utilized rather than the intended taps,even though it was on the right.

The squat wc

Mr and Mrs Patel are not able to use this wc as joint stiffness renders it impossible for them to reach a squat position; they, therefore, use the upstairs pedestal wc. Kanu and Chandu can manage, but prefer to use the upper floor facilities as balancing in squatting is difficult.

Savita is the main user of the ground floor wc, achieving a level of independence in this room that does not occur in any other activity of daily living. She is able to crawl into a

sitting position over the aperture, propping herself up on the floor and can reach the washbasin and taps, although she does not use the rail over the washbasin that was intended for her to pull up on. This independence, that only requires help in flushing the wc, is vital in a household where the fittest member, albeit very disabled himself, might otherwise be called upon to help his sister, but is forbidden to do so by their culture.

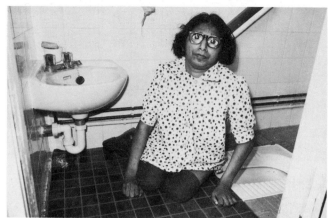

Savita is the main user of the squat wc compartment

BATHROOM
* 400mm high wc retained; toilet frame and 825mm high horizontal grab rail fitted.

* Washbasin lowered to give rim height of 640mm.

* Bath removed and replaced with shower tray set at 360mm from floor, as first adaptation.

* Shallow steps installed to give access to base.

* Blockwork wall constructed to enclose area on third side.

* Thermostatically controlled shower, with head mounted on slide rail, and controls at 1325mm above base level fitted on wall.

* Horizontal grab rails fixed to shower walls at heights 960mm and 1240mm above floor level.

* Bathroom floor covered in linoleum.

The wc is used by all members of the family in preference to the ground floor one. Kanu and Chandu can pull themselves onto the seat using the toilet frame and grab rail. Mr and Mrs Patel find the toilet frame useful to support and lift themselves and Savita finds it useful in balancing and adjusting her position when she is lifted onto the wc.

The washbasin was lowered to a compromise height for use from the floor or in standing. As a result it is uncomfortably low for Mr and Mrs Patel, especially for activities that involve stooping, such as cleaning teeth. It is too high for Kanu who can only balance himself when sitting on the floor, but Savita can use it when pushed up to it by the nurse.

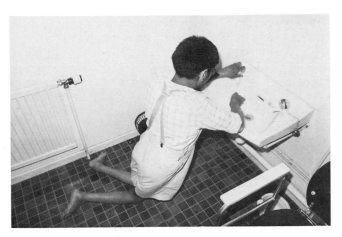

Chandu can kneel up to the washbasin and finds the height suitable, as he identified when acting as interpreter for the needs of all the family

Problems emerged during conversion of the bathroom, since the builders were unable to install the waste pipe for the shower base below the floor boards because of central heating pipes across the position required. Their solution was to raise the shower base and to install shallow steps and rails, rather than reroute the pipes, and they informed the the occupational therapist and welfare officer afterwards. Chandu and his parents were the only family members able to negotiate the steps to the shower, but Chandu could not operate the high controls independently and Mr and Mrs Patel did not like showers. As a result, the steps and base were removed and the bath reinstated.

The shower was retained and additional grab rails were fixed vertically, starting at height 1000mm above floor level at the shower end of the bath and at 1000mm at the entrance to the room.

The bath is accessible to all members of the family who use varying methods to achieve independence. Mr and Mrs Patel use the Autolift or pull themselves up on the rails, depending how they feel. Kanu and Chandu can use the hoist, but tend to find it a slow and laborious process and so use a combination of rails for support. When in the bath, neither feels confident in rising from the non locking Autolift seat, which they need to do to operate the taps and insert the plug. It is intended by the occupational therapist that a locking device will be fitted in due course.

Kanu's method of entry to the bath is to squeeze into the 395mm space between the Autolift and the wall and to haul himself up on the two facing handrails to eventually kneel on the bath rim. He then drops onto his knees on the base of the bath, thence achieving a sitting position propped against the side and end of the bath for bathing.

Chandu climbs over the end of the bath by pushing up on the toilet frame and by pulling himself into position on the edge of the bath. His descent to the base is more controlled than Kanu's and, because of greater trunk control, he can sit more easily in the bath.

The shower is only accessible from standing and is not used by any family member, but is useful for the nurse to give Savita frequent and speedy showers rather than always attempting the longer process of lowering into the bath.

An Autolift bath hoist was installed to the new bath and the taps resited 235mm back from the end onto the remaining blockwork wall to the side of the bath, in order that clearance could be improved for the Autolift chair to swing over the unenclosed end of the bath

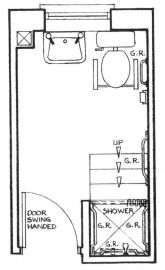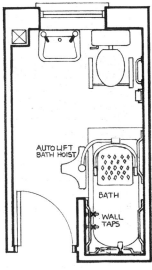

Bathroom, plan of first adaptation at left, second at right

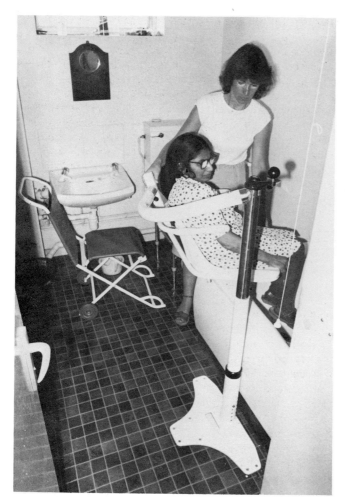

Savita is lifted onto the hoist seat and is lowered and washed

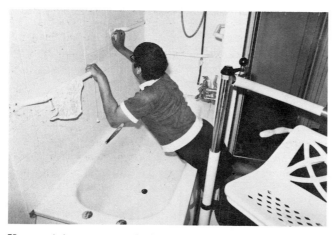

Kanu gaining access to the bath

BEDROOM

No adaptation was made to the bedrooms, other than to the fourth for lift shaft installation.

Bed heights vary between 420mm, that allows Savita to roll out of bed onto the floor, and 560mm which is a better height for Mr Patel. Kanu and Chandu share one room and Mrs Patel and Savita another, leaving Mr Patel who has respiratory difficulties a room to himself. A fourth bedroom is for the use of guests.

COSTING

1984		
Lift		£3,764.00
Electrical, plumbing and building		2,610.00
Replacement of bath, taps and ramping		890.00
	Total	£7,264.00

FUNDING

City council housing budget		£3,500.00
Improvement grant		3,764.00
	Total	£7264.00

CONTRACTUAL PROCEDURE

The work was put out to tender by the city council housing department and a local builder was nominated for the work. Stannah Lifts Limited were contracted by the council, acting as agents for the family, to install the through ceiling lift, following preparatory work done by the builder.

Two years later, the sum of £600.00 charged by the lift engineers for the additional time spent on the installation has yet to be paid, as the housing department, social services and the builder are not prepared to accept responsibility for the error made in the siting of the shaft aperture.

EVALUATION

The Patel family background of wealth, comfort and life in a warm climate enabled the health problems of a multiply handicapped family to be minimized. Servants assisted in all aspects of personal care of the disabled children and in the entire running of the household, with low expectations of independence being a matter of course. Following the trauma of a hasty departure from the country of their birth, loss of all their possessions and removal of their earning capacity, there was accommodation in a reception centre, a cold climate, language difficulties and dependence on state aid.

Adjustment would have been difficult under any circumstances, but was made worse by the need to find resources within the family in care of the physically handicapped members, in a manner to which they were not accustomed and in a country which valued self reliance. Conflict inevitably arose between the expectations of a family, used to ordering affairs in their own home, and those of statutory agencies with strict parameters of their own assessment of need and who were not accustomed to being considered as servants. Staff allocated to assist the handicapped were diverted into what were seen as tasks that family members could undertake, and they had difficulty in handling the low status of Savita, who was the main focus of their work.

The aggregation of disabilities in the family has meant that there was not the emphasis on any one family member who, as the only handicapped person in another family, might have received a lot more attention and individual provision. Mrs Patel appears to have a severe visual handicap, but is not registered as blind, and has difficulty in accepting and undertaking her new responsibility of cooking and cleaning. This is not, however, given a high priority in staff time and her attitude, stemming from a history of organizing servants and habits such as spreading newspaper over the house to keep it clean, does not endear her to home care workers. The intervention of an ethnic key social worker might have helped the family to make an easier adjustment to their new country, with a lessening of tension over misinterpreted motives and language barriers.

The occupational therapist has a good rapport with the family built up over a period of time, with trust given in response to her efforts to ensure service and equipment provision in testing circumstances. It proved impossible to ascertain the exact functional levels of the Patel children, as they never had any opportunity or desire to develop individual skills, and roles in the family tended to be determined by cultural status and not by degree of handicap. That the occupational therapist and the housing welfare officer could not agree on adaptations required was unfortunate, but perhaps predictable when assessment was so difficult, owing to the limited opportunity to demonstrate skills in unsuitable housing, language barriers and the complexity of needs in the family. Chandu acted as interpreter and, inevitably, focused on his own requirements. He was not greatly aware of his brother's needs, and was positively denied consideration of his sister's methods of personal care by their cultural ethos.

The multiplicity of problems was not a challenge that the housing authority or other statutory services could hope to rise to. Purpose built accommodation might theoretically have been a solution, but it was not available, and the best that could be done was allocation of the four bedroomed house. It alleviated the situation for the Patels as it gave adequate heating, sufficient space and the possibility of adaptation to meet some of their practical needs.

There were intractable problems. A **lift** had to be incorporated, and it was not installed correctly. It is used by all the Patels, although it proves most suited to the ambulant ones as it is rather too small to take Savita's chair and an attendant and causes some problems in management of the doors for those using the floor. The size of the lift was governed by the space available in the ground floor storeroom, although removal of the non structural walls and repositioning of the kitchen door could have allowed a larger model with a side opening and greater freedom of wheelchair movement to and from it. An alternative method of holding open the fire door on the first floor would also improve use of the lift for Kanu and Chandu, who risk injury to their legs in the present situation. However, building regulations demand that the lift company install a half hour fire resistant door that must engage in a positive way to be effective, so a strong spring closer is used.

The ground floor **cloakroom** has given Savita a level of independence previously denied her, although this is limited to the mornings by her inability to get from the floor into the wheelchair she uses during the day. It is regrettable that there was misapprehension of the position of the Asian wc and some thought might have been given to reorganization of doors to improve wheelchair access, which could have been directly across the lobby from the kitchen door.

The original **shower** would have been manageable for the floor mobile people had it been possible to install a level or minimally raised base and if the controls had been placed at a low level. The latter would not have been helpful

however, for Mr and Mrs Patel who, anyway, disliked showers; a fact that was not apparent at the time of planning. It is regrettable that the blockwork wall was not removed from the **bathroom** at the same time as the shower base, as it greatly restricted the siting of the Autolift; makes setting the shower from outside the bath very difficult; creates difficulties for Kanu who must squeeze between the hoist mast and the wall to reach the rail to pull up on; has meant resiting of the taps to a less accessible point. The washbasin height is a compromise that is not really suitable for anyone, except Chandu who organized it, as it is too low from standing and too high from the floor for those who cannot kneel up to it.

The young people manage more independently than they previously did. Mr Patel's health has improved to some extent, by the move to a warmer house that he saw as a basic essential for life in a cold climate, as well as for his own health. Mrs Patel does the cooking and no cleaning, has made little progress in language or in contacts outside the home and appears to be quite handicapped visually. The men in the family are not expected to participate in the domestic running of the house and Savita is the only one who could help with chores, but is the least able to do so. Language difficulties, coupled with poor eyesight and severe physical handicap have, with cultural expectations, placed the greatest burden on Savita, who has the lowest status in the family and the least opportunity to use her intelligence.

The principles applied in planning the major adaptation were as sound as was perhaps possible in the circumstances of language barrier, the family's low interest in self reliance and the lack of suitable housing for a large family with complex difficulties. However, the occupational therapist and the housing welfare officer could not agree on provision for the bathroom and neither could forsee, or were consulted about, the problems of the pipes that resulted in a high level shower base that neither wanted. There were misunderstandings about positioning of the ground floor wc and the Patels' fears about the lift being a danger to young children meant that optimal access to it was not permitted.

While the Patels acknowledge that the move helped to overcome some of the family's difficulties and removed the more crucial architectural barriers to independence, it is nevertheless hard for them to be enthusiastic about a lifestyle so far removed from that to which they were accustomed.

MISS ALISON FRENCH

Aged 19. Athetoid cerebral palsy.

Living with parents and brother.

Adaptation of a ground floor, district council flat under construction.

Miss French's athetosis was identified soon after her birth. In order to support her mother in the care of two highly dependent children when her brother was born, day attendance at a centre for spastics was organised when she was two years old. She transferred to a local day school for handicapped children at the age of five and from thence, at eleven, to a senior school as a weekly boarder at a specialist unit.

At the age of sixteen she gained sponsorship for further education and vocational assessment at a residential college for disabled youth. Her successful response to training in skills of daily living enabled her to transfer from the college accommodation to the local youth hostel and to develop an enthusiasm for independence. At the end of the two year course, however, she returned to live at home with her parents and brother.

She immediately put her name down for council accommodation and saw the disablement resettlement officer about opportunities available in the local area, to which she was now a stranger. She asked for placement on the youth opportunity programme and gained full time work with a youth and community scheme. She found it difficult, however, to adjust to living with her parents again. Friction occurred as they tried to find the balance between encouraging her full potential yet protecting her from disappointment.

Attention was drawn to her difficulties and aspirations when she participated in a television documentary for the 1981 International Year of Disabled People. She was interviewed by the district council senior housing officer and offered a ground floor flat in a development already under construction in the centre of the local town. She enthusiastically accepted the tenancy and worked closely with the social services occupational therapist, who was asked to become involved to advise on special features required.

The occupational therapist found that the flat was designed to mobility standards, the outer shell of which could not be changed. She visited Miss French and discussed special features for inclusion to overcome potential difficulties. Functional assessment produced the information for this, and for briefing the district council and architect on the adaptations needed:

Mobility. Miss French walked in an uncoordinated and unsteady manner. Left sided weakness resulted in unreliability of her left leg when she was tired or unwell. She could not walk long distances and had difficulty in gaining balance in an upright position after stooping low. She used a wheelchair in which she could be pushed for long distances or for support in getting up from the floor, for transporting shopping and heavy items around the house and, on the days when walking was particularly unsteady, she manoeuvred herself around in it using her feet.

Dressing. She was independent, although morning preparation in readiness for work could take two hours, as her problems in fine coordination were most apparent then. Fastenings, socks and tying the laces of her support shoes were her greatest difficulties.

Wc. She used a raised toilet seat and a rail at home and found it impossible to rise from a standard height wc.

Bathing. She could not rise from a bath seat and had difficulty negotiating the bath rim, even with the use of a board. She needed plenty of space in the bathroom to avoid injury caused by limbs flailing against fitments.

Personal care. Fine motor coordination was improved by bracing her elbows on surfaces or into the side of her body to bring her hands up to a useful position at mid chest height. Hair washing was very difficult and she could not rub in shampoo.

Bed. She rolled out onto her hands and knees when feeling most unsteady first thing in the morning.

Eating & Drinking. She used a combined spoon and fork for eating and a plastic straw for drinking.

Domestic tasks. She was able to prepare and cook meals providing equipment used could be stabilized and she wore protection against burning. A front loading washing machine was used for laundry and she could hang out small amounts of lightweight washing on the line. She was independent in doing her own ironing, but had to be very careful to avoid burning herself. She had no difficulties with day to day domestic tasks, but needed help with occasional heavy work and window cleaning, which her family were happy to offer.

Hobbies & Interests. She enjoyed an active social life, pop and rock music and making contacts through her citizen band radio.

The occupational therapist and the architect for the project met on site and agreed special features required, to include a change to the proposed locks and switches, replacement of a bath with a level access shower, elimination of all steps and raised thresholds, kitchen reorganization and an alternative construction of internal walls to allow fixture of rails.

It transpired, however, that main drainage had already been installed and there was no scope financially to remake the system to lower the 230mm high waste outlet pipe made for a bath. In addition, the district council's chief architect could not agree a change in wall construction material from the stud partition which, while simple and inexpensive to build, was unsuitable for secure fixing of rails.

In consultation with Miss French, the occupational therapist suggested a compromise of enlarging and reorganizing the bathroom to allow sufficient space for shallow steps and a floor fixed rail to give access to the high shower base. During the work the occupational therapist left and was not immediately replaced, so that the builder ultimately had no specialist in disability with whom to discuss changes in specification relating to technical problems. In addition, recommendations made by the occupational therapist in her final summary for work to adapt the window and central heating controls and to advise on choice of kitchen appliances, methods and organization, were never picked up.

The work was completed in the autumn of 1983; Miss French moved in and was delighted with her flat and the rediscovery of independent living. She was, however, geographically close enough to her family for visiting, and personal relationships that had recently been under strain were restored. Following the youth opportunity placement, she was offered a job as a youth worker, liaising at national and local level with clubs and societies specializing in opportunities for disabled people. Beyond this, sponsorship from the education department has been secured for a two year diploma course in youth and community work which will mean finding suitable accommodation near the college, with return to her flat at weekends.

Front view of the block of flats

THE PROJECT TEAM

Miss French.
County council social services occupational therapist.
District council architect.
Builder.

THE AIMS

To promote independence in all activities of daily living. To promote safety and efficiency in the home and to avoid dependence on fine motor coordination.
To meet requirements of work, leisure and an active social life.

THE PROPERTY

A one bedroomed ground floor flat in a block of six flats under construction in 1982.

Gross internal floor area 46.6m² unchanged.

The site for the new flats was part of a programme of infill development of council land close to the centre of a small town in a semi rural area. Construction of the block was of timber with a skin of facing bricks, and while no adaptation was permitted to the external shell, layout of rooms and provision of special features was allowed on designation of the flat for use by a disabled person, within strict expenditure limits.

THE ADAPTATION

Alteration to plans and building of a ground floor flat.

A small garden was made to the rear with access to a hardstanding area for car parking and a level tarmacadamed area for rotary clothes driers. Kerbed access to the car park was ramped in asphalt and the space nearest to her flat was reserved for her with a notice painted on the ground.

The flat is within easy level distance of town centre shops and enables Miss French to buy small amounts frequently or to transport larger amounts on the seat of the wheelchair, which she pushes.

The garden has been laid to a rockery, pond and small lawn area and is usually tended by friends of Miss French. Local residents have respected the reserved parking space which has greatly alleviated problems that occur when she is only able to park at a distance from her destination.

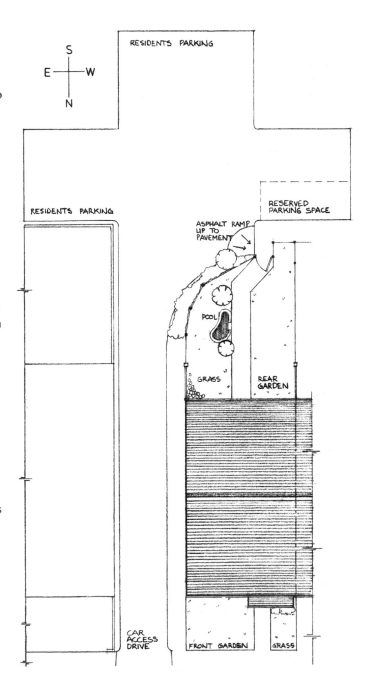

Site plan. 1:200

However, in bad weather, she would appreciate a garage or carport as it takes some time to load the car with the wheelchair and she is often soaked before she starts her journey.

She would also have liked an outdoor store for the wheelchair, as bringing the chair directly into the flat in wet conditions causes unsightly markings of the carpet.

EXTERNAL DOORS AND PATHWAYS

* Front door with latch lock in long recessed porch.

* Half glazed door to rear, initially fitted with mortice lock, later replaced by latch lock.

* Duraflex threshold at rear door; metal extension bar fitted to bottom of door.

* Front pathway sloped to eliminate front step.

* 1040mm wide concrete path made from parking and clothes drying area to rear door of flat and sloped to come level with threshold.

* Iron gate fitted to rear garden boundary chain link fencing.

Miss French had difficulty in managing the full turn key in the mortice lock and finds the latch lock half turn much easier, providing she can use her right hand. The back door also does not need to be locked behind her when she goes out and can be easily slammed shut for automatic locking. The same arrangement is available at the front door but, as the lock is sited for left hand use from outside and necessitates use of her less controllable hand, she tends not to use this door. In addition, a full length draught exclusion curtain, that draws open to the hinge side, limits the full opening of the door which makes passage of the wheelchair difficult.

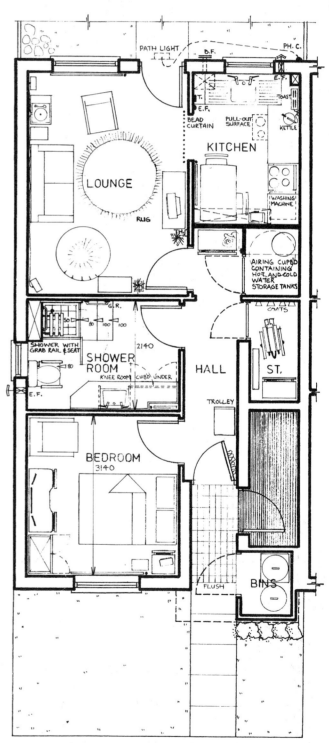

Plan of the adapted layout. 1:75

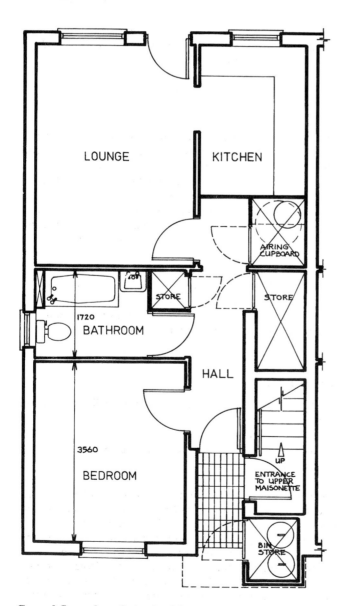

Ground floor plan of standard layout. 1:75

The combination of the flexible rubber strip threshold and metal plate successfully excludes weather penetration at the exposed back door and there is no problem at the front where the door is well protected by the porch.

The concrete path in the rear garden can present a problem at the point of direction change when Miss French uses the wheelchair as there is no kerb and the downward slope can cause the wheels to override the bend

The refuse collection area that is in the entrance porch is easily accessible and Miss French has had her dustbin put up onto a 570mm height table, which brings the bin lid into a more accessible height of 1300mm for her. The help of the resident upstairs is sought for lifting heavy bags and for inserting a new bin liner.

She would have liked to have had a handrail along the rear path length to help support and steady her when the slope becomes slippery in icy and snowy conditions. She can operate the slide bolt of the gate, but usually leaves it open for greatest convenience.

WINDOWS
* Sash windows with lifting rails at 600mm and 1300mm from floor.

* Cill heights of 500mm in bedroom and living room.

* Cill heights of 960mm and 1150mm respectively in kitchen and bathroom.

* All windows fitted with swivel locking catches, as standard throughout development.

The sash windows, designed with a very close fit to exclude draughts, are very stiff to operate. Miss French has to use both hands to open windows and finds the small knurled knobs that lock the catches impossible to unfasten if someone else has closed and tightened them fully. She is unable to reach the 1520mm high central bar to the kitchen window over the sink and the 1630mm high one in the bathroom, and relies on extractor fans for ventilation in these rooms.

The district council would not permit any alteration to the exterior of the flat and the windows could not therefore be changed, even though their unsuitability for Miss French was apparent.

ELECTRICAL WORK
Large rocker light switches set at 1250mm from floor throughout.

* Switched power sockets at 840mm above floor in all rooms except kitchen.

* Power points set at 340mm above worktops in kitchen.

* Extractor fan in kitchen with operation switch at doorway.

* Extractor fan in bathroom linked for automatic operation with pull cord light switch.

* Light sensitive external light over back door, with overriding switch by back door.

Miss French finds the rocker switches easy to use as they have a large area at which she can aim, and her father has fitted clear plastic surrounds to protect wall decorations. The socket heights are manageable but, as the switches are flush with the plate in the off position, they are very difficult for her to locate. She has it in mind to fit hooks next to the power outlets to hold plug leads when changing equipment as, presently, they often fall to the floor and are difficult for her to retrieve.

The external light can be switched from a master switch in the kitchen to come on automatically at dusk, which can ensure she always has light over the pathway and door when she returns home at night.

HEATING
* Gas central heating boiler mounted on wall over worktop in kitchen.

* Radiators with individual thermostatic controls throughout.

The small knob on the thermostat and central heating timer require fine control and Miss French relies on others to set timing and temperature for her. The siting of the thermostatic control valves on the radiators at 150mm from the floor means that she needs to bend to reach them, increasing her coordination problems. The kitchen always remains warm enough for her not to need the radiator and she uses the wall space for placement of a table, which is an important additional work surface for her.

HALLWAYS AND DOORS

* No adaptation made to 775mm clearance width of internal doorways.

* Lever handled door furniture used through out.

On the days that she needs to use the wheelchair, right turns from the 1020mm wide hallway into rooms are difficult, as is getting the chair in and out of the hall cupboard where it is stored. The need to house the wheelchair indoors, under the stairs, takes up space conceptually designed for general storage. The kitchen trolley is often kept in front of the front door when not in use, as the only vacant space available, although this is no great problem as this door is rarely used. Miss French has installed a bead curtain to divide the living area and the kitchen which affords a visually attractive screen and obviates the need for a door.

LIVING AREA

No adaptation was made to this room.

Smooth pile carpet was fitted as a standard feature throughout. Miss French has added a circular rug, which she finds more attractive, but this presents a serious trip hazard. She has furnished the room with a small dresser, easy chairs, push button television and a record deck. Furniture has to be moved to give space for the board for ironing, which she does using a power point in this room.

KITCHEN

* 600mm deep x 920mm high worktops incorporating single sink with double drainer and lever taps.

* Pull out shelf with two bowl cut outs and floor mounted cabinets below.

* Triple wall cabinets set at 1230mm from floor at one end of room.

* All cupboards fitted with autolatch catches.

* Sheet linoleum floor covering.Miss French uses a front loading washing machine, refrigerator with right hand door opening and a floor standing electric cooker. In addition, she has added a small table and two chairs which, although only occasionally used, constitute the main dining area.

Choice of cooker was governed by availability and cost of a secondhand model. Miss French can manipulate the large oblong knobs for the hot plates, but cannot manage the fine grip and control needed for the oven timer. She only uses the oven when there is someone to take pans out for her, as she needs one hand to support herself when bending to the oven and has insufficient grip and coordination in only one hand for safe handling of dishes. She also has difficulty in stooping to the refrigerator and the right hand hung door means that she has to use her weaker left hand to take things in and out.

One floor cabinet was fitted with pull out storage baskets which she finds easy to use. The bowl holding board does not, however, have a lip or handle on the outer edge for her to latch her fingers onto in order to pull it out, and she

The bowl holders are vital for stabilizing items for food preparation

has to reach underneath and over the refrigerator to grasp it through one of the holes.

Miss French preferred to have the dining table in the kitchen rather than having it taking up space in the living area. It doubles as an extra working surface, but takes up a considerable proportion of space in the small room and means that the trolley, needed most frequently in this room, cannot be stored at its point of use. There was no vacant wall or cupboard space for the refuse bin which has, therefore, to be free standing and presents an obstacle to use of the washing machine and wall cabinets.

The sink is used to contain spillages in tasks requiring fine coordination and control. The position of the sink bowl allows the draining board to be used as work space

The linoleum floor covering becomes very slippery when wet, creating a problem for Miss French who spills things easily. A metal threshold strip divides the kitchen floor from the carpet of the living area and necessitates lifting of the trolley to negotiate the rise when she transports things between the rooms.

BATHROOM

* Space from bedroom and storage cupboard annexed to enlarge room to 3000 x 2140mm from that planned.

* Wc set on plinth to give seat height of 490mm.

* Grab rail on adjacent wall, later replaced by toilet frame.

* Wall mounted washbasin with rim height of 740mm and lever taps.

* 535mm deep worktop mounted just below washbasin rim and extended over cupboards and around radiator to side, installed as later addition.

* Triton Powerflow pillar mounted adjustable head shower.

* Obscured glass shower cubicle over 280mm high base and rim.

* Two 100mm steps and 470mm long handrail at an 18° angle constructed to give access to cubicle.

* Fibre backed linoleum laid to floor, and to steps with addition of rubber moulded edging.

As the wc was placed centrally between the shower cubicle and the wall, the adjacent grab rail was almost inaccessible. When Miss French fractured her right wrist, a toilet frame was installed as a speedy solution to difficulties and has since proved useful with the raised height wc.

Miss French has added the worktop and cupboards, as she found she needed a larger surface upon which to rest her elbows to give stability for optimum use of her hands at the washbasin.

She has no problem in using the taps or sitting at the basin, but has no mirror at a suitable height for use from this position. She has installed her own mirror fronted cabinet above the tiled splashback which is useful to her when standing. The additional storage afforded by the cupboard is very useful, but heat received from the enclosed radiator is reduced, despite the use of louvre doors.

The shower cubicle size of 720 x 720mm is too small for Miss French and uncontrolled movements mean that she continually bangs herself on the sides. She has to use both hands on the rail to mount the steps and reaching across from the handrail to the grab rail, which she had fitted at the back of the cubicle, is precarious. The shower controls prove difficult as, while she can use the large knob for management of water flow, the lever temperature control is so close and obscured that, whenever she tries to change the temperature, she turns off the water flow.

The original free standing wooden shower seat, supplied by the builder, became rotten and had to be replaced. The seat chosen by the new social services occupational therapist was a folding type installed to a batten between the wall and back of the shower cubicle. This only allows a

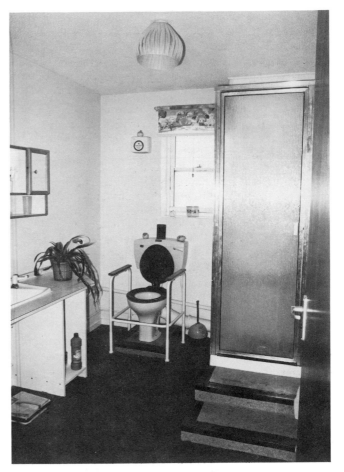

The shower room

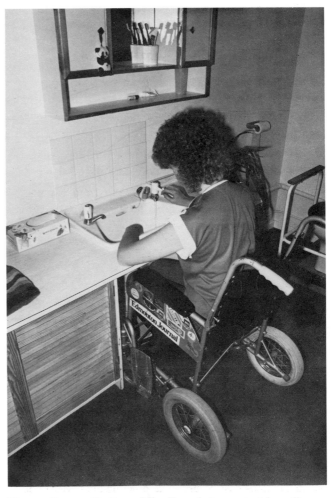

The vanitory unit allows Miss French to support her elbows when she uses the washbasin

300mm knee clearance in the small cubicle; Miss French finds she constantly kicks the door off its light roller closure catch. As she is not safe standing to shower, she uses the shower head held in her hand to spray it over herself while sitting. She is not, however, able to hook it back afterwards onto the slide rail, which is set at a height where she has particular coordination problems.

The linoleum becomes very slippery when wet and adds to the already hazardous steps for Miss French. In addition, the fibre backing soaks up water with the result that the top has curled and peeled back, compounding the problems.

There being no alternative permissible to the high shower base and cubicle, the occupational therapist suggested enlargement of the bathroom to permit installation of the steps that were to take up a large proportion of circulation space in the room. She also recommended two types of thermostatically controlled showers that would be suitable, suggested use of a pivoting cubicle door to reduce the opening arc over the top step and the use of a hinged wooden seat to be installed through the cubicle wall. It later transpired however, that the cold water storage tank in the airing cupboard gave insufficient head of water and a pump was needed for the shower. The builder chose a type that was easily available to him, in the absence of specialist advice on its suitability for operation by Miss French. In addition the shower cubicle was set forward from the adjacent walls to clear pipework and the builder felt unable to get a good fixing for the seat and so made a free standing one.

Once the shower cubicle door is wide open, Miss French cannot reach to close it again

BEDROOM

Bedroom reduced in size from approximately $10.7m^2$ to $9.4m^2$ by enlargement of bathroom.

Miss French uses a small free standing wardrobe for clothes storage, which limits space for manoeuvre in the room and means that wheelchair access is only possible to one side of the bed. However, as the area nominated for wardrobe space between the door and adjacent wall was lost to the bathroom, there was no other alternative.

COSTING

1982
Wc plinth, shower seat, rails and provision of
a shower instead of a bath   £150.00.

FUNDING

District council capital budget, general improvement works for the development project.
Housing budget allocation for the disabled for the contract variation of £150.00.
The costs of all other structural features for Miss French were absorbed in the sum for the total project.

CONTRACTUAL PROCEDURE

The entire scheme was put out to tender and a local builder contracted by the district council for the work. Subsequent changes made for Miss French were incorporated in the overall agreement.

EVALUATION

Miss French does not see herself as disabled in any way and believes that it is not her problem that not everyone else has similar balance and walking difficulties. She can see the amusing side of being refused drinks on the grounds of drunkenness, to which her unsteady gait can be attributed and is, no doubt, the victor in explaining the real situation. She tends to regard tasks that are difficult for her as a challenge and her cheerful personality enables her to make contacts and friends easily. In spite of her enthusiasm for life however, she can get very tired on a long and busy day.

She is delighted with her flat in that it affords the independence that she wanted which, at the time of planning, was considered at almost any cost. The delight at being offered the property did not make her greatly motivated, however, to insist on the provision of particular features when technical difficulties made them more complex to install than was originally envisaged. Even now, while she is critical of poor design concepts for her needs in the flat, she has not pushed for change other than when unavoidable, as seen in need for the replacement shower seat and equipment associated with her fractured wrist.

The flat that was under construction had an internal floor area that was slightly larger than the minimum of $45.5m^2$ recommended for a two person unit, and could have been suitably adapted for Miss French's particular needs, had it been a shell with no internal planning constraints. However, from decisions already made, the disposition of the rooms was fixed as was the fenestration and infrastructure of the plumbing. The plumbing could not be changed to enable installation of the correct height shower base and consequent adaptations did not make the flat convenient for use by a physically handicapped person. The bathroom was enlarged to accommodate steps to the shower to give greater space where Miss French most needed it. The bedroom, however, was reduced in size and this has created its own problems.

The **shower** base, cubicle and steps are far from ideal and, as the occupational therapist's request for wall structure to which rails could be fixed was not answered, positioning of rails was determined by the studwork within the timber frame construction, and not on suitable location for Miss French. The reduction in designated **storage** space has meant the need for an additional cupboard in the bathroom and, since the only vacant wall space for this was also that of the radiator, some heat is lost. The loss of one of the storage cupboards was necessary to give space to the bathroom, but, with the only other one being used for the wheelchair, storage space in the flat became insufficient for Miss French's needs. A 2.0m² storage shed in the rear garden might have been provided to conform with recommendations for the provision of external storage space.

Some features of the **kitchen**, such as the pull out baskets and bowl holders, are particularly useful to Miss French. Problems of the cooker and refrigerator could be resolved by suitable alternative types, but Miss French was limited to availability and price of secondhand models. In any case, low priced and readily available new refrigerators most commonly have right hand opening doors. The size of the kitchen and the area available for work surfaces does not lend itself easily to the provision of a split level oven; while it would remove the need for Miss French to bend and could allow pans to be slid along tops, it would reduce food preparation space even further. Storage of the frequently used trolley is precluded near to its point of use, because of the siting of the dining table.

The principle of providing a well recessed shelter to the front door has proved a good one, but, in this case, the width of 890mm left no space to the left of the opening jamb to facilitate operation of the door. **Access** to the rear of the site and the parking area does not require Miss French to negotiate steps and does not create any difficulty, except when she needs to use the wheelchair or the weather is icy, for which kerb edging and a handrail to the path would be helpful. A garage or car port would also assist her in wet weather, although it is questionable whether the small parking area allowed to the rear of the block could have sustained one that was wide enough for the full car door swing and wheelchair manoeuvre, without complaints from other residents about space being lost from that already allocated for general use.

The architect cooperated with the occupational therapist in provision of features where immediately possible, but did not use the best and most imaginative methods to overcome the technical problems. The occupational therapist could not ensure that her recommendations were complied with, as she had been brought in as an advisor from a department that had no jurisdiction or financial commitment to the building work. She left during the project and it fell to the builder to do the best he could to find suitable fitments, when those originally recommended were found to be technically inappropriate in the particular situation.

Special features for Miss French were kept to a minimum in a project that was economical overall. Had Miss French's tenancy been assured at the time of planning the whole building project, a different choice of windows, heating control and plumbing might have been made that was equally cost effective, but more suited to her needs. To change these features would have been costly, but the flat could have been more convenient for Miss French to live in.

99

H

SIMON JOHNSON

Aged 14. Brain Damage.

Living with parents, two brothers and a sister.

Adaptation of a five bedroomed, owner occupied semi detached house.

Simon Johnson's mother contracted poliomyelitis at the age of eighteen months and, while this affected both legs, she was brought up not to allow handicap to create dependence. Her own mother had lost a leg in an accident at the age of two, had made an independent life for herself and did not allow her daughter to be overprotected. This did not change when, at the age of fifteen, Mrs Johnson, as she was later to become, was involved in a road accident that badly injured her left leg and caused severe burns to her back. For a while she had to depend on a wheelchair for mobility, and over the next five years had many hospital admissions for treatment before she was able to walk with full length calipers as well as she had prior to the accident.

In 1967 she was married and two years later they had their first child. The birth was straightforward and they were delighted with their healthy baby boy. Simon's early months were without problem except for a short episode of sickness in reaction to vaccination, for which they did not bother their general practitioner. At ten months, and following a booster vaccination, he reverted from the walking he had just learned to crawling and his left hand began to clench into a tight fist. A high fever quickly developed with convulsions and an intolerance to light. He was admitted to the general medical ward of the local hospital and encephalitis was diagnosed. Convulsions continued in the next forty eight hours until he became drowsy and drifted into a coma, from which he appeared never to regain full consiousness. During this time, his spine became increasingly arched to the point where his head almost touched his feet behind him.

When Simon was eventually able to be brought home, still in a comatose state, he was dependent on a regime of tube feeding and large doses of phenobarbitone and valium. By the patient efforts in feeding by mouth, Mr and Mrs Johnson found it gradually became possible to reduce his medication and to stop tube feeding, to the point where it was only needed to boost fluid levels. Management was, however, extremely difficult, particularly on account of positioning difficulties relating to the arched back.

Using her experience of passive tendon stretching exercise that her father had used on her own polio damaged legs, Mrs Johnson exercised Simon and improved his posture as well as, incidentally, repositioning his dislocated hip. She persistently requested physiotherapy, eventually getting him accepted at a local clinic for three half hour sessions per week, which she supplemented with continuing passive exercise at home.

In 1972, when Simon was three, she heard about the Dolman and Delacato method of total body stimulation and was successful in getting Simon referred to a local trained person in the following year. Although he was thought to be more brain damaged than was appropriate for the treatment, he was accepted because of his parents'

enthusiasm. The treatment involved patterns of exercises, to be done five times daily by five people at a time. Mrs Johnson successfully advertised for help and, over the subsequent four years of intensive treatment, more than one thousand patterners helped Simon, some of whom remain good and close friends of the family. In addition, Mrs Johnson's youngest sister moved in with them, helped in the patterning and provided considerable stimulation and attention to Simon.

In 1974, the Johnson's second son was born and the family thought about moving to larger and more suitable accommodation than their small three bedroomed bungalow that was on a steep slope. Mrs Johnson's parents agreed to combine into one household with them in order to share in Simon's management. They found a four bedroomed house nearby that they felt was suitable in size and that had full central heating. They had double glazing and cavity foam insulation installed throughout and the original bathroom, that had been superseded by a recent extension to the house, was converted to become Simon's bedroom.

A point was reached in Simon's treatment where no measurable progress was made for more than twelve months, following some success over three years and, when in 1977 Mrs Johnson found she was pregnant again and very tired and despondent about Simon's lack of progress, they reluctantly agreed that the patterning should cease and he should attend a local school for physically handicapped children. Without the patterning however, Simon's spasticity increased and he was put on muscle relaxant drugs, which helped to a certain extent, although his health was later seen to have deteriorated from this point.

In 1979, arthritic deterioration in the joints of Mrs Johnson's mother's leg caused management of the stairs to become very difficult and she and her husband decided to move to a flat. They were able to find one locally and continued the considerable practical support to the family on a daily basis. Mrs Johnson's sister left to get married in 1980, but also continued to live in the area and to maintain good contact.

An opportunity arose for Mrs Johnson to open a shop selling babywear and haberdashery and she saw this as a means of keeping Simon with her at work and in touch with the world outside their home. Simon's health was not good, however, and he slowly lost weight until an episode of total loss of temperature control that developed into hypothermia and pneumonia, severe loss of weight and muscle wasting necessitated hospital admission. Doubts were expressed about whether he could survive the crisis.

He did recover, however, as he did in several similar episodes in the next years, including a drop in weight to two stones, spinal collapse and diagnosis of anaemia and a hiatus hernia. The hernia problems were controlled by diet and effects of the poor swallowing reflex overcome by draining by his mother, if food was inhaled.

The family had little help from the primary health care team who considered that Mrs Johnson's exceptional rapport with her son and excellent management of his physical needs were of an order far higher than they could offer. Mrs Johnson was content with this arrangement until she needed to ask for help in management of Simon's needs during the day, his continuing poorliness, her fourth pregnancy and the need to look after the other children in the long summer holiday. Although she was finding it very difficult to cope, her request for assistance in postural drainage of Simon could only be met one week before the birth of the baby, a girl. A month later, their youngest son developed meningitis, from which he recovered after special care.

In 1983, Mrs Johnson's unstable leg gave way at the top of the stairs and she fell the length of the flight. She broke bones in her foot and had to use a wheelchair while she was in plaster. Shortly after becoming ambulant again, she tore tendons in her wrists when Simon and a moulded seat insert slipped from her grasp when lifting him from the front of the car. She found herself, as a result, greatly afraid to carry Simon especially down the stairs as was a daily routine occasioned by her husband's long working day.

When the lease of the shop came up for sale in 1983, Mrs Johnson decided to give up the business, hoping that the profit made would pay for special transport needed as difficulties increased in managing Simon in her Mini. Delays in the sale of the shop and reduction in stock value, however, left her with a large overdraft. The family had already contracted to buy a Sherpa van with a tail lift, in order that the whole family could go out together and in a way that was most comfortable and manageable for Simon; high heating bills to maintain a warm even temperature, with boosts in anticipation of Simon's undressing, added to their financial difficulties. Despite full attendance allowance for Simon and mobility allowance for both him and Mrs Johnson, Mr Johnson found himself working up to eighty hours a week in order to meet bills and debts.

The couple realized that the effects of arthritis in her damaged joints, added to the wasted muscles associated with poliomyelitis, were now causing increasing problems in Mrs Johnson's management of Simon. She suffered several further falls and injuries caused by awkward lifting and carrying, with particular difficulties encountered on the stairs, at the front door and steps and in getting him and his wheelchair into the car. They were prompted to obtain a manufacturer's quotation for a stairlift, but were unprepared for the cost that would substantially add to their already highly committed financial status. Mrs Johnson contacted the local social services department to enquire whether they could help financially. The occupational therapist who visited could not agree to the idea of a stairlift on which Mrs Johnson expected to carry Simon on her lap, but decided that the option should be tested, before other avenues could be wholeheartedly explored. A joint visit to a local aids and assessment centre flat proved how difficult and hazardous it was to carry Simon on a stairlift; his action of extending his back under stress and the insufficient width of their stairway caused the idea to be abandoned. It was agreed then that a more comprehensive plan to facilitate management of Simon's care should be considered.

Simon's level of function and needs, coupled with Mrs Johnson's methods of skilful management, were discussed in detail so that precise requirements could be identified:

Mobility. Simon had no functional movement, was blind and displayed relatively little response to stimulus. A model 9 DHSS wheelchair, with a moulded inset seat mounted on a frame and strapped to the chair, was used. Compensation for increases in spinal extension was made by tilting the seat forward on a block, although this tended to throw Simon's weight forward and so risk overbalancing the chair. This was countered by hanging objects of weight on the back of the chair rather than by adapting the inset seat, since surgery for insertion of spinal rods was contemplated and the seat would anyway need to be changed. Simon was carried up and down stairs by either parent, although Mrs Johnson's own deteriorating mobility meant that there were hazards. The family used a small saloon car in addition to Mrs Johnson's DHSS Mini in which she carried Simon and his wheeled car chair.

Bed. Simon slept in a bunk bed fitted with a lift off cot rail and, because of the limited access to the bed, the base was loose laid on a box construction so that one end could be easily raised to facilitate postural drainage.

Wc. Incontinence was managed by towelling nappies used over disposable ones. This method was usually sufficient except occasionally at night. A manual bowel evacuation was given by Mrs Johnson weekly.

Bath. Simon was lifted in and out by either parent. His head needed to be supported and no aids were used.

Personal care. All activities carried out by Mr and Mrs Johnson.

Dressing. Done on the bed. Simon wore thermolactyl underwear and soft leather fur lined bootees to help maintain body temperature.

Eating & drinking. All food needed to be blended before feeding with a spoon. The process was long and laborious to activate his limited swallowing reflex. Drinks were given in a feeding cup with a spout.

Social. Simon was included in all activities of the immediate and extended family. The people who had helped in the patterning treatment and who were interested in him maintained contact and made him the focus of a continuing fund raising exercise to help other brain damaged children in the area. His mother had enormous patience with his needs and an empathy which anticipated the needs he could not express, which she attributed to her own childhood experiences of being bedbound, uncomfortable and sore.

The occupational therapist organized home help support for Mrs Johnson, and with the family began to consider various options for structural alteration to the house, as Simon's fluctuating condition and survival of crises in health became recognised as a pattern. A through ceiling lift to transport Simon, and to allow Mrs Johnson a means of avoiding the stairs herself, was suggested, as was an overbath shower and bath hoist to reduce lifting.

The most suitable positioning for the lift was from the ground floor wc rising to the area of the shower cubicle above, but this was rejected because Simon would have to travel alone, the second wc would be eliminated, space would be taken from the bathroom, alignment to the narrow first floor corridor would be difficult and the size of Simon's bedroom already made use of a wheelchair difficult. An extension to the rear of the property to provide ground floor bed and bathroom facilities was also considered, but discounted because of the technical difficulties in getting sufficient light to the kitchen area, the

Front view of the house

extensive building that would be required and the undesirability of reducing the small garden for three lively children.

The conversion of the integral garage and ground floor wc into a bedroom and bathroom was the option finally decided upon, and plans were drawn up by the architect in September 1983. The proposed work was agreed by building control and the grant authority in February 1984 and work commenced three weeks later.

The building work proved extremely disruptive to the family as for several weeks only scaffold boards bridged the entrance and pathway while work was done at the front door. It was impossible to get Simon out in his wheelchair and Mrs Johnson and her mother found the unstable surface very difficult to negotiate. For some time there was also a hole in the floor of the area used for cooking because of pipe laying and, as the central heating had to be extended to the new area, it was very difficult to keep Simon warm when it was turned off. In addition all the children got chicken pox and had to be nursed at home and the strain on Mrs Johnson became so intense that she wondered if the family could come through it intact. The support of the occupational therapist was greatly valued and Mrs Johnson was able to use her to ventilate feelings and to attempt to maintain a perspective, even though they could do little to influence the course of the building work, which was completed in May 1984.

THE PROJECT TEAM

Mr and Mrs Johnson.
Metropolitan district occupational therapist.
Architect.
Environmental health officer.

THE AIMS

To achieve total care of Simon on the ground floor.
To provide special facilities to help maintain the health and energy of the prime carer.
To give wheelchair access to the house, all parts of the ground floor and the patio.
To acknowledge the needs of family life.

THE PROPERTY

* A three bedroomed house built in 1956 and later extended and adapted to give five bedrooms.

* Gross internal floor 114.0m^2 before and 127.0m^2 after adaptation.

The house was built as part of an estate on the outskirts of a small Midland town. The site at the end of a cul de sac allowed no on street parking and only a small turning area. The ground floor originally consisted of an open plan kitchen and dining area, a separate sitting room and an integral garage. The upper floor had three bedrooms, a small bathroom and a separate wc. To this had been added, at a later date, a utility room and a cloakroom on the ground floor to the rear of the garage with a bedroom and a bathroom over and a single storey rear extension to the dining room. The Johnsons had further modified the house by conversion of the shell of the original small bathroom and wc into a bedroom for Simon and the installation of double glazing throughout.

THE ADAPTATION

Modification of a five bedroomed house and conversion of the integral garage to a bathroom and bedroom.

In the major project for Simon, the solid external garage walls were drylined with thermal insulation board and the

102

front was extended by 1125mm to come level with the entrance porch. A bedroom was formed in the front section with an en suite bathroom behind. The existing ground floor wc was removed and Simon's upper floor bedroom incorporated into the adjacent room by removal of the dividing wall.

EXTERNAL DOORS AND PATHWAYS

* Front entrance porch demolished and rebuilt as integral part of new front bedroom extension.

* Aluminimum frame, double glazed sliding door installed with clear passage of 730mm and threshold step of 60mm.

* New front pathway constructed in concrete with level areas outside porch and at midway turning point, linked by two 2300mm long ramps with gradients of 1 in 7 and 1 in 8.

* 100mm step incorporated either side of midway level platform. 900mm high wooden guard rail installed along length of pathway.

* Concrete hardstanding area made for car in front garden, ahead of sitting room window.

* Patio raised and extended to rear, and enclosed by brick walls topped with decorative wrought iron work. Shallow steps formed from patio to rear garden.

The patio was raised and extended

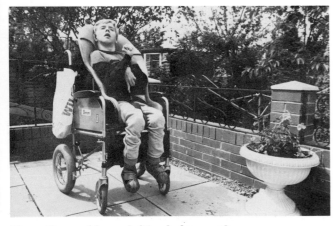

The patio provides a sheltered place outdoors

Mrs Johnson finds the reduced height step easy to negotiate with the chair, although furniture has to be moved in the lounge to gain clear access to the patio doors

Access to and from the house with the wheelchair presents no problem, with the level platform turning areas allowing sufficient space to tilt the chair for negotiating the shallow steps. The hardstanding is barely large enough for the Sherpa van, although it was sufficient for the Mini once owned. The van has to be taken out onto the road for there to be sufficient level space to operate the tail lift, although this does not create any great problem in the quiet cul de sac.

The patio to the rear of the property is used extensively by the family in the summer as a sitting out or eating area, and was raised in height and extended so that it was large enough for Simon to share, as is acknowledged by his Christmas present to the family of an additional garden bench. Raising the surface level reduced the 315mm original step down from the patio doors to 150mm.

The insistence by the planning department that on site parking must be retained initially created problems. The forward extension, necessary to ensure a sufficient size of bedroom, reduced the length of the hardstanding to less than five metres from the house to the pavement; this was not acceptable to the planning officer. Mrs Johnson suggested that, as an alternative, the hardstanding should be re formed to the other side of the front of the house where there was sufficient space, so allowing the area in front of the new room to be used for the path access to the main door. The depth of frontage here, however, meant that there was insufficient space, with the shape of pathway chosen, to achieve a ramp gradient that was suitable for the wheelchair and for Mrs Johnson's mother who found steep slopes difficult to walk on. The two shallow steps which were inserted present no problem to Mrs Johnson in pushing the chair.

The porch had to be replaced, rather than adapted. It had a side facing door that would have been lost in the new forward extension and the opportunity was taken to provide new double glazed sliding patio doors for improved wheelchair access.

Considerable work to raise the rear patio was required in order to construct retaining walls in the garden which sloped steeply away from the rear of the house. These brick retaining walls had to be built up by 1300mm, giving an upstand 260mm above the surface area.

WINDOWS

* Sealed unit, double glazed bow window with leaded lights and cill height of 780mm installed to new bedroom.

* Small, high level openable window fitted to bathroom.

* Extractor fan positioned over wc.

Although Simon appears to have no response to light and cannot see, the room is light and airy and pleasant to work in.

The bathroom window is not opened in winter because of Simon's temperature control problems, so the extractor fan is used as the means of ventilation to the room.

ELECTRICAL WORK

* Double socket power outlet, combined shaver socket and pull cord light switch, and intercom alarm installed in new bedroom next to proposed position of bed.

* Connection for Hydro spa bath motor and electric shower with pull cord operation housed in boxed area in far corner of bathroom, and isolation switch in utility room.

Tape cassettes, talking book machine, shaver and hair dryer can all be used conveniently for Simon when he is on the bed, which is where most activities of personal care are undertaken. The position of the Hydro spa bath motor and pull cord was chosen to avoid the other children playing with it. The intercom alarm that is linked to his parents' bedroom was considered to be important as Simon's new room was more remote and there was concern that his requirements for assistance would not be as easily heard. In practice, it is redundant since Mrs Johnson's strong rapport with her son has meant that she senses his needs, wakes and is able to attend to him before the alarm is sounded.

HEATING

* Turbo instant hot water boiler installed to provide domestic hot water and feed central heating system, including two single high efficiency radiators in new rooms.

* Cavity wall insulation in new building.

A high output system was necessary. The large surface area provided by the deep corrugations of the new radiators maintain the required temperature. The system can be

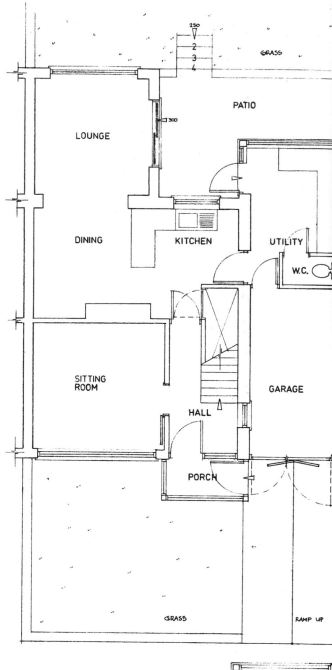

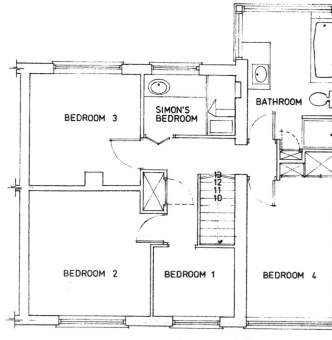

Ground and first floor plans before adaptation. 1:100

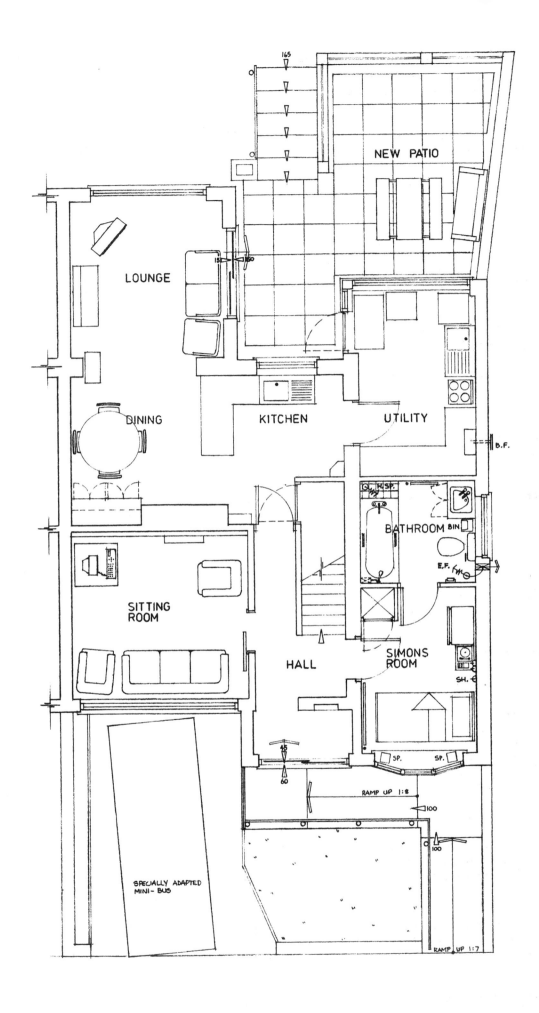

NEW PATIO

LOUNGE

165

DINING

KITCHEN

UTILITY

B.F.

**SITTING
ROOM**

BATHROOM BIN

E.F.

**SIMONS
ROOM**

SH.

HALL

SP.   SP.

45

60

RAMP UP 1:8

100

100

**SPECIALLY ADAPTED
MINI - BUS**

RAMP UP 1:7

Ground floor plan after adaptation. 1:75
THE JOHNSONS' HOUSE

boosted in advance of Simon being undressed and bathed and is more economical than the previous method used, as no hot water is stored. The pressure means that two taps cannot be used at once because the water flow drops to an unacceptable level, and it also takes a long time to fill a bath.

HALLWAYS AND DOORS

* Inner door from porch to hall removed and archway formed.

* Clear opening of 720mm allowed at doorways to new rooms.

* Utility room opening repositioned farther along same wall.

There are no problems of weather penetration or loss of heat by the omission of the inner door to the porch, which was necessary to allow straightforward wheelchair access to and from the front external door. No turns are required at the new internal doors which allow sufficient space for passage of the wheelchair, although Simon is usually carried to and from the bathroom from his bedroom. Relocation of the utility room door afforded a more useful layout of the room on removal of the cloakroom.

LIVING AREAS

No adaptation was made to these areas.

Lightweight furniture is positioned around the edges of the rear room to allow space for moving and parking the wheelchair in the family group. Wheelchair access to the patio doors requires, however, that the settee be moved. The front room is used as a quiet room for the children and houses their computer.

KITCHEN AND UTILITY ROOM

* Utility room enlarged by removal of partition wall and ground floor cloakroom.

The kitchen area is used for general food preparation and serving and the utility room for cooking as well as other general domestic tasks.

In place of the original wc, a doorway and lobby to the new bathroom from the utility room was suggested to give alternative access to the new bathroom than through Simon's bedroom, in order to preserve his privacy. The family decided against this as it would have again reduced the size of an area vital to the household. In addition, if Simon were ill in bed, the other children could use the upstairs wc and it was thought that Mrs Johnson would in any event use the ground floor facilities when she was so involved in the rooms in connection with Simon's care.

BATHROOM

* Standard wc with seat height of 400mm.

* Washbasin and vanitory unit at height 800mm from floor.

* Hydro spa bath with electric shower over.

* Fitted carpet to floor.

The wc is not used by Simon but is a necessary facility for Mrs Johnson, who organizes her day to use the stairs as

little as possible. The hydro spa bath is comfortable and buoyant and Simon can relax in it. He appears to derive pleasure from the stimulation of the jets of water over his whole body and this is one of the few things to which he shows a positive, if slight, response. The bath is also a helpful therapeutic medium of leg massage for Mrs Johnson and is popular with other members of the family, who acknowledge its use as something Simon is able to contribute in a life that otherwise yields little opportunity for giving. The shower allows for hairwashing but Simon is sensitive to the slight drop in temperature as the hose is lowered. The temperature control, therefore, has to be adjusted with the shower head at the lowest level, which makes the task a two person operation since it is not possible for one person to simultaneously support Simon's head and make the necessary adjustments to the shower.

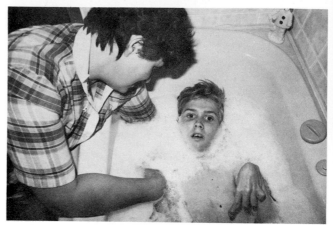

The hydro spa bath is a medium to which Simon will respond

The position of the bath and shower was determined by the need to carry Simon into the room with his feet first and so enable him to be put directly into the bath without the need to turn within the room. The carpet helps to keep the warm temperature required.

BEDROOM

* Lockable storage cupboard built between bedroom and bathroom doors.

* Fitted carpet to floor.

The cupboard is used for storage of incontinence equipment, spare sheepskins, clothes and drugs. Despite the large size of the storage area, bulky items such as boxes of disposable pads have to be stacked in the bathroom.

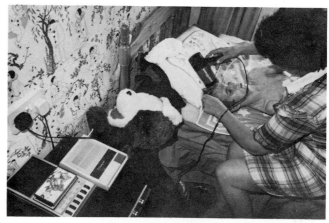

It is easiest to attend to much of Simon's personal care as he lies on the bed

The room is bright and cheerful and decorated in a manner as might be appreciated by a teenager. As the bedroom is opposite and close to the front sitting room, Simon is included in activities undertaken there, which would not be possible if the other children had to disappear upstairs to use their computer.

COSTING

1984

Building work		£6,063.00
Materials and fittings		1,784.00
Hydro spa bath		1,350.00
Fees, additional costs and builders		
differential		1,047.00
	Total	£10,244.00

FUNDING

Improvement grant 90% of eligible expense		£9,038.00
10% interest free loan from social services		
repayable on sale of property		1,004.00
Additional costs incurred after grant		
allocation, met by social services		202.00
	Total	£10,244.00

* The 90 per cent improvement grant was given on grounds of financial dependence on state benefits.

CONTRACTUAL PROCEDURE

As the borough concerned did not employ architects to work with disabled people, a private architect was engaged by social services acting as agent for the family to draw up plans and liaise with the Johnsons, occupational therapist, environmental health officer and planning department to the point where plans were passed. Mr and Mrs Johnson engaged the builder; only one tender was required by the grant authority and the environmental health officer supervised the building work.

EVALUATION

Simon's fluctuating health, fears for his survival and the management of a series of crises coupled with his mother's own physical handicap presents a picture that would daunt most families. Instead, here is a loving family, a mother with an incredible rapport and communication with her son, children who want to include Simon in their activities where possible and who vie with each other to help feed him and to attend to some of his personal care.

Mrs Johnson uses her own experience of physical handicap to understand Simon's needs and approaches new difficulties in an intensely practical manner as they arise. Her skilful and dedicated care is, on their own admission, greater than could be offered from statutory agencies, although this lack of regular contact with health care workers proved problematical in getting a help regime set up when it was requested and needed. In addition there was no regular contact with social services who only became involved in response to the crisis of Mrs Johnson's fall on the stairs and request for financial help for a stairlift.

The house, chosen by the family as being more suitable than their previous bungalow, did not lend itself easily to the needs that later arose for Simon and for Mrs Johnson. The property already had a history of adaptation and extension, with some unusual designation of rooms as a result and as seen in the ground floor layout of two separate areas for food preparation, one of which had a wc without a lobby leading from it.

The proposal to lose the garage in favour of a sixth bedroom must have been difficult to justify in principle, but there was no other realistic solution using existing internal space. It did however, prove to be the most acceptable solution in terms of the general use, family life and layout of the property as well as meeting Simon's specific needs. Anomalies that could have occurred were usefully avoided by the conversion of Simon's old bedroom to become an integral storage and dressing area to the adjacent bedroom, so allowing a larger room for his brothers. The opportunity was taken to undertake other building work at the same time, and the utility room was given a better layout for food preparation for Mrs Johnson by removal of the wc that was being replaced in the new area.

The problems of the sloping site have been successfully overcome at the rear with the raised **patio** which allows sufficient accessible space for all the family. Furniture has to be moved to gain wheelchair access to the patio door in the rear lounge; this difficulty is outweighed by the alternative lounge being the childrens' room for quiet activities which can include Simon. In addition, this lounge could be converted to a bedroom, while still preserving sufficient living space, should stairs become too difficult for Mrs Johnson.

The **ramping** and steps at the front present no problem to Mrs Johnson, although it might be questioned whether the gradient of 1 in 8 will remain accessible if there is any further deterioration in the mobility of Mrs Johnson or her mother. A shallower slope ramp without steps might have been doubled back across the frontage, but this would have removed any possibility of a garden at the front of the property, and would have considerably lengthened pedestrian access to the house. Parking for and access to the large family vehicle is not the problem it would be on a busier road, although street parking would avoid reduction of light to the front room.

The bedroom and bathroom position and layout remove the need for Simon to be carried up and down stairs, and allow his mother to keep her own use of stairs to a minimum. The **spa bath** might be viewed as a luxury, but was astutely recognized by social services as a medium to which Simon could respond. It is a useful therapy for Mrs Johnson and, while its primary achievement is an apparent improvement in the quality of Simon's life, it has the added feature of being a contribution to the family's pleasure that Simon can give. No strengthening was made, however, to the ceiling joists to allow for any future provision of an overhead tracked hoist, as might need to be considered if Simon gained weight or lifting were to become difficult or impossible for Mr or Mrs Johnson.

The **heating** of the new rooms is effective and comparatively economical. The reduced water pressure throughout the house is a major problem in a large family, and use of the overbath shower for Simon is not the single handed operation that it was carefully designed to be.

The undoubted success of the adaptation for the varying needs of all family members is affirmed by the Johnsons, who are now able to care for Simon in a more efficient and safe way that presents less risk to his fragile health and the wellbeing of his principal carer. The design of the house now positivly assists his inclusion in all major activities of family life and has allowed incorporation of features for Mrs Johnson's special needs and safety within an improved layout for continued long term use of the property.

MR HARRY WATTS

Aged 74. Parkinson's disease and a left hemiparesis.

Married.

Modification of a semi detached council house.

Mr Watts worked for many years as the manager of the news section in the local branch of a large chain of newsagents in the south west of England. His job necessitated long hours and an early start in order to organize the morning paper rounds. During 1973 he noticed that he had increasing difficulty in initiating movement in his legs after periods of sitting, and that long days in the shop took more and more out of him. Parkinson's disease was diagnosed and he attempted to reduce his working day to conserve his dwindling energy. He found this impossible, however, with the demands of his job and decided to retire a year early in mid 1974.

He maintained contact with the firm, mainly through the regular visits of the welfare officer and developed his hobbies of stamp collecting, playing skittles and whist, and running a youth club. His wife also led a busy life in voluntary work and activities in the neighbourhood, despite a hiatus hernia, enlarged heart, high blood pressure and osteoarthritis.

Movement, especially walking, became more difficult over the years for Mr Watts and he grew to rely on the support of two walking sticks indoors or a bicycle for distances outside the house, as pedalling remained a comparatively easy means of mobility. By 1980, however, movement was so difficult for him that the occupational therapist, to whom the family had been referred, requested the supply of an outdoor, attendant operated powered wheelchair and had a ramp installed to the front door to permit its use.

Difficulties relating to the stairs were also discussed with the family and the house owning district council. Options considered were to install a stairlift and so give access to the upper floor bathroom and bedroom facilities; to convert the dining room into a bedroom with provision of ground floor toilet facilities or to seek rehousing in more suitable accommodation.

The family did not wish to move as they relied on the support of their daughter and family, who lived three doors away, on their son in the same town, their local church, and on informal contacts in a neighbourhood where they were well known. The occupational therapist applied to the house owning authority to supply and install a stairlift, but this was turned down on the grounds that it would take up one sixth of the total annual budget for disabled people for the district and, instead, offered purpose built wheelchair standard housing about half a mile away. This the family decided against on the grounds that help was available in their locality and that the alternative was in a complex for elderly people, where help would be needed, rather than given by neighbours. They were not keen on the idea of a chemical wc, as offered in conjuction with conversion of the second reception room to a bedroom, and decided to continue as best they could in the present situation.

During 1980, Mrs Watts had to have a gall bladder operation and Mr Watts was temporarily admitted to the local hospital. On his return to his wife's care, a district nurse was requested to help with the daily management of dressing and bathing him and this developed into a permanent arrangement. Stairs remained a great problem, however, and put physical strain on Mr Watts, his wife and daughter.

In early 1982, discussion of the problem with the welfare officer from Mr Watts' old company led to an agreement for funding for a stairlift from the benevolent fund. Mrs Watts was supplied with a list of local installations which she visited in the knowledge of her husband's problems and needs, as nausea when travelling rendered him too unwell upon arrival to assess for himself. Several models were discounted before the type most suited was found and installed in mid 1982.

With the staircase problem resolved, there was focus on other activities where there were equal, if less hazardous and time consuming problems. The occupational therapist was asked to visit again and discussions followed on all areas of functional problem.

Mobility. Mr Watts had difficulty in initiating movement, but was able to walk with help to guide rather than support. He used an outdoor attendant operated wheelchair, but rarely went out owing to the upright seating position and type of movement that induced nausea caused by spinal arthritis and a flexion deformity of the neck. Transfers were achieved by his wife facing him and holding his hands to pull him up, using her foot on his to act as a pivot. While this method was contrary to advice, the use of his impetus and her body as a counterbalance was considered by them to involve the least strain on either. Medication, used to successfully reduce tremor and rigidity, had caused confusion and aggression in Mr Watts and had, therefore, been modified. While this was of consequent detriment to tremor and rigidity, it was deemed preferable to the alternative of the extreme side effects.

Dressing. Maximum help was required with clothes that were put on while he was in a seated position. Lower half items were pulled up as he supported himself on a rail in a standing position.

Wc. He was able to transfer to a commode chair with the support of a helper and a rail, but had difficulty in transferring to and rising from the wc, as space was too confined to allow the most effective support from a helper. He used a bottle during the day or, if tremor made this impractical, he transferred to the commode chair which was kept on the ground floor.

Bathing. A bath seat and board was used and maximum assistance given by his wife in an activity that was becoming increasingly difficult and hazardous.

Chair. He had an armchair raised on blocks to give a seat height of 460mm. A high backed model giving the same seat height had been tried, but the straight back gave him no head support, because of his neck flexion deformity, and the upright sitting position increased his tremor to the point where he could shake himself out onto the floor.

Bed. He was unable to get on or off the bed or to sit up without help.

Personal care. He was shaved by his wife using an electric razor and required help in washing and hair care.

Eating & drinking. He could not cut meat, but was able to feed himself at times of reduced tremor, using a casserole lid placed on a cork mat, with the lid rim used as a barrier against which food could be located. He used a straw for drinking from a beaker held for him.

Hobbies & interests. Mr Watts enjoyed the television and radio and having news items read to him. His inability to travel without increasing sickness rendered him virtually housebound, but he maintained contacts in the area via the many informal calls from friends and neighbours.

Plans were made for adaptation work and the supply of further equipment to enable easier methods of care. To make lifting more manageable, the occupational therapist arranged for Mrs Watts, and a lady in a similar situation, to visit a disabled person with a hoist installation; this developed into a light hearted session of experimenting with slings and lifting methods in a relaxed manner, their feeling being that there was no great pressure for the use of such sophisticated equipment, at the time. Confidence was gained, however, and they were able to look generally at improved methods of managing spasticity and tremor.

The session was to prove additionally valuable however, as a hoist became necessary two months later when Mr Watts suffered a slight stroke resulting in left sided weakness, speech loss and an inability to give any help in the process of transfers. Mrs Watts wanted to look after her husband at home and the occupational therapist was able to get an electric hoist and overhead gantry installed on A frames and operational within two days.

Daily visits from the community nursing service were initiated to get Mr Watts up and dressed and a physiotherapist instituted a treatment programme at home, that Mr and Mrs Watts meticulously followed. A ministry wheelchair was used for ground floor mobility and a castor wheelchair was supplied for the upper floor. Transfer to the stairlift was achieved, on the ground floor, via a perching stool and directly from the castor wheelchair on the upper floor.

Mr Watts made a good recovery from the stroke, but services of the nurse were continued and the hoist gantry replaced by a more permanent arrangement of ceiling tracking, both of which proved essential when Mr Watts had particularly bad days.

THE PROJECT TEAM

County council social services occupational therapist.
District council senior housing maintenance officer.
District council building inspector.
Mr and Mrs Watts.

THE AIMS

To provide safe and easy access to the house and the upper storey.
To promote ease of care, lifting and daily living in a locality where additional support was readily available.
To observe the physical limitations and health of the principal carer by provision of facilities suited to these needs, as well as those of the recipient.

THE PROPERTY

* A semi detached, district council house built in 1958.

* Gross internal floor area 80.6m².

The house, situated in a crescent shaped road on the outskirts of a rural town, was set on a level plot laid to

Front view of the house

garden to the front and rear. No provision was made for on site garaging of cars, but parking was available in specially designated areas to the side of the road.

They enjoy their garden, which is well tended by Mrs Watts, and there is a good view of the street from the living room.

THE ADAPTATION

Modification of a three bedroomed house.

EXTERNAL DOORS AND PATHWAYS

* 760mm wide x 1080mm long x 175mm high timber ramp installed to threshold step at front door.

* Raised weather bar removed and replaced by Duraflex threshold strip.

* Small ramp infill to interior cill.

* Front gate rehung to open against fencing to give 950mm width opening directly onto 880mm wide concrete pathway.

Mrs Watts has some difficulty in getting the wheelchair up the 1:6.2 gradient ramp and the infill, although the equidistant battens that have been fitted across the width give improved control of the chair. Mrs Watts is reluctant to accept the occupational therapist's solution of a level platform at the top of the ramp because it would extend further into the garden and require a larger concrete base for its permanent position. Mr Watts does not go out very often and usually only when others can assist if necessary.

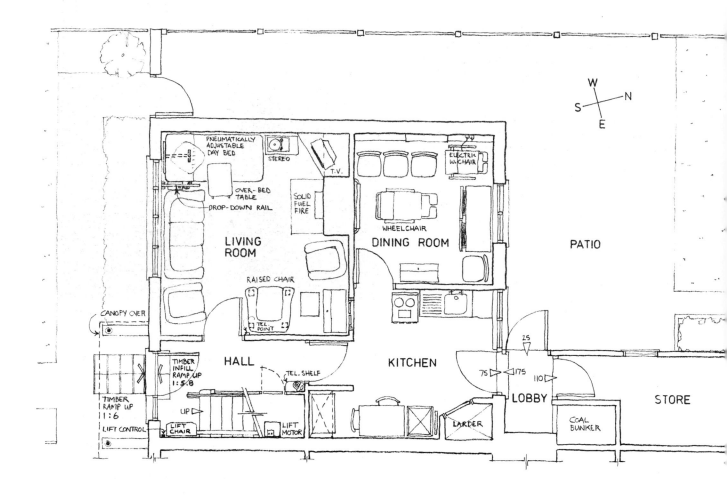

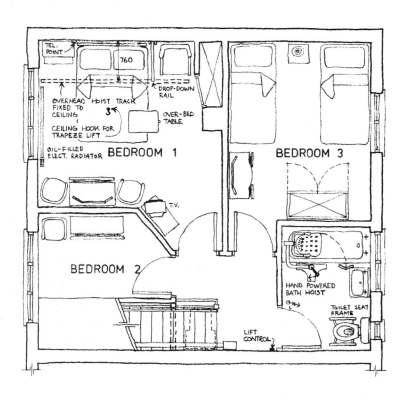

Ground and first floor plans. 1:75.
MR WATTS' HOUSE.

The front ramp is also the only means of access to the rear garden, via the concrete pathway that extends along the side of the house, as the wheelchair cannot negotiate the threshold steps, two doors and tight turns through the rear door lobby.

As the outdoor chair is infrequently used, Mrs Watts wanted a moveable ramp, although its size means that it is heavy to move. However, it can be taken up when not in use and its storage under the front porch helps to protect it from the worst effects of weather. Manoeuvre of the chair at the front boundary used to be very restricted, but rehanging of the gate has allowed a more direct and easy access without the need for path widening, as had been considered at one stage.

WINDOWS
* Cill heights of 900mm on the ground floor and 1000mm on the upper floor. Latch furniture was not altered as Mr Watts' lack of mobility meant that he was not expected to operate the windows.

Mr Watts' view of the garden and road from his sitting position in the living area is limited by the high cill. This was not altered, however, because of the high cost involved and the couple's reluctance to increase upheaval to the home.

ELECTRICAL WORK
* Additional power points installed at base of stairway to serve stairlift and in bedroom to supply electric hoist.

* Motor for stairlift housed in understairs cupboard with power cable and housing projected upwards through stair to supply lift at approximately mid point of flight.

The 290 x 270mm size motor is housed in a previously unused space and, although it would be awkward to reach the manual winding gear in the case of power failure, it is a compact and unobtrusive installation.

HEATING
* Solid fuel back boiler in living room fireplace, serving radiator in dining room and hot water system.

The back boiler and radiator, supplemented by additional electric radiators used selectively in the bedroom and hall, a convector heater mounted in the kitchen and a radiant heater in the bathroom, allow an even temperature of between 65° and 70°F to be maintained.

INTERNAL DOORS
No alteration was made to the 760mm wide doorways.

HALLWAY, LANDING AND STAIRS
Coat rack and telephone resited from their position at foot of stairs to allow installation of stairlift.

STAIRLIFT
* Gimson Stairmaster stairlift set to allow footplate to rest level with floor at base of stairway and to abut landing at first floor.

* Controls mounted 1200mm above ground floor and 1100mm above first floor level to allow operation from these points, as well as from arm of chair.

* 220mm protrusion of footplate guide rail at base of stairs boxed in and carpeted.

The stairlift seat projects only 270mm from the wall when folded

The arms of the stairlift seat fold back to ease sideways transfer from a wheelchair, although Mr Watts is usually able to walk with help to the lift and step onto the footplate, while supporting himself on his wife and the newel post, before seating himself in the chair. Mrs Watts has sole control of the lift as Mr Watts' hand pressure is too inconsistent to use the button push on the chair arm.

Requirements sought by Mrs Watts on behalf of her husband were that the stairlift should have a large seat, as Mr Watts' large frame and tremor might cause him to slide off a small one; an ample footplate was necessary, as rigidity precluded feet being tucked back; stations should allow level access both at the top and bottom of the stairway. They consider that they have successfully met these aims and find the stairlift to be very helpful to the extent that they continued to use it at a time of further reduced mobility, caused by the stroke.

The lift track projects 135mm from the wall leaving a clear width of 680mm on the stairway when the lift is not in use. The guide rail was boxed in to remove the risk of feet being caught underneath. However, attention is still needed to avoid it and Mrs Watts warns those unfamiliar with the house.

LIVING AREA
* Drop down rail giving horizontal height of 680mm installed on wall next to 480mm high day bed.

Mr Watts spends his day in this room with time divided between the raised armchair and the day bed. Mrs Watts assists him in transferring and lifts his legs up onto the bed as he supports himself on the rail and an overhead bed pole. A Marcon bed elevator and triangular cushion allow a variety of positions on the bed to counteract flexion rigidity and give relief from headaches, sickness and increased tremor that occurs if he sits upright for long.

KITCHEN
No adaptation was made to this room for Mr Watts' use.

BATHROOM
* Partition wall between bathroom and wc removed and one entrance doorway blocked up and made good.

111

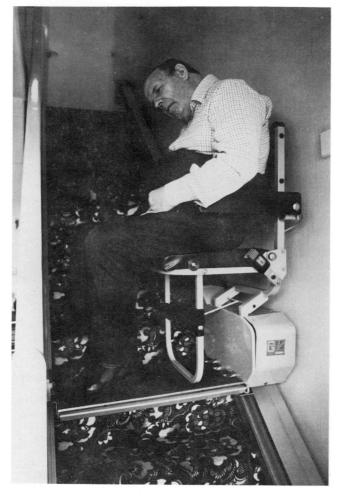

The seat size of 430 x 380mm is sufficient for Mr Watts and the footplate projection beyond the seat of 280mm allows sufficient space for his feet.

* Autolift bath hoist installed with base plate set 570mm back from head of bath.

* High level cistern replaced and wc pan sited farther out from rear wall, floor fixed toilet frame fitted.

* Washbasin mounted on the wall at height 850mm.

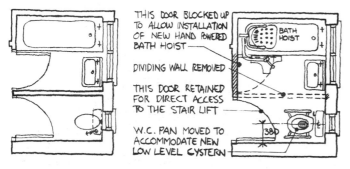

THIS DOOR BLOCKED UP TO ALLOW INSTALLATION OF NEW HAND POWERED BATH HOIST

DIVIDING WALL REMOVED

THIS DOOR RETAINED FOR DIRECT ACCESS TO THE STAIR LIFT

W.C. PAN MOVED TO ACCOMMODATE NEW LOW LEVEL CYSTERN

BATH HOIST

380

Bathroom alterations 1:75. The bathroom and wc were individually too small to allow space for the assistance needed by Mr Watts

The new large bathroom allows sufficient space for two helpers as is required when Mr Watts is bathed by his wife and the nurse. The Autolift is successful, although Mrs Watts complains about the lack of drainage holes at the back of the seat, which causes water to collect there and cascade off into the room when her husband transfers for drying.

The small size of the original two rooms made the task of assisting Mr Watts more difficult in the confined space. The high level cistern was in a poor state of repair and the council accepted the work of replacement, with positioning of the pan out from the wall to allow provision of a low level cistern. While they agreed also to the removal of the partition wall, they were not prepared to block off the second doorway, suggesting the door should merely be kept locked. The family felt they wanted both jobs done and decided to combine them in one operation to be done themselves, with the council's permission and use of a builder friend aided by Mr and Mrs Watts' son.

The Autolift bath hoist

BEDROOM

* Trapeze lift installed from ceiling fixing 700mm from bed head wall.

* Drop down rail mounted alongside the bed at height 750mm from floor.

* Wessex hoist mounted on overhead tracking fixed to reinforced joists to take necessary bolts and weight transference.

The hoist positions to centre 760mm from the bed head wall with a track length sufficient to permit transfer from an adjacent chair to the bed. A one piece sling with commode aperture is used without the leg pieces crossed as this makes for easier adjustment and positioning of the sling. The drop down rail used in conjunction with the trapeze lift and a double bed Marcon elevator allows him to alter his position and assist in the process of sitting up and rising from the bed.

The bedroom and hoist arrangement

COSTING

1981	
Trapeze lift	£16.00
1982	
Gimson stairlift	1514.00
1983	
Installation of overhead tracking	48.00
Materials to remove bathroom wall and doorway	150.00

FUNDING

The W H Smith benevolent fund initially paid for the supply and installation of the stairlift, although some of this was later reimbursed by the British Legion, local charities and friends of the family. It was agreed by Mr and Mrs Watts that the stairlift should become the property of the benevolent fund, should it no longer be needed. Costs for an annual servicing agreement on the stairlift have been met from various charities or Mr and Mrs Watts, and not by social services or the district council. The hoist, rails, toilet frame and bath lift were supplied by social services and the family paid for the removal of the bathroom wall and doorway.

CONTRACTUAL PROCEDURE

The W H Smith benevolent fund acted as the client in arranging supply and installation of the stairlift by Gimson Limited, having first obtained the permission of the district council for the installation in their property. Social services contracted direct to Mecanaids Limited for the Autolift and to a local electrician for the urgently required supply to the gantried hoist. The ceiling tracked hoist was installed from social services'stock by the district council, who used their price book for labour charges in contracting one of their usual jobbing builders.

EVALUATION

Some of the difficulties that Mr and Mrs Watts continue to have in their home can be attributed to the design and layout of the property, which might have been overcome by a move to purpose built accommodation. They do not, however, regret their decision not to move and value the support they receive in a neighbourhood where they are well known and respected. They have many spontaneous visitors, which is important both as a stimulus to Mr Watts, who rarely goes out, and as support in his physical care to Mrs Watts, who might otherwise have become isolated.

The couple maintain close contact with their daughter, son and families, and with the community nursing service who visit on a daily basis. They also have a good relationship with their general practitioner who calls regularly and with the occupational therapist, who acknowledges Mrs Watts' expert and capable care and will, therefore, visit when needed. She keeps in touch with events through the district nurses in this supportive community.

The problems of access to the house have only been partially resolved by the provision of the **ramp**, as it is rather too steep and of a construction that is unlikely to be resilient to bad weather. The Watts elected, however, to have a type that is removable, which would not be the case with a larger, shallower gradient type incorporating a platform as is most suitably required at this threshold. As it is, it is not easy to move the heavy ramp and must cause the family to consider additional help when taking Mr Watts out on the rare occasions that his health and feelings of nausea will allow. This would be a considerably more serious problem, however, should more frequent, spontaneous or independent outings need to be contemplated.

The **stairlift** was a successful provision and Mr Watts continued to be able to use this even at a time of reduced mobility associated with the stroke. He and his wife acknowledge, however, that the time may come when transferring may become too difficult or hazardous, particularly at the top of the stairs, but prefer to consider the option of ground floor living, by conversion of the dining room to a bedroom, to that of a move. The method

Space is limited in the hall for assisted transfer from the wheelchair to the stairlift

of transferring to the stairlift from the wheelchair was shown to be difficult, particularly at the bottom of the stairs where the confined space could not allow optimal positioning for sideways transfer when this became necessary. A through ceiling lift that would take a wheelchair might have been considered as a long term measure, although a district council that refused to fund the less expensive stairlift might have been unwilling to assist.

The occupational therapist was wise in forseeing the possible need for further lifting aids and was successful in enabling provision of an electric **hoist** within two days, with the cooperation of a knowledgeable electrician and the availability of a suitable hoist and gantry from the social services store. The earlier demonstation and teaching session in a relaxed manner ensured that Mr and Mrs Watts could confidently use the hoist and slings when this became necessary.

In the **bathroom** the aids supplied work well and the additional space given by removal of the partition wall gives the space necessary for assistance to the wc. A castor commode type chair could also be used, if necessary, to be pushed over the wc or for transfer to the bath. The present arrangement allows the provision of a more useful and sophisticated bathing aid, which could not have been included or have allowed transfer in the smaller room. The retained wc door gives the best and most direct access to the bathroom from the stairlift.

Mr Watts' future management will depend to a large extent upon his wife's health and the course of his medical condition. The couple would seem well equipped, however, to cope with many of the difficulties that might arise. There are neighbours and local people who wish to return some of the support and interest they have given over the years to their community. They are in full control of their lives and are well able to make decisions on how they will use services and in a manner that will assure sensible and practical continuation of their lifestyle.

MR JACK KIDSLEY

Aged 49. C6 complete lesion tetraplegia.

MRS ANN KIDSLEY

Aged 41. C5/6 complete lesion tetraplegia.

Purchase and conversion of a semi detached house.

Mr Kidsley sustained a spinal injury in a diving accident in 1961. Following treatment at a spinal unit, the direction of his life was relatively quickly moved outward into the community, with considerable apprehension on his part and little prior preparation for the psychological and social consequences.

In September 1962 he was discharged to a minimally adapted council prefabricated bungalow, and the onus of care fell directly on his young wife. After a period of increasing stress, the marriage broke down irrevocably in July 1964. By this time, however, with help from a disablement resettlement officer, he had completed a course of vocational training and was holding down a full time clerical job.

Care was offered and accepted from his supportive mother and brother, although their home was unsuitable for a wheelchair user, and they all eventually moved to a new bungalow in 1967. During this period, Mr Kidsley learned to drive an adapted car and became more independent in self care, although, apart from regular visits from a district nurse, the basic assumption prevailed that the family was the appropriate source of support.

However, by 1972, when he met his wife to be, he had consciously changed his life direction, resigned his job and was studying with the Open University. Up until the time of their meeting at the spinal unit, however, the course of their post injury lives had been very different.

By contrast, Mrs Kidsley had known only institutional forms of care since her whiplash injury, sustained in a car crash in Beirut, in 1966. The event was surrounded by trauma, the death of her father preceded her paralysis by four weeks and was followed by her mother's nervous breakdown. The course of her rehabilitation in 1967 was marred by depression, and a negative prognosis of tetraplegia led her to break off relations with her fiance.

Her struggle to return to work as a state registered nurse was beset with disappointment, as hopes of a career in nurse training were first raised, then dashed by the final decision of the matron of a teaching hospital. A dialysis unit, which had offered her a job before the accident, also turned her application down on the grounds that the hospital was inaccessible to a wheelchair.

Her mother's frail health meant that, instead of returning home from hospital, she was consigned to a series of segregated institutions, in the absence of appropriate housing and support services. Although she had supplemented her training by taking a number of courses in specialist nursing, her skills were used first as a receptionist, and then in folding sterile towels in a hospital workshop for therapeutic earnings pay.

Shortly after Mr and Mrs Kidsley met in 1972, they became determined to make a life together. However, at first they could see no clear alternative to the institutional settings that had constrained Mrs Kidsley's economic and social rehabilitation, and had undermined her emotional strength and confidence.

However, when they became members of the Union of the Physically Impaired, they soon discovered that their situation was not unique and, through discussions with fellow members, were able to obtain a fresh perspective on their situation. Although their lives had developed in different directions, they came to see that they shared many of the same fundamental problems. Drawing on the strength of their peers, they gained greater determination to seek a course to overcome their accommodation and care difficulties and, by the time that their attention was drawn to a seminar on the housing needs of disabled people, they had the embryo of an idea of a solution.

At the seminar they met the director of a housing association, who was interested in their idea of linking three of the basic components of independent living and offered his support in principle. The couple considered, that if they could obtain well designed accommodation, the right aids and live in sufficiently close proximity to willing helpers, there was a real alternative to the prospect of residential care. Shortly afterwards they were able to draw together friends who were themselves interested in the idea of the new group living arrangement.

A search for suitable accommodation near to his home, to allow his fiancee to visit on holiday, brought Mr Kidsley into contact with a local vicar with his knowledge of what might be available in the parish. He was helpful and became interested in the long term accommodation difficulties being encountered. He was able to identify a plot of church owned land and to secure agreement to its sale to the housing association that had offered support.

The concept of a group support scheme captured the imagination of all concerned, including a group of architects willing to work with the potential tenants on design, and the complex of three ground floor flats with three units above for support carers was eventually completed in September 1976. The group living scheme was based, as planned, on concepts of good design, appropriate provision of aids and equipment and the use of statutory support care as well as that of the support carers. A system of democratic participation of all tenants and a payment system for care additional to that available from home helps and community nurses was set up.

In general the features proved very useful, and Mr and Mrs Kidsley's projected need of thirty three hours of help per week, identified from past experience of residential care, became eight hours in practice. The other flats were allocated and the system worked well. Mr and Mrs Kidsley enjoyed the flexibility of the care system, their personal privacy and opportunities to do things for themselves. However, after a lengthy and exhausting process of proving that she was capable of undertaking traditional household tasks, Mrs Kidsley realized that she had no spare time in which to take an active interest in other issues that concerned her. She had to adjust her perceptions to accept more help with personal and practical tasks in order to free time for both social and political interests.

In 1981 the couple felt that they had begun to outgrow the project and could see that their flat would be useful to others looking to develop an independent lifestyle. They saw the challenge of moving to a house on their own, and enlisted the support of another housing association, this time under the Improvement for Sale scheme of the 1980 Housing Act. They could more accurately assess their requirements for care in the light of their experience:

Mobility. Mr Kidsley used a self propelling wheelchair indoors and an electrically operated one for distances outdoors. Using a sliding board, he could transfer independently to seat heights similar to that of the wheelchair and also to and from the car.
Mrs Kidsley used a Roho cushion in a self propelling wheelchair, which she operated with the protection of hand gloves. Anything more than a very slight gradient was difficult for her to manage in the chair.

Dressing. Mr Kidsley was independent with casual clothes. Mrs Kidsley had successfully taught herself how to dress, using specially designed garments with which she did not need help.

Wc. Using appropriate aids, they were able to manage their incontinence problems and to help each other accordingly. Electric hoist transfer and two piece slings were used for transfer to the Clos o mat wc that was necessary for personal hygiene.

Shower. Showers were taken in an old self propelling wheelchair over a level access base.

Bed. Hoist transfer was required and hooks into ceiling joists were used for strap pulls to adjust position in bed.

Domestic tasks. Both enjoyed cooking and had planned their kitchen to maximize efficiency, to eliminate the need to lift heavy pans and to reduce the risk of dropping things on the floor. All but the most heavy housework could be achieved independently between them, but was very time consuming. In order to conserve energy and to allow themselves time to work and to follow other pursuits, they used domestic help for shopping, washing and heavy work and their Home Link computer for management of bills and household organization.

Work & interests. Mr Kidsley worked full time for a disabled peoples' organization. Both were active and articulate campaigners for the rights of minority or disadvantaged groups. They were involved in local organizations and politics and enjoyed an active and varied social life.

Their financial position made it possible for them to consider property for sale in the area. They soon found that bungalows were outside their mortgage limit of the £20,000, but otherwise they needed to place no other restriction on the type of house they could consider. Primarily they wanted a property that they liked and would feel happy about living in, and was large enough to allow conversion for easy circulation of two wheelchairs.

They found a three bedroomed semi detached house in good decorative order which they liked and, although a full

structural survey could not be carried out before purchase, the housing association agreed that it met the improvement for sale criteria. The association bought it, having established that a building society mortgage was available to the Kidsleys, and that a home improvement grant and social services' funds were agreed for the specialized adaptations and equipment needed, to add to the £7,500 maximum improvement for sale grant of the time. As the scheme was new in concept, a considerable amount of work and time was envisaged to be spent on preparing the design brief, dealing with structural repair, researching equipment and adaptations, and working through complicated procedures, and a research grant was obtained to meet the extra over cost.

The housing association's consultant on housing for disabled people worked closely with Mr and Mrs Kidsley to produce a very detailed design brief from which the association's architect worked. The scheme was not straightforward as, on opening previously inaccessible places, extensive dry rot was found which escalated the repair costs. In order for the district council to give an improvement grant, the house had to be in the ownership of Mr and Mrs Kidsley and this was made possible when the building society agreed to release the mortgage funds before the house had reached the stage of practical completion. Problems arose in overseeing the work for the Kidsleys, since they could not get onto the excavated site in their wheelchairs, which they found very frustrating.

Mr and Mrs Kidsley were finally able to move in during April and found that use of their new home generally lived up to their best expectations and detailed planning. A programme of helpers was organized which evolved into two hours of private help each weekday morning to speed the process of rising for work, being ready for meetings and domestic requirements. In addition, domestic tasks were undertaken by a social services home care aide employed in the afternoons for evening meal preparation and minor personal tasks. Further help was contracted on an ad hoc basis to help Mrs Kidsley when her husband needed to be away from home overnight. Only morning helpers came in over the weekends when privacy was otherwise jealously guarded.

The Kidsleys' work with organisations of disabled people was an important source of help in achieving new approaches to the problem of housing and care. Their association with supportive colleagues and professional workers helped to pioneer interdependent group living ideas and full integration into the community.

THE PROJECT TEAM

Mr and Mrs Kidsley.
Housing association chief administrator.
Housing association design consultant.
Architect.

THE AIMS

To allow sufficient space for access to all facilities and movement of two wheelchairs throughout the house.
To provide features and equipment tailored to the needs of the user and to promote independence in all aspects of daily living.
To facilitate activities that required additional help.
To provide an attractive and stimulating environment for development of work and personal interests.

THE PROPERTY

* A semi detached house built in 1910 on a long narrow plot, as part of a development on the outskirts of a small mining town.

* Gross internal floor area 122.7m² before and 135.3m² after adaptation.

Garages built to form the rear boundaries to the houses were reached via a service road, with access to the garden and house through a door in the rear garage wall. Concrete slabs had been laid to the front garden and to form a patio at the back, with steps leading from this to accommodate a level change down the garden.

THE ADAPTATION

Conversion of a three bedroomed house and site for two wheelchair users.

Main construction work to the house involved bringing the outbuilding into the main structure, the installation of a through ceiling lift and reorganisation in the use of rooms. In addition, the roof and guttering was repaired and the damp course and floors replaced.

EXTERNAL DOORS AND PATHWAYS

* Partition wall in outbuilding removed and lintol inserted to give opening of 1770mm.

* External door from kitchen bricked up and new opening made.

* Timber framed lean to with corrugated clear plastic sheeting roof made against boundary wall to connect outbuilding to kitchen.

* 1000mm doorway formed in new wall and inward opening door, with lever handles, fitted.

* Small area outside door enclosed with fence and gate to garden.

* Terry step lift installed next to steps in garden.

* Paving slabs in poor state of repair replaced to give improved access around garden and to garage.

Front view of the property

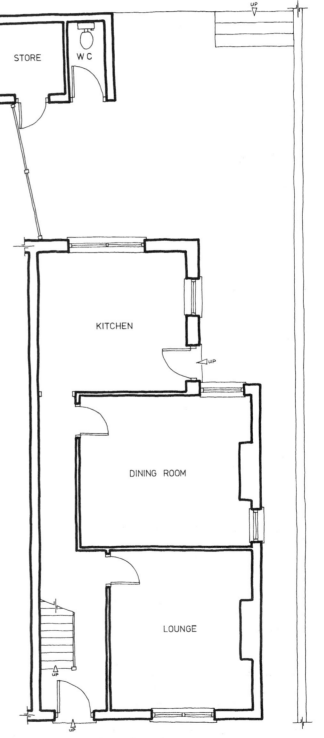

Ground floor plan before adaptation. 1:75

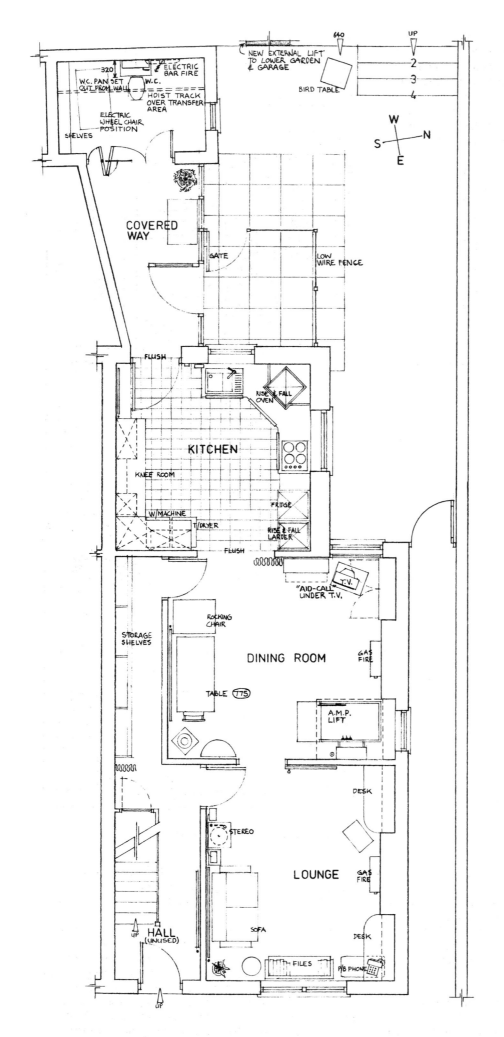

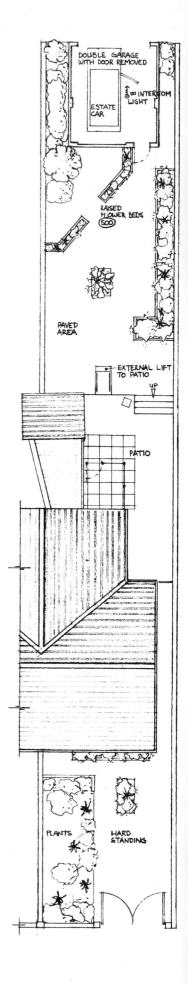

Ground floor plan after adaptation. 1:75

Site plan. 1:200

The 1000mm wide door leaf gives a good line of access in a wheelchair either from the kitchen or from the end of the covered way, where the electric wheelchair is stored next to the wc and the battery charger. The fenced area allows the Kidsleys to let their dog out into an easily monitored area, eliminating fears of the dog getting onto the road if the side or front gates are inadvertently left open by callers.

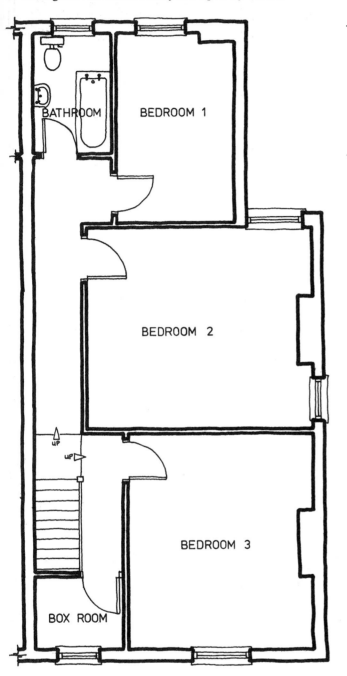

First floor before adaptation. 1:75

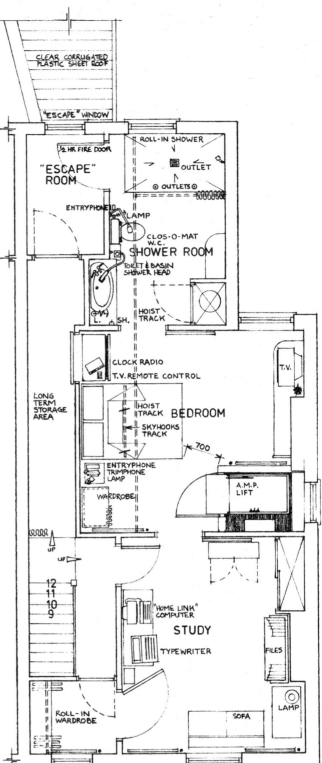

First floor plan after adaptation. 1:75

Wheelchair circulation is possible to all parts of the site with the step lift used to give access to the rear portion of the garden and the garage. The lift was chosen for its ease of operation and minimal preparation work for installation and has proved successful in use. However the Kidsleys find that its pneumatically operated mechanism can be temperamental in extremes of temperature, although it has never let them down completely.

Traffic to and from the house is via the rear external doorway as the front door is neither negotiable nor operable by the Kidsleys. All regular callers know this and there has not been any problem with the arrangement in an

area where it is customary to call at the back door. In addition, a sense of security is given in that use of the front door bell indicates that there is a caller unfamiliar to them.

A portable intercom tied to a rafter in the garage over the position of the driver's door of the car allows Mr Kidsley to announce his arrival to his wife in the house or to summon assistance from the family aide if he is particularly tired and therefore unable to transfer without help. It had been intended to provide a remotely operated garage door but, when the costs of the project escalated because of the dry rot, savings needed to be made and the garage was left without a door.

Rear view of the property.

The covered way connects the kitchen to the ground floor wc

WINDOWS

* One kitchen window made smaller to allow new door opening to covered way.

* Second opening to kitchen and to second bedroom partially bricked up to give raised cills and top hung windows.

* Top hung window fitted in new opening to outbuilding.

* Lower half of old bathroom window blocked up in wooden construction that could be removed from outside by firemen, to allow escape from upper floor in case of fire.

* Sash window frames to dining room and one large bedroom repaired.

* Crank handle opening devices installed to front bedroom, kitchen and lounge windows.

The Kidsleys later installed secondary double glazing to all windows. As a result, they are not able to use the openable parts of some windows except by removing the fixed panels.

Sliding panel type double glazing was fitted to the bathroom window and is manageable, allowing cross ventilation on the upper floor between this window and that of the front bedroom.

ELECTRICAL WORK

* House rewired with light switches and power points set over work surfaces in kitchen and at height 900mm from floor in all other rooms.

* Power meters and fuse box at height 770mm sited in cupboard in dining room.

* Television points given to dining room and main bedroom.

* Telephone points to kitchen, dining room, lounge and main bedroom.

* Entryphones to operate rear external door sited in lounge and by proposed position of new first floor wc.

* Provision of power to Clos o mat, showers and anglepoise lamp in bathroom.

The receiver to the communication system that Mrs Kidsley uses is housed under the television and linked to the telephone point in the dining room. Pop out fuses had been intended to be used, but were eliminated from the contract when costs had to be cut. The Kidsleys plan to replace the conventional type that were used; this will then give them independent management.

HEATING

* Gas fired back boiler fitted in dining room chimney to feed radiators throughout house.

* Warm air space heaters mounted on walls of bathroom.

* Thermostatic valves fitted to top of radiators.

* Top control gas fires installed in lounge and dining room.

* Domestic hot water tank and airing cupboard sited in new bathroom.

Mr and Mrs Kidsley find the central heating system easy to use and consider the thermostatic radiator valves help to save fuel in keeping the desired temperature of 21°C. The space heating from two outflows in the bathroom allows boosting of the temperature in the room, which is important in view of time spent there. Mrs Kidsley has difficulty in using the gas fires, which require the knobs to be pressed down and turned; their position on top of the appliance is awkward for her.

HALLWAYS AND DOORS

* Doorway and adjacent wall to new bathroom removed and partition wall formed to abut doorway of old bathroom.

* New 900mm wide openings and sliding doors with D handles made from middle bedroom to rooms on either side.

* Sliding door to new bathroom reduced in height after contract completed, as it snagged hoist cable and motor.

* New opening made to old bathroom from new and fitted with casement door to half hour fire resistant standard.

* Inward opening door from landing to main bedroom widened and replaced by sliding one.

* New inward opening half glazed door made to opening from covered way to kitchen.

* Opening dividing outbuilding from covered way fitted with bifold doors.

* Sliding doors with D handles made from dining room to lounge and to kitchen, corresponding with those on first floor.

* Much of original hallway fitted with shelves.

All the sliding doors are easily operated but are usually left open to facilitate movement between the rooms. A bedside cabinet is usually positioned in front of the sliding door from the landing to the main bedroom as there is no requirement to use this doorway, as access to the front boxroom that is used as a wardrobe is through the front bedroom/study. If visitors are staying, however, privacy is given to the front bedroom by the family aide collecting clothes using the sliding door and the door to the boxroom from the landing, which are otherwise kept closed. The outward opening door to the boxroom from the front bedroom is awkward to use as it opens into the room space and not against the wall. The extra storage space in the hall proves useful for bulky items that might otherwise interfere with wheelchair circulation if housed elsewhere.

THE LIFT

* 80mm deep 1200 x 790mm well created in dining room floor.

* Equivalent area aperture cut and trimmed in joists of floor above to enable installation of AMP home elevator.

* Half height timber and plasterboard wall partition formed on first floor to enclose lift on third side.

Both Mr and Mrs Kidsley enter the lift forwards and reverse out. Mrs Kidsley has some difficulty with the small gradient of the ramp/gate when she is very tired and finds it impossible to enter the lift backwards. They are generally pleased with the lift operation, the easy controls and its reliability.

The contractor sited the lift 280mm forward of the external wall and not in the position specified against the wall. This did not become apparent until near the end of the contract, as the Kidsleys were not able to gain access to the bedroom until the lift was installed. To gain sufficient space for a wheelchair to pass between the corner of the lift and the bed, the bed head had to be positioned directly against the wall, by sacrificing the shelf intended to go behind it. Overhead tracked hoisting, accurately installed for the original position of the bed, therefore, was not in the optimal position and could not be moved because of the line needed to the Clos o mat. The contract could not have been extended without incurring additional costs and the Kidsleys, having moved into the house, were loathe to face having the work altered. The return of the builders would

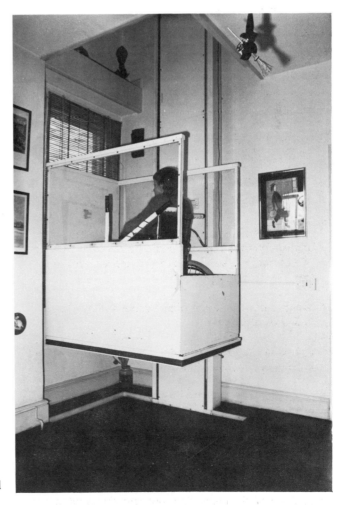

Mrs Kidsley is only able to enter the lift forwards

121

have meant considerable upheaval and the requirement for the Kidsleys to move out and find suitable alternative accommodation for the period of work.

LIVING AREAS

* Fireplace surround removed.

* Woodblock flooring installed to lounge and dining room, chosen and funded by Mr and Mrs Kidsley.

The Kidsleys find the flooring attractive, easy to clean and it presents no friction to the easy passage of wheelchairs. It also facilitates furniture movement, depending on how the rooms are to be used, meetings and visitors. For added warmth in winter they have a tight pile carpet put down and secured at the edges under furniture.

KITCHEN

* Prototype kitchen assembly comprising corner unit of elevating oven, static ceramic hob, sink, worksurfaces, refrigerator and elevating drawer storage units installed to one half of kitchen.

* Pine units of work surface with wall cupboards above, combined washing machine/tumble drier and small freezer under to other side of room.

Work surfaces were set at 750mm as being the optimum safe working height for Mrs Kidsley as, although a greater height was useful to Mr Kidsley, absence of triceps power meant that she could not gain control at a higher level and risked pulling things down onto herself.

The use of a diagonal corner unit was a familiar one to the Kidsleys who had used it to good effect in their flat, as it enabled them to reach oven, hob, sink and worksurface by pivoting from the central point. However, the dimensions of the new arrangement were slightly larger than their previous one; the sink and hob being out of reach unless the wheelchair was moved. No pivoting was possible owing to the position of the oven housing under the work surface, which impeded movement of the wheelchair footplates. The limited work surface space usually meant that the area in front of the oven was used for food preparation and had to be cleared in order to move pans to and from the oven. It was not possible to extend the worktop forward, however, as this would have rendered the oven out of useful reach.

They find the flat hob and its switching easy to operate but cannot easily regulate degree of heat, see into pans to judge simmering or have enough space to move things off the boil. Aluminium pans cannot be used and they find the alternative materials heavy and expensive.

Mrs Kidsley can operate the large controls of the washing machine/tumble drier. They intend to replace the ex contract prototype unit with a different type based on the design of the kitchen in their flat as finances permit.

Use of the prototype kitchen corner unit

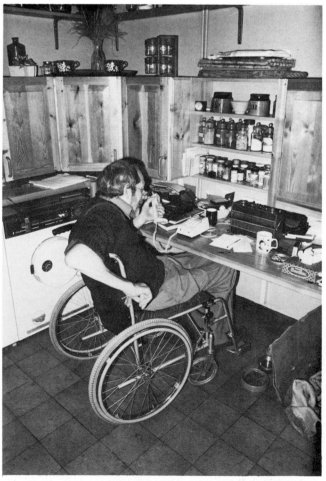

The pine units, made and installed by a local carpenter, are attractive and provide a useful work and storage area

BATHROOM AND WC

* Floorboards to shower area removed, joists chamfered to give fall to two waste outlets and area covered in 6mm marine plywood.

* Entire bathroom floor covered in Altro safety flooring with bonded corners and raised to skirting level.

* Clos o mat with seat height of 480mm.

* Two Ideal standard lever operated pillar attached showers.

* Oval washbasin with lever taps set in vanitory unit at height 780mm from floor.

The whole bathroom can be designated a wet area, if required, or the shower area divided off completely by a curtain. Storage of regularly used items is either on the vanitory unit or the easily accessible shelves. The washbasin taps are easy to use but the central waste pipe limits knee space and there is a risk of scalding from heat transferred from hot water discharge into the pipe.

When redesigning the ground floor wc, it was set forward to allow the hoist track to be used both for access to the wc and for hoisting to wheelchairs on each side, with battery recharging facility for Mr Kidsley.

BEDROOMS

* Floor of main bedroom covered in vinyl cushion flooring and front bedroom/study in short pile carpeting.

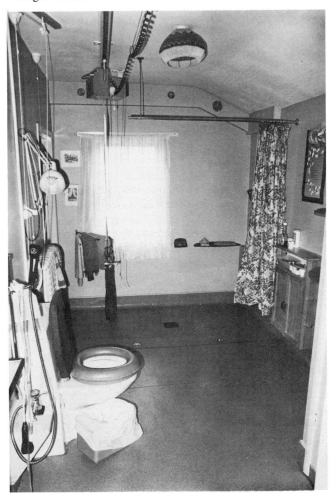

The shower room.

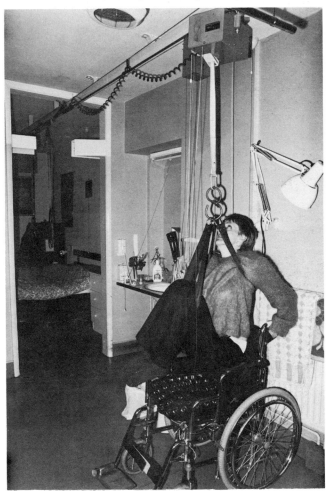

Mrs Kidsley is able to transfer independently to the hoist in the shower room

* Wessex electric hoist fitted to overhead tracking running in direct line from bedroom wall over Clos o mat into shower area.

* Storage shelves made to bathroom and adjacent fire resistant room.

* 480mm seat height standard wc and Wessex overhead tracked hoist to original outbuilding on ground floor.

Direct hoisting is possible from the bed to the Clos o mat and for transfer to a self propelling wheelchair that is used and stored in the shower area. There is sufficient space on either side of the Clos o mat for transfer and the shower here can be used equally well from the wc and washbasin.

* Battery back up service installed in case of power failure to hoist.

* Skyhooks and straps on 2250mm track parallel to hoist were fitted over bed.

On either side of the bed there is ample room for transfer in the main bedroom using the hoist but, because of the forward positioning of the lift and the consequent repositioning of the bed, the hoist tracking line is no longer the optimal planned. Although the strap pulls enable Mr and Mrs Kidsley to adjust position, more effort is required than would have been the case had the plan been carefully adhered to.

The floor can be easily cleaned and presents no friction for the wheelchairs or problem of water that may be brought from the bathroom. The communication system acts as further security in an event of total power failure that would eliminate the battery back up service to the hoists.

The front bedroom is generally used as a study and as passage way to the dressing and clothes storage room, which has shelves and low hanging rails. It can, however, easily be restored to a bedroom with use of the settee that converts to a bed.

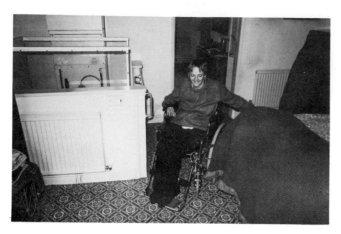

Although the bed has been moved back, there is only just enough space for wheelchair manoeuvre between it and the lift enclosure

COSTING

1982

House purchase		£16,000.00
Basic repairs, fees and legal costs		11,000.00
Special adaptations		6,375.00
Aids and equipment		6,950.00
	Total	£40,325.00

FUNDING

Purchasers, deposit and mortgage		£19,500.00
Housing corporation improvement for sale		7,500.00
Improvement grant, 75% of £8,500 maximum		6,375.00
Social services for equipment		6,950.00
	Total	£40,325.00

CONTRACTUAL PROCEDURE

The housing association architect worked with Mr and Mrs Kidsley and the design consultant on the brief and plans. The contractor engaged by the housing association by competitive tender carried out all repairs and installation work. Sub contractors for the through ceiling lift were AMP Engineers Limited and Terry Lifts Limited for the Step Lift.

EVALUATION

Mr and Mrs Kidsley became paralysed at a time when the survival of people who had suffered severe neck injury had only relatively recently become the norm. The rehabilitation they received was, in their view, limited, and centred on containing their condition rather than developing their capacity for independent living and full participation in the life of the community. It assumed that the family was the primary source of support, with all the concomitant physical and emotional stress involved. In the absence of family support, residential institutional provision was the only alternative and the Kidsleys were convinced that this was fundamentally wrong.

They carefully developed strategies to break the constraints which hindered their full integration in the community and this recognised the importance of good housing as one factor in a number of interlocking elements vital to achieving full social participation.

The improvement and adaptation to their house bears this out. The change of a bedroom to a **bathroom** on the first floor was designed specifically to place the main bedroom adjacent to toilet facilities. The purpose of this was to facilitate the most economical use of the overhead tracked **hoist**. The hoist combines a number of transferring functions and interrelates with other factors, such as the need for care support, since both Mr and Mrs Kidsley can choose to complete a number of tasks independently. The financial and social consequences of this are considerable by reducing the number of hours of care support needed and relieving helpers of the need for heavy lifting.

Similar interlocking factors can be seen elsewhere in the redesign of the old outbuildings to a **ground floor wc**. The resiting of the wc allows access both sides, one side being reserved as a battery charging/parking space for a powerchair. The hoist not only permits transfer to the wc, but also from a self propelling chair directly to the powerchair for Mr Kidsley. The design of the covered way and surrounds permits easy access and egress for the powerchair and the choice of independent functioning. There was no alternative site within the existing structure for a ground floor wc, that did not remove space that was otherwise more usefully designated, and incorporation of existing plumbing and building structure was more economical than building on a new room.

The choice of the property in the context of the local environment becomes apparent as it is well within powerchair reach of all local shops and other amenities. When they choose, the Kidsleys can operate independently of care support, taking part in the life of their local community and using wheelchairs chosen to help overcome some of the physical barriers involved. Their immediate environment however is designed to facilitate functional integration, as can be seen by the way Mr and Mrs Kidsley have redesigned the **garden** to paved areas combined with raised garden beds. The **steplift** gives vital access to the car by overcoming a level change on the site. Without the lift, the pathway would have had to be sloped to eliminate the step and it is doubtful whether Mrs Kidsley would have been able to manage the gradient, and access to the garden on either side would have been a problem. The intercom in the garage is imaginative use of equipment in a different setting to that traditionally used.

The incorrect placement of the **lift** creates some difficulties in the use of the bedroom, which were not planned, but to which the Kidsley's have now adapted. As the Kidsleys could not get on site, or to the first floor until the lift was installed, the positioning was not checked or amendments made at the time of installation. It was fortunate that a shelf had been planned at the back of the bed, which allowed some of the problems to be overcome by its removal, although the Kidsleys lost a storage space that they had originally deemed necessary, and still have difficulty in using the hoist. The 280mm involved could have made the difference between independence and dependence, to which supervising staff, who could get on site should have been alert.

The **bathroom** is sufficiently large to allow movement of two wheelchairs in it simultaneously. The construction method used has proved successful as it does not impede wheelchair access and there have been no problems of leakage into the ceiling below.

Equipment and bulky items that may be needed from time to time in the room are stored conveniently close to the point of use in the adjacent room, that also doubles as a **fire protected escape route**. Fire might render the lift inoperable and the open shaft could be the focal point of transferring fire and smoke between the floors. If trapped on the upper floor, the Kidsleys have the use of a room that is sufficiently large for two wheelchairs, with some fire protection. It is commendable that this safeguard has been considered, although the pitch of the roof of the extension below would not make it the easiest place for firemen to reach from outside.

Space that was difficult to use in a wheelchair has been successfully converted to **storage** as is required for bulk buying and housing of large domestic equipment, that is neatly placed out of sight and general room area.

The design of rooms, with two doorways to each room, allows flexibility in use as the front upper floor room can be a **study**, unless resident guests preclude this, and the ground floor front room can be closed off without detriment to access to the upper floor or the rest of the house. There are other areas that can be easily used for writing in each of the ground floor rooms, and the Clos o mat upstairs is also used as a study area with extra lighting over. Easy circulation is available on both floors for two wheelchair users, with rooms having varying uses depending on the needs of the residents.

The space and layout of the large house works well towards promoting the individual needs of Mr and Mrs Kidsley and they are able to develop their individual, as well as communal interests at will. They were successful in finding the right property to meet these needs in the area in which they wanted to live, but did not over commit themselves financially to accommodation that they greatly enjoy, but which they may not wish to be their residence for the rest of their lives.

MRS COLLINS

Aged 90. Mild osteoarthritis and generally frail.

Adaptation of daughter and son in law's house to provide a self contained flat annexe.

When she was widowed in 1974, Mrs Collins moved to a first floor maisonette in the town in which her daughter lived. She settled well, being close enough for her daughter to help if required, yet following the independent lifestyle she wished. Physically, her joint stiffness increased and the stairs became more difficult, but this problem was largely resolved by provision of a second bannister rail, installed by her son in law. She had successful hip replacement surgery and later made a good recovery from a fracture of her left ankle.

In the following years, however, it was acknowledged that Mrs Collins required more and more help from her daughter, to the point where she became totally dependent upon her daughter for most aspects of her daily life and care. It was suggested that she move in with the family, but she remained resistant to the idea until a well appointed self contained flat was assured in this arrangement. The decision to build over the drawing room was made in mid 1983 and her son in law, Mr Carter, commenced the planning.

The Carters had increased the size of their home in 1972 by a single storey extension to form a large drawing room and double garage on one side of the property and by conversion of the existing garage to a study/work area on the other. This work had taken the property up to the side boundaries and, while there was ample space for further extension on the first floor, there was no scope to extend on the ground floor.

In terms of the property as a whole, they had seen the value of a second storey to the extension, but had not been able to justify the additional space with their children living away from home and no need for additional bedrooms. They were concerned about the prospect of stairs for an elderly person, but resolved to find a suitable lift, as there was no possibility of a flat meeting the requirement of self containment on the ground floor.

Mr Carter used his knowledge as a chartered engineer, and long experience in voluntary work with an association for disabled people, to ensure provision of suitable facilities, as well as observation of Mrs Collins' difficulties and requirements.

Mobility. Mrs Collins could walk short distances with the support of a walking stick, but stairs were virtually impossible.

Dressing. She could be independent, but tended to need supervision with organization of clothes.

Wc. She had frequency and urgency of urine.

Bathing. She required considerable help in a task which was difficult and time consuming.

Bed and chair. She could rise independently providing seat levels were not particularly low.

Domestic tasks. She tended to neglect herself and had grown to depend on her daughter for most aspects of her care.

Interests. Her life seemed to focus around eating, sleeping, warmth and watching snooker on television.

The basic requirements were for a living area, kitchen, bedroom and bathroom; that all provision should be finished to a high standard with large low cilled windows that would allow good visibility; that the bedroom should be large, in case Mrs Collins became bedfast and a warm even temperature would need to be assured. Mr Carter drew the plans himself and obtained planning and building regulation approval, allowing work to commence in January 1984.

During the process of planning and building, Mrs Collins' health deteriorated and she was not well enough to comprehend or be involved in planning the conversion. Hospital admissions were required and with these the acknowledgement that it was no longer merely desirable, but essential, that she should not live on her own. She was discharged from a local hospital directly to the new flat in May 1984, without return to her old accommodation. Her reaction to the work was immediately favourable and the stimulus of a new lifestyle, in which there was encouragement to do some things for herself, has resulted in a marked improvement in her health.

The front of the house showing the external door to the new flat annexe.

THE PROJECT TEAM

Mr and Mrs Carter.
Builder.
Representative from the lift company.

THE AIMS

To allow independence and privacy in a setting where help could be readily and easily available, on a regular basis. To maintain a comfortable lifestyle and existing social contacts. To provide facilities tailored to particular needs resulting from old age, frailty and joint stiffness.

THE PROPERTY

A three bedroomed detached house built in 1948 and extended in 1972.

Gross internal floor area of flat annexe 37.5m².

The property stands in a quiet residential road on the outskirts of a small town. A large, mature garden is sited to the front and rear of the house, which has extensive views over hills and woodland.

THE ADAPTATION

A first floor addition to an owner occupied house to form a self contained flat.

A flat with a large bedroom, a bathroom, a living room and a kitchenette was built over the drawing room, with access via a lift installation from the exterior or through the third bedroom of the main house internally.

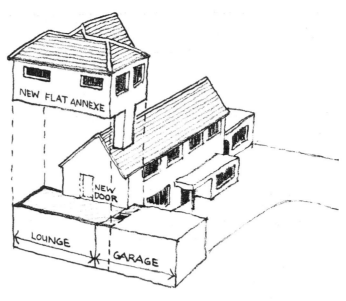

The flat annexe design concept.

Access to the flat is easy and fast for Mr and Mrs Carter through the bedroom, which would also serve as an adjoining room for a nurse or live in carer, should this ever be required. Mr and Mrs Carter usually have lunch and tea with Mrs Collins and Mrs Carter provides all meals, domestic and personal care as required during the rest of the day. Mrs Collins does, however, lead her own life and receives her own friends and visitors.

EXTERNAL DOORS AND PATHWAYS

New external door and 100mm step formed between garage and drawing room extension, by resiting of garage wall to central storeroom.

Rear view of the property.

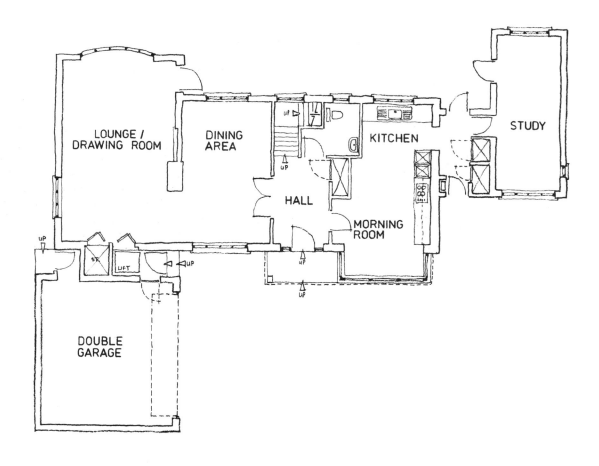

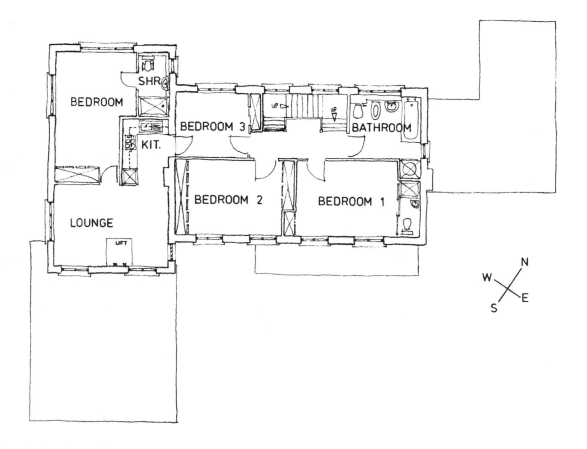

Ground and first floor plans after adaptation. 1:150.

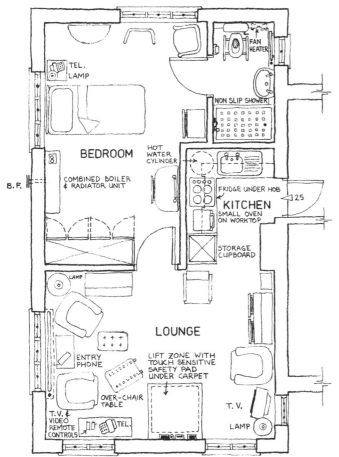

Plan of flat annexe. 1:75.

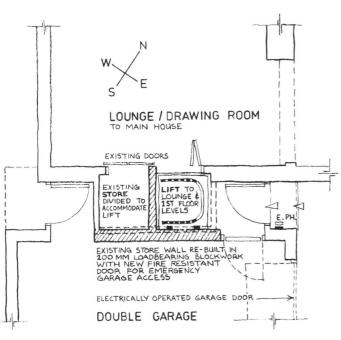

Plan of ground floor adaptations. 1:75.

The new door gives direct access to the upper floor flat from the ashphalt driveway. Mrs Collins can manage the front door step, but does not go out alone. The close proximity of the garage and drive to the external door require only a few steps to a car.

WINDOWS

* Casement windows with lever handles at height 790mm to match existing windows.

* Cill heights of 560mm.

* High level window over proposed position of bed.

* Additional round porthole type window to living area.

The position of the flat and the generous number of large windows allows sun in rooms at all times of the day. Mrs Collins can open the windows with ease and has good views of the rest of the road as well as of some beautiful scenery to the rear of the property. The high window on one wall of the bedroom increases light to the room, but does not allow casual overlooking of the neighbour's property. The porthole window provides an attractive feature and an asset to the flat as well as to the house as a whole. Integral weather stripping to the openable parts of the windows keeps draughts to a minimum.

ELECTRICAL WORK

* Light switches set at 1350mm throughout.

* Spotlights and concealed strip lighting over kitchen work surfaces.

* External light to ground floor door linked to table lamp in flat to allow operation on this floor as well as by switch at main door.

* Power points set at 280mm above floor level.

* Time switch installed to outlet serving electric blanket.

Mrs Collins has easy control of lighting and is unlikely to leave the external light on all night as it is switched off with the table lamp. Power points are low for optimum use, but Mrs Collins does not need to use appliances independently.

The family did consider an intercom connection between the two establishments, but decided it would compromise the sense of independent living. Telephone links are used instead, to supplement the regular and frequent visits to the flat during the day. When dining in the flat, Mr and Mrs Carter take a radio telephone with them, to know of incoming calls to the main house in their absence.

HEATING

* Servowarm central heating supreme plus system with boiler, pump and radiator arrangement sited in bedroom.

* Temperature control at height 850mm on top of main unit.

* Radiators in each room.

* Hot water cylinder in kitchen.

* Fan heater and heated towel rail in bathroom.

The central heating system is efficient and compact, taking up hardly more space than a radiator and with an easily accessible mechanism for maintenance. Mr Carter has fitted an automatic thermostat as the high input of sunshine on bright days could cause the temperature setting to be too

The guide rails and aperture have little effect on the living area when the lift is not in use.

high at certain times of the day. A separate system to that of the main house was chosen as Mrs Collins needs heating to be on all the time, as is not the case for the rest of the family.

HALLWAY LANDING AND STAIRS

Through ceiling lift installed in shaft to connect external door and living area of flat.

LIFT:

* Portcullis home lift installed on cavity wall bolts.

* Additional station, to that at each floor, for access to drawing room of main house.

* Floor area of shaft lowered by 100mm for necessary clearance of lift.

* Walk in cupboard reduced to accommodate lift shaft with access retained from drawing room of main house.

The lift was chosen as a type that could serve the three stations required, the drawing room one of which was only 260mm up, and at right angles, to the ground floor entrance door. The lift was adapted to Mr Carter's specifications and as a result of technical restraints of the site.

The hipped roof to the front of the new extension prevented the lift motor from being placed in its normal position directly above the lift shaft. It was decided to incorporate the motor in the lift body itself, with the result that the internal headroom was reduced to only 1660mm.

The lift gives Mrs Collins access to the front door and living area above, as well as to the main drawing room of the house via double doors sited at one end. The lowering of the floor in the shaft allows the platform to rest level with the surrounding floor. As she is not very tall, the reduction in head clearance does not worry her. The lift has a manual emergency release handle sited in the car which can lower the lift by degrees, should power failure occur. Problems existed, however, with there being three stations not equidistantly apart, in that the lift could confuse at which station it was resting and, consequently, not move the correct distance to the next one. Mr Carter devized suitable circuit changes to overcome this with the lift company.

LIVING AREA

The lift guide rails, positioned in the centre of the external wall, are unobtrusive. The lift is stored at ground floor level when when it is not in use and the carpeted floor cut out fits neatly into place to give access to whole floor of living area. The touch sensitive safety pads under the floor cut out prevent the lift being brought to first floor level if anything is standing on it. The room gives a sense of spaciousness and brightness and is furnished with favourite pieces of furniture selected from Mrs Collins' previous, larger home.

KITCHEN

* Small kitchenette formed to open directly from living area.

* Sink unit and single drainer, with cupboards under.

Mrs Collins spends much of her day in the living area.

The bathroom.

* Full length storage unit, two wall corner units with shelving, and three units of cupboards and drawers installed with autolatches and contrastingly coloured handles.

* Hob with side controls mounted in worksurface with extractor hood over.

* ICTA convectionaire oven positioned on work surface.

The kitchenette was designed to provide sufficient facilities for the preparation of light meals and hot drinks, and is used as such by Mrs Carter. It is not used by Mrs Collins who relies on her daughter for her meals, although she had been interested in and still able to bake cakes at the time the project was planned. The room is an efficient base and was considered a necessity by the family, in terms of the long term use of the property.

BATHROOM
* Standard height wc.

* Wall mounted washbasin at rim height of 740mm, with mirror over.

* 750mm x 1200mm shower base with 230mm step over.

* Adjustable head, pillar attached shower and mixer fitted to rear wall of shower area.

* Cushion type vinyl floor covering.

Mrs Collins uses an integral toilet frame and raised seat to give a height of 520mm, a half step to the shower and a free standing shower chair as supplied by the social services occupational therapist. She has independent use of the wc and washbasin but is assisted in the shower by a nurse or Mrs Carter.

The shower is not thermostatically controlled as the flat has its own cold water tank and there are no problems in fluctuating pressure, as Mrs Collins is the only user.

BEDROOM
* Standard flat pack wardrobe, incorporating shelves, hanging space and internal lighting adapted to be built in.

The bedroom is large and airy with excellent views of countryside afforded over the low window cills from the bed. There is sufficient space to allow additional furniture and storage, should Mrs Collins need to be nursed or to spend more time in bed.

COSTING
1984		
Structural work		£19,000.00
Lift		4,000.00
	Total	£23,000.00

FUNDING:
Mrs Collins agreed a sufficient provisional sum for the project. No grant was applied for, but the conversion is subject to rate relief.

131

K

CONTRACTUAL PROCEDURE

Mr Carter contracted a local builder for the structural work and Portcullis Fabrications Limited for the preparatory and installation work to the lift.

EVALUATION

Mr and Mrs Carter must have doubted the wisdom of moving Mrs Collins to a first floor flat that depended entirely upon a **lift** for access to and from the flat, since she could not manage stairs as an alternative. Not only would she be trapped if there was a power failure or lift breakdown, but she might well have not taken to the management of controls or the movement of the lift and its opening into the living area. As it was, she responded well, and the entire move was a stimulus to her mental and physical health.

The lift has, however, had serious teething problems with long periods when it would have been inoperable but for Mr Carter's specialized knowledge in overriding circuits to allow its use. Mrs Collins does not go out often, and never unaccompanied, so this loss of independent management is not as important to her as it might be to other people.

The **kitchen**, although not used by Mrs Collins, is nevertheless well organized and relative in size to the rest of the flat to allow flexibilty in long term use. The layout with units in close proximity promotes efficiency and allows ample storage and appliance provision for Mrs Collins' meals to be prepared in this room when required.

The family have only had contact with an occupational therapist for the provision of aids in the **bathroom** and did not seek to involve her in any way in the planning or fitting out of the adaptation. It seems regrettable that a half step to the shower, a raised lavatory seat and free standing rails have had to be supplied to be added to the finished work, when the occupational therapist might have been able to suggest features that could have been less obtrusively included in the building work. The Carters consider, however, that the aids used can be easily removed, as becomes necessary when young grandchildren visit.

The flat is well appointed and gives Mrs Collins varied views, either over countryside or over activities in the road. The large **windows** and south facing position allow sun in the main rooms throughout the day and create an impression of space and brightness, particularly in the **living area** where she spends most of her waking hours. No space in this room is lost by the lift installation, with the platform stored in the downward position when not in use, and with guide rails that are unobtrusive and do not detract from a room where attention has been given to achieve as pleasant and stimulating an environment as possible.

To ensure health and safety, the electric blanket cannot be left on all night, as it is controlled by a time switch. In addition, the linking of the external light to a table lamp in the flat ensures that the external light is not overlooked when Mrs Collins goes to bed.

The size of the rooms would allow wheelchair circulation, if necessary, and the position of the bathroom off the bedroom allows for ease of access if Mrs Collins were to need more in the way of nursing care. There is sufficient space in the lift for a small wheelchair and ample room at the external door for a ramp to the step. The position of the third bedroom would allow for a live in nurse, and is presently useful as such when Mr and Mrs Carter go away on holiday.

It was fortunate that Mrs Collins could fund the project prior to the sale of her maisonette. This enabled all building work and upheaval to be resolved before the move and allowed a smooth transition, as might not have been the case had the family all had to live together with reduced facilities in the interim. The success is also attributable to Mr Carter who was enthusiastic about the project and applied his interest and knowledge to the successful design and planning work. In addition, he had a cooperative and efficient builder who completed the work quickly and to a high standard.

It would have been desirable to achieve ground floor facilities and so eliminate problems of stairs and a total dependence on a lift. However, as is not infrequently the case because of space limitations, no other solution was possible. While, in this instance, there was space for an extension to the rear, it would not have permitted the accommodation to be self contained as was an important condition requested by Mrs Collins. Facilities in the main house would also have been at a greater distance for her to reach, at times when she wishes to be with her daughter and son in law in their house, and a further imbalance between the two floors would have occurred in terms of the property as a whole.

Mrs Collins' decision to move to the flat suits all the family. Mrs Carter is able to support her mother in an efficient way while pursuing her own interests in a manner that was not possible when she had to travel across the town to the maisonette. Help can be summoned by telephone, or by the walking stick banged on the table, if it is necessary beyond the frequent visits made to the flat. Mrs Collins is able to join in with activities in the rest of the house, as and when she wishes, but each establishment can retain its individual lifestyle and the property as a whole has been improved.

MR NORMAN HENRY

Aged 58. Right hemiplegia.

Adaptation of a ground floor flat in a housing association terrace to give wheelchair standard amenities.

The more active elements of Mr Henry's life, as director of a civil engineering firm, member of the territorial army and keen gardener, came to an abrupt halt in 1976 when he suffered a cerebral haemorrhage. This resolved into a dense right hemiplegia and total loss of speech, which was treated with intensive rehabilitation in the following six months. Walking with the aid of a caliper and tripod was established and stairs managed with the support of a handrail. Communication improved to the level of limited voice projection and imperfect articulation.

The decision, made before the cerebral haemhorrage, for he and his wife to separate was effected by divorce during the time he was in hospital and he was left in the devastating position of having no home, no family to care for him, no job and no prospects. The hospital social worker looked for long term care for him and eventually found a place in a unit for younger disabled people which was in the city near to the town of his birth. The fact that his mother and old friends would be nearby was the only thing about which he could be positive and, six months after the stroke, he transferred to the unit in which he was to stay for five years.

Whilst he had daily physio and occupational therapy, standing was not utilized, except for transfers, at any other time and his ability to walk declined to the point where he became entirely dependent on a wheelchair for mobility. To improve his future job prospects and to fill his considerable free time, he took a correspondence course in accountancy, passing the preliminary and intermediate examinations with distinction and developed an interest in the idea of running a small business.

In 1982, a complex of bungalows for assessment, rehabilitation and long term independent living was established in the grounds of the hospital and he became one of the first to occupy a bungalow. With the provision of appropriate equipment and adaptation, he only needed additional help with bathing and with putting on his socks.

At his instigation, the hospital social worker began to seek suitable accommodation in the community and, within a month of the move to the assessment bungalow, the interest of a housing association was established. The association was already involved in an extensive programme of housing rehabilitation in the local area and had a substantial stock of accommodation, several types of which Mr Henry, his social worker and a community occupational therapist were able to visit.

The occupational therapist's work with Mr Henry was largely confined to discussing availability and types of equipment, as Mr Henry's knowledge of building and construction, in conjunction with an accurate appraisal of his condition and functional ability, enabled him to plan and organize the adaptations that would be required. Conversion of the house was based upon the assessment made during his stay in the bungalow.

Mobility. Mr Henry had a dense right hemiplegia with spastic paralysis and some flexion contracture of the upper part of the spinal column. Indoors he used a left hand only driven manual wheelchair of overall length 1140mm, including toe restraining strap, and a large electric kerb climbing wheelchair outdoors. Although manoeuvre of the manual wheelchair was cumbersome and its length required a large turning circle, especially when turning to the left, Mr Henry preferred to retain its use indoors to meet his individual daily living needs. He was able to transfer forwards providing there was rail support for his left hand, but could not transfer sideways owing to lack of lateral movement.

Dressing. He could manage the top half and getting lower clothes to his knees from a sitting position, but needed a rail to pull up on to finish the process from a standing position. Help was required for socks as spasticity in his right leg eliminated the possibility of his reaching far enough forward for the operation. Shoes, however, were no problem.

Wc. He could manage transfer to a standard height seat and management of clothes in conjunction with a grab rail for left hand use when standing from the wheelchair, and on the left side when rising from the wc.

Bathing. He required maximum assistance and considered a shower more suited to his needs.

Bed. He used a Nesbitt Evans 600mm high bed with integral overbed pole and a side rail at 780mm from the floor, for getting in and out of bed, adjusting his position in bed and for support into standing for transferring to and from the wheelchair.

Eating and drinking. A non slip mat under the plate allowed meat to be cut with a standard knife prior to eating with a fork.

Domestic tasks. Mr Henry could self cater independently with the use of an accessible hob and oven, electric can opener, bread buttering board, spike board for vegetables, jar opener and lightweight electric jug kettle. He needed help with laundry and some cleaning, but could do his own ironing with a standard board.

Hobbies and interests. He enjoyed reading, music, gardening and board games. Future plans were to include computer programming and final accountancy exams with a view to starting his own business.

Properties considered were assessed both for present suitability and potential for change that could incorporate the special features that Mr Henry would need. In addition, factors such as proximity to shops and other facilities were important. In practice, the team were drawn towards larger ground floor flats which could allow wheelchair circulation without the need for very precise alignment and turning, and which could accommodate his two wheelchairs and special equipment, as well as his considerable gadgetry and books for work and hobbies. The housing association had a number of properties in the process of rehabilitation and, as an economy measure, it was decided to adapt one on which building work had not yet commenced.

The choice came to be between two ground floor flats in the same road which, while they were of the same size and proximity to shops, had different internal organization. Ultimately, the decision was made against the one that had the bedroom at the front, as Mr Henry wanted his living area to be where there were more interesting views than at the back. It was also not possible to get an acceptable layout in the mid room to form a bedroom and passageway to the kitchen that was at the rear right of the property.

Once the choice was made, a series of meetings followed to plan the adaptation work that was additionally required and the special features for Mr Henry's particular needs. The occupational therapist, the architect contracted by the housing association and Mr Henry worked closely on plans and reworking ideas on paper prior to detailed specification. Although this process was finalized within six weeks, the speed and impetus could not be sustained, as the work was part of a larger contract and had to take its place in the schedule of work planned by the builder. The team had to settle for this as no great urgency could be justified, other than Mr Henry's own eagerness to get on with the project, as pressure was not being exerted for his bed at the unit and he could not therefore be considered homeless.

When work started in March 1983, Mr Henry took a keen interest in it and, once the floors were completed, was able to visit the site and to suggest modifications. In addition he researched fitments he would require and made his own arrangements for the odd job work of installing domestic necessities. The architect involved him in the choice of colour schemes and carpets, and the occupational therapist found a suitable door release mechanism that he could operate. The work was completed by mid August 1983 and he moved in shortly afterwards, with only some minor adjustments to household fittings still unresolved.

THE PROJECT TEAM

Mr Henry.
Metropolitan borough social services occupational therapist.
Social worker.
Architect.
Housing association development officer.

THE AIMS

To provide facilities tailored to specific functional needs within a programme of property rehabilitation.
To promote maximum independence and safety in all aspects of daily living.
To give opportunities for development of work, leisure and social interests.

THE PROPERTY

A pair of flats built in the 1890s as part of a terrace, of a type peculiar to the north east of England, and scheduled for extensive rehabilitation.

Gross internal floor area 78.4m² unchanged.

The flats had earlier been the subject of a conversion to provide bathrooms inside, but were otherwise in a poor, neglected state and had been bricked up for some time. Internal reorganization of rooms was required; the position of doorways caused very difficult turns into rooms from the hallway; the original opening to the bathroom precluded wheelchair access; neither of the bedrooms nor the kitchen was large enough for reasonable wheelchair circulation,

although the flat was large as a whole. The special features required were effected along with the necessary general repairs.

THE ADAPTATION

Conversion of a flat for one hand drive wheelchair use.

* Rear boundary realigned where external wc removed.

* Internal walls dividing bathroom, the two small bedrooms and hall removed and realigned to give larger hallway, one large bedroom and square bathroom.

* Wall dividing kitchen and dining room removed and external walls dry lined.

* Decayed timber floor replaced in concrete 200mm below previous level.

* Bonded, heavy duty waterproof nylon carpeting laid to all floor surfaces, except tiled kitchen and shower area.

The change in the boundary created a useful dustbin storage area close to the back door. Although the dry lining is 80mm to 90mm deep, this space is not missed in such large rooms. As the original timber flooring was in a poor state of repair, the opportunity was taken of forming a new level to eliminate the two steps at the front entrance. Level access to the street is achieved instead of the 1 in 6 gradient that would have otherwise been necessary.

The front of the house, showing the level access, boundary wall flower bed, the opener and closer over the main door and environmental control sub station to the side.

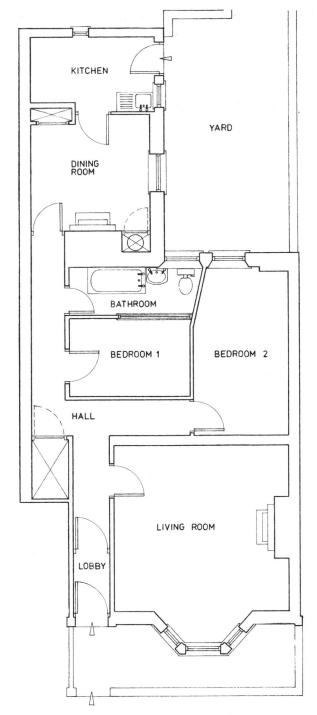

Ground floor plan before adaptation. 1:100.

EXTERNAL DOORS AND PATHWAYS

900mm wide new rear door with latch lock, internal bolts and lever handles hung to open against kitchen wall.

* Water exclusion bars installed across front and rear door thresholds.

* Clear plastic corrugated canopy sited over rear door.

* Step to pavement at front gate eliminated and transition to sloping pavement effected by new concrete path to front door.

* Back yard lowered to 200mm below new floor level.

1 in 12 ramps and handrails installed from back door to yard and from yard to back gate.

* 525mm high flower bed built to form front boundary wall.

* 560mm high flower bed formed against side boundary wall at rear.

Mr Henry has difficulty propelling himself out over the front threshold as the small wheels of his manual chair lock sideways against the 15mm water bar upstand, although he can cope with the 10mm one at the back door. The ramp at the rear door is rather steep for Mr Henry and the handrail was installed for left hand use to help in pulling himself up the ramp. The condition of the rear pavement is poor and the extra distance required to travel along the back of a long row of terraced houses is time consuming and inconvenient to the extent that he does not use this route to go out.

The back yard slopes laterally to a drainage point, which can cause problems as the chair tends to drift sideways, requiring additional effort for the upward slope to the planter.

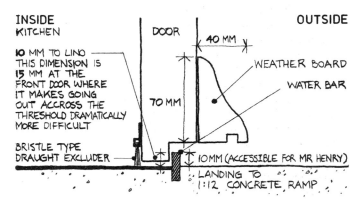

Rear door threshold. The 10mm high water bar, run off and sheltered doorway allow wheelchair access, but prevent rain penetration.

WINDOWS

* One kitchen window opening realigned and enlarged for installation of new back door.

* All other original openings retained with cill heights of between 900mm and 1070mm.

* Poor condition frames replaced with top hung casements.

* Louvres set above to be operated by drop rod pulls sited at 1300mm from floor.

* Push bar cam stays to operate lower windows.

The lower windows are easily used and those out of direct reach can be operated with a long handled reaching aid. The long window pole that is used to open the top louvres takes practice and precision for one handed use, and Mr Henry finds that this type of window creates draughts even when closed.

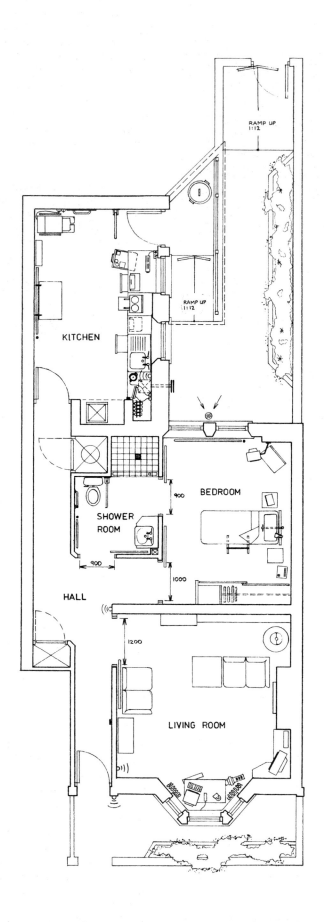

RAMP UP
1:12

KITCHEN

RAMP UP
1:12

BEDROOM

900

SHOWER
ROOM

900

HALL

1000

1200

LIVING ROOM

Ground floor plan after adaptation. 1:100.

The flower bed gives a good working height for use of standard gardening tools, and plants are chosen for their ease of care and all year round interest.

ELECTRICAL WORK

* Flat rewired.

* Power sockets mounted at heights between 960mm and 1280mm from floor level.

* Two double sockets in bedroom, three double in living area and two double in kitchen.

* Light switches set at height 1000mm from floor.

Boiler control moved onto front of kitchen chimney breast at height 1020mm.

* Extractor fan installed in bathroom and linked to pull cord light switch for simultaneous use.

* Fuse board relocated to new understairs cupboard, at height 580mm from floor.

* Intercom door release system installed to front door with operational sites in living area, kitchen and bedroom.

* Pressure plate sited in hall to operate door opener and closer.

* Ten station environmental control system by Scientific Systems Limited installed with operation from living area, and substations in kitchen, bedroom, hall and outside front door.

* Pull cord in bedroom to close off substations at night.

Additional sockets have been installed, as Mr Henry found the original provision to be insufficient for the many appliances he uses. He has chosen the conventional siting above the skirting board, as he considers the multisocket adaptors he uses and trailing flexes from plugs set higher in the wall to be unsightly; he is able to reach the new sockets by leaning sideways out of his chair. The worktop mounted sockets in the kitchen are useful for equipment used infrequently, although most appliances are left plugged in and switch controlled on the equipment itself. The boiler control is easily accessible, as is the fuse box master switch.

Three double power sockets in the living area were insufficient for Mr Henry's range of electrical equipment.

The environmental control equipment is linked to a television, a video recorder, a radio, a standard lamp, curtains in the living area and bedroom, the door lock and release, the door opener and closer and an external alarm. The door opening device can be operated either sonically from the stations or from the pressure plate. Three room locations for operation were necessary as the flat is large and Mr Henry's movements slow. A dead lock with another electric keep, later installed in addition to the latch lock, has eliminated the need for bolts to protect against intruders, as had proved necessary with only the latch lock. Both electric keeps are connected together and operate as one. Mr Henry's reason for wanting an electrically controlled fully secure service unit was that, if taken ill, he would not have to get out of bed to unbolt the door to let in help.

The first intercom door release system chosen was inexpensive, but was not successful, as the amount of static and interference that was picked up made Mr Henry's already limited speech inaudible. Handsets on the replacement proved more suitable to overcome problems of lack of speech projection than the boxed microphone type originally tried. However, the door opener and closer operated by the environmental control system gives better control by the user, needing one command to open and a separate command to close the door.

Mr Henry is generally pleased with the environmental control system that affords easy use of electrical equipment, including that of the long curtains required at the living room windows, which would be too heavy for him to operate manually. He likens the system control box to an item of high fidelity equipment. Equally, the door opener mounted outside the front door looks like a burglar alarm; this serves to deter intruders, while it also avoids advertising vulnerability.

The occupational therapist spent long hours trying to resolve problems of door opening and environmental control, and, while the system chosen was ordered well in advance of the move, installation was not completed until after the builders had finished. Teething problems persisted for some time, including an occasion when lightning struck, causing the system to malfunction and then jam, the front door and curtains to open and lights to go on in the middle of the night. The pull cord closing off switch over the bed is an attempt to avoid operational faults at night when he is in a position to do least about it and which can be reactivated as necessary.

HEATING

* New hot water tank sited in hall to replace old one removed from kitchen.

* Solid fuel heating system replaced by small gas fired boiler, mounted on kitchen wall.

* Radiators in all rooms and hall.

* Wall mounted gas fire with right side controls sited in living area.

Mr Henry leaves the radiators on to their fullest setting and controls heating from the boiler which is usually left on a twice daily automatic setting. He finds control of the gas fire difficult as the knob is stiff and the location awkward to manage with the left hand.

HALLWAYS AND DOORS

* Inner lobby door and large understairs cupboard removed.

* Shallow understairs cupboard formed.

* 900mm wide door openings from bedroom and from hall made to new bathroom.

* Opening to living area enlarged to 1200mm width.

* Opening to bedroom from hall widened to 1000mm.

* Sliding doors with vertical D handles fitted.

* Side opening kitchen door rehung to open against wall.

* Kick panels fitted throughout.

The extra opening problem of the secondary lobby door was eliminated, without any problems of weather penetration resulting, and this allows easier access to and from the front door. The hall cupboard is sufficient for storage of the vacuum cleaner, in addition to the fuse board sited here, and Mr Henry has easy access to both.

Access to the rooms from the corridor is comparatively easy as right turns, which are easier for left hand propulsion of a chair, are required. Doors are generally left open and, as the bathroom door faces the front entrance, Mr Henry has installed a plastic strip curtain through which he may pass easily, but which conceals the view of the bathroom through the open door. A towel rail on the back of this door allows him to close it when seated at the washbasin.

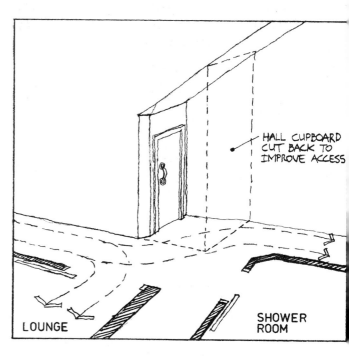

HALL CUPBOARD CUT BACK TO IMPROVE ACCESS

LOUNGE

SHOWER ROOM

The understairs cupboard was removed to improve circulation space and access to main rooms from the 900mm wide corridor.

LIVING AREA

* One long wall left clear of radiators and sockets to allow space for Mr Henry's substantial library.

* Purpose designed shelving for television, video, record player, cassette deck, environmental control unit, intercom handset and tape carousels on another wall.

The living room is spacious with high ceilings and furniture placed well back to allow optimum circulation space. Lightweight furniture that can be easily moved is placed in front of the bookshelves, but the position of the desk at the window, to gain best light, created problems in access to the windows for opening.

KITCHEN

* Phlexiplan system of 800mm high worktops with drawers, cupboards, shelves, pull out surfaces and mobile trolley set along one wall on 220mm metal supports.

* Shallow bowl sink, with left handed drainer and lever taps, mounted on side panels giving 650mm clearance under.

* 200mm radius cut out in front edge of panel adjacent to refrigerator.

* Wall mounted double cupboards with autolatches and base shelf of 1115mm above floor sited over radiator.

* Small cooker set on shelf to allow radiant rings to come level with adjacent worktop.

Cooking and food preparation area.

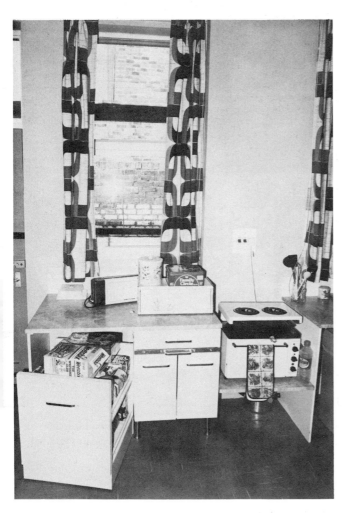

The cut out in the panelling allows Mr Henry to turn to the refigerator without having first to back out from his position at the sink.

* Refrigerator/freezer set in position of old chimney.

* Floor covered in asbestos vinyl tiles.

Tins and packets are stored in the mobile trolley next to the drawer containing the electric can opener and scissors. Above the trolley is the socket for the can opener, and saucepans are kept alongside the drawer close to the hob. The result is that all cooking assembly can be done in one place with almost no need to move the wheelchair.

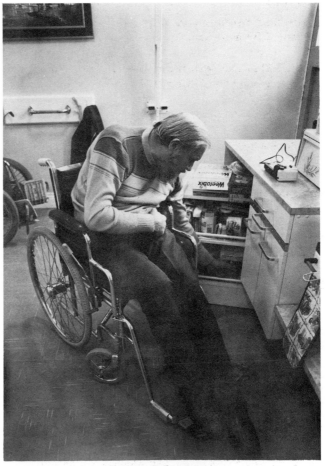

The trolley is useful for Mr Henry, as it holds a large amount of heavy provisions in easily accessible form.

While storage space is limited, it proves sufficient for such a well organised person and is supplemented by the storage trolley which is housed under a worktop when not in use. Pull out surfaces at 650mm adjacent to the sink and cooker give varying heights and avoid the necessity for all work tops to be reserved for wheelchair access. Shallow open shelves provide an easily accessible and visible storage area.

The old chimney area also houses kitchen steps, dustpan, bucket and broom, and an easily pulled out wine rack is stored on the otherwise inaccessible worksurface alongside.

One end of the kitchen is devoted to storage and recharging of the outdoor electric wheelchair, and for standing practice with a drop down rail. The large size of the room easily allows for this and for clear access to the back door. As the original wall mounted position above the radiator was too high to be useful, Mr Henry has had the table lowered to a height of 755mm by cutting down the two uprights and supporting the rear of the table with a towel rail on the double radiator. He does not need to put any great weight upon the surface of the table.

BATHROOM

* Wc set at standard level and seat raise later installed to give overall height of 450mm.

* Right angled rail mounted on wall next to wc with leading vertical section 20mm forward of wc pan and horizontal section 760mm above floor.

* Drop down rail at height 840mm installed to other side, giving extension of 760mm forward from back wall.

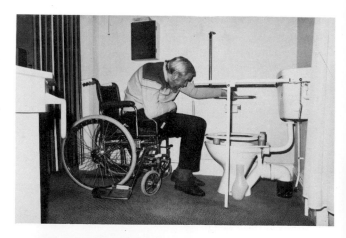

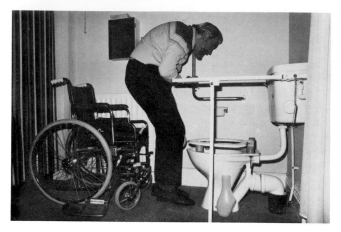

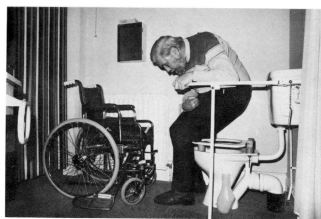

The increased seat height of the wc used in conjunction with the right angled and drop down rails is successful and Mr Henry uses a bottle at other times of the day.

* 1250 x 1080mm shower area formed against rear wall of airing cupboard, with studded ceramic tiles sloping to central drainage point, and 20mm deep gulley type flood barrier to front edge.

* Hinged shower seat mounted on wall 465mm above floor level.

* 830mm high drop down rails set on each wall of shower area.

* Heatrae Sadia Touchflo slimline shower, with removable head on slide rail, sited on wall adjacent to shower seat.

* Vanitory unit with washbasin and lever taps inset to give front edge 590mm forward of the wall.

The shower area showing the hinged rails.

* Vanitory unit mounted to give knee clearance of 650mm.

* Small shelf and mirror installed immediately above 150mm high splashback.

With the installation of appropriately sited grab rails, Mr Henry had anticipated being able to shower independently and, with the drop down rail on the wall facing the cubicle entrance, is able to effect transfer to the shower seat from the wheelchair. However, reliance on another drop down rail on his left, to help him stand from the shower seat, effectively blocks his exit from the area as he finds himself surrounded by rails. A nursing auxiliary is involved, therefore, to lift the rail out of the way and to speed up the operation of showering.

The drainage gulley was installed as back up to the central waste outlet, and prevents flooding if the central grill becomes blocked; the shower area has no measurable fall, and the nurse finds herself standing in water as she moves the rail. Wall fixing of rails needed to be particularly strong as Mr Henry puts a lot of weight behind their use. Drop down design allows versatility of use while still preserving circulation space.

BEDROOM

* Full height wardrobes with ceiling hung sliding doors on flat floor guide rails, purchased by Mr Henry after completion of the contract and installed to one wall.

The washbasin and useful area on the left hand side is highly successful, allowing Mr Henry optimum positioning and use.

Mr Henry chose a lamp with integral switch clamped onto the bedhead instead of a pull cord light as he finds a hanging cord difficult to locate in the dark. A television on wall brackets and two bedside cabinets to house a clock/radio, master telephone and intercom are all easily usable from the bed.

The clearance between the corner of the wardrobe and the doorway might have caused problems, but for the wide opening sliding door to the room. This allows Mr Henry to approach at an angle, although he has to concentrate on getting this right in order not to catch his fingers when entering the room. The problem of the dogleg turn from the bottom of the bed to the bathroom is easily overcome by turning at the foot of the bed to reverse into the bathroom, which leaves him facing the washbasin.

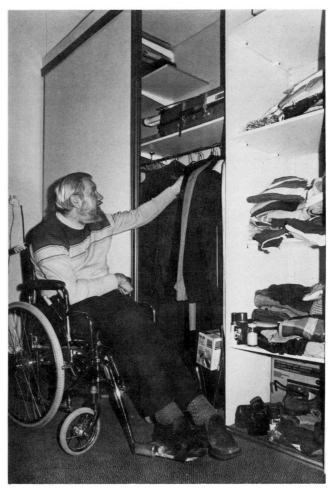

The hanging rail and open shelf storage is easily accessible over the flat threshold to the wardrobe in the bedroom.

COSTING

1983

Environmental control system		£1,250.00
Purchase and repair of flat		18,200.00
Ramps and repositioning of walls		1,200.00
	Total	£20,650.00

FUNDING

Housing association allocation for purchase and repair of each flat under the ehabilitation scheme	£18,200.00
Housing corporation supplement for adaptations required for occupation by a disabled person	1,200.00
Social services for the environmental control system, remote and master phone, intercom and rails	1,250.00
Total	£20,650.00

CONTRACTUAL PROCEDURE

The architect negotiated the contract for the rehabilitation of a number of properties with a builder whose work was known to the housing association. The structural features needed by Mr Henry were made part of the larger contract and the tender was renegotiated accordingly. Social services contracted a local electrician for installation of the second intercom and for the adjustments to the environmental control system.

EVALUATION

Mr Henry was fortunate that the period in the assessment bungalow could be so quickly followed by the opportunity to live in the community and that, in addition, there was a wide choice of accommodation and a willingness by the housing association to adapt it as necessary. Despite the choice available however, adaptations required were substantial and this is in part attributable to the type of housing generally found in inner city areas, and which is not usually favoured with good facilities for wheelchair use. However, substantial work was in any case required to meet Mr Henry's precise and particular needs.

Circulation around the almost 80m² size flat is good, with the reorganization of internal walls and door openings allowing for spacious rooms, good organization and adequate turning space for single hand wheelchair propulsion. Access is not impeded at any point by storage of equipment, and Mr Henry is generally able to move around without over attention to alignment of the chair.

A common access problem of many such terraced houses is steps opening almost directly onto the pavement. Even where a small forecourt area affords the opportunity for ramping, the gradient needed is often too steep to be practical. The decision to lower the **floor** levels by 200mm might seem a radical solution but, in this instance, the property had rotten suspended floor timbers which were due to be replaced in any case. The decision to take advantage of this was a good one, but it is a pity that some of this advantage is lost by Mr Henry's difficulty in negotiating the raised water exclusion bar at the front doorway in his manual wheelchair.

The lowering of the back yard to bring it 150mm below the damp course level, as required by building regulations, necessitated the provision of **ramps** to bring the access level back up again for ease of wheelchair use. Limitations of space, however, meant that it was only possible to get a gradient of 1 in 12, which is rather too steep for Mr Henry's use.[1] The steep lateral slope to the drain for surface water run off seems unecessarily extreme and creates a further difficulty in a confined space where the wheelchair has to be turned through 180° against the slope of the ground.

Although several **electrical sockets** were installed in each room, these proved insufficient for Mr Henry's range of electrical equipment, especially in the living area. The use of adaptors to increase the number of outlets meant that raised sockets caused flex to trail down the wall in an untidy manner. Despite some dramatic teething problems, the **environmental control system** and **intercom door lock** are successful and allow use from several points in the flat. Substations allow Mr Henry a sophisticated degree of control without the need to constantly return to the core unit, which would be time and energy consuming in terms of his limited mobility.

Mr Henry finds the **kitchen** quite adequate to his needs. He relies heavily on packaged and processed foods, and his good organizational management has concentrated all the elements of food preparation into a confined area.

However, positioning of work surfaces along one long wall might prove more inefficient and tiring if he were required to do more cooking. The mobile storage trolley is useful as additional cupboard space and allows a flexibility in its use and that of the work surface under which it is generally housed.

In the **bathroom**, the positioning of the rails and the height of wc seat allows Mr Henry the exact requirements for independent transfer, and the washbasin and its surround is ideally sited for his use. It is regrettable however, that such near independence in showering still requires the visit of a nurse. As a mobile shower chair is not used, the fall to the centre grill of the shower floor might have been greater to eliminate the ponding that occurs.

The comparatively smooth operation of house adaptation and transition from residential care is attributable to good working relationships, communication and Mr Henry's own drive and experience. The team were able to recognise the potential in the house chosen and paid attention to detail in a comprehensive specification to which the builder adhered. Undoubtedly, Mr Henry found the project and the prospect of his own home again very stimulating, and used the energy generated, in conjunction with his knowledge of engineering, in a constructive way. The resultant independent living has been of unquestioned value in helping him to pick up the threads of his life again and to face a more positive future.

---

[1] Drainage grating for ramps, see page 199.

MR ALAN STOKES

Aged 35. Multiple sclerosis.

Separated, living with his parents.

Adaptation of a three bedroomed, local authority house into two self contained flats; one for a wheelchair user.

Confirmation in 1980 of the diagnosis of multiple sclerosis was a relief to Mr Stokes coming, as it did, after years of increasingly florid symptoms and inconclusive test results. This meant an end to energy being wasted on speculative experiment and the end of insinuations that some problems were hysterically based. Plans for a future, however difficult, could now be made.

Five years earlier Mr Stokes had suddenly found himself unable to walk across the car park one day after work. Three subsequent days of feverishness seemed to see the end of the matter, although he noticed that he tended to tire more easily and particularly in hot weather or after a hot shower. His work as a bass guitarist in a band began to suffer as he took longer to warm up for sessions and could not always manage the more intricate finger work at which he had been so successful. As difficulties increased, a consultant neurologist diagnosed peripheral neuritis, although it was at this time that Mr Stokes began to suspect his real condition, having come into hospital contact with multiple sclerosis sufferers whose symptoms appeared remarkably similar to his own.

In 1977 he left the band to marry and moved back to his home town where he found work with a firm of publishers. While the work was sedentary, it could only be reached via two steep flights of stairs and the office itself was on three floors. He managed the stairs for four years until, one humid September day, his legs collapsed under him, he failed to get beyond the first landing and had to be taken home. Two months later he resigned, acknowledging that his difficulty in walking, frequent falls and low tolerance to fatigue made it impossible for him to continue in the post. Some contact with the disablement resettlement officer followed, but no work was ever found. In the first weeks of unemployment his marriage failed and he returned to live with his parents in their five roomed rented cottage on the edge of a west country town.

Mr Stokes had been known to social services for some time and provision of minor aids and adaptations to the bathroom had been made. On his move, the occupational therapist referred him to her colleague in the new district and a visit was made in response to this and his own request for bath aids. The discussion that followed concluded that the cottage with its spiral staircase, single small reception room, presently being used as Mr Stokes' bedroom, and external door steps presented far greater problems than just the identified bathing ones.
A social worker was assigned who, with the occupational therapist, worked closely with the family to resolve the difficult living situation. Levels of independence that Mr Stokes could achieve were discussed as a means of ascertaining short and long term needs:

Mobility. Mr Stokes had difficulty in lifting his arms against gravity and could not get his hands above eyebrow level.

He could just manage to walk in the living area by supporting himself on furniture. He was unable to leave the house unaided because of steps at the external doors and could not propel an outdoor manual wheelchair very far owing to problems of fatigue. He accepted that future plans should encompass use of an indoor electric wheelchair.

Dressing. He could manage his top half with well chosen clothes, but needed considerable help from his father for the lower half.

Wc. He was independent with the support of a grab rail.

Bathing. A lot of help was needed for him to negotiate the rim and to rise from a bath seat.

Personal care. He was able to use an electric shaver by supporting his forearm to put his hand in a functional position. He could not reach his hair and had difficulty in gripping implements.

Eating and drinking. He used a mug for drinking and could manage food, except for cutting meat. He found the heat of a meal and the process of eating and digestion very debilitating.

Domestic tasks. Mr Stokes was interested in cooking, but found that the effort required to prepare even a simple meal left him with no energy or strength to eat it.

Hobbies and interests. His life revolved around music including composing and use of a computerized system to a four track mini studio.

Minor work, such as the installation of grab rails, was done but the main focus of intervention centred upon finding more suitable accommodation for Mr Stokes. Options considered were that the cottage be adapted and extended, that alternative and more suitable accommodation be found for Mr Stokes, or a move be made by the whole family. All agreed that the cottage had no feature to allow it to be considered for adaptation for a wheelchair user and the landlord, anyway, was totally resistant to the idea of major structural change.

No guarantee could be made that statutory agencies could meet the amount of care Mr Stokes needed if he lived on his own, and it was resolved that accommodation should be sought which would allow his parents to continue to support him, while giving some privacy to both. In addition, the property was to allow the independent use of a wheelchair and was to be within the area that Mr and Mrs Stokes senior had always lived and had their friends. Coincidentally, they were happier at the prospect of a move than they might have been, as recent building had reduced the size of their garden, with overlooking by the new development.

Mr Stokes had insufficient capital to be an owner occupier and was dependent on state benefits. Equally, his parents did not want to change habits of a lifetime and, close as they were to retirement age, probably could not have attracted a mortgage anyway.

Three applications were made and accepted onto the housing lists of two local authorities. One was made to Mr Stokes' previous authority for him to live alone with the support of a suitable package of care. Otherwise, the present and previous authorities were approached with the view to the three family members living together.

Ground floor flats were offered by each authority quite quickly, but were not found to be suitable: they did not allow good wheelchair circulation, they only marginally improved privacy, and one was in a remote area. Although the local authorities were sympathetic to the reasons for rejecting the properties, it was very difficult for the family to turn the flats down, as even a small improvement seemed attractive compared to their present situation. However, it was recognised that the move could not be viewed as a temporary one, as it was unlikely that authorities could go on making offers in response to the limitations of a second property, once a move had been effected.

The occupational therapist suggested converting a three bedroomed property into two self contained flats, giving a ground floor wheelchair standard one for Mr Stokes and first floor accommodation to his parents. Such a plan would allow levels of independence and privacy for all the family members and scope for possible changes in living arrangements, such as Mr Stokes remarrying. The occupational therapist and the social worker approached his old authority, whose area the occupational therapist also covered, and found them to be enthusiastic about the idea.

The case was discussed at the regular tenants' panel meeting and agreement was reached to look for a suitable property for conversion. A warning was given, however, that the plan could take some considerable time to realise, as they had only a few houses of a type thought to be suitable and none vacant. In addition, planning, funding and building arrangements would also be time consuming in such a major project. The family elected to hold out for this, as it afforded separate yet interdependent living. It was agreed that the occupational therapist would assess any property before an offer was made, to ensure that necessary facilities were, or could be, included.

There were many times in the following year of waiting that all seriously doubted whether they had made the right decision. Mr Stokes developed severe sciatic pain, thought to be as a result of infection from an early diagnostic test, which not only further restricted his mobility but also left him feeling very depressed. While relationships in the family were good, additional strain was placed upon them in the claustrophobic living situation and admissions to hospital for pain regulation were seen as a break for all and a positive factor in allowing Mr Stokes the opportunity of contact with new people.

In December 1982 the family were offered a council house in an area that they happened to most like and, despite its poor state of repair, accepted it with alacrity. The occupational therapist was then asked to view the property and, fortunately, agreed that it was suitable for adaptation and had features to commend it in terms of access and position. There was sufficient space at the side and rear of the site to allow for the extension that would be needed and the internal layout lent itself to reasonably easy conversion for wheelchair circulation.

The particular needs of Mr Stokes and of his parents, in relation to the property now identified, were discussed thoroughly and a site meeting set up between the occupational therapist, architectural assistant and housing manager from which the firm plans were formulated.

The housing manager warned Mr Stokes that it would be six to nine months from the start of building to completion, and this would only be after the lengthy process of making planning and funding arrangements. In practice, the latter took nine months and building five and a half with the move being made in February 1984. This period turned out to be the blackest time for the Stokes family, resulting in a desperation to move in ahead of schedule.

THE PROJECT TEAM
County council social services occupational therapist. Borough council principal housing management officer. Borough council technical officer.

THE AIMS
To promote independence and privacy in a living arrangement that could permit help to be given regularly and easily.
To provide facilities tailored to Mr Stokes' needs and to allow for possible future changes in living arrangements and health.
To facilitate individual and separate interests of family members in a setting of interdependence.

THE PROPERTY
A three bedroomed, semi detached house built in 1929.

Gross internal floor area 82.0m² before and 121.4² after adaptation.

The house was one of six properties built at the same time in a residential road on the outskirts of a village, close to a large west of England town. Considerable refurbishment needed to be done at the same time as the adaptations.

THE ADAPTATION
Conversion of a three bedroomed semi detached house.

* Lean to shed removed at rear of property.

* Two storey extension formed to give lobby and large bedroom to each flat.

* Single garage with up and over door built to side.

* Garage roof extended forward to cover concrete hardstanding area.

It had been hoped to allow a second bedroom, by division of the large living area in the upper flat, in case live in help was needed to support Mr and Mrs Stokes in the care of their son in later years. Costing of the whole project, however, came out higher than had been budgeted by the council and this had to be sacrificed along with decorating of the upper flat and a reduction in the planned patio size, as cost saving measures.

EXTERNAL DOORS AND PATHWAYS
* Original front door to property retained as main entrance to upper flat.

* Double glazed door with lever type latch lock and Duraflex threshold given to 840mm doorset, as main entrance to ground floor flat.

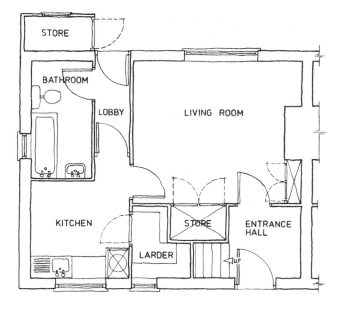

* Double glazed external door with mortice lock lever handle and Duraflex threshold installed to give immediate access to back garden.

* Delivery shelf made next to main door.

* 1830mm wide patio formed across width of house to new building and extended as a pathway to link with front driveway.

* Driveway lowered to give gentle gradient to dropped kerb at road and finished in concrete flag stones.

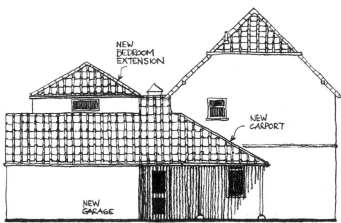

The south elevation.

* 5000 x 3300mm car port formed to front of garage.

Mr Stokes has no difficulty in using either of the main doors or in gaining access to much of the site via the pathways. The sheltered position of the patio makes it a pleasant place at which to sit and there are no problems of rain penetration at the back door threshold that is sheltered from the prevailing wind, and the front that is well protected by the covered way.

WINDOWS
* Existing plain glass units incorporating high ventilator openings retained.

* Windows in new building set to match with cill height of 850mm.

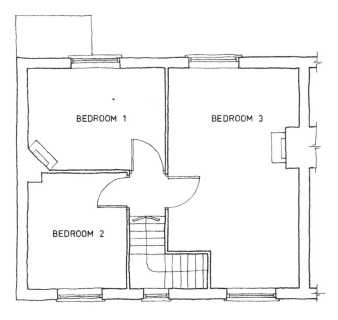

Ground and first floor plans before adaptation. 1:100.

Front of house showing new driveway with level access to pavement and road.

The garage and bedroom extension from the rear garden.

The low cill heights afford good visibility from a wheelchair but the ventilators are too high for Mr Stokes to reach and the kitchen one over the sink is inaccessible even from a standing position. One quarter light winding gear per room, to be operated at height 500mm, was allowed in the original specification, but was lost in the revision to reduce costs.

ELECTRICAL WORK

* Switched socket outlets and rocker light switches set at 800mm throughout.

* Double switched socket outlets at 1100mm above floor and 60mm above worktop installed in kitchen.

* Double switched socket outlet and light provided in garage.

* Intercom door lock installed to main door, with operational site mounted at height 800mm by living area door to hall.

* Fuse box set at 800mm from floor at side of chimney breast in living room.

Points and switches are all easily accessible, although the rocker switches are very stiff to operate. The close proximity of the socket outlets to the work surface makes insertion of plugs difficult for Mr Stokes, who needs to rest his forearm below the level of his hand for greatest functional capacity. His father arranges overnight recharging of the wheelchair batteries from the socket outlet in the garage.

HEATING

* Gas fired heating boiler mounted on wall in kitchen.

* Large single radiators installed to living area and bedroom.

* Small double radiators in entrance lobby, kitchen and bathroom.

* Thermostats set at height 800mm in living room.

* Central heating clock set at height 900mm adjacent to boiler.

The heating system maintains a warm and even temperature, which Mr Stokes supplements with a small fan heater for his feet in very cold weather. The central heating control clock is difficult to manage because of its close proximity to the boiler on one side and a switch on the other. Mr Stokes' fingers tend to get caught in the small gap and there is insufficient space for the finger flexion he needs in order to manipulate the dial.

HALLWAYS AND DOORS

* 2920 x 1235mm entrance lobby formed to open from inner hall leading off living area.

* Rear lobby access to kitchen blocked off by formation of airing cupboard and store.

* Door from front hall to living area retained.

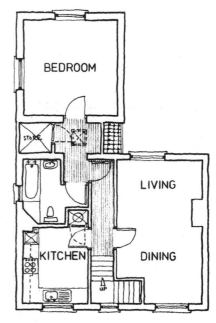

Plan of first floor flat. 1:150.

* All other doors on ground floor replaced by 860mm door sets and sliding doors operated by D handles.

The sliding doors run smoothly, can be easily opened by Mr Stokes and allow easy passage between the rooms. Doors are mainly left open, except in very cold weather, when the lobby needs to be closed off from the living area. If wishing to close a door, Mr Stokes backs into the room in order to be positioned to reach the D handle and this can be particularly difficult for him to manage from the confined space of the small inner hall into the living area.

LIVING AREA

* Fireplace blocked up.

* Built in cupboards removed from alcoves beside chimney breast.

* Storeroom access closed off from lounge, with new stud partition wall, and access given from original hall.

* Telephone point moved from hall to living area.

The size of the room is sufficient for a two piece suite, hi fi equipment, occasional tables and ample wheelchair circulation space.

KITCHEN

* Understairs larder retained.

* Hot water tank resited in new airing cupboard.

* 600mm deep worktops set at height 780mm and supported on metal props to floor.

* 140mm deep sink and single drainer at height 805mm, with 780mm width clearance under, installed below window.

* Ceramic hob mounted in adjacent worktop.

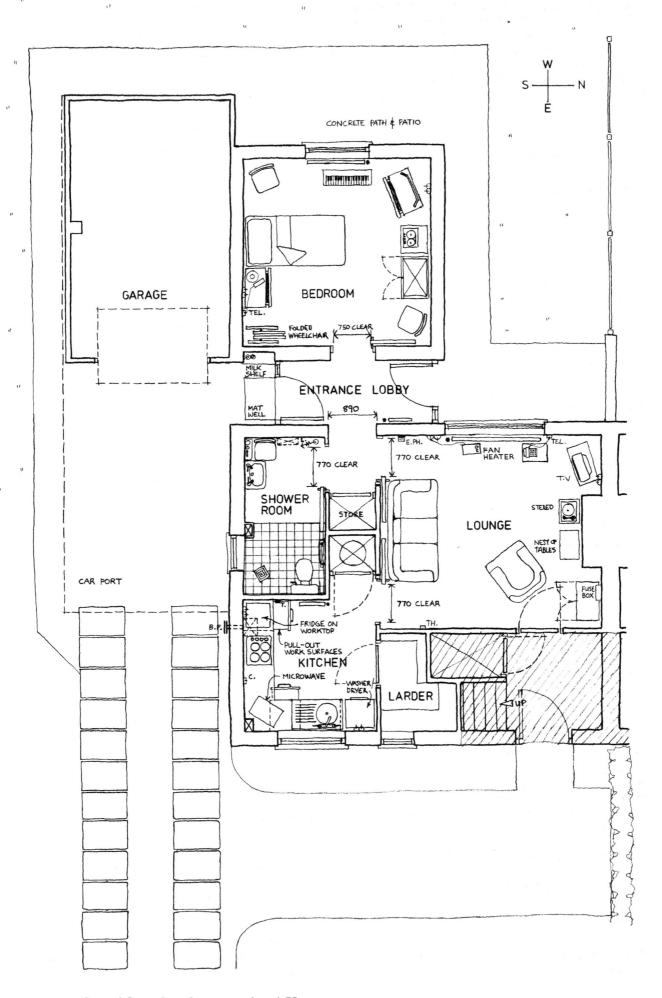

W
S — N
E

CONCRETE PATH & PATIO

GARAGE

BEDROOM

TEL.

FOLDED
WHEELCHAIR

750 CLEAR

MILK
SHELF

ENTRANCE LOBBY

MAT
WELL

890

CAR PORT

E.PH.

FAN
HEATER

TEL.

770 CLEAR

770 CLEAR

T.V

SHOWER
ROOM

STORE

LOUNGE

STEREO

NEST OF
TABLES

FUSE
BOX

770 CLEAR

T.

B.F.

FRIDGE ON
WORKTOP

TH.

PULL-OUT
WORK SURFACES

KITCHEN

C.

MICROWAVE

WASHER
DRYER

LARDER

UP

Ground floor plan after conversion. 1:75.

147

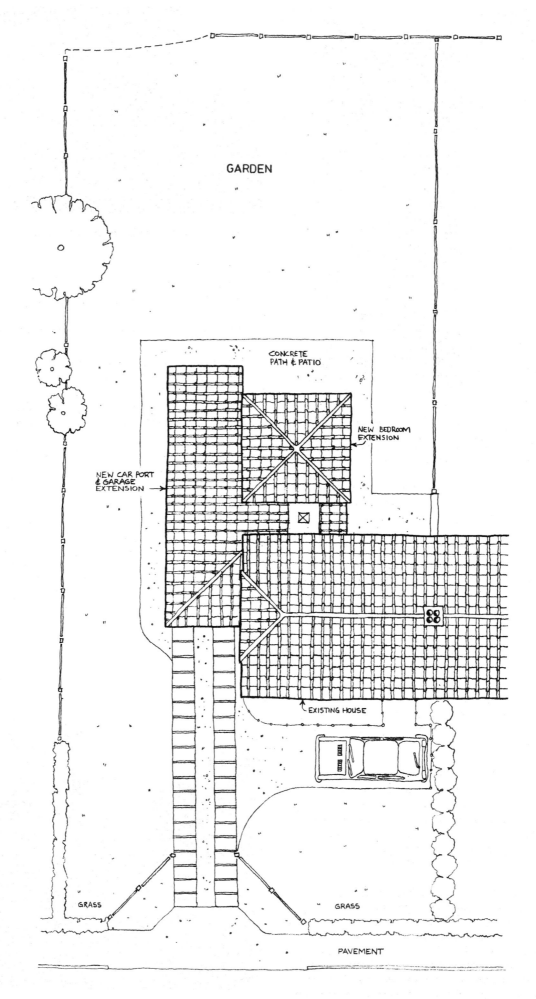

GARDEN

CONCRETE
PATH & PATIO

NEW BEDROOM
EXTENSION

NEW CAR PORT
& GARAGE
EXTENSION

EXISTING HOUSE

GRASS

GRASS

PAVEMENT

Site plan. 1:150.

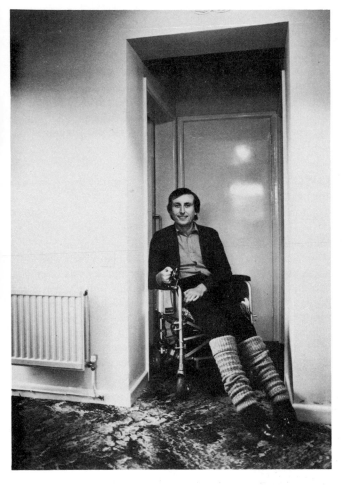

The turning space from the living room through the inner hall to the entrance lobby is tight, although Mr Stokes is able to cope by careful alignment of the wheelchair.

* Two sets of two drawer units with pull out work surfaces above set under worktop to allow footplate clearance of 280mm.

* Plumbing for automatic washing machine.

A sliding door to the larder had been proposed, but there proved to be insufficient wall space when the sitting room door was resited to allow positioning of the hot water tank and airing cupboard. In practice, however, Mr Stokes has no problem in gaining access to the large pantry although it is a disadvantage that the door has to open across the washing machine.

The system of worktops and drawer units works well and there is sufficient space for a top mounted refrigerator and microwave oven, which prove sufficient to Mr Stokes' needs. His limited involvement in domestic tasks and reliance on his mother led to the planning of a simple kitchen, meeting basic requirements and promoting efficiency in management by his carers.

Mr Stokes does little more in the kitchen than make hot drinks from a standing position, supporting himself on his old walking frame. Recent deterioration in his condition makes active lifting of his arms against gravity very difficult and he, therefore, finds it easier to work from a standing position. Mrs Stokes provides most meals from her kitchen upstairs and the microwave allows speedy provision of meals by a home help or Crossroads care attendants, who relieve Mr Stokes' mother on certain days of the week.

The wheelchair accessible kitchen work area.

BATHROOM

* Original wc, washbasin and bath removed.

* 440mm high seat, low level cistern wc installed.

* Wall mounted washbasin and lever taps, set to allow knee clearance of 600mm under.

* Floor excavated to give 1360 x 1550mm shower area sloping to an offset gulley and finished in non slip tiles.

* Mira 722 lever controlled shower mixer with pillar attached head fitted over.

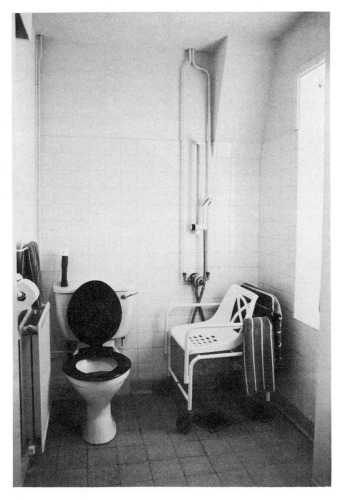

The wc and shower area.

* Mirror fronted cabinet, shelf and toothbrush holder added next to washbasin by Mr Stokes.

Mr Stokes transfers forwards to the wc, supporting himself on a securely fixed towel rail that is sited on the adjacent wall, and is independent in toileting. He transfers from the bed in the morning to the castor shower chair that he uses and is pushed into the shower area by a helper, from whence he showers independently.

The large size of the shower area and simplicity of fitments means that there is no requirement for a shower curtain and water drains away efficiently to the gulley. Mr Stokes sees no need for a grab rail by the wc when he can use the towel rail.

It had been intended to adjust the height of the washbasin and to install a grab rail by the wc before the builder left the site but, as this would have further delayed their move, Mr Stokes asked that the building be handed over for him to take responsibility for this work. He has intended to ask for alteration to the height of the washbasin, but has not got round to it and does not consider the difficulty to be great.

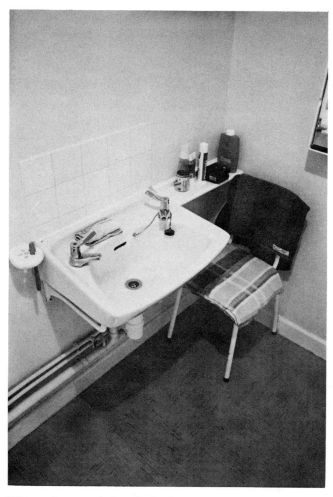

600mm clearance below the bathroom washbasin precludes access in either of the wheeled chairs and transfer to a kitchen chair is required for activities here.

BEDROOM
* Large bedroom constructed off entrance lobby with joists suitable to take overhead tracking, if required.

* Telephone point installed next to bed.

Mr Stokes has ample room for his music equipment in this room as well as furniture of a single bed, wardrobe, dressing table and bedside cabinet. The room was deliberately large on account of the required size of a double bedroom for his parents above, it being agreed that both flats should allow double occupation if necessary and that fluctuations in Mr Stokes' health might require him to spend additional time and have nursing care in this room. He does not use the wardrobe, as his mother organizes his clothes at his direction.

COSTING
1983/84
Total cost   £29,549.00

Estimate of the costing to the agreed specification for tender came out at approximately £29,000, which was above the budget allocation. The discrepancy was largely accounted for by extensive and originally unforseen work needed to the foundations of the extension, because of the position of a drain. The specification had to be revised to eliminate any refinements that were not essential to the wheelchair standard flat or the basic essentials of the accommodation above. The final costing included the sum of £1292.00 for the previously unforseen work.

FUNDING
Borough council HIP allocation   £29,549.00

CONTRACTUAL PROCEDURE
Tenders were invited by the borough council and the contract awarded to a local builder with no subcontracting involved.

EVALUATION

In a short space of time there had been the failure of a marriage, loss of work, considerable physical deterioration and a return to dependence on parents in a home that was no longer structurally suited to needs. That Mr Stokes and his parents coped with this and the very confined living arrangements is a tribute to the good relationships within the family. These were, however, strained to the limit as they waited for suitable accommodation and had to cope with extra pressures of pain and depression. While they were able to see the advantages of the final plan and to recognize that it was worth waiting for, it must have been tempting to opt for less useful, but vacant, accommodation. Equally, the staff who saw the strain under which the family were living must have worried about there being no time horizon for the move and questioned whether the situation could be held long enough for the plan ever to be effected.

Good working relationships existed between the social worker and the occupational therapist, both of whom supported the Stokes in the interim waiting period, and with the housing authority who were enthusiastic about the project and sympathetic to the needs of a family living in the private sector. In the main there was good communication among staff, although the oversight of not informing the occupational therapist about the property before the offer was made, and the hopes raised of the family, could have had a dramatic and serious effect on a family in crisis, had she found the house to be unsuitable.

In the event she was able to plan for a housing arrangement that had been her idea and could subsequently be suitable for other wheelchair users and their carers. In addition, the housing authority used a generous policy, as is their general practice towards the needs of disabled people, with importance attached to good design and informed briefing. In view of their committment to such projects, they were particularly disappointed to find that they could not qualify for any form of joint funding support. Careful planning and imaginative design of the conversion by the architect has led to the provision of an attractive home which blends well with the site and the area. Good wheelchair circulation is possible around the site and to the road, with the covered hardstanding providing sheltered **access** to the main door as well as space for a second car, if required on reallocation of the property.

Internal rooms are of a generous size and allow ease of movement, except at the lounge door to the inner **hall** where turning space is tight and would be impossible if Mr Stokes used extended footplates. As it is, he has to be very careful in alignment to avoid catching his feet on the wall and this grows more difficult as hand weakness limits the most precise control of the electric wheelchair.

Design and fittings have been kept simple and as such are very effective. The **bathroom** layout is good and allows ample space for the wheelchair or shower chair and an assistant, if necessary. The shower works efficiently and is still manageable for Mr Stokes, despite the recent deterioration in power of his arms.

It seems regrettable that he has to transfer to another chair to use the washbasin, and it cannot be recommended either that the towel rail be used as a grab bar, despite its firm installation. However, as Mr Stokes has used it consistently for a year without problem, it is perhaps understandable that he does not wish to bother with a change.

The **kitchen** is sufficient for Mr Stokes' needs and facilitates tasks required of a carer here. He could use the pull out work surfaces to provide a lower working height and therefore ease his problems of lifting his arms against gravity, but considers standing to be good practice and exercise.

There is sufficient **storage** provided by the large larder, easily accessible airing and hall cupboards with the size of the bedroom allowing for more freestanding units if required. Space is also available for musical equipment without wheelchair circulation space being affected.

Some detailing appears, however, to have been overlooked as with the siting of the central heating clock and the **sockets** placed too close to the worksurfaces in the kitchen. It also seems unecessary for the rocker **switches** to be so stiff and questionable why **windows** that Mr Stokes could have operated were omitted as a reasonable cost cutting exercise.

The overall impression of the project, however, is of unquestionable success. Members of the family have privacy which allows them to pursue their own interests and social lives within an arrangement that provides the help and support required in an uncomplicated manner. Mr Stokes depends greatly upon the care of his parents who are able to help efficiently and when required. In addition, they are supported by care attendants and a home help, which allows them some relief on prearranged days.

Mr Stokes enjoys his attractive and spacious flat in which he can entertain his own friends and pursue his interest in music in surroundings that need not interfere with the lives of others, in a manner he had felt unable to do in the small and overcrowded cottage. He is highly appreciative of the social services and housing authority staff who were very supportive to him and his family through a difficult period in their lives, and who were imaginative in helping to create the change and improvement to his situation. He acknowledges that this has allowed him the strength and possibility of resuming responsibility for his own life and planning for the future.

STUART HURRELL

Aged 12. Dystonia musculorum deformans.

Living with parents and younger brother.

Adaptation of a three bedroomed semi detached house.

It was Stuart's tendency to drag his left foot, apparent at the age of five, that prompted his mother to seek advice from their general practitioner. Referral was made to the paediatric department of the local hospital and then to a consultant neurologist specializing in children at a London teaching hospital. Over the next four years numerous tests were made and possible causes examined for his increasing clumsiness and numerous falls. No diagnosis could be made or treatment prescribed and the family became more anxious as Stuart's fine motor coordination, handwriting and school work were affected and he had a low tolerance to fatigue.

Shortly before his eighth birthday, the headmaster of Stuart's primary school suggested to the family that special education was required. He felt his school did not have the resources needed, and was concerned about Stuart's safety in the playground. The family were shocked, since Stuart was happy at school, was doing well academically and was settled at a time when many other things were uncertain about his future and medical prognosis. Their initial reaction was to resist a move, especially as Stuart could not understand why he was being judged as failing when he worked hard and was well placed in the class.

The education authority, not having a special school of its own, decided that a transfer should be made to one in a neighbouring London borough, and a place was offered. Mr and Mrs Hurrell were not happy that the decision was made without consulting them, but decided to visit the school and assess its potential for their son. They refused the placement however, on the grounds that low emphasis placed on academic achievement would be frustrating for Stuart, and they resolved to seek an alternative.

They found it difficult to get information and did not know to whom to turn for advice as their friends and aquaintances in the neighbourhood only knew about local schools, of which there were none offering special education, and could offer no suggestions as to resources that could be tapped. The family were not keen on the idea of residential schooling, but faced this as it seemed to be the only possibility until Mrs Hurrell was invited through a relative to join a group of parents of handicapped children in a neighbouring borough. Here she obtained support and advice and then visited several special day schools before finding a suitable one to which the education department could agree sponsorship and transport.

During this time, Stuart's medical diagnosis of dystonia musculorum deformans was made and the family told of its rarity and that physical impairment might be severe, although there would be no intellectual involvement. No indication could be given by the hospital of the speed at which effects might be manifest and it was recommended that treatment and management should be on the basis of dealing with symptoms as they arose.

The local hospital occupational therapist provided feeding aids and referred Stuart to a colleague in social services for provision of alterations to the home. In her working hours, Stuart was only available after school which was a time when he was most tired and, so as not to duplicate the numerous tests that he had undergone, much of the functional assessment done by the community occupational therapist was based on informal observation of Stuart, a history given by his mother and contact with the key workers in the two hospitals.

Mobility. Stuart's left foot tended to invert and he ran in a bizarre manner. Constant involuntary movement was present in the trunk and legs and manifested itself in clumsiness and difficulties in activities requiring fine movement and coordination.

Dressing. Mrs Hurrell had adapted fastenings with velcro and Stuart could dress independently providing he could sit with his feet on the ground to steady himself, using the assistance of gravity. Management of trousers and socks was most difficult.

Wc. He supported himself in sitting by keeping his feet on the floor, then pulled up on the toilet roll holder. He had difficulty in cleaning himself since, as soon as he let go of support, involuntary movements increased.

Bathing. Involuntary movement increased when his legs were in extension, as they were when sitting on the floor of the bath. His mother had difficulty assisting him owing to back pain, which increased as she reached over the high sides of the bath.

Chair. Stuart could sit most comfortably in a child's tubular steel framed chair used at home; he could hook his feet around the chair legs for support and so reduce involuntary movement.

Bed. He used a low divan bed, from which he had fallen on occasions.

Eating and drinking. He could use a combined knife and fork with a rocker action and a mug rather than a cup.

The occupational therapist supplied a shallow bath insert, adapted by the social services technician with stabilizing blocks to counter the effects of involuntary movement, a second bannister rail and rails on either side of the wc.

Stuart immediately liked the new school that he went to in September 1982. A taxi and escort was provided to transport him on the ten mile journey to and from home. The hospital, school and community therapists kept in close touch to ensure correct provision of equipment and adaptations necessary both at home and school, while a social worker in the local hospital remained as the keyworker.

In October, Stuart developed intense muscle spasm and his health deteriorated to the point where hospital admission became necessary. Heavy sedation was used to control muscle activity and he was often very poorly as attempts were made to gain control on a drug regime that sometimes had marked and unpleasant side effects. He was able to return home for Christmas, but could hardly walk or sit and was most comfortable in a prone position using extensor muscles in combination with gravity. Involuntary movement was intense; it increased on activity and it was often easiest for him to get around the house by wriggling on his bottom. He had to be carried up the stairs to the bathroom, wc and his bedroom on the upper floor, and his brother devised a method of getting him downstairs in a sleeping bag to watch early morning television, if their parents were not up to help. The occupational therapist supplied an armchair commode for use during the day when Mrs Hurrell was unable to get Stuart upstairs on her own, and in which he could be supported in sitting. A child's over wc commode chair was also tried, but proved too flimsy to sustain Stuart's strong movements.

Stuart returned to school and in February 1983 began using a wheelchair for distances and outdoor activities, of the type used by friends there and with which he had previously played. A change in transport to school to accommodate the wheelchair was organized and the community occupational therapist talked to the family about possible structural adaptation to the house. Their initial reaction was to avoid any further upheaval in a changing situation that was hard enough in itself to cope with. However, as Stuart's condition deteriorated they realized that longer term plans were necessary. They thought about moving to a bungalow, but found that most were outside their price range and would anyway need considerable adaptation. They also felt it important to remain in the neighbourhood where they were well known and Stuart had friends; his schooling outside the area and mobility problems made it harder for him to make new contacts.

The occupational therapist had considerable experience with similar properties in the area and suggested that the house was suitable for adaptation. An option considered was a lift; this was discounted on the grounds that it would be difficult for Stuart to operate alone, the family would lose essential living space, the bedrooms were small and the necessary reorganization of the first floor bathroom, wc and central corridor would have meant major adaptation with only limited useful results. They considered converting the garage but found that the construction material was inadequate and, as they would have lost their direct access to the rear of the property, discounted the idea of garage demolition and loss of use. While the two reception rooms had attracted them to the house at the time of purchase, they acknowledged that the best plan was to convert one room into a bedroom and add on a shower and wc on the ground floor. In terms of its access and general layout with the virtual impossibility of moving the wheelchair in the small kitchen, they decided to convert the kitchen to a wc and shower room, and replace it in an extension to the house. The occupational therapist obtained social services agreement to a reimbursement payment and the management support to press for additional living space to house the many large pieces of equipment used by Stuart. She arranged a joint visit with the borough council improvement grant surveyor who agreed the idea in principle and suggested that the family had plans drawn up for formal grant application and planning permission.

Since Stuart's prognosis was unclear, it was not easy to determine how much adaptation work should be done. The community occupational therapist could not so well identify changing requirements as the therapists who saw him regularly at the hospital in London or daily at school. Close contact was kept between the agencies, but staff at school were limited in the advice they could give by the lack of knowledge and medical guidance available on the rare condition and no appreciation of the house for adaptation. Good communication and working relationships were required both to plan the structural work and to devise equipment to maintain sitting posture, reduce effects of spasm and allow a means of communication as Stuart's speech became affected. Contact with the clinic at the local hospital was reviewed and considered an unecessary duplication to the work being done at the hospital in London and at school and, when the key social worker left, this role passed to a community social worker in the same team as the occupational therapist involved.

The community and hospital occupational therapists worked on finding a seating position for Stuart that was comfortable, supportive and helped reduce muscle spasm. It proved difficult for the DHSS appliance centre to keep up with the changing needs in wheelchair provision, as chairs offered could not meet such specific demands and technicians could not respond as quickly as was required. It was found that by tilting a chair insert to assist the effects of gravity, Stuart's involuntary movements were lessened. The best and most comfortable solution came to be inserting Tumbleform seating into Stuart's manual wheelchair, recommended by the London hospital occupational therapist and fitted, on special mountings, by the hospital technician. The results were successful, although this made a very large and high chair to manoeuvre around the house.

The community occupational therapist arranged through social services for the kerbs to be lowered both sides of the road at the house to facilitate wheelchair mobility when Stuart joined in outdoor games with his friends. The Hurrells commissioned a building surveyor who drew up plans for the house adaptation and made application for planning permission in June 1983. Changes in the layout of the shower room to allow for sideways transfer to the wc and provision of a new porch was requested by the occupational therapist and agreed by the family, who took on the management of the contract. The drawings were amended, submitted and approved and sent for copying to obtain builders' estimates. However, the plans were mislaid and considerable time was lost before anyone realized that they had not been returned from the incorrect addressee and that new ones needed to be drawn.

By the end of 1983 all estimates for the structural work had been received and were sent for improvement grant approval. Financial constraints in the grant authority meant, however, that formal agreement would not be made until the new financial year. The family felt unable to take the risk of commencing building work, as was suggested by the improvement grant officer, until the amount granted was confirmed in writing. This was done at the beginning of April, but by this time the builder was unable to give a commitment to commence until June for work he assessed would take eight weeks.

Towards the end of June 1984, work started and was still in progress at the end of October when Stuart was taken seriously ill and was admitted to hospital with uncontrollable muscle spasm. In the intensive care unit he was heavily sedated in an attempt to gain control of muscle activity. For three months Mrs Hurrell stayed at the hospital during each week and was relieved at weekends by her husband. No monitoring of the day to day building work could be made and little progress seemed to be achieved. The plan had been to minimize the extent to which building work would disrupt family life, but Mrs

Hurrell often returned at weekends to find the whole house dirty with construction dust and her washing machine, needed for the week's accumulated laundry, disconnected in the middle of a plumbing process. On one occasion the entire front garden was flooded with a delivery of ready mixed concrete and for some time there was no flooring to the central corridor, necessitating travel from the kitchen to the only useable reception room via the garage.

The builders finished work in February 1985 and although the workmanship was generally good, a few minor errors were never rectified as the family could not face the prospect of contractors again in the house.

As a result of the hospital treatment, Stuart's condition stabilized to the point where involuntary movement was controlled. An electric wheelchair with adapted controls and reclining supportive seating was supplied for independent mobility indoors. Referral was made to the community nursing service for an adjustable height bed that would allow Stuart to be washed and dressed at a height that was comfortable for his helper and could be lowered for ease of transfer. Nursing help was requested for management of bowel evacuation and this service developed into Stuart's inclusion on the evening back to bed round. Tube feeding that was needed for a while after hospital discharge was managed by Mr and Mrs Hurrell.

Planned or informally organized breaks evolved through the work of the community social worker and occupational therapist, using foster care funding, to provide a skilled friend for the family who could either act as a home sitter, or accommodate Stuart and his brother during the day in her own home, as required. It is intended that Stuart should be able to stay overnight, but adaptations are needed to the second house and there is no improvement grant eligibility. The social worker and occupational therapist are currently pursuing the idea of a portable cabin that could be moved elsewhere if changes so demanded.

THE PROJECT TEAM

Mr and Mrs Hurrell.
London borough social services occupational therapist.
Social worker.
Building Surveyor.
Improvement grant officer.

THE AIMS

To eliminate the need to use stairs.
To provide as flexible an environment as possible to accommodate any future and largely unknown changes in functional capacity.
To allow wheelchair circulation on the ground floor and to the exterior.
To promote educational and leisure activities and the overall needs of general family life.

THE PROPERTY

A three bedroomed semi detached house built in 1936.

Gross internal floor area 84.3m² before and 103.7m² after adaptation.

The house was part of a large private housing scheme in a quiet residential area. No change had been made to the layout of two reception rooms and a small kitchen on the ground floor with three bedrooms and a separate bathroom and wc above.

THE ADAPTATION

* Reorganization of the ground floor for wheelchair use.

* Kitchen chimney stack removed.

* Kitchen divided to form wc and shower room on one side and corridor on other.

* Flat roofed, single storey extension built to rear of property to form new kitchen and larger living room.

* Front reception room converted to bedroom.

The building line precluded extension of the house towards the road. Extension at the south facing rear used the light important to the lengthened room with only one wall available for windows. Woodworm infestation was found in the timber floorboards of the hall and these were removed and replaced with a new concrete floor, as in the shower room and the new extension.

EXTERNAL DOORS AND PATHWAYS

* Front porch removed and replaced with storm porch of 1920 x 850mm internal dimensions and inward opening door.

* Original front door retained and hall floor ramped to 40mm raised threshold.

* Inward opening, half glazed rear door made to new kitchen, and 130mm long concrete ramp installed to internal 45mm raised threshold.

* Level platform at porch door and 1 in 32 concrete ramp with 90mm brick upstand kerb edges formed to front pathway.

* Level platform and 1 in 20 ramp with brick upstand edges made from rear doorway over new concrete patio area in garden.

Access through the front porch is straightforward. The gradients of the ramps are gentle and the inward opening doors do not impede access over the platforms. However, the builder originally omitted the platform at the rear, a fault identified while he was still on site, and had to alter the ramp after it had been completed. The ramp was not lengthened, however, and a raised cill was formed at the

The door threshold is difficult to negotiate in a wheelchair, but is eased to some extent by the internal concrete ramp installed by Mr Hurrell.

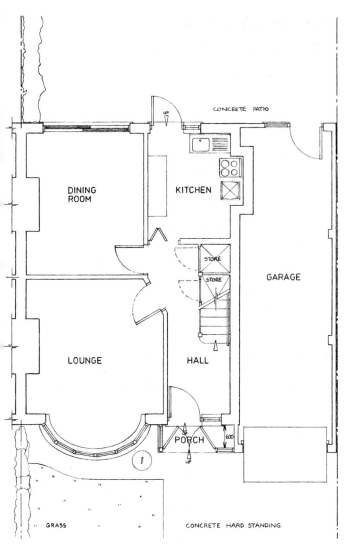

Ground floor plan before adaptation. 1:100.

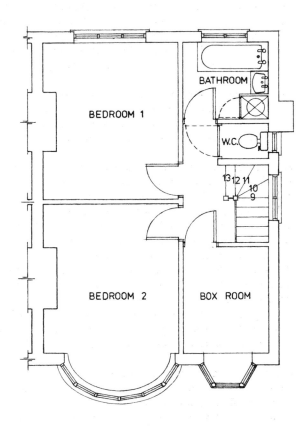

First floor plan, unaltered. 1:100.

lower end of the run. The Hurrells could not face the prospect of the builder's return to rectify this, and the 40mm appro can be negotiated reasonably well in an electric wheelchair.

The family intends to extend the small patio and to give paved access to all the garden. In the meantime the patio is a sufficiently large sitting out area for all the family with one side of the ramp forming a boundary.

WINDOWS

* Window in rear wall of garage blocked up and internal wall lined with insulating material and plasterboard.

* Window to original kitchen blocked up.

* Casement windows installed in new rear wall to give light and ventilation to new kitchen and extended living area.

The decision not to resite the patio doors from the old living area external wall to the new one was difficult for the family to make, as maximum light was required and they enjoyed the good view of the garden. However, space for wheelchair access to the doors could not be preserved in the now single reception room and they considered that two rear doors, each with a ramp, would create too great an impact upon the rear garden.

Front view of the property.

ELECTRICAL WORK

* Double power points set at height 1070mm in living area, front room, hall and over work surfaces in new kitchen.

* Light switches installed at height 1070mm throughout ground floor.

* Additional lighting given to exterior over rear ramp.

* Extractor fan operated automatically with light switch installed to shower room to give three air changes per hour, with outlet over garage roof.

* Sufficient points were allowed in the front room for use of a television, cassette player, hairdryer and lamp and, over the proposed position of a work surface, for a computer and other appliances for school and leisure activities.

HEATING

* Balanced flue gas boiler mounted on wall in kitchen extension and connected to existing radiator and hot water system.

* Long single radiator in hall replaced by double to give same capacity in less space, and sited on opposite wall.

* Low level double radiators installed to front room, shower room and kitchen.

* Large double radiator and single one installed to extended living area.

The house can be kept warm easily and relatively economically. The radiator was moved in the hall so that it did not impede wheelchair access to and from the front door, and the low level radiators in the kitchen, bathroom and bedroom were to allow installation of worksurfaces or vanitory unit over.

HALLWAYS AND DOORS

* Suspended timber floor replaced by concrete floor.

* Frame to original kitchen door removed and archway formed over.

* Corridor extended to new kitchen.

* Rear reception room doorway blocked up and new opening formed opposite that for new shower room.

* Sliding door with finger panel and mortice lock set to shower room.

* All ground floor doorways widened to give clearance of 790mm and front room door rehung to open against wall.

The hall was planned to be a wheelchair cleaning area with vinyl flooring, which would avoid soiling of carpets in other rooms when the wheelchair is brought in from outdoors in wet weather. The design of the ground floor with its central corridor meant that turns into rooms in a wheelchair would be tight, despite wider doorways. Stuart now needs to use a reclining chair, with a much longer wheelbase than he did at the time of planning, and the chair has to be manually pivoted for turns to some doorways, with consequent risk of damage to paintwork.

Rear view of the property.

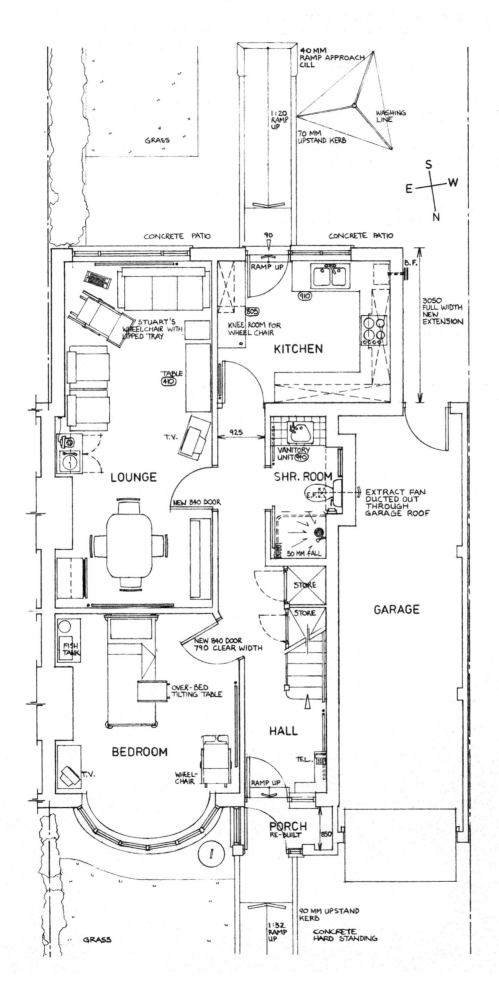

Ground floor plan after adaptation. 1:75.

The hallway.

A sliding door to the bathroom preserves space both in the hall and the room. The lightweight door and sliding mechanism works easily with a mortice lock on a block fitted to the door frame.

LIVING AREA

New decorations and carpeting made to extended rear reception room.

The sitting room furniture was removed from the front room to form a new arrangement in the extension. The living room is sufficiently large to allow use as a dining room and sitting room and yet allows reasonable wheelchair circulation and access to the television and other equipment for Stuart.

The sitting end of the living room viewed from the dining area.

KITCHEN

* Rendering removed from old external wall and surface plastered to match new walls.

* Floor and wall units, double sink, hob and oven purchased by family from specialist kitchen supplier and fitter.

* Matching 810mm high work surface with knee room under and drawers to side fitted specifically for Stuart's use.

Provision had originally been planned of a microwave oven, remote control taps and knee room under the sink to allow use from sitting. When Stuart's condition deteriorated, it was decided to omit the features and allow their provision at a later date if required.

Stuart has clear access into and through the kitchen to the back garden. All the family is pleased with the new layout and fitments.

BATHROOM

* Low level wc with 400mm seat height, and washbasin with corner set lever taps inset in 940mm high vanitory unit installed to converted old kitchen.

* Thermostatically controlled shower with pillar attached head sited over dished floor area falling to 160mm diameter gulley.

* Entire floor area covered in Altro safety flooring extended with sealed joints to height 100mm up walls.

While Stuart is no longer able to achieve the sideways transfer to the wc that was allowed for in planning, the space provided enables assistance for transfer to the Chailey shower/commode chair that was modified to give a less upright sitting position. The vanitory unit allows ample space for storage of personal items within easy reach of a helper for the shower and wc. Boxing in of pipework underneath does however, impede access to the wheelchair footplates and caused the basin to be too far away for Stuart's own use or for optimum help from a carer. Transfer from the wheelchair to the shower chair is made in the bedroom, where Stuart is undressed lying down, being then pushed to the bathroom and helped with showering.

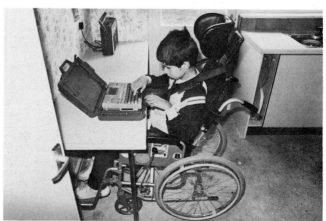

The worksurface with knee room under allows Stuart to participate in kitchen activities or do homework.

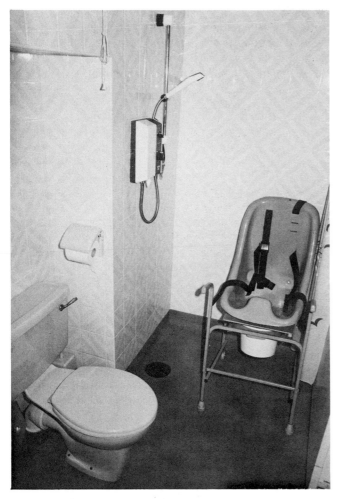

The wc, Chailey chair and shower area.

BEDROOM

* Front reception room converted to bedroom and floor covering replaced in short pile carpet tiles.

A body worn alarm call system is used at night, easily heard in his parents' bedroom on the upper floor. The flooring presents no impediment to the movement of a wheelchair and tiles can be individually lifted and replaced by spares for cleaning of any spillages. The family intend to complete the room eventually with shelves and a notice board so that Stuart has immediate visual access to his belongings. They feel that without the ability to tidy

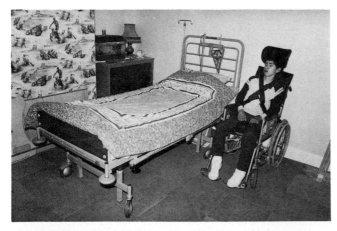

The bedroom allows ample space for Stuart's adjustable height bed, drip stand, wheelchair storage and electrical equipment.

cupboards or search for items when trying to find something to do, he would lose awareness of his posessions and their stimulation.

COSTING

1984

Building work	£14,500.00
Kitchen units and fitting	2,300.00
Fees	330.00
Total ex. VAT	£17,130.00

VAT exemption was given on the ramps, bathroom fitments and door widening to the sum of £6,000.00. No exemption was given on the structural work of the extension as would have been allowed had it been a new provision of a bathroom rather than a replacement kitchen.

FUNDING

Improvement grant 75% of maximum £13,000 and revised on account of changes in VAT legislation	£10,350.00
Client contribution	6,280.00
Social services reimbursement payment	500.00
Total	£17,130.00

CONTRACTUAL PROCEDURE

The builder was contracted by Mr and Mrs Hurrell, to whom the improvement grant was paid directly.

EVALUATION

Planning the type of structural work and the features to be incorporated was exceptionally difficult as so little was known of the course of Stuart's condition. In addition, time could not be exclusively allocated to the adaptation work by staff or the family owing to crises in his health and the need to find solutions to problems of posture, communication and mobility. At one stage the house adaptation was being planned by staff who could see Stuart least often and had to depend on questioning and reporting skills of others. The fact that the project was ultimately successful is of merit to the close working relationships, good communication and thorough research of the staff involved.

The loss of the original plans, the temporary embargo on improvement grant applications and the protracted building work added pressure to the family at a time that was already stressful. The adaptations project took a disproportionate amount of time to achieve and the family were not supported in their absence from the home by any successful attempt to get the builder to finish the work more quickly.

The house did not lend itself to any simple adaptation solution owing to its limited size, layout and the juxtaposition of rooms. An advantage was that the two reception rooms had not already been adapted to form one room, as was popular for the type of housing in the area, and the front room could be a ground floor bedroom.

Division of the kitchen into a shower room and a corridor disposed of a room that was not suitable or easily converted for use in a wheelchair. The layout of the shower room was however important as space was confined. The extension to form a new **kitchen** allowed a room in which Stuart could freely move in his wheelchair and which enabled all the family to be present at once. Circulation space here also duplicates as the line of direct access to and from the external rear door and the garden.

Without the extension to the rear reception room the adaptation would not have been nearly so successful, as **living** space would have been very constrained and would have left little scope for placement of Stuart's large wheelchair in the family group for watching television and other activities. The inclusion of this extension in the application for funding through an improvement grant was an important factor in encouraging the family to go ahead with the plan.

The gradients of the two **ramps** are sufficiently gentle for Stuart to manage in his electric wheelchair and do not present any problems to the people who push him in the manual chair. However, the raised cills at the external doors are an obstacle as the electric wheelchair has to be lifted over the thresholds and its independent use is therefore eliminated. Some improvement has been made by Mr Hurrell with the small ramp inserts and he intends to work further upon this in preference to the return of the builder, who it was intended should have done this work originally.

Turns to and from the narrow central corridor are difficult at the living area and bathroom **doors**. The door openings, even though they have been widened, proved insufficient when Stuart needed a reclining chair with consequently increased size wheelbase. It is hoped that Stuart will eventually be able to tolerate a more upright sitting posture, thereby eliminating a long wheelbase, and use a proportional control electric wheelchair that would make driving more precise and facilitate turns into rooms. Finding the optimal seating and equipment for Stuart remains a challenge as he gets bigger and his needs change.

The **shower room** layout has proved flexible enough to accommodate changes in equipment required, with assisted rather than independent use of the room. It is easily reached from Stuart's bedroom, promoting efficiency in managing personal care. The **bedroom** is also sufficiently large for access with a large wheelchair and permits educational and leisure pursuits in a quiet atmosphere. In such a compact house, Stuart's ground floor bedroom is not a great distance from the rest of the family and his alarm call can be easily heard on the upper floor.

The family is a close knit one, with members who have sustained each other through many difficult and uncertain times regarding Stuart's health. They are supported by good community services and an imaginative use of foster care that allows Stuart and his brother a sitting service, the stimulation of a change of environment for them and a break for their parents from the demands of continuous care.

The consultant neurologist who treated Stuart acknowledged that, for lack of confidence as to how Stuart's condition would evolve, he could only respond to problems that presented. The adaptations team could not tackle their job in the same way since such short term management aims could not be applied in planning major structural work aimed to meet future as well as present needs. For the staff responsible for the task, planning challenged the good practice of using thorough and

informed advice as the basis for response. The results achieved are, therefore, a credit to the good relationships of the staff and the family and their ability to combine thought and resources in a manner that allowed the skills and experience of each to be flexibly utilized.

MISS JANE THOMAS

Aged 36. Cerebral palsy.

Living with her mother and stepfather.

Adaptation of a chalet bungalow.

Jane Thomas was born at home, two and a half months prematurely and weighing two and a half pounds. By the sixteenth day, her weight had dropped to two pounds and her legs began to swell. She was admitted to hospital, where she was kept in an incubator for the next six months, by which time her weight increased to nearly seven pounds and she was allowed home.

As the baby grew, Mrs Thomas became concerned that her daughter did not reach the normal development milestones and during a holiday at her sister's London home, she had the baby referred to a consultant paediatrician at a specialist hospital for children. Cerebral palsy was diagnosed, attributed to injury caused during the fifty hours of labour and the breech birth. No referral was made for treatment or further contact and the family returned home to Wales. Mr Thomas and his mother had great difficulty in coming to terms with the diagnosis, and when Jane was three years old, he and his wife separated.

Although assisted by her mother, Mrs Thomas had no other support physically or financially in the care of her child and returned to her previous occupation as a hairdresser. From the age of five to sixteen, Miss Thomas attended a school for the physically handicapped, initially as a boarder and later as a day pupil. She used a wheelchair for mobility, but had little other attention or practice in independence skills with problems of adduction deformities at her hips only highlighted when she came to cope with menstruation. A tendon release of the shortened adductors was performed, allowing her to walk short distances with a frame, for the first time at the age of fifteen.

A year later, back problems prompted a referral from their general practitioner to a consultant orthopaedic surgeon. He diagnosed scoliosis, but was not prepared to operate and suggested the use of a spinal support corset. Miss Thomas found, however, that she could not adjust to wearing this and her spine remained unsupported.

At the age of sixteen, Miss Thomas left school. A series of twenty three operations followed, concerned with tendon release in her hips, feet, ankles and wrists and laminectomies to improve circulation and remove the pain in her legs. When able, she worked as a receptionist in her mothers thriving hairdressing business and lived at home with her mother caring for her.

In 1970, Mrs Thomas remarried and her husband, Mr Jones, came to live with them in their bungalow on the edge of a seaside town in south Wales. In 1978, Mr Jones had to retire early from his work as a transport supervisor following a gastric haemorrhage and surgery to remove part of his stomach, and the development of emphysema. At the same time Mrs Jones was diagnosed as having a hiatus hernia, angina and disc problems as a result of many years of lifting her daughter.

Affected by all these problems, they recognised that the bungalow was unsuited to their needs, and in 1980 purchased a chalet bungalow on a new estate in a less hilly area, nearer the sea and the town's amenities. It proved much easier to take Miss Thomas out in her wheelchair and Mr Jones found he could manage his breathing difficulties with less frequent use of oxygen. However, in the same year, he had an acute attack of rheumatoid arthritis and became dependent on his wife for many aspects of daily living.

At about the same time, Miss Thomas developed very severe headaches and it was found that her spine had started to collapse. She was admitted to a university orthopaedic hospital in September for surgery to insert spinal rods and was encased in a full length plaster for seven months, during which time she came home in time for Christmas. In the meantime her stepfather's health had deteriorated following three heart attacks. To limit his use of the stairs, social services provided a chemical wc in his first floor bedroom, the only wc being on the ground floor. At the same time the social services occupational therapist was alerted by the hospital of Miss Thomas' impending discharge and arranged provision of a mobile hoist with a divided leg sling, mobile commode chair with footrests, spring lifter seat, bed raising blocks, a cantilever table and temporary ramps to the side door.

Miss Thomas arrived home feeling very unwell and vomiting. In hospital she had not been able to use a bedpan from the horizontal position in which she had to be nursed and was, in effect, incontinent. Mrs Jones found she could not reach her arms around the plaster to lift in the manner to which she was accustomed, and rapidly had to learn to depend on the hoist. The day to day practicalities of managing the new equipment, the cumbersome plaster and Mr Jones' poor health made it a difficult and testing time for the family.

A short time after her discharge from hospital, Miss Thomas developed a thrombosis in her leg and was admitted to a local hospital. On her recovery and discharge, a Crossroads care attendant was organized to get her up in the morning and onto the castor commode chair, which could be pushed over the wc without the need for transfer, and Mr and Mrs Jones were able to get her back to bed at night. She was far from comfortable in the plaster; when it was finally removed it was discovered that the acute pain in her right hip had been caused by a disclocation. Surgery to relocate the head of femur and a period in a frog plaster followed before she was free of plaster for the first time in nearly a year.

Mr Jones' health improved, although he still needed to spend time in bed, and the family decided to install a washbasin and wc in the en suite dressing room of the front first floor bedroom. The occupational therapist suggested an improvement grant, but the Jones decided to go ahead on their own, and found the additional facilities when completed to be very helpful.

In the following two years Mrs Jones continued to care for her daughter, using methods with which they were most familiar. There was some contact with social services for the provision of aids, and in 1982 the occupational therapist arranged provision of an Autolift bath hoist. Positioning was not straightforward because of the small size of the bathroom; the resting position over the bath impeded access to the washbasin and they needed to keep the door open to ensure sufficient space for transfer from the wheelchair.

The occupational therapist, aware of the shortcomings of the situation, began discussions with the family about structural adaptations to the ground floor. The problems centred on Miss Thomas' inability to use the stairs, her difficulties in the bathroom and in gaining wheelchair access to the house and kitchen. In addition, her stepfather was able to offer little in the way of help, because of his own poor and fluctuating health, and her mother had a hiatus hernia and back problems.

Options considered were to move into council owned, purpose built accommodation or to adapt the present house. The Jones were reluctant, however, to consider a move to council property as Mrs Jones felt particularly proud of the fact that she had brought her daughter up without support, developed her business into a thriving one and had bought her own bungalow, which she did not wish to give up.

A stairlift was investigated to give access to the upper floor, particularly for Mr Jones, but the small size and layout of the accommodation made this impractical. An externally mounted lift shaft as an alternative was discounted by the family as major work was unwarranted when the dining room could be converted into a bedroom for Mr Jones, if needed, and Miss Thomas could live quite satisfactorily on the ground floor.

To gain a clearer picture of the methods and equipment which might promote independence, the occupational therapist referred Miss Thomas and her mother to a national assessment and rehabilitation centre. During the six month wait to gain a place, Miss Thomas was admitted to hospital with suspected meningitis which, on investigation, was associated with a protruding spinal rod at the top of the spine; shortly afterwards, the other became detached at the base and both had to be removed.

Early in 1984 Mrs Jones and Miss Thomas attended the assessment centre and a report was made to the referring occupational therapist.

Mobility. Miss Thomas used a DHSS self propelling chair in which she was pushed. Sitting balance was poor, she had pain in a hip and walking was limited to short distances with a frame. There was increased muscle tone in adduction and extension, but a general decrease in muscle power. Her mother transferred her using a pivot method. A different type of hoist and a hammock sling were recommended, along with a castor commode chair for use over the wc.

Dressing. She was dressed by her mother.

Wc. She was dependent on her mother for all assistance. A Clos o mat was recommended.

Bathing and personal care. She was dependent in all aspects of personal care. Washing was done as she sat on the wc and a bath hoist was successfully used, although the size of the bathroom at home made this less than ideal.

Bed. Her mother helped in all transfers and slept beside her when she was known to need help following operations or in ill health. Miss Thomas was otherwise able to sufficiently adjust her position in bed.

Eating and drinking. She had good grip and fine finger dexterity, but full functional use was lost by increased spasm on effort. She needed food to be cut up, but was able to feed herself using a knife and fork that she did not wish to see adapted. Involuntary spasm meant that she was unable to hold drinks safely and so she used a straw.

Domestic tasks. She thought she might be interested in cooking, but was unable to get into the kitchen in her wheelchair and was not required to carry out any domestic activity.

Hobbies and interests. She was active in youth leadership, enjoyed swimming, embroidery and horse riding and sought opportunities for public speaking, particularly on the needs of disabled people.

On their return to Wales, the hoist was supplied as requested, but Miss Thomas and her mother soon returned to their previous methods of lifting and transfer. The hoist was retained, however, for use in the convalescent stages of proposed further surgery on her spine. The occupational therapist felt that an overhead tracked hoist might be managed with more confidence, but the family were not prepared to have such an obtrusive piece of equipment in the bedroom. A rotating car seat was supplied and successfully used to ease methods of transfer to and from the car.

Application was made for an improvement grant in principle, but it was found that there would be a three month delay for approval until the new financial year. Mr Jones drew a sketch plan of the proposed work, which was discussed on site with the occupational therapist and the grant officer, and a draughtsman drew up the plans for grant and planning permission application. The specific requirements were detailed in a letter from social services to Mr Jones and this formed the basis upon which he sought three estimates from builders. He appointed a contractor who was already known to have done work to a high standard for another disabled person and application was made to social services, through the senior occupational therapist, for a grant to meet the IO per cent shortfall in the agreed eligible sum for the improvement grant. The work commenced in October 1984 and took approximately six weeks. Mr Jones immediately reengaged the builder for the project of widening the entire garage, in preference to the provision in the grant to install a wheelchair accessible door with a canopy.

THE PROJECT TEAM

County council social services occupational therapist.
Borough council improvement grants officer for handicapped and disabled people.
Mr Jones.

THE AIMS

To give wheelchair access to the property, throughout the ground floor and to allow transfer from a wheelchair to the car, under cover.
To provide facilities suitable to the needs of two disabled people.
To permit conversion of another ground floor room to a bedroom as a future option.
To allow some domestic involvement, if desired.

Front view of the chalet bungalow.

THE PROPERTY

A semi detached chalet bungalow built in 1980.

* Gross internal floor area 95.5m² before and 103.8m² after adaptation.

The property was constructed in a cul de sac as part of a small housing estate on the edge of a seaside town. Level access was possible to local shops and the town centre and sea, some mile and a half away. There was a small garden to the front and rear with driveway access to a single garage.

Subsequent to their move, when Mr Jones' health demanded that he have accessible facilities without using the stairs, the family installed a wc and washbasin in the en suite upper floor dressing room, with half height louvre doors to divide the area from the bedroom.

THE ADAPTATION

Extension of a bungalow to give increased bathroom and kitchen space and facilities.

* Double steel box lintol inserted in external wall of kitchen and brickwork below removed.

* Construction of flat roofed extension with concrete blockcavity walls and glass fibre insulation.

* External walls finished in smooth white render to match rest of house.

* Internal wall between kitchen and bathroom removed.

Rear view of the property.

* 100mm concrete block wall formed in old kitchen area to give larger bathroom.

* Garage widened 640mm by repositioning of external side wall constructed in concrete blocks with piers and damp proof course.

* Timber joists extended over new wall and corrugated asbestos cement roof and concrete floor extended into new garage area.

* Opening of 838 x 1981mm made in new wall to garage adjacent to house and externally hung sliding door fitted.

The car is reversed into the garage and transfer is possible from the wheelchair to the pivoting front passenger seat in the garage as a result of the widening. The sliding door gives a clear access to the house that was not previously possible at the narrow rear door from the garage to the garden.

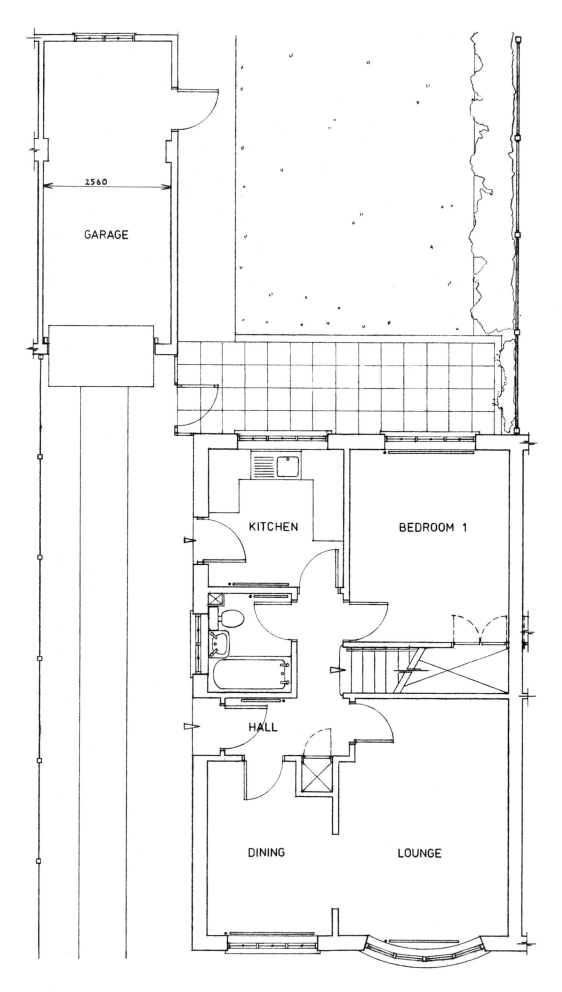

2560

GARAGE

KITCHEN

BEDROOM 1

HALL

DINING

LOUNGE

Ground floor plan before adaptation. 1:75.

MR AND MRS JONES' BUNGALOW.

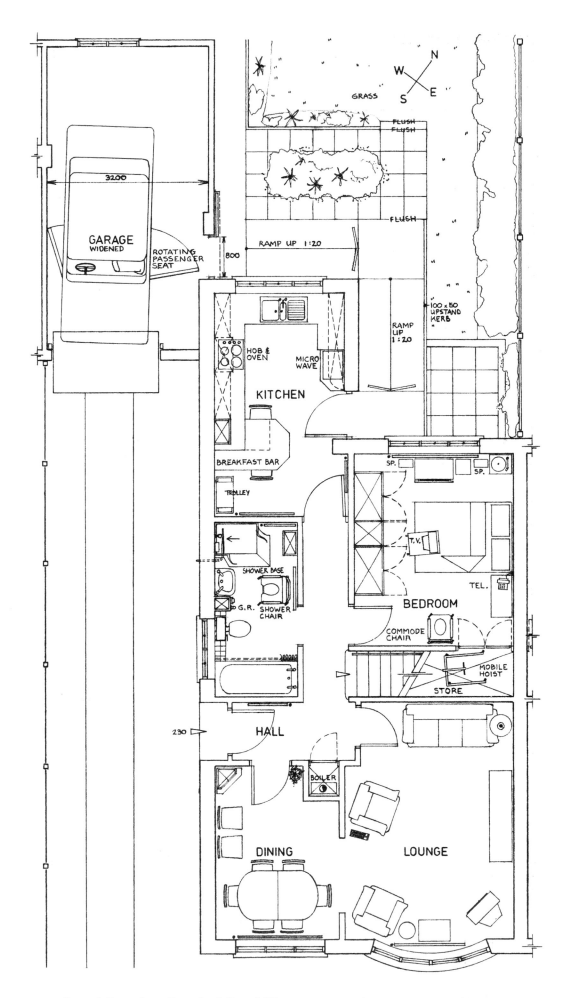

Ground floor plan after adaptation. 1:75.

MR AND MRS JONES' BUNGALOW.

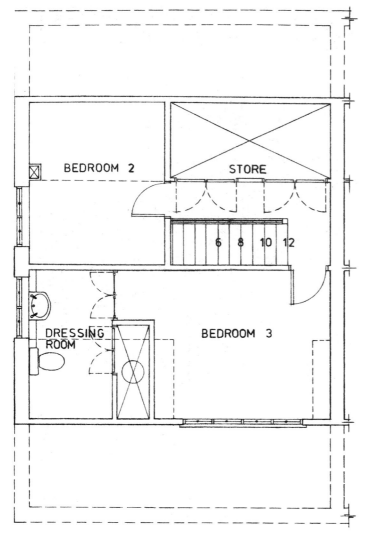

First floor plan. 1:75.

EXTERNAL DOORS AND PATHWAYS

* Fully glazed back door with lever handle and mortice lock installed in side wall to kitchen, giving clearance width of 775mm.

* Pre formed storm guard threshold inserted in concrete.

* 1200mm and 1300mm wide ramps with 100mm kerb upstands laid from back door to garden and to garage with overall gradient of 1 in 20.

Wheelchair access to the house is via the garage, ramps and back door. The ramps also give access from the house to the rear garden, the small paved area and the lawn, and are of sufficiently gentle gradient for easy management by Mrs Jones in pushing her daughter in the wheelchair. The threshold strip has been installed to give a 25mm upstand at the point where the ramp meets the door, which necessitates backward tipping of the wheelchair to negotiate it.

The 230mm high step and raised weather bar in the small porch of depth 550mm could not be easily ramped and the approach would have needed to extend across vehicular access to the garage. The garden is neatly laid to lawn and shrub borders with plants chosen for ease of maintenance by Mr Jones, who spends a short time most days on the work. Miss Thomas does not do any work in the garden.

WINDOWS

* Old kitchen window resited in new extension with cill height of 1050mm.

The kitchen cill is too high to give a useful sight line from a wheelchair, but the fully glazed back door gives a view over the patio and flower borders at the side of the new extension. A large bay window at the front of the south facing house has a cill height of 710mm and allows good views of the front garden and roadway.

ELECTRICAL WORK

* Additional lighting given to kitchen.

* Light installed over shower area, with pull cord switch in corner of room.

* Power points installed over work surfaces in kitchen and under sink.

* Additional power point in garage for freezer.

* Electrical connection made for shower, with pull cord isolation switch in kitchen.

All other switches in the house were left at a standard height of 1380mm with sockets at 350mm above floor level, but there is no necessity for Miss Thomas to operate any of them. She can reach the power point under the sink, which was sited well forward to allow her to use it for the washing machine, should this be necessary in the event of both Mr and Mrs Jones being unwell.

HEATING

* Radiator, removed from first floor at time of dressing room adaptation, sited in kitchen with addition of new radiator.

* Radiator resited on new wall beyond shower base from original position next to wc.

All radiators are fed from a gas fired boiler sited in the hall. The 630mm long radiator gives sufficient heat to the bathroom in a generally warm house. The two radiators at the dining end of the kitchen make this a very comfortable area to sit in, as appreciated by Miss Thomas when she joins her mother in the room during meal preparation.

HALLWAYS AND DOORS

* Side hung inward opening door to bathroom removed.

* New opening formed with sliding door leaf of 840mm and clear entrance width of 680mm.

* Knob fitted to each side of sliding door.

* Door to kitchen resited in new opening, giving clear width of 780mm.

The position of the bathroom door opposite the bedroom gives direct wheelchair access between the rooms. The turns from the 905mm hallway into either of the rooms are, however, a little tight and would be more difficult if the wheelchair were self propelled. The position of furniture and opening of the door into the lounge impedes wheelchair access, so Miss Thomas is wheeled through the dining room to the main living area.

LIVING AREA

Miss Thomas usually sits in the archway that connects the rooms when the lounge is being used. From this position, she has a good view of the whole room and the television and is close to the bay window that lets in maximum sunshine during the day.

KITCHEN

* New kitchen fitted with storage units operated by large D handles, to incorporate built in oven, hob, double sink and drainer, washing machine and refrigerator.

* 1500 x 1000mm peninsular unit of breakfast bar over storage cupboards, with knee clearance of 720mm height and 390mm depth.

* Small corner shelf mounted on wall brackets at height 760mm above floor level beside back door.

It was originally intended by the occupational therapist that the kitchen should be made suitable for Miss Thomas' independent use and would incorporate low level units, a small oven and hob, and a shallow sink with knee room under. However, it was agreed that it was unrealistic to expect her to take a full role in the kitchen, having made no previous contribution to domestic activity and the kitchen needed to be useful primarily for Mrs Jones. The compromise agreed was to install the small shelf at a useful height for a microwave oven for Miss Thomas' use and to make some storage easily available.

The facilities encourage Miss Thomas to do some baking, but the rest of the scheme is centred upon the needs of Mrs Jones as a busy housewife. The dining area of the kitchen easily incorporates wheelchair space and gives a pleasant place for Miss Thomas to keep her mother company in the kitchen. The peninsular unit could be used as the main dining area of the house, if the dining room were to be converted to a bedroom for Mr Jones.

BATHROOM

* Washbasin resited with rim height of 780mm alongside retained soil pipe duct and mirror fronted cabinet mounted over.

* Wc resited with cistern 130mm away from duct and closer to bath, with seat height of 390mm.

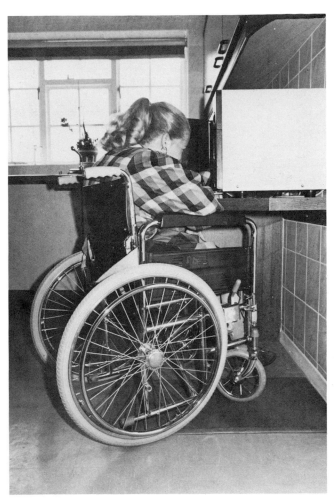

Miss Thomas can use the microwave oven independently and has developed an interest in baking.

* Invadex Opendeck shower base installed in corner of new area.

* Triton T80 thermostatically controlled shower with controls at 1200mm over base.

* Vertical grab rail fitted alongside wc.

* Former kitchen unit included in room for additional storage.

* Floor finished in thermoplastic tiles.

Swing out wire trays provide easily accessible storage space adjacent to the microwave oven.

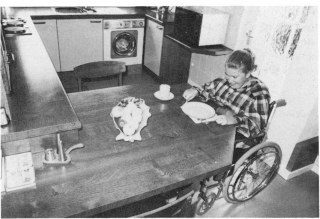

The peninsular unit in the kitchen can be used as a dining area.

Pivot transfer is made from the wheelchair to the commode chair that is positioned over the wc for use in the morning.

The shower area.

Resiting of the wc was necessary to give easier access on both sides for assisting Miss Thomas at the wc and in pivot transfer to the wheelchair; this method is used during the day, with the commode chair being easily pushed over the wc in the morning.

The washbasin is much more accessible than in its previous position overhanging the bath, but the pedestal impedes close access with the wheelchair or commode chair unless Miss Thomas' legs are abducted, which she finds somewhat uncomfortable. The siting of the shower next to the washbasin, with a hose that is long enough to reach well over it, allows hair washing without the need to take a full shower. This might have been made easier if the slide rail head mounting had been fixed on the lefthand side of the controls, next to the washbasin.

For using the shower Miss Thomas is pushed in backwards for hair washing and forwards for showering. The small internal size of the shower base leaves little room for knee clearance beyond the overall 640mm length of the shower chair that is used. In addition, the chair has to be lifted over the outer rim of the raised base and Mrs Jones finds the ramped edges rather too steep a gradient over which to push the chair. Owing to space limitations, the shower chair gains access over the corner of the shower ramped base with the two cambers at the edges making the manoeuvre precarious.

When the structural work was completed, the occupational therapist discussed provision of a combined commode and shower chair but, on seeing the equipment proposed, Miss Thomas and her mother opted for a small shower chair and retention of the castor commode. The commode was replaced by the health department and social services provided the shower chair.

The builder chose the shower base as an easier and less costly option to that of making a level access shower area.

The washbasin and wc.

BEDROOM

Miss Thomas' bedroom was not adapted.

The double bed at height 580mm is useful for Mrs Jones to stand, pivot and sit Miss Thomas in transfer from the wheelchair, commode or shower chair. Mrs Jones kneels on the bed at the other side to that of transfer and lifts her daughter under her arms into a comfortable sitting or lying position in bed. Miss Thomas sits supported on a triangular pillow and has a tilting table over the bed for a small portable television, needlework materials and books to be within easy reach. A stereo unit and dressing table are stood against the window wall and wardrobes on the length of one wall provide ample clothes storage. A push button telephone at the side is accessible and easily operated from the bed.

The understairs cupboard allows for storage of large items including the hoist for use during convalescence or for emergency use if Mrs Jones' back becomes problematical. Although the bed is set rather far towards the window to be used conveniently as a double bed, the area of floor on Miss Thomas' side of the bed was to allow for manoeuvre and turning of the wheelchair, commode, shower chair and the hoist when needed.

COSTING

1984

Adaptation to bathroom, kitchen and external pathways		£5417.00
Garage adaptation		482.00
Kitchen fittings		2900.00
	Total	£8799.00

FUNDING

90% improvement grant		£4868.00
Social services top up grant		542.00
Social services grant for 10% of estimated cost of the garage canopy		16.00
Client contribution: garage		473.00
kitchen fittings		2900.00
	Total	£8799.00

CONTRACTUAL PROCEDURE

Mr and Mrs Jones contracted the builder for all projects. The builder was concerned that payment via an improvement grant would be delayed and requested three intermediate payments. As Mr Jones did not know that he could arrange this with the grant officer, he approached his bank for a loan which was agreed as an interest free short term bridging loan.

EVALUATION

Miss Thomas and her mother have a close relationship of mutual support and affection which has survived through difficult times of pain and ill health, as well as the unremitting responsibility and demands of Miss Thomas' total care. They have devised their own methods of transfer and lifting, invariably reverting to them when other methods have been suggested, but not found to suit as well as those developed over years of practice.

Mrs Jones found herself in a position of having to bring up her child alone and successfully developed a hairdressing business to support them. In addition, she also managed to buy a home for them and to fit it out in the attractive and comfortable manner of which she is justly proud. Her reluctance to move is, therefore, understandable, although the application for council housing was made in the knowledge that this was the only means of acquiring already built wheelchair standard housing in their area.

The decision to adapt the existing accommodation proved to be sound as Miss Thomas has wheelchair **access** to all areas of the ground floor, to the garden and to the street. It is unfortunate, however, that a flush threshold strip was not used at the back door for getting the wheelchair in and out of the house. It presents an additional unecessary threat to Mrs Jones' back as the wheelchair has to be tipped backwards for it to negotiate the doorway. Wheelchair access to the driveway was removed by the kitchen extension and, in view of the impossibility of ramping the main door to the bungalow, there was no alternative but to give passageway through the garage. The same space is used for transferring to the car, which is now achieved under cover. Although the canopy suggested by social services would have met the essential requirements of weather protection, the family elected to pay for more substantial work done and in a manner they considered to be more in keeping with the rest of the property.

Wheelchair access to the **kitchen** was not possible before the extension was built and this led to an assumption that it was only this that precluded involvement in domestic tasks. Miss Thomas had not, however, shown any interest in being involved in the running of the home and, while major adaptations to the kitchen were considered, it was more important to tailor the kitchen around Mrs Jones. In practice, the accessible height microwave oven, storage and breakfast bar prove sufficient for Miss Thomas to use when she wishes. The dining space of the kitchen is sufficiently large to become the main eating area, were the dining room to be converted to a bedroom to meet Mr Jones' health needs.

Enlargement of the **bathroom** permitted retention of the bath and a shower to be added, with just enough space for movement of the shower or commode chair and the person who is required to assist in all activities in this room. Repositioning of the pillar attachment of the shower would improve accessibility of the shower head over the washbasin for hairwashing at times when it is not to be combined with full showering.

Some of the problems with the **shower base** can be attributed to the inability to gain a direct approach other than across the two cambers of the corner, owing to the position of the washbasin on one side and the storage unit on the other. Even if the store cupboard in the corner were to be removed, direct access to this side would still not be possible because of the restriction in floor space to carry out a right angled turn. Had a dished base been used, the problems presently encountered could have been eliminated. A combined commode and shower chair would have reduced the amount of equipment that has to be stored when not in use, although the design of these chairs did not appeal aesthetically to the family and would not have made access to the base any easier.

The earlier adaptation to the first floor to provide a wc and washbasin allows Mr Jones to remain on the upper floor when he is unwell. It also provides a second facility when the wc, integral to the ground floor bathroom, is

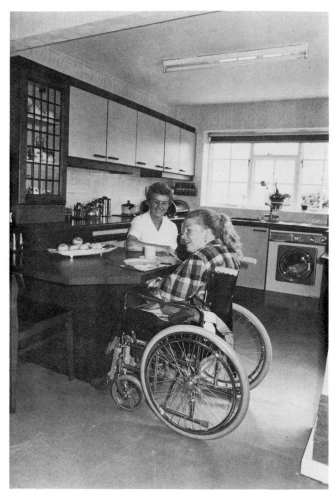

Miss Thomas is able to keep her mother company in the large kitchen that easily accommodates the wheelchair.

unavailable during other personal care activities that can take some time to complete. The area on the upper floor was presumably originally designed to become an en suite bathroom if required, as the only possible entrance is from the bedroom and the size of 1665 x 2980mm is too small for consideration as another bedroom. This has proved to be helpful, not only in terms of the particular needs of this family, but also in allowing upgrading without the need for structural adaptation.

The family are very pleased with the work that has been done to a high standard of finishing, which was closely supervised by Mr Jones as semi confinement to the house enabled him to always be on hand. No supervision was required of the occupational therapist or the grant officer, except in the case of specific requests made on individual equipment and, even so, the choice of shower base was overlooked. The property has been improved overall, helped by the family's choice and purchase of high quality kitchen units. Their home has always been an important focus and interest for the family and the high standard has been maintained in an attractive, yet economical manner, to meet present and future needs of two disabled members.

MR JOHN THORPE

Aged 73. Right hemiplegia.

Married and living in a three bedroomed house.

Adaptation of a mobile home.

Mr Thorpe had always led a very active life with much of his leisure time dominated by his love of football. He managed youth teams, taking an active role in coaching, training and in organizing playing trips abroad. His second marriage, to a woman fifteen years his junior, centred his life in London and upon their five children from previous marriages. He and his wife both worked, with Mrs Thorpe continuing in her post after her husband's retirement at the age of sixty five.

Three years after retiring from his work with London Transport, Mr Thorpe suffered a cerebro vascular accident which resulted in a right hemiplegia and expressive dysphasia. His wife gave up work to care for him and he had to relinquish his retirement pursuits, the greatest loss being his football interests. They applied to social services for the provision of aids and for help in completion of the central heating system that they had started to install in the three bedroomed house which they owned. An efficient heating system was needed all the more urgently now because of Mr Thorpe's sedentary lifestyle, but they could no longer afford the work they had planned as Mrs Thorpe had ceased paid employment.

An occupational therapist visited and supplied bathing and feeding aids, but turned down the request for help with heating as Mr Thorpe was not considered to be very severely handicapped. She agreed, however, to make approaches to charitable organizations for help but, while small sums were offered, the total was never reached and the work was not completed.

Mr Thorpe made good progress to the point where he could manage steps and stairs and regained much of his speech. A year later, however, he had a second and more severe stroke which resolved into a dense right hemiplegia, total speech loss and a reliance on help for all aspects of his care. Little improvement was ever made, resulting in permanent functional limitations on which they had to base a different kind of future than the one they had planned:

Mobility. Mr Thorpe was dependent on a ministry model 9 wheelchair and could not transfer independently, although he could take his weight sufficiently in standing to assist his wife to move him.

Dressing. His wife had to dress him.

Wc. He was doubly incontinent unless taken frequently to the lavatory, with needs having to be anticipated by Mrs Thorpe. An armchair commode and a urine bottle were supplied by the community nursing service as it was impossible for him to be got to the ground floor bathroom and wc owing to a floor level change and the confined space within the room.

Bathing. Mrs Thorpe gave him a daily bed bath.

Personal care. He was dependent in all aspects of his care.

Bed. They bought a bed settee for use in the living area when Mr Thorpe became unable to walk or use the stairs to reach their bedroom. They slept together with Mrs Thorpe attending to her husband's needs during the night.

Chair. He spent his day either in the wheelchair or a low seat armchair.

Eating and drinking. He was generally spoon fed as limited strength and poor coordination made it difficult for him to use implements himself. He could hand feed but this tended to be rather a messy process.

Hobbies and interests. Mr Thorpe appeared interested in television and in being taken out on trips for shopping and bingo. However, he was totally dependent in all aspects of daily living, lacked control of bodily functions and was unaware of his needs. His wife assumed a maternal role which allowed the transition from wife to mother with no evidence of reproach in her attitude to him.

While the bathroom and wc were on the ground floor of their three bedroomed terraced house, they could only be reached via a step from the kitchen. The result was that Mr Thorpe's total care was undertaken in the living area as the only place where there was sufficient space and heating, the rest of the house being cold and damp.

The previous unsympathetic response to their request for help did not cause Mrs Thorpe to see any value in making contact again with social services, although they did have the support of a district nurse. The routine and expert day care that Mrs Thorpe gave her husband, however, led her to make an arrangement that the nurse would not call regularly, but only on demand and this system worked well. Mr Thorpe's health was maintained at a stable level, except for the occasional respiratory disorder which sometimes necessitated an admission to hospital for treatment.

The daily routine of making and remaking the bed settee, carrying water and living in a cold damp house, however, began to get Mrs Thorpe down and, on a visit to her brother in his mobile home on a rural site, she thought seriously of making a similar move. She felt that the convenience of a compact single level home would ease the care of her husband and could more efficiently assure a warm even temperature. They had nothing to keep them in the London area, as their family had all moved away, so she enquired about the possibility of finding a suitable mobile home that could be adapted to their own special needs. Her brother's help and support was assured, so it was decided that they should move to the same site, especially as it was in an area that they liked.

Mrs Thorpe visited a mobile home demonstration centre and chose a model that she considered to have useful features for their needs. She arranged for the doorways to be widened in the process of construction and for a ramp to be installed to the external doors to the living area once the unit had been set on site. She contacted the social services department of the area to which they intended to move and understood that she would receive financial help with the adaptations on production of the receipted final accounts. They put their house up for sale and awaited an offer that would allow them to put a deposit on the mobile home and so start its process of manufacture.

During this time, Mr Thorpe suffered a severe and debilitating bout of diarrhoea and was admitted to hospital for several weeks. Mrs Thorpe remained active in his care when visiting and discovered it was easier to transfer him to the high seat armchair next to the hospital bed than it was to the low one used at home. When he was discharged she approached the local social services department who supplied a similar chair to the hospital one, although in long term use this proved to be uncomfortable for Mr Thorpe.

During the visit of the occupational therapist, the idea of the mobile home and its special features of widened doorways and ramping was mentioned and she suggested that they should also consider adapting the bathroom, and avail themselves of the opportunity to avoid duplicating their present unsatisfactory situation. Mrs Thorpe's expectation that the new authority would be more generous than the old, was somewhat dampened, however, when her occupational therapist said that payment was unlikely from a local authority without a formal application and agreement to costs prior to commencement of adaptations. The occupational therapist agreed to liaise with her counterpart in the authority to which the Thorpes were moving. Mr Thorpe's functional difficulties were explained, together with the proposed plan and the value of the support of Mrs Thorpe's brother, and social services agreed to meet the costs of the special features.

However, agreement to the specification and price estimates in advance of the work commencing was a provision that had to be adhered to and the mobile home company were not keen to give a detailed estimate. An overall price is usually all that is offered, but they finally agreed to meet the requirements because of the exceptional circumstances involved.

When the specification for the ramp was received, it could not be agreed as the gradient was considered to be too steep for safe use, although this was somewhat improved by the decision to resite the doors farther back along the living area wall to allow a longer ramp with little protrusion beyond the front of the home. Mrs Thorpe's reaction to the fact that the ramp was still steep was that she would be able to cope and, if not, her brother would help and that

they did not want any larger installation than the one proposed. At the same time, they received and accepted an offer on their house and ordered the construction of the mobile home to include adaptations to the bathroom to allow wheelchair access, wider doors and an external ramp of gradient 1 in 5.6. The house sale proceeded smoothly and they moved to the home of one of their sons for a seven week period until all work was completed on the new home to which they moved in mid 1984, some four years after Mr Thorpe first became ill.

THE PROJECT TEAM

London borough social services occupational therapist.
County council social services occupational therapist.
Sales manager of the mobile home company in conjunction with the construction company.

THE AIMS

To provide a suitable environment in which constant care and attention could be most easily given.
To enable wheelchair circulation and access to all necessary facilities in the home.
To promote interests outside the home by ensuring that a wheelchair could be efficiently moved between the accommodation, the car and the rest of the site.

THE PROPERTY

A Donnington 32 twin mobile home.

* Gross internal floor area 57.0m² unchanged.

The mobile home was purchased as a fully fitted and furnished unit set on a site at the edge of a new town development. The site incorporated spacious grassed areas and trees with easy vehicular access to the homes and around the site. Car parking was in bays.

The model was chosen as the only one with wide double external doors from the living area; the room that would be most frequently used by Mr Thorpe during the day. In addition, there was a washbasin included as a standard fitment to the main bedroom, which would be useful in the nursing care likely to be performed in the room.

The mobile home on site.

The home was only mobile in that it was prefabricated, in two sections, and transported to the site where it was permanently situated. The construction in twin sections gave a central partition line that determined the shape and size of bedrooms, bathroom and kitchen with a relatively large lobby.

THE ADAPTATION

Incorporation of special features in a newly purchased mobile home.

EXTERNAL DOORS AND PATHWAYS

* Double doors from living area resited from standard position.

* 1220mm wide x 3820mm long, 1:5.6 concrete ramp with continuous handrail formed to arrive at 1220 x 1220mm level platform at main double doors.

The 750mm wide pathway to the unit from the site road gives good access from the parking bays. The ramp is steep, although Mrs Thorpe copes well and would not wish to see any changes to make the gradient more gentle, as this would incur a longer and, therefore, more obtrusive installation.

The external doors were moved back to allow as long a slope as possible, without ramp extension forward of the unit. The level platform makes for easy manoeuvering in the right angled turns to and from the doors, which are opened fully to maximize space. The 670mm wide back door opens directly from the kitchen and is too narrow for the wheelchair and so is not used by Mr Thorpe.

WINDOWS

660mm cill height for bay windows in living area, 920mm for kitchen and all others at 840mm.

As the mobile home is set at 720mm above ground level, sightlines from the low seat chair that Mr Thorpe uses are limited by the 840mm high window cills. Mr Thorpe does not, however, show interest in what is happening on the site and focuses attention only on the home.

ELECTRICAL WORK

* Additional power supply made to bathroom for electrical shower.

* Pull cord extractor fan sited in bathroom.

No other alteration was made to the standard provision in this type of home, as Mr Thorpe is unable to use switches or power points.

HEATING

* Gas fired back boiler installed to feed three radiators in living area, one in bathroom and one in each bedroom.

Delivered calor gas is used and, although the mobile home is compact, it does not have good insulation. Fuel bills are extremely high, if the warm even temperature needed for Mr Thorpe is to be maintained.

The ramp with level platform and handrail.

HALLWAYS AND DOORS

* Doorway from living area to central corridor eliminated and replaced by archway.

* 760mm wide door leaves fitted to all other internal door openings to give clear opening widths of 710mm.

The archway was formed to allow sufficient turning space for manoeuvering the wheelchair from the living area to the bathroom. The new DHSS model 10 wheelchair can be passed through all doorways with greater ease than the previous model 9 pushchair, and there are no raised thresholds internally. The archway does mean, however, that as the living area cannot be as effectively closed off there is consequent heat loss into the rest of the accommodation.

LIVING AREA

Mr Thorpe spends his day in this room, taking meals off a cantilever table and watching television.

The resiting of the double external doors, to allow for the ramp, has also meant that furniture can be usefully positioned without impeding access to the doors, which would have been the case with the doors in the centre of the wall length.

KITCHEN

No adaptation was made to this room as Mr Thorpe can take no active part in domestic activities.

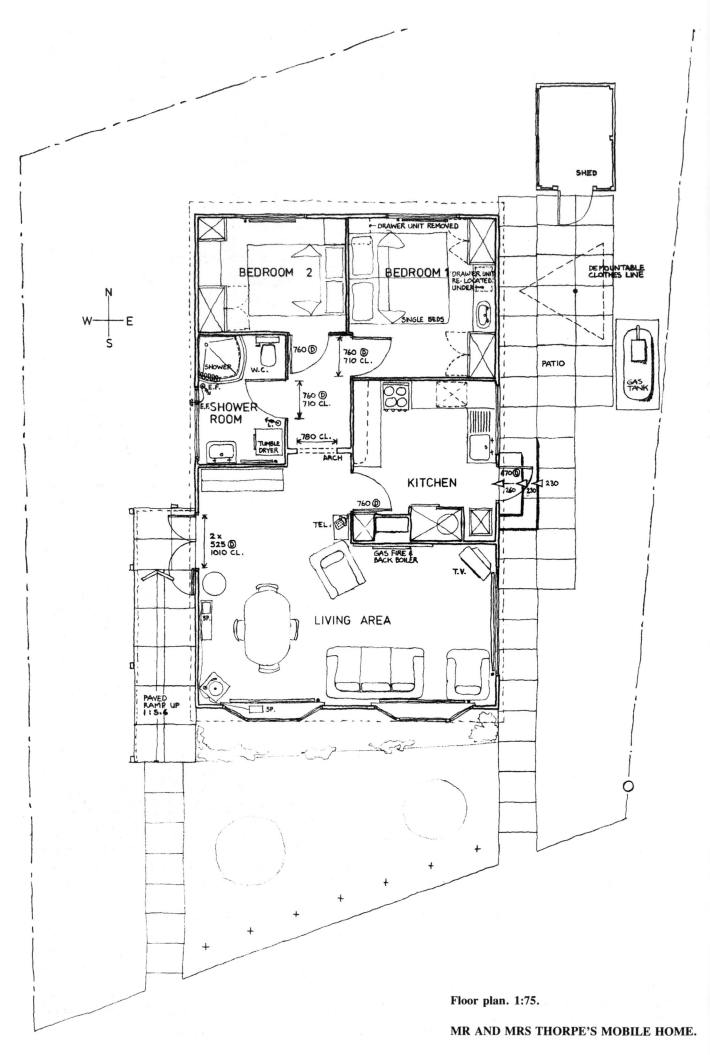

Floor plan. 1:75.

MR AND MRS THORPE'S MOBILE HOME.

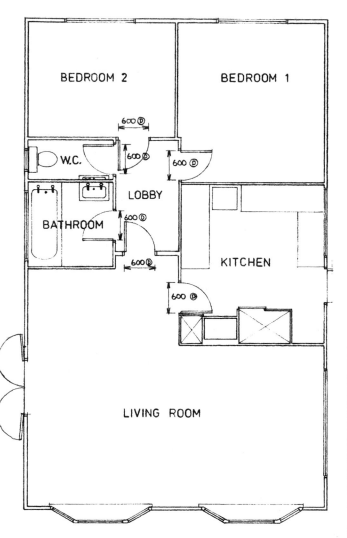

Standard layout of bathroom and doorways in a Donnington 32 twin mobile home.

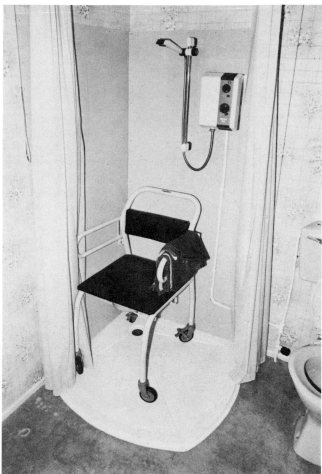

The shower area.

BATHROOM

* Partition wall between wc and bathroom removed and wc door blocked off.

* Low level wc positioned behind door.

* Pedestal washbasin mounted adjacent to radiator and heated towel rail.

* Triton electric shower installed in conjuction with Invadex Leveldeck shower base.

* Shower area lined with coloured perspex sheets.

The layout of the room would be improved if access to the wc and shower in the commode/shower chair, supplied by social services at the time of the move, was not obstructed by the inward opening door. Once in the room with the door closed, however, the chair can be pushed easily over the wc and then into the shower, which Mrs Thorpe operates from outside the partially closed curtains.

The electric shower was chosen because there was insufficient water pressure from the tank in the kitchen to supply direct hot water. Water drains away well and there are no problems of splash or leakage from the shower area. The extractor fan was added to compensate for the loss of the enclosed lobby and creates negative pressure which

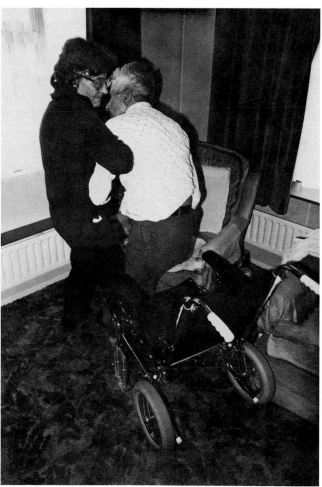

Mr Thorpe requires help with all transfers.

draws air from the other areas, as an effective means of keeping stale air from the living areas.

BEDROOM
* Washbasin set in vanitory unit opposite position of bed as standard fixture.

The washbasin is useful for Mrs Thorpe to give her husband the daily morning bedbath, which is necessary in addition to the shower used in the evenings. The widening of the doorway meant that there was insufficient room for a bedside locker; since this was at the side where Mr Thorpe slept and he would not have independent use of it, this was not an important factor. Later substitution of twin beds for the original double one, in order that Mrs Thorpe could make use of the incontinence laundry service for her husband's sheets, required that the other bedside locker be rehoused beneath the washbasin as there was no longer space beside the wider system of beds.

COSTING
1984

Ramp, platform and handrail	£500.00
Door widening	23.00
Bathroom adaptations	208.00

The provision of the shower unit was included in the usual price of the mobile home as it replaced a standard feature upon which savings could be made.

FUNDING
Mr and Mrs Thorpe funded the project as a whole and claimed the sum for the extra adaptations from social services, who met this from their aids and adaptations allowance. There was no eligibility for an improvement grant, mobile homes not being considered as permanent accommodation.

CONTRACTUAL PROCEDURE
Mrs and Mrs Thorpe contracted directly with the agent for the mobile home company to manufacture the unit with the special features incorporated. The agent contracted a local builder for the construction of the ramp once the home had been set in position on the site.

EVALUATION

Mr Thorpe receives devoted and skilled care from his wife, whose physical strength and comparative youth enables her to take on some heavy lifting tasks without complaint. Their earlier home was unsatisfactory with its inaccessible bedrooms, bathroom, and wc and cold and damp conditions. In addition, they found social services unable to support them in the manner they considered most useful, and Mrs Thorpe found this attitude difficult to accept at a time when demands were being made upon her to adjust to a new lifestyle totally committed to her husband's care. It was fortuitous that the social services occupational therapist called on another matter, otherwise they might have had a similar experience over payment for the proposed adaptations with the department of the area to which they were moving.

It cannot have been easy to organize the adaptations and assure funding between staff from authorities set many miles apart. The functional assessment, upon which

justification for funding the proposed structural work was founded, was done by an occupational therapist who was not required to assure funding from her own authority and who would not ever see the completed project. In addition, she did not know the site on which the mobile home was to be set and had only an outline sketch plan of the standard model upon which to base recommendations. She was required, however, to convince colleagues in the other authority of the necessity of the work, for which they were being asked to pay, for a client they would not see until the adaptations were complete. However, the trust that there was between professional colleagues enabled the adaptations to be funded and the Thorpes to begin a relationship with the new authority that would allow support on a more positive foundation.

The success of the move and improvement in Mr Thorpe's health and morale is undoubted. Wheelchair circulation space in the areas used by Mr Thorpe is good and the removal of the **doorway** from the living area to the corridor has allowed for ease of turning into the bathroom, which would not have been possible with the original doorway design. The archway is also an attractive feature, although the resultant heat loss of not being able to close the room off effectively from the rest of the accommodation is a disadvantage. The **living area** is sufficiently large for their needs and is a pleasant room in which Mr Thorpe spends much of his waking hours. Space for a dining area was available with positioning of furniture not needing to impose on access space to the external doors.

Internally, the layout of the **bathroom** allows efficient care in a comparatively small room. However, direct access to the wc from the doorway is obstructed by the door itself, which opens across the front of the wc. An internal sliding door or one hinged from the other side would have obviated the need for additional manoeuvering in the confined space. Once in the room, with the door closed, the position of fitments allows ease of access for the chair over the wc and then into the shower, which is the usual order. Mr Thorpe can be seated easily at the washbasin in this room and the bedroom one is helpful for the daily bed bath.

The **ramp** is too steep for optimal use, although Mrs Thorpe's physical strength overcomes the difficulties that some people would have in pushing or self propelling over such a gradient. She is entirely satisfied with the ramp, which she considers would not be the case with a larger and more obtrusive installation.

The choice of gas central **heating** over that of solid fuel was sound in terms of ease and convenience of use, but maintaining the constant comfortable temperature using calor gas has resulted in very high bills. Heat is lost through the single glazed windows and poorly insulated walls and floors in the lightweight construction of this type of unit.

Mr and Mrs Thorpe have settled well in the new neighbourhood and are additionally supported by Mrs Thorpe's brother, with whom they also enjoy a social life. It is less of a major undertaking than at the house to get the wheelchair in and out of the unit to the rest of the site and for outings in the car, with the result that they are far less isolated than they were in London. Mrs Thorpe feels better supported and has gained from the move to a smaller living unit, which has a layout that lends itself to Mr Thorpe's care and the efficient running of a household.

Mr and Mrs Thorpe do not regret their decision to move from their inconvenient London home to a mobile home in the country. It is easier for Mrs Thorpe to care for her husband and to manage household tasks in the new home, and it is advantageous that Mrs Thorpe's brother is nearby and can help. The occupational therapists concerned backed the move for these reasons and the success of this mobile home is proven in this instance. It does not, however, demonstrate that a mobile home is generally suitable for adaptation to meet the needs of a severely disabled person.

MRS VERA CHAMBERLAIN

Aged 73. Poliomyelitis, osteoarthritis, chronic bronchitis and mild cardiac failure.

Married with one son living at home.

Adaptation of a caravan.

Mrs Chamberlain was five years old when she contracted poliomyelitis that principally affected her right leg. The problems of a weak knee and foot drop were exacerbated some years later by a fall which caused dislocation of the right hip and consequent shortening. She remained ambulant however, during her forty three years as a machinist in the hosiery industry, although difficulties in mobility increased with age and the development of arthritis and chronic bronchitis.

Upon their retirement in 1970, Mr and Mrs Chamberlain bought a caravan on a corner plot of a rural site and moved from their four bedroomed house in the nearby town. Their belief was that such accommodation would be easier and more economical to manage, clean and heat than a large house with stairs and surplus rooms. This largely proved to be the case, although they had overlooked the two deep steps at the entrance to the caravan, which were very difficult for Mrs Chamberlain to negotiate.

Mrs Chamberlain coped until 1977, when she developed pneumonia whilst on holiday, and from which she never recovered her ability to walk. Mr Chamberlain had been a coalman and haulier all his life; he saw no problem in lifting his wife around the caravan and bought a secondhand wheelchair to assist with greater distances. Referral was made to the local authority occupational therapist who had the wheelchair replaced by a ministry pushchair and attempted to get Mrs Chamberlain independent in transfers using a lifting seat and walking frame. This did not prove successful however, and the couple continued to use the lifting methods until, two years later, Mr Chamberlain dropped his wife while lifting her up the steps to the caravan, and she fractured her femur. Admission to hospital was followed by a period of living with her daughter until a ramp could be installed at the main entrance of the caravan to allow wheelchair access. Referral was made to social services for the ramp by the Chamberlain's daughter, and the occupational therapist asked the general practitioner to endorse the application to enable provision as a matter of urgency.

The ramp, at 1:6.6, had to be steep owing to the clearance needed for the second external door. The family were able to manage, however, and acknowledged that being able to use the wheelchair directly from inside the caravan was an improvement.

As the time came for a replacement caravan, Mr and Mrs Chamberlain decided on a two bedroomed model so that the living room did not need nightly conversion to a bedroom, as had previously been the case so that their son could have his own bedroom. However, door widths were not checked and it proved impossible for the wheelchair to enter any of the rooms. In addition, the layout of the new caravan required the external doors to face onto the site, instead of onto the sheltered side away from the other dwellings as with the previous model. They did not want to turn the caravan around to avoid this, as it would have removed Mrs Chamberlain's view of the site from her daytime chair in the living room.

The ramp was resited against the new caravan, with its platform now being 200mm too low for the new threshold. They uncomplainingly managed to cope, with the wheelchair lifted over the step, and Mr Chamberlain decided to give the exposed timber ramp some weather protection by installation of a timber framed fibreglass sheet cover.

In 1983 a visit by a planning officer to inspect all constructions, in consultation with a fire officer, resulted in the requirement that the ramp covering be removed, as the necessary twenty feet to protect against the spread of fire between the caravans had been reduced to fifteen. As the ramp was anyway deteriorating, the Chamberlains made further contact with social services for a review of their situation and the provision of a narrower wheelchair for use indoors. An occupational therapist visited and made an assessment upon which plans for adaptations were based.

Mobility. Mrs Chamberlain was unable to walk or stand and was moved by her husband lifting her indoors or in an attendant pushed wheelchair outdoors. No doorways were wide enough for the chair she used, although a castor wheelchair was found to pass through the kitchen/hall doorway.

Dressing. She could dress herself but for stockings and pants.

Wc. She used a chemical wc that was stored in the bath when not in use. She needed to be lifted onto the wc.

Personal care. She washed daily from a bowl in her lap and her husband gave her a weekly bed bath.

Eating and drinking. Meals were taken on a tray in her lap in the living room where she spent her day.

Domestic tasks. Mr Chamberlain did all the cooking and cleaning, although his wife took responsibility for decisions on menus and provisions to be bought on their weekly shopping trips to the supermarket.

Hobbies and interests. Mrs Chamberlain enjoyed reading and working on two dolls houses which her grandchildren also appreciated.

A castor wheelchair was provided and plans made to facilitate management at the entrance and indoors, and to counter cold and damp conditions which were affecting her respiratory condition. Grants for heating were not available from the local authority or in a special needs payment from DHSS, although the latter did agree to meet interest repayments. The occupational therapist applied to local charitable organizations, with some success, and the rest of the heating installation bill was met via a loan from a finance company to the family.

THE PROJECT TEAM
County council social services occupational therapist.
Social services technician.
Heating and ventilation engineer.
Lift representative.

The adapted caravan and immediate site.

THE AIMS

To enable Mr Chamberlain to move his wife around the
caravan with ease and safety.
To provide a safe means of wheelchair access in accordance
with fire regulation standards.
To provide an adequate means of heating the whole
caravan without the problem of fumes.

THE PROPERTY

A two bedroomed caravan on a corner plot of a fifteen unit
site, situated half a mile from a village and four miles from
a large town.

Gross internal floor area 32.0m² unchanged.

THE ADAPTATION

Conversion of a caravan.

EXTERNAL DOORS AND PATHWAYS

* 3300mm long timber ramp and 1000mm square platform
  with handrail and non slip surfacing installed to 500mm
  high entrance threshold of first caravan and later moved
  to second one.

* Timber ramp subsequently replaced by AMP steplift at
  700mm wide and 700mm high threshold main door.

* External concrete pad of 1070 x 1010mm built to lift
  manufacturer's specifications outside door to take lift
  mounting and power gear.

* Controls placed at 900mm on lift safety rail for attendant
  operation and internal control switch sited just inside
  door.

* Lift rise predetermined at 700mm to take platform flush
  with the level of internal floor.

* Old ramp resited, without its cover, at other external
  door that opened from passageway.

The steplift was chosen by the occupational therapist as the
second external door opening and necessary clearance
precluded use of a ramp with a more gentle gradient. In
addition, a more permanent arrangement of ramping would
not necessarily be serviceable in the event of a further
change of caravan. The old and badly worn ramp is
retained for use in the event of power failure or lift
breakdown and is rarely used, but means that wheelchair
access is possible from both doors to the paved pathways
and small island beds that form the garden, and to the rest
of the site.

Mr and Mrs Chamberlain like the lift and feel confident in
its use. The 1100 x 770mm platform allows the attendant to
travel with the chair and operation proves easy, although
teething problems in the first week caused the platform to
override the stop mechanism and to come up under the
door that had been left slightly open. The door and the
platform were damaged, and there was a risk of the whole
caravan being pushed over. However, the faulty stop switch
was replaced with no further problem, although Mr
Chamberlain is careful to ensure that the door is left fully
open when the lift is in use.

WINDOWS

Top hung, outward opening windows, which are typical of
caravans, cannot be reached by Mrs Chamberlain who has
no independent mobility and is rarely left alone.

N

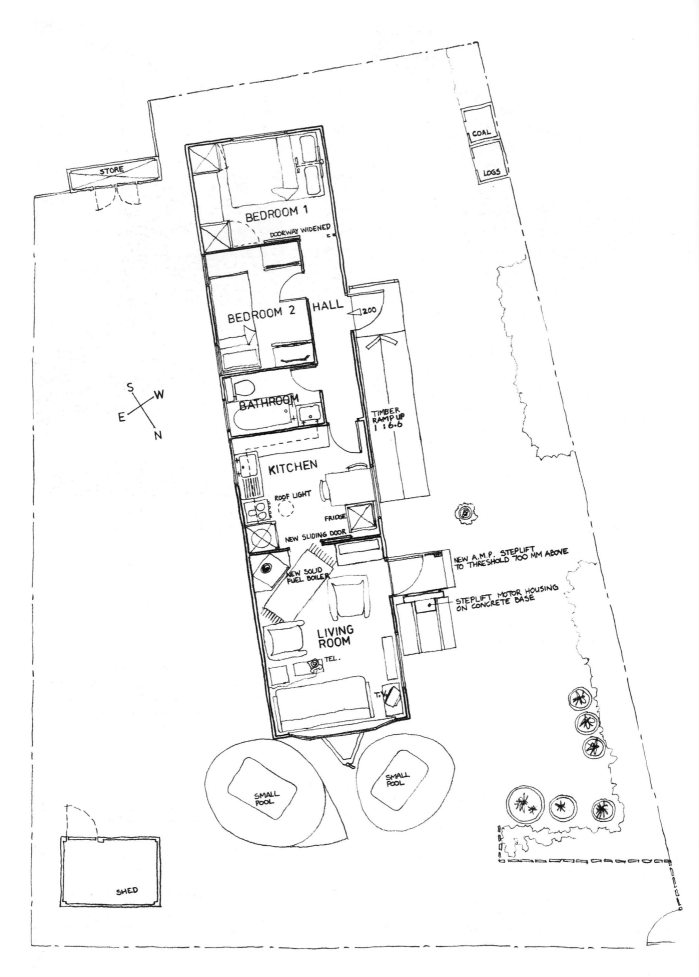

Floor plan. 1:75.

THE CHAMBERLAIN'S CARAVAN.

180

Mr Chamberlain positions the wheelchair on the steplift for entry to the caravan.

Mr Chamberlain raises the platform to the living room door threshold for backwards entry to the caravan.

ELECTRICAL WORK

* Power supply for step lift taken from separate fuse box mounted underneath caravan.

* Light switch moved to allow installation of sliding door to replace concertina door between living room and kitchen.

HEATING

* Open coal fire in living room replaced by solid fuel back boiler with radiators in bedroom, bathroom and passageway.

The living room and kitchen are heated directly through the boiler casing and a warm even temperature is maintained. This and the lack of insulation jacket on the hot water tank in the kitchen means that extra demand is put on the temperature control of the refrigerator.

The caravan had been cold and damp in the winter and the fumes from the coal fire were found to exacerbate Mrs Chamberlain's bronchitis. The general practitioner recommended a change and upgrading of heating, and the Chamberlains find the type chosen to be more efficient and economical than the open fire supplemented by a bottled gas heater that they had previously used.

HALLWAY AND DOORS

* Doorway to bedroom widened by 115mm to 625mm by removal of part of hardboard infill panel and sliding door fitted.

* Concertina door to kitchen removed and replaced with sliding door.

* D handles fitted to kitchen door and recessed pull handles to bedroom door.

The corridor width of 740mm is narrow for the right angled turn that would be required into the bathroom and second bedroom if Mrs Chamberlain should attempt to use these rooms. The sliding doors give greater clearance for the castor wheelchair with ease of closure allowing good control of heat in the living room and bedroom.

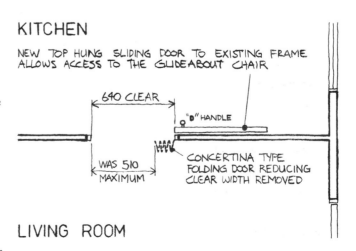

KITCHEN

NEW TOP HUNG SLIDING DOOR TO EXISTING FRAME ALLOWS ACCESS TO THE GLIDEABOUT CHAIR

640 CLEAR

"D" HANDLE

WAS 510 MAXIMUM

CONCERTINA TYPE FOLDING DOOR REDUCING CLEAR WIDTH REMOVED

LIVING ROOM

Plan of the living room/kitchen doorway.

Mr Chamberlain brings his wife into the living room from the steplift. The confined space demands precise manoeuvering.

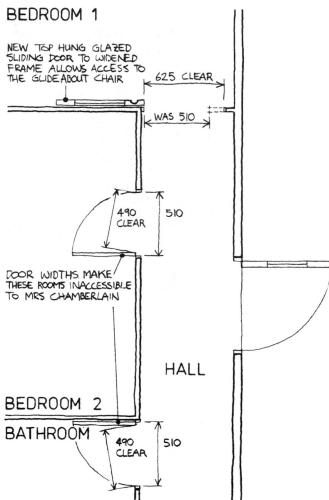

BEDROOM 1

NEW TOP HUNG GLAZED SLIDING DOOR TO WIDENED FRAME ALLOWS ACCESS TO THE GLIDE ABOUT CHAIR

625 CLEAR

WAS 510

490 CLEAR   510

DOOR WIDTHS MAKE THESE ROOMS INACCESSIBLE TO MRS CHAMBERLAIN

HALL

BEDROOM 2

BATHROOM

490 CLEAR   510

Plan of the bedroom and bathroom doorways.

LIVING AREA

Mrs Chamberlain spends most of her day in an armchair in this, the largest room in the caravan, from which she can look out onto the garden, the roadway and the rest of the site.

KITCHEN

No adaptation was made as Mrs Chamberlain is not involved in domestic activities other than to direct operations from her position in the living area. Space is adequate for wheelchair manoeuvre through the room for access to the rest of the accommodation.

BATHROOM

No adaptation was made to the bathroom, although widening of the doorway and removal of the bath for shower installation had been suggested.

Mr and Mrs Chamberlain resist the idea of further major alteration as they do not wish to change or lose the second bedroom, as might have been the case to accommodate a wheelchair accessible shower; they are content with the present method of a daily wash, weekly bed bath and use of a portable chemical wc.

BEDROOM

The sliding door gives direct access to the room and Mr Chamberlain is able to transfer his wife sideways to the bed by removing the arm of the castor wheelchair. An overbed

lifting pole assists position change, turning and sitting up and the castor wheelchair is housed in this room when not in use. The wheelchair used out doors is stored in the car.

COSTING

1979	
Ramp and widening of one door in the first caravan	£125.00
1984	
Installation of a Parkray heater and four radiators	622.00
Supply and installation of an AMP Steplift and guard plate	1365.00
Preparatory work: electrical	171.00
concrete base	200.00
	£2358.00

FUNDING:

Social services aids and adaptations budget for the ramp and steplift   £1861.00

* A small grant from a local welfare group and social services, plus a loan from a finance company, with the interest paid by DHSS, for the heating system.

CONTRACTUAL PROCEDURE

Work for the ramp and the preparatory work for the lift installation were put out to three builders for tender as normal practice by social services. Door widening was done

182

Transfer is made to the castor wheelchair that is used for internal circulation.

by the technician advised by the occupational therapist, and AMP Engineers Limited were contracted for supply and installation of the lift. Heating and ventilation engineers were engaged directly by Mr Chamberlain for the installation of the central heating system.

EVALUATION

Mr and Mrs Chamberlain have coped with increasing difficulties with fortitude and determination. The decision to move from a spacious house to a caravan was unsound in terms of wheelchair manoeuvering space, but when retirement was planned, there were no thoughts of wheelchair dependence. The floor raised above ground level and confined space of a caravan do not lend themselves to independent wheelchair living, but there have been advantages compared with the large house.

The accommodation is easily managed by Mr Chamberlain, with his wife always being close to tasks performed. The provision of the castor wheelchair has considerably reduced the need for lifting and it would be possible to alter the bathroom to allow use of it in this room, with a model that could go over the wc, and so remove the need to lift at all, should the family so wish.

Mrs Chamberlain appears to have a history that only generates useful help as a result of crisis, as seen at the time of her fractured femur and the enforced change to the ramping arrangement. The occupational therapist who

visited following the pneumonia episode did nothing about the difficulties and potential hazards of the steps to the raised floor of the caravan, and it was left to the Chamberlains' daughter to generate a solution after Mrs Chamberlain was injured in a fall at this site. The **ramp** when it was installed improved matters, although its unavoidably steep gradient was not ideal and may explain why the family accepted the further limitations on its use created by the higher floor of the second caravan.

The **steplift** overcomes the wheelchair access problems with ease and safety. While the lift may be more expensive than some other solutions to access problems, it may be the only one suited to caravans whose small size and raised floor necessitate large and costly ramping. In addition, extensive slopes can use up all or more than a plot size and also create trip hazards to transverse traffic in areas that are not always well lit at night.

The **heating** problems are not those usually associated with a small area that should, theoretically, be easy to heat. However, heat is lost through the 40mm external walls and the suspended floor of the caravan, exacerbated by the long narrow shape that gives a high ratio of surface area to enclosed volume. In addition, the fumes from the coal fire aggravated Mrs Chamberlain's bronchitis. The solution of central heating from a solid fuel boiler gives the desired even temperature in a more efficient and economical manner, although heating bills remain high.

Door widening did not prove to be a difficult task with reduction in the infill panels allowing for resiting of door frames. Wall space for sliding door movement did need to be assured, however, and this might not always prove to be practicable in the confined space of a caravan which needs to house many of the same domestic appliances and equipment for home life as do larger properties.

For the Chamberlains, the merits of caravan life outweigh the disadvantages, including the considerable problem that no adaptation will enable convenient wheelchair living to be achieved. They enjoy caravan life and the idea of applying to the local council for a move back to a house or bungalow does not appeal to them. They find their present situation quite satisfactory, with the option of further changes still possible to improve the bathroom, before a move would need to be contemplated or effected.

MISS SHELLEY SMITH

Aged 24. Renal failure.

Living with parents.

Extension of a house to provide a haemodialysis treatment room.

The need for a splenectomy in September 1980 was Miss Smith's first contact with illness and medical treatment in an otherwise healthy life. She recovered quite well from surgery, but three months later returned to her consultant with symptoms of persistent and frequent vomiting. He immediately diagnosed renal failure and referred her to the specialist unit of a London hospital.

During the five month admission that followed, peritoneal dialysis was tried without success before Miss Smith could be stabilized on a haemodialysis regime. Towards the end of the admission, weekends were tried at home before she was finally discharged with thrice weekly visits arranged to the unit for dialysis. However, she disliked the treatment, the haemodialysis machine and the travelling, and some months later persuaded her consultant that she could try continuous ambulatory peritoneal dialysis.

The method proved successful this time and she was able to return to her full time clerical job with the local district health authority, who allocated a room for her use for treatment when required during the day. The arrangements worked extremely well for eighteen months until thickening of the peritoneum developed to a point where fluid transfer became interrupted and she was readmitted to hospital and returned to the old haemodialysis regime.

In 1983 she was offered a kidney transplant which was successfully performed, despite problems in controlling her blood pressure during and after surgery. Her condition settled, until the following September when she awoke one morning to a very severe headache and loss of sight. She was able to call the renal unit before losing consciousness and was admitted to the hospital as a medical emergency. It was found that her blood pressure was abnormally high and that the kidney had been so damaged as a result that there was no alternative but to remove it.

Stabilization, again on haemodialysis, meant that she became well enough to return to work early in the following year. Treatment at the renal unit was organized during the day on Mondays and overnight on Tuesdays and Thursdays, enabling her to work four days a week. The hospital car service could offer help with transport during the day and so took her to and from the unit for the Monday sessions. This proved to be the most useful time as, if she was to feel at all unwell, it was likely to be on that day as it followed possible weekend excesses in diet and was at the end of the longest period without treatment. The other sessions were less likely to have problems and she found that she was well able to cope with driving to and from them.

She wished, however, to return to full time employment and approached her consultant about the possibility of home dialysis, which had been discussed prior to the

transplant. She also recognized that haemodialysis was the method that proved to be most benign for her continued good health. The medical team agreed and the home dialysis administrator and building surveyor looked at options available for a treatment room in the family home.

It was undesirable to use her bedroom, which was anyway too small to house all the equipment. The spare bedroom was discounted as it contained the central heating boiler and, being at the front of the house, was farthest away for connection to the water and drainage systems of the rest of the house. The use of this room was not a popular option with the family either, who did not want to see any reduction in the use of space in their already small house. The alternative was to build a room onto the ground floor.

The building surveyor drew up plans and obtained the approvals from building control and the water authority, together with estimates for the work. Mr Smith commenced visits to the renal unit to learn the procedures for assisting his daughter in treatment. The building work started in March 1984 and was delayed by bad weather. In addition, the whole of the ground floor and family life was disrupted by the need for all materials, machinery and workmen to pass through the house from the front door, as there was no other access to the back of the house from the road.

The construction work was completed in mid July and treatment at home commenced during August, following installation of the necessary equipment and completion of Mr Smith's tuition. A nurse from the renal unit was available to help with the first sessions and the family's confidence grew, especially when they successfully coped with an initially temperamental dialysis machine.

Miss Smith finds that she keeps well and is able to adhere to the diet required without much difficulty. It was more difficult for her to adjust to the reduction in fluid intake as she had habitually drunk a lot of liquids and got very thirsty in the early weeks of the reduced intake. She does not feel that her lifestyle has greatly altered or that she is unable to do anything that she would really like to do. She does, however, need to have a blood transfusion every six weeks to help maintain blood levels.

She is engaged to be married in the next year and her fiance is already learning how to help her with treatment. They intend however, to remain living in the area and for her to continue to use the treatment room at her parents' home, as was envisaged when the project was first mooted.

THE PROJECT TEAM
Home dialysis administrator.
Building Surveyor.
Builder.

THE AIMS
To provide a suitably sized and positioned extension to the family home for use as a haemodialysis room.
To allow a pleasant environment for treatment and to avoid isolation of the user.
To preserve existing space within the home.
To permit straightforward reinstatement, if required.

THE PROPERTY
An owner occupied, mid terraced house built in 1939.

Front view of the house.

Gross internal floor area 64.4m² before and 71.2m² after adaptation.

The house was constructed as part of a small terrace on an estate on the outskirts of a large town.

A hardstanding for the parking of two cars was formed to the front and a small, well laid garden at the rear.

THE ADAPTATION

Extension of a three bedroomed house to provide a haemodialysis room.

* Flat roofed extension to form one room built to dining area at rear of house.

* Pathway and 650mm high retaining wall made to garden beyond.

* Soil and vent pipes to first floor bathroom relocated and additional branch drains and inspection chamber made.

The decision to extend to the rear of the property means that there is no interference with the car parking space and that the room does not get the evening sun.

WINDOWS

* Sash and part of window opening at rear of dining area removed.

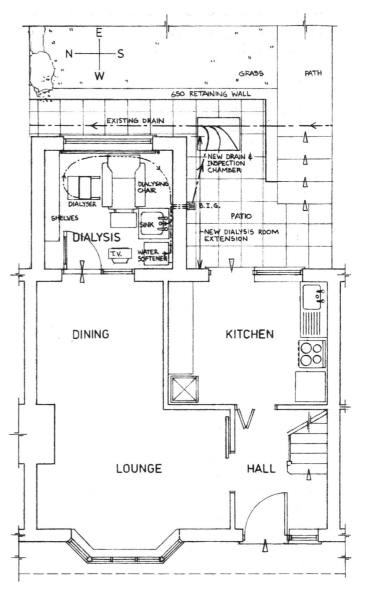

Ground floor plan after extension. 1:75.

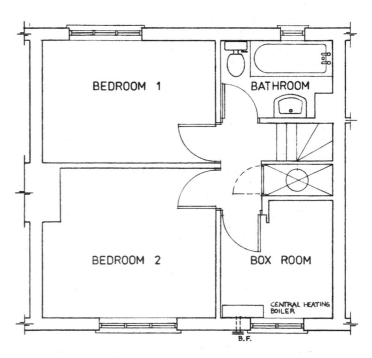

First floor plan unaltered. 1:75.

Rear view of the house showing the new extension.

* Large, sealed unit double glazed window with high level ventilators installed to new rear wall of extension with cill height of 905mm. Sidelight made next to opening for door to new room.

The use of the sidelight and such a large window was governed by the need to get light into the long living area and this has been successfully achieved.

ELECTRICAL WORK

New electrical service, run separately from mains intake via fused isolation switch to new consumer unit located in treatment room, to serve dialysis equipment only.

* 13amp single gang earth leakage circuit breaker socket outlet, on separate circuit, set 1550mm above floor level to serve dialysis machine only.

* Single gang 13amp switched socket outlet; 13amp switched and unswitched fused connection units with neon indicators and flex outlets installed at height 1680 above floor to serve sink pump and water softener.

* Three sets of double power points at height 450mm, wired into house ring main.

* Twin tube fluorescent light, with single pull cord switch by door, mounted in centre of room.

* Alarm bell to ring in hall fitted with pull cord next to proposed position of chair.

* Telephone installed for direct contact with renal unit.

The double sockets are usefully placed for a television and other electrical equipment Miss Smith may choose to use during treatment. The alarm bell has never been used, as a verbal call for help is easily heard within the small house.

HEATING AND WATER

* Large double radiator resited from rear of living area to position under new window.

* Eighteen litre cold water tank with lid mounted on shelf at height 1910mm over proposed position of sink and water softener.

* Trapped back inlet gulley to receive waste from sink, softener and dialyser, formed with sealed cover plate.

* Rising water main service to dialysis room taken as first branch off existing house service; gate valve installed at sink.

* Non return valve installed at highest point to new service to prevent back syphonage of dialysis water into house supply.

* Hot water to sink taken from existing hot water system.

A warm even temperature can be maintained in the room with the radiator that is always left on during treatment, and there is no need to close the door to the living area to maintain temperature levels, even in the coldest weather. While a spur outlet was provided for an infra red wall heater in case it was needed during the summer months when the central heating was turned off, additional heating appliances did not prove necessary.

DOORS

* Clear glass panelled door with lever handle fitted to new doorway.

* 75mm raised threshold formed to link extension to living area.

Frosted glass was suggested for the door and sidelight to counter the dominant view of the treatment room from the living area. Miss Smith decided against this; she felt it would isolate her from the rest of the family. The clear glass helps to maximize light penetration, although it means that the new room and its equipment is clearly visible from the living room. This does not worry the family. The door is usually left open, allowing Miss Smith to feel part of family activities during treatment and enables the passage of heat from the large source in the new room to the living area.

THE TREATMENT ROOM

* Vinyl sheet flooring laid with hospital coving secured to raised threshold and to walls to height of 95mm.

* Six 1829 x 305mm melamine faced shelves at regular intervals starting at 580mm from floor to 2135mm.

* Haemodialysis machine with integral drip stand, sink unit, formalizing pump, water softener and reclining chair installed by hospital technicians.

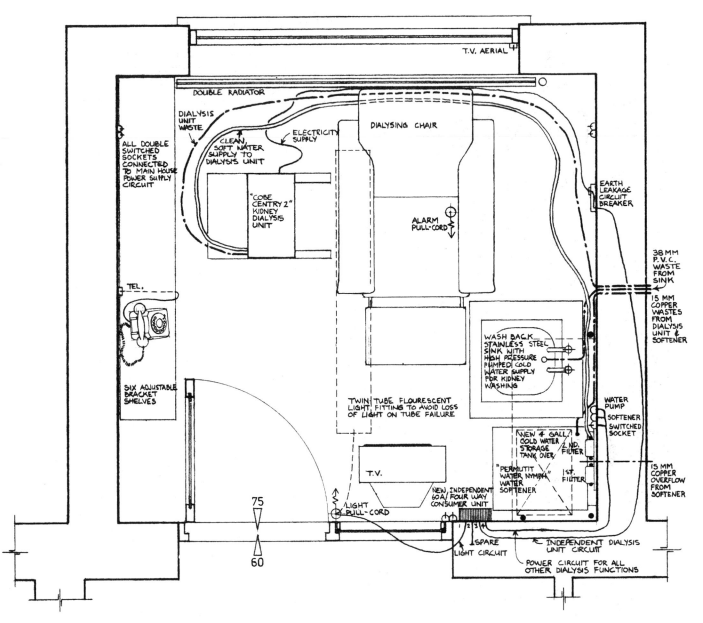

Labels within the plan:

T.V. AERIAL

DOUBLE RADIATOR

DIALYSIS UNIT WASTE

CLEAN SOFT WATER SUPPLY TO DIALYSIS UNIT

ELECTRICITY SUPPLY

DIALYSING CHAIR

ALL DOUBLE SWITCHED SOCKETS CONNECTED TO MAIN HOUSE POWER SUPPLY CIRCUIT

"COBE CENTRY 2" KIDNEY DIALYSIS UNIT

ALARM PULL-CORD

EARTH LEAKAGE CIRCUIT BREAKER

TEL.

38 MM P.V.C. WASTE FROM SINK

15 MM COPPER WASTES FROM DIALYSIS UNIT & SOFTENER

WASH BACK STAINLESS STEEL SINK WITH HIGH PRESSURE PUMPED COLD WATER SUPPLY FOR KIDNEY WASHING

SIX ADJUSTABLE BRACKET SHELVES

TWIN TUBE FLOURESCENT LIGHT FITTING TO AVOID LOSS OF LIGHT ON TUBE FAILURE

WATER PUMP

SOFTENER SWITCHED SOCKET

T.V.

NEW 4 GALL. COLD WATER STORAGE TANK OVER

2ND. FILTER

"PERMUTIT WATER NYMPH" WATER SOFTENER

1ST. FILTER

15 MM COPPER OVERFLOW FROM SOFTENER

75

60

LIGHT PULL-CORD

NEW INDEPENDENT 60A FOUR WAY CONSUMER UNIT

SPARE LIGHT CIRCUIT

INDEPENDENT DIALYSIS UNIT CIRCUIT

POWER CIRCUIT FOR ALL OTHER DIALYSIS FUNCTIONS

Plan of services to the dialysis room. 1:20.

The floor is easily kept clean and spillages or splashes from the sink are contained and removed within the room with its raised threshold. The open shelves are used to store essential materials and small equipment needed during treatment, and as a back up store. The room also allows sufficient space for stacking additional boxes of supplies which are ordered to cover an eight week period.

Miss Smith dialyses on Monday, Wednesday and Friday evenings following work. Her father returns home at lunchtime and puts on the artifical kidney to rinse, puts the lines onto the machine, checks the water is soft and sets up the saline and heparin drips. This can usually be done in half an hour. Being on flexi time enables Miss Smith to be home at about 4.45pm and she is usually on the machine by 5.15pm. The chair is used fully extended and a television is brought into the room if she wishes. Dialysis takes about five hours during which time she takes her evening meal. She usually feels quite well after treatment, but finds it helpful to be able to go straight to bed, while her father clears up.

CONTRACTUAL PROCEDURE

The home dialysis administrator engaged the building surveyor he usually used and he, in turn, prepared the plans for both the extension and dialysis requirements and nominated a builder. Contract price was agreed for the building construction and services with the contractor and the district health authority. Installation of the specialised equipment was made by the hospital technicians.

EVALUATION

Dialysing at home has meant that Miss Smith is able to hold down a full time job and, while working for a health authority was no doubt helpful to the assurance of her special needs, she no longer has to seek special attention or consideration. Her parents are supportive as seen in the manner in which Mr Smith learnt about and assists in treatment. The whole process is further helped and speeded by Mr Smith's ability and willingness to return home at lunchtime to spend time on the necessary preparation. For Miss Smith, this means that treatment can be undertaken outside working hours.

Miss Smith and the family are content with the work that has been done and see the extension to the rear of the

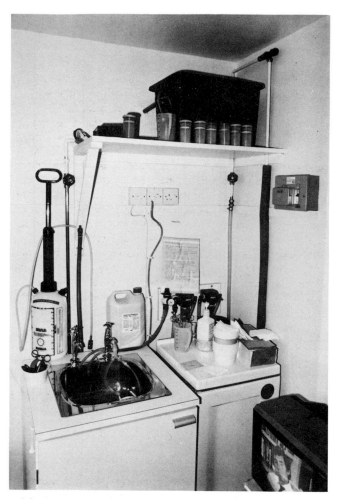

Dialysis equipment.

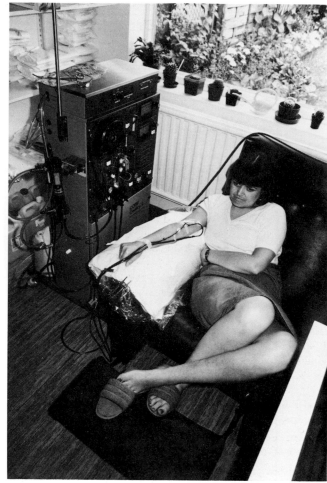

Miss Smith receiving treatment.

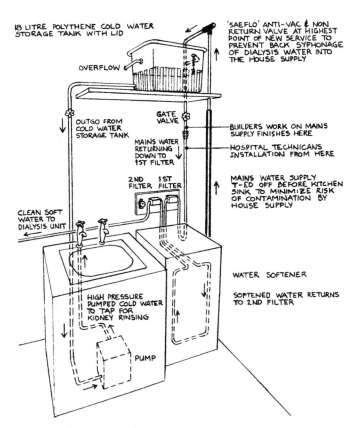

18 LITRE POLYTHENE COLD WATER
STORAGE TANK WITH LID

OVERFLOW

OUTGO FROM
COLD WATER
STORAGE TANK

GATE
VALVE

MAINS WATER
RETURNING
DOWN TO
1ST FILTER

2ND   1ST
FILTER FILTER

CLEAN SOFT
WATER TO
DIALYSIS UNIT

HIGH PRESSURE
PUMPED COLD WATER
TO TAP FOR
KIDNEY RINSING

PUMP

'SAEFLO' ANTI-VAC & NON
RETURN VALVE AT HIGHEST
POINT OF NEW SERVICE TO
PREVENT BACK SYPHONAGE
OF DIALYSIS WATER INTO
THE HOUSE SUPPLY

BUILDERS WORK ON MAINS
SUPPLY FINISHES HERE

HOSPITAL TECHNICANS
INSTALLATION FROM HERE

MAINS WATER SUPPLY
T-ED OFF BEFORE KITCHEN
SINK TO MINIMIZE RISK
OF CONTAMINATION BY
HOUSE SUPPLY

WATER SOFTENER

SOFTENED WATER RETURNS
TO 2ND FILTER

Water supply to the treatment room.

living area as the best of the options originally considered. Despite its dominance on the living room, they do not find the treatment room unattractive and see no need to camouflage something that is an integral part of their lives. The room could be easily reinstated, as would become necessary if Miss Smith had to move out of the area, or her parents decided to retire elsewhere. The water and electricity supplies that are separate from those of the main house ensure that the dialysis equipment could be easily removed, to leave only the three standard double switched socket outlets for connection to the house ring main.

The dialysis room is sufficiently large to allow easy positioning of equipment for efficient use and to allow circulation space even when bulk supplies are heavy and storage space is needed beyond that of the usually sufficient and easily accessible shelves. The positioning of electrical and water services meant that the internal organization of the room had to be planned well in advance and there was, consequently, little scope for flexibility in moving furniture and equipment. This has created no real problem except that Miss Smith cannot decide to look out onto the garden during treatment, as she might wish in the light evenings of the summer months.

Miss Smith is very much part of the family and of activities that go on in the lounge in the evenings during treatment. She has her evening meal and can watch television with the others, in the same manner in which she may spend other evenings.

MISS BELINDA DUDLEY

Aged 19. Renal failure.

Living with mother and a brother.

Provision of a haemodyalisis treatment area at home.

Continuous weight gain and its assessment by friends and family as being typical of teenage years was endured by Miss Dudley with deepening feelings of depression and loss of self confidence. At a time when she wanted to develop an active social life, she found herself withdrawing more and more as her weight grew without apparent check or response to reducing diets. In two years her weight had increased to over 10 stones and when this combined with new symptoms of swollen ankles and feet, she resolved to go to her general practitioner for help.

She was sent to hospital for tests and then to a specialist renal unit in London. Diuretic and steroid therapy was commenced and she was discharged after four weeks. At home her weight increased to over 12 stones and she was readmitted to hospital, a marked drop in urine output indicating that the treatment was not beneficial.

Various methods to control kidney function were tried over the next two months; she frequently felt very unwell and encountered additional complications of a shoulder infection following insertion of a stoma into the subclavian vein for a procedure of dialysis. Eventually, she was established on a dialysis regime and allowed home, with returns to the unit three times each week.

Her need to remain on the machine for six hours meant that she often missed the earlier transport home. Hospital visits developed into long days which had to be managed at a time when she felt least well to cope with them. She tried public transport instead and this proved more successful, as did her treatment which was reduced to five hours per session as she grew stronger and fitter.

Eight months after the diagnosis of renal failure, Miss Dudley was considered by the medical and nursing team to be a suitable candidate for treatment at home. The hospital home dialysis administrator was asked to organise the project and he discussed the implications with the family, who were enthusiastic. Consideration was given to ways in which a treatment room could be incorporated in the home and the building surveyor regularly used by the hospital was commissioned to prepare suitable plans. Permission for the necessary adaptations was obtained from the house owning authority, with the district health authority undertaking to reinstate if necessary. As standard procedure, the building surveyor submitted plans to the water authority for approval, in order that they would be aware of the implications of any interruption in supply or possible contamination. Mrs Dudley commenced a programme of studying and assisting with hospital dialysis in order to help her daughter with the procedures at home, and continued to do this for about two months until fully confident. Once agreed, the aim was to complete the building work as quickly as possible, in order to release time on the hospital machine for another's use; this was achieved in five weeks. A nurse from the renal unit visited Miss Dudley and her mother for the first few sessions at home, with continued contact with the renal unit assured as and when required.

Establishment on the artificial kidneys has meant that Miss Dudley has regained her health. She finds that she walks a little more slowly and has some difficulty with hills but, as she had never been very energetic, this makes little impact on her life and her disco dancing remains unaffected. She found it hard to adjust to a salt free diet and restrict her fluid intake to one pint per day, needing to plan ahead for social outings such as to the pub. She was also able to return to her previous office job with a local company who had made temporary arrangements to cover for her sickness leave. As she could only manage two short days per week to start with, a colleague increased her own hours on a temporary basis that allowed job sharing. In addition, the firm paid for taxi transport in order that her travelling time be kept to a minimum and the sum of her therapuetic earnings remain intact. A return to full time employment and dialysing in the evenings is Miss Dudley's aim, in the determination that the treatment necessary to her life should disrupt it to the absolute minimum.

THE PROJECT TEAM

Home dialysis administrator.
Building Surveyor.
Builder.

THE AIMS

To allow provision and use of home dialysis equipment in an area where hygiene requirements could be maintained.
To provide a pleasant environment for treatment without impinging on general family life and the needs of the patient outside the treatment time.
To allow bulk delivery of essential items by provision of adequate storage.

THE PROPERTY

A district council three bedroomed, semi detached house built in 1955.

Gross internal floor area 87.3m² unchanged.

The house was sited on a corner plot, with a large open expanse of garden to the front and a small, secluded one to the rear.

THE ADAPTATION

* Storeroom forming corner of house adjacent to side gate modified to provide treatment room.

* 2090 x 1510mm wooden shed built in rear garden for storage of bulk supplies.

The storeroom was the only area possible fortreatment, within the existing property, as there was no spare bedroom and the hospital would not consider conversion of Miss Dudley's bedroom.

The wooden shed houses the eight week bulk supplies for the machine and salt for the softener. Its position next to the side gate gives ease of delivery and access from the

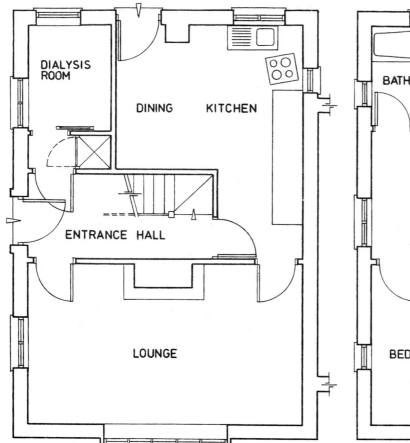

The ground floor after adaptation. 1:75.

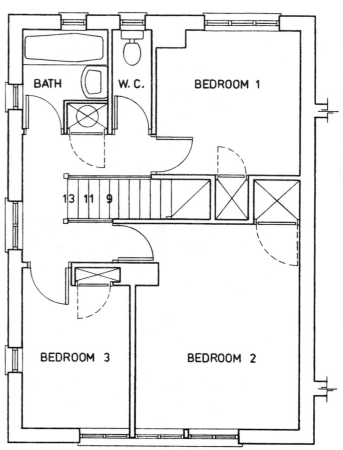

The first floor, unaltered. 1:75.

house, so that materials may be brought in quickly when the weather is bad. Although the wooden shed is substantial and of a good size, the equipment for dialysis takes up a good deal of the space and leaves little room for storage of bicycles, steps and garden equipment, once housed in the integral storeroom to the house.

EXTERNAL DOORS

* External door to storeroom infilled with timber panel construction to internal cill height 1535mm.

The choice of materials to block up the doorway was made to facilitate reversion to the original state on reallocation of the house.

Front view of the house.

WINDOWS

* High level window made above infill of old external door opening.

* 905mm cill height window at front of house retained.

The large window affords a good view of the whole corner and a road junction from the chair, although Miss Dudley rarely takes notice of what is going on outside when she uses the room.

ELECTRICAL WORK

* New electrical service, run separately from mains intake via fused isolation switch to new consumer unit located in new meter store, to serve dialysis equipment only.

* New consumer unit to serve: 13amp single gang earth leakage circuit breaker socket outlet on separate circuit installed for dialysis machine; single gang 13amp switched socket outlet; 13amp switched and unswitched fused connection units with neon indicators and flex outlets installed at height 1250mm above floor to serve sink pump and water softener.

* One double socket outlet at height 410mm above floor connected to house ring main to serve television, radio and additional heating appliances.

* Pull cord switched twin fluorescent tube lighting.

* Pull cord alarm bell beside proposed position of chair.

* Separate line telephone for direct contact with renal unit in emergency.

The external door to the storeroom was blocked up to form a new window, but could be easily reinstated if required.

The alarm bell, if used, rings in the main house to summon help and the telephone gives contact with the renal unit. A small television or a radio can be easily brought into the room for use during treatment as desired.

The provision of a separate electricity supply allows for the facilities in the room to be driven by a generator, if necessary, and for dialysis equipment wiring to be easily stripped out on reinstatement of the room.

HEATING AND WATER

* 750w infra red heater with pull cord mounted on wall above proposed position of reclining chair.

* Eighteen litre cold water tank sited on shelf at height 1870mm and connected to give direct supply to wash back sink unit and water softener under.

* Hot water to sink taken from existing service to house.

Good heating was considered essential since it is usual to feel the cold more when dialysing. The external cavity walls, in this instance, were not insulated and the room can be cold.

A first tapping of the water main and a non return valve prevents the possibility of contamination of the main house supply.

HALLWAYS AND DOORS

* Gas and electricity meters retained in storeroom and partitioned off to form small lobby between hallway and dialysis room.

* Meter area enclosed by louvre door.

* 75mm high door threshold formed and 760mm glazed sliding door fitted.

* Door to dialysis area from main house rehung to open outwards into hall.

Gas and electricity boards do not like their meter readers to enter dialysis rooms if in use and this necessitated, in this instance, division of the room to allow a lobby to contain the meters, with the result that the treatment room had to be reduced in size. The glass door does, however, help to create an illusion of greater space, but is usually left open unless the weather is very cold. The original internal door was rehung as there was insufficient space for it to open inwards because of the position of the partition wall and the sliding door.

THE TREATMENT ROOM

* Brick walls plastered and painted.

* Vinyl sheeting with welded seams applied to floor, continued against raised threshold and up walls to height of 95mm.

* Six 305 x 915mm shelves starting at 750mm from floor to height of 2000mm.

* Haemodialysis machine, wash back sink, water softener, drip stand and reclining armchair supplied and fitted.

Owing to the small size of the room and the partition wall, a smaller than usual water softener had to be used and positioned under the sink which was the only space available. The open shelves allow for storage of towels, stethoscope, blood pressure pads and bulk supplies for a week. The small table is used for initial preparation and take off packs and for a portable television that can be brought into the room for watching during treatment. The chair chosen allows better and more comfortable positioning for treatment than a bed.

The floor can be easily kept clean and its waterproofing avoids damage if there is a leak from the machine. The room does not have to be clinically sterile, however, there not being the same danger of cross infection as in hospital.

Miss Dudley attaches the needles, sets the machine and sits on the reclining chair for five hours. She reads, dozes and watches television. In an emergency, a bell rings on the machine and she is usually able to rectify the problem or call for help from the house or renal unit. Following treatment, Miss Dudley requires help to be removed from the machine and her blood pressure is taken to determine whether a dextrose or saline solution is required as the final washback is made into the system.

Miss Dudley uses the machine every Monday, Wednesday and Friday with completion of treatment at approximately 3.30pm. Preparation takes about one hour and cleaning up

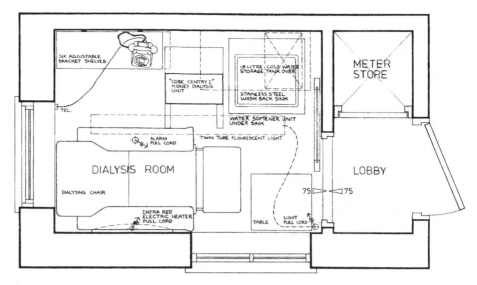

Plan of dialysis room layout. 1:20.

a further one. The return to full time employment is planned on the basis that Mrs Dudley will take over the procedure of preparation which will allow her daughter to go onto the machine as soon as she gets back from work, the evening meal being given to her during treatment.

CONTRACTUAL PROCEDURE

The home dialysis administrator contracted the building surveyor usually engaged for such projects in the catchment area of the hospital. The building surveyor nominated the builder most frequently used and, therefore, experienced in the special field. The price tendered was acceptable to the district health authority who contracted the builder, without the need for other prices to be sought. All preparation of services was made by the contractor with final connections of the equipment made by the hospital technicians.

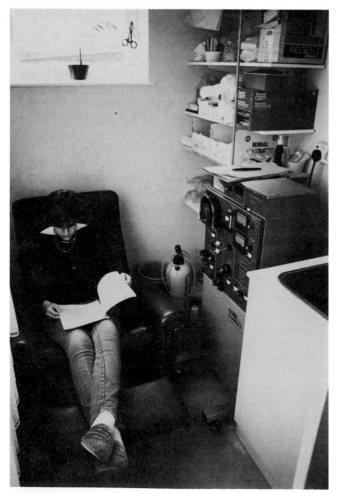

The chair cannot be fully reclined owing to space limitations.

EVALUATION

Dialysis at home has allowed Miss Dudley to reduce the impact of her need for treatment to the minimum. There is no lengthy travelling and waiting time, as was encountered in visits to the unit. With a little sensible planning and thinking ahead, she is able to pursue the same interests as her peers and to contemplate return to full time employment. Essential also, however, is her mother with whom she has a close relationship and upon whom she depends for help throughout the dialysis procedure. It was fortunate that Mrs Dudley was not in employment and could, therefore, more easily give time to learning the necessary skills and to assisting with the dialysis procedure.

The position of the room within the house means that Mrs Dudley can come and go easily, as treatment procedure may dictate, and Miss Dudley need not feel cut off from the rest of the family. A house extension would have involved a far lengthier process, upheaval and expense, and the layout of the whole site did not lend itself to provision of a prefabricated portable dialysis room.

It is regrettable that the family continues to have problems with storage of such items as garden equipment and bicycles that cannot be easily transferred to internal storage areas. The provision of the new shed in the garden has not made up for the loss of the storage area to the treatment room as it is only sufficient, as intended, for keeping bulk supplies from the hospital. Provision such as a new shed is included in the specification for home dialysis work only when there is no existing storage space for bulk supplies, and not in response to replacing space used for the adaptation.

The site chosen for the treatment room allows a discreet provision that has no detriment to general home and family life. The presence of the room is not apparent elsewhere in the house as no alteration has been necessary to the living areas, other than to rehang a door. Although the room is small, it is sufficient to house the necessary equipment and supplies and yet give the impression of a light and pleasant room. It seems remarkable, however, that the size of the room had to be reduced to create a lobby to house power meters and that no more appropriate site could be found for them, although this would have considerably increased the expenditure on the project. The new room is viewed as a treatment area, permitting diversions to help pass the time of dialysis. There is no other connection to Miss Dudley's or her family's daily living activities and, as such, no effort has been made, or would be appropriate, for it to become a more homely room.

SUPPLEMENTARY TECHNICAL REPORTS:

Gardens (1)

CONVERSION OF A SUBURBAN GARDEN TO
ALLOW WHEELCHAIR CIRCULATION AND
MANAGEMENT OF PLANTS FROM SITTING OR
STANDING

As standing tolerance and walking ability became limited, a
lifelong interest in gardening was maintained by redesigning
the vegetable plot to allow management principally from an
electric wheelchair.

An area of 18.0 x 4.5m was lowered by removal of 200mm
depth of top soil, which was subsequently used to fill ten
open ended raised beds of various sizes made of second
hand paving slabs. The beds were formed by sinking the
slabs on end in 150mm deep concrete, with a single layer of
bricks across the width to keep the base in position. Steel
cord or rope ties were secured around each bed for added
safety.

The wide pathways between the beds were paved with
similar slabs set in sand and an original pathway down the
side of the garden was retained.

A 3.0 x 2.2m aluminium frame greenhouse, with sliding
door entrance and additional concrete slabs used to form
an internal paved area and a surrounding raised bed was
set at the lower end of the plot.

Additional varied plant containers were achieved using
upright sewer, rainwater and chimney pipes, wooden
barrels and pierced five gallon paint pots.

The garden is reached by a Terry step lift to allow transfer
from the 430mm high patio to ground level, with a 1 in 12
ramp giving access to the plot at the lower end of the
garden.

An organic system of cultivation is used and facilitated by
annual use of manure based compost including hops and
comfrey which, with careful crop rotation, ensures soil
health. Restriction of space demands intensive sowing;
potatoes, for example, are spaced at 300mm intervals and

**The beds are tended from a sideways position to allow close
contact with the plants without stretching.**

194

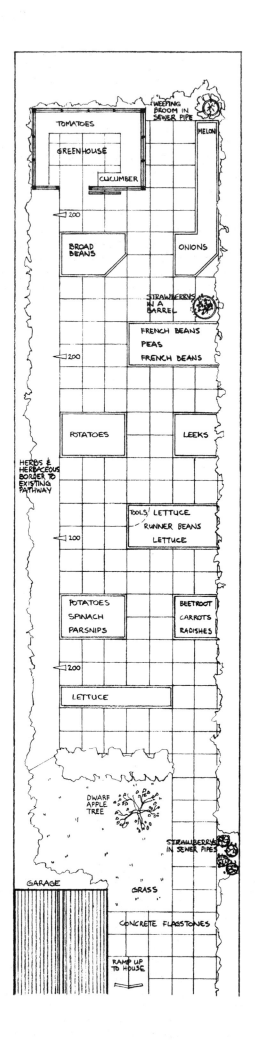

Plan of the garden. 1:100.

banked up with well rotted leaf mould and grass cuttings at soil level. Peas are trained against wire racks and runner beans on wooden frames that allow support and management from standing.

Garden tools are adapted from conventional implements or household equipment, for example: a shortened garden fork and rake, a blunt paint scraper for hoeing and a table fork for fine weeding. Cloches are made from large clear plastic sweet jars with the tops removed.

Although wheelchair access is not possible in the greenhouse, standing is reduced with management of plants achieved from sitting at a light bench seat which clips across the top of the slabs. Automatic ventilation is used in the greenhouse and watering, with an adjustable spray nozzle, is facilitated by a hose running from the main house.

Planning of the dimensions of the raised beds was based upon the most comfortable and safe arm reach of 600mm from a wheelchair. Costs were kept to a minimum using second hand paving slabs at a total cost of £180 and construction by members of the International Voluntary Service.

Gardens (2)

GREENHOUSE GARDENING BY A WHEELCHAIR USER AND AN AMBULANT PERSON WITH LIMITED REACH

An interest in gardening, and a desire to combine this into a semi commercial venture in which both husband and wife could participate, led to this development of plant raising under glass. The work is a joint project with skills and abilities of each member used to complement those of the other.

An aluminium frame 2600mm glasshouse by Robinsons of Winchester, consisting of glass walls with metal base panels and a double sliding door of 1220mm clearance was used. The sliding doors were suspended from the top of the door frame, with lower guidance in a shallow groove in the flat metal strip forming the base of the door frame. No base walls were required to the greenhouse, as anchors could be set directly into concrete in the ground to secure the main frame to firm subsoil foundations.

Ventilation was achieved through two sets of six louvre windows set in the walls and four top ventilators, two of which were fitted with solar powered automatic openers.

Gas heating was supplied in 10mm microbore copper pipe covered in a plastic waterproof casing, terminating in a rigid bayonet fixing for attachment to a small gas heater via flexible hosing.

Power was given via weather protected cable from the main house for the propagating bench, extended artificial daylight, three power points and a 3kw fan heater.

A water tap was mounted on the outside corner of the house, next to the greenhouse door, and a hose was connected for plant watering.

Single tier aluminium staging at height 760mm was used throughout, except for a small two tier area for the propagating bench, with 20mm deep gravel trays reversible to form flat work benches around the perimeter. In addition, two purpose built propagating benches, with domed plastic covers, were positioned close to the power source.

The entire area, including the surrounding garden and pathways, was laid to concrete slabs.

There is sufficient knee room under the single tier staging for forward access to plants from a wheelchair. Plants at

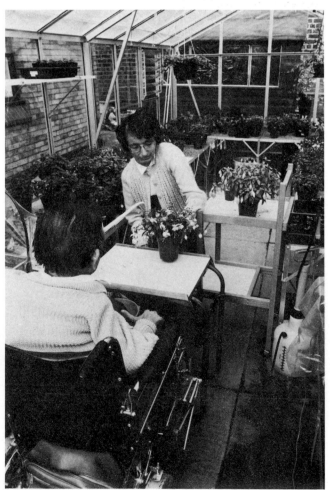

Plants are passed for individual attention on a cantilever table used from the wheelchair.

The threshold strip does not impede wheelchair or wheelbarrow access, and the metal base panels of the greenhouse act as kick plates.

195

O

the back of the bench can be reached by the ambulant person if there is a risk of damaging tall, fragile plants by leaning over from a seated position. Work at the two tier bench is possible from a sideways sitting position, and a free standing table is used as a base for individual work.

An Etwall trolley and an Easywheeler barrow are used for carrying such items as potting compost, which is bought in bulk and scooped into a plastic bucket for transportation to the work area. The heater is housed on a low trolley for wheeling into the centre of the greenhouse for most efficient night heating and the thermostatically controlled fan heater is used as a back up in case of gas failure, or to boost the temperature when needed.

The modular design of the greenhouse and the staging means that the system can be extended if required. The entire paved floor of the greenhouse is maintenance free and allows maximum turning space between the benches.

The louvre window operating handle at 65mm above the level of the back of the bench makes it inaccessible to anyone but the most able bodied and, although ventilation is controlled to some extent automatically, the limit for opening does not give the flexibility in temperature control needed for varying plants. The lightweight plastic domes over the propagating benches are easy to reach and move when more ventilation is required.

The spray gun attachment on the end of the hosepipe does away with the need to return to the tap. Routine watering is achieved by capillary matting or standing plants on expanded clay granules.

The secondhand concrete slabs were laid for £100.00 and the greenhouse price was reduced by 25% to £750.00 in 1984, as it had been a demonstration model.

Mains services were installed by friends and a grant of £500.00 was given by the Gardens for the Disabled Trust.

A hosepipe with lance spray allows fine mist spraying from a wheelchair.

Doorways (1)

REORGANIZATION OF LAYOUT AND OPERATION OF DOORS TO PERMIT WHEELCHAIR CIRCULATION

* Automatic door openers by Wessex Medical Ltd.

The requirement to use an electric wheelchair and to have straightforward access to all parts of the bungalow called for alterations to most rooms in a property that was poorly designed for ease of circulation. An extension was formed to the side of the house to give a larger kitchen/dining area and a carport. The partition wall dividing the bathroom from the wc was removed, and the corridor leading to the study was incorporated into the bathroom. Radical reorganization of doorways was required to give access to the study and to give wheelchair turning space into rooms from the narrow central corridor.

The study door from the corridor was blocked up and new access to the room made from the lounge. An automatic door opener with hit switch operation, of the opener located on the top of the study side of the door, mounted at height 240mm on either side of the doorway. An electro magnet was also linked to these switches to keep the door from being pushed open by the dog.

The lounge door from the entrance hall was blocked up and new 45° splay doorways to the corridor made to the lounge and bathroom.

A UPVC framed French door was used to replace the single leaf door leading from the study to the garden and a radio controlled automatic door opener was fitted.

The new door from the study to the lounge enabled restrictive corridor space to be annexed to form a larger bathroom, and so permit installation of an overhead tracked hoist with wheelchair circulation. The splayed doorways took little usable space from the lounge to give essential circulation space in the corridor at the point of interlinking of the main rooms. In addition, the much used link between the lounge and the study requires negotiation of one door, instead of two.

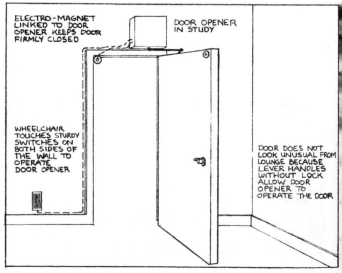

The lounge/study door.

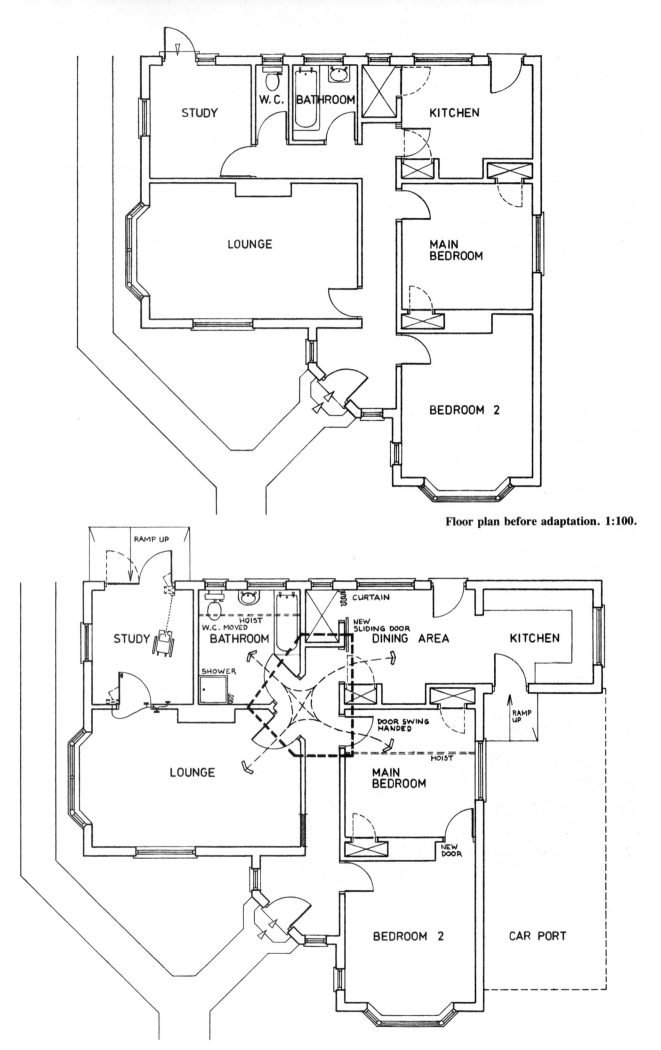

Floor plan before adaptation. 1:100.

RAMP UP

STUDY

W.C. MOVED
BATHROOM

SHOWER

HOIST

CURTAIN

NEW
SLIDING DOOR
DINING AREA

KITCHEN

RAMP
UP

DOOR SWING
HANDED

HOIST

MAIN
BEDROOM

NEW
DOOR

LOUNGE

BEDROOM 2

CAR PORT

Floor plan after adaptation. 1:100.

197

The height of the switches permit an electric wheelchair to be driven against them for speedy use of the door and, although the system appears rudimentary, it works well and needs little attention.

At the external study door the close proximity of the top of the metal framed doors to the ceiling did not allow a conventionally mounted door opener. This is operated by a radio controlled unit sited underneath the door opening mechanism, and activated by a transmitter mounted on the wheelchair. Instructions are needed both to open the door and to close it, and the cycle cannot be interrupted once begun. The door is held rigidly open for twenty seconds and, if no instruction is given to close it, will flap freely in the wind. There is no permanent hold available as would be useful on occasions.[1]

The single link switch to opener of the internal door is reliable. The more complex and expensive double link of radio signal to switch to opener of the external door is likely to be more prone to breakdown.

Doorways (2)

TWO HEIGHT AUTOMATIC DOOR OPENER

* Electric door locks by Tunstall Telecom Limited.

* A system of door opening was required, to be operated by a phocomelic disabled person, at conventional height when artificial limbs were worn and at floor level when these were removed.

The external door was secured by an electric keep, operated by any of four key switches sited in pairs inside and outside. The upper switches were set at height 1225mm for use from standing and the lower set at 545mm for use from the floor. Lever door handles, without mortice lock or latch, were set at 990mm height on the door.

The door keep unlocks as soon as the switch is turned off, and locks thirty seconds after the switch is turned on. The delay is sufficient to admit visitors with a simple on/off turn of the key, which reduces the risk of the door being left unlocked accidentally.

The external study door.

The door can be operated at two heights.

[1] Subsequent modifications to an early prototype used in this instance allows the door to be held open until commanded to close, if required. A range of activating devices is now available, including a small hand held transmitter and receiver.

Doorways (3)

TO PERMIT ENTRY TO A SMALL WC COMPARTMENT WITH A WALKING FRAME AND THE DOOR TO BE CLOSED

* Ellipse door by Reduced Swing doors Ltd.

Design of small wc compartments with inward opening doors in a residential home for elderly people meant that those who used walking frames were unable to close the door behind them when using the wc. Reversing the swing of the doors to open outwards was not possible as the 830mm door leaves would have created a hazard to those walking in the transverse corridor outside.

Ellipse doors were fitted to the existing frames on the other side of the door stops, with the stops moved out slightly to accommodate this. Use of the folding door meant that the total floor area needed for the swing was reduced to less than half that of the previous door.

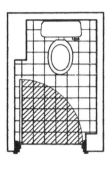 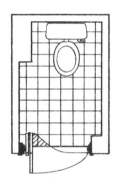

The reduced swing door. 1:50. The new door reduces the area of door swing within the compartment to almost a tenth of its original size.

Clear opening width was reduced by only 60mm, protrusion of the door swing into the corridor being 250mm. The folding of the doors keeps the handles within easy reach for closing. Access to the compartments is not impeded, as there are no guide rails at floor level, and walking frames can be taken in and the doors closed without difficulty.

The door does not obstruct corridor or compartment.

Ramping

TO REDUCE RISK OF DAMP PENETRATION IN A WALL ABUTTED BY A RAMP BRIDGING THE DAMP PROOF COURSE

Ramping was considered as a means of overcoming the problems of a 160mm high threshold step for residents at the main entrance to a block of sheltered accommodation. As part of the ramp had to abut one of the external walls of the building, a special detail was used to prevent it from transmitting dampness into the wall above the level of the damp proof course.

The ramp and doorway.

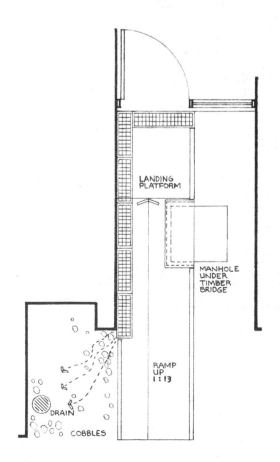

Plan of the ramp and grating. 1:50.

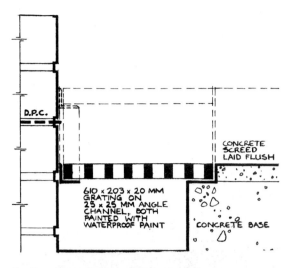

Section through the ramp and grating.

The concrete ramp was built to within 170mm of the wall and the door threshold. A 25mm x 25mm steel angle channel, painted with waterproof paint, was fitted to the wall. 610mm long x 203mm wide x 20mm deep standard channel grating sections, painted with waterproof paint, were laid to span the channel and ramp base.

20mm leveling screed was laid on top of the concrete to finish flush with the edge of the grating, forming a rebated edge to the ramp. A removable timber bridge section was used to give access to a manhole.

The ramp is sheltered by the shape of the building, and the detail allows the ramp to abut the wall without causing excessive dampness. Access for cleaning and maintenance is achieved by the easy removal of the gratings which are held in place by their own weight.

Windows

LOW LEVEL OPENING OF HIGH WINDOWS

* Solopak gear by Teleflex Morse Limited.

The requirement was to give control of window opening for a person who moved around on the floor for some of the time, but who could, despite limited reach, have access to window latches at conventional height when wearing artificial legs.

Window opening gear consisting of cable in conduit to the operating handle was used to open and close small high level windows. The handle was set at 540mm from the floor as required by the resident.

The conduit can be bent and the cable made up to 3m in length, to enable positioning of the winding handle at a point most accessible to the user. The handle is easily operated, although friction increases with the length of the cable.

The handle can be set at a height to suit the user.

Stairlifts and Hoists (1)

A STAIRLIFT IN A COTTAGE WITH A VERY SMALL LANDING AND HALL, AND A 57° ANGLE STRAIGHT STAIRCASE

* Silver Rail stairlift by Stannah Lifts Limited.

Doctor's advice that climbing stairs was to be avoided meant conversion of the one small reception room to a bedroom in this country cottage. Although there were difficulties of overcrowding in this room, there was no desire to move from the home of birth, and the site was unsuitable for house extension. A stairlift was considered as the only means of allowing the home to be used more fully.

The choice of lift with a motor under the seat meant that no space was lost for motor housing from the landing or hall.

The slim rail and seat allowed sufficient knee clearance for use on a narrow stairway.

Adjustment of the stairlift seat height helped to compensate for the unusually steep angle of arrival at the top of the stairs and enabled the platform to rest 100mm over the landing, giving an easily managed step and sufficient space for alighting.

The Silver Rail stairlift in use.

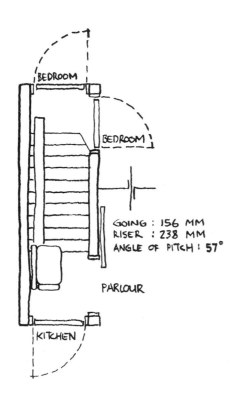

GOING : 156 MM
RISER : 238 MM
ANGLE OF PITCH : 57°

Plan of the 57° stairlift. 1:50.

201

Stairlifts and Hoists (2)

A STRAIGHT STAIRLIFT ALLOWING SPACE FOR HELP WITH TRANSFERS ON A NARROW LANDING

* Swivel seat stairlift by Fred Brookes Limited.

The requirement for mechanical assistance to get upstairs, and the unsuitability of house layout for a through ceiling lift, led to consideration of a stairlift. The hall allowed sufficient space for transfer from wheelchair to lift seat, but the small, transverse landing and bannister extension was too confined a space for the assisted transfer needed on the upper floor. However, by removal of the bannisters at landing level, additional space could be given, providing the hazard of exposing the open stair well could be overcome when the lift was not in use.

The newel posts and bannister rails were removed from the landing on either side of the stairs and were replaced by a pair of matching wrought iron and wooden handrail supports.

One handrail was fixed permanently into position. The other was fitted with floor insertion pegs and a slide bolt into the wall at handrail level to allow it to be easily removed when required.

Removal of the top bannister is essential to allow the stairlift seat to swivel to enable the helper to assist transfer on the upper floor.

When the lift is not in use, the replacement of the removeable rail affords protection across the landing from the open stairway.

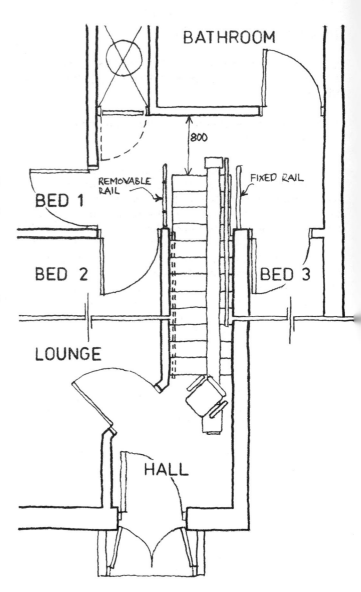

Plan of the stairway. 1:50.

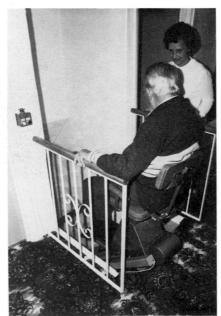

Space is made by removal of the bannister rail at the top of the stairs.

202

Stairlifts and Hoists (3)

LEVEL ACCESS FROM A STAIRLIFT STANDING PLATFORM AT THE TOP OF A STRAIGHT FLIGHT OF STAIRS

* Standing platform stairlift and adaptation by Fred Brookes Limited.

Limitations in the depth of the landing and the position of the bathroom door precluded siting of the stairlift motor farther away from the top of the stairs, with the result that the stairlift platform stopped level with the landing, leaving a gap above the adjacent lower stairs.

A wooden platform, supported on two legs and hinged to a bracket fixing between one leg and the landing, was constructed to bridge the gap at the top of the stairway. The outer leg was hinged to drop back flat against the platform when this was raised and a magnetic catch was fitted to the newel post to hold the platform in position.

A pull cord from the corner of the platform was tied to the bannister, to be easily accessible for use in controlling lowering of the platform. The platform gives a firm surface, level with the landing for alighting and is easily operated either from the lift or the landing.

Free pedestrian access is given to the stairway when the lift and platform are not in use.

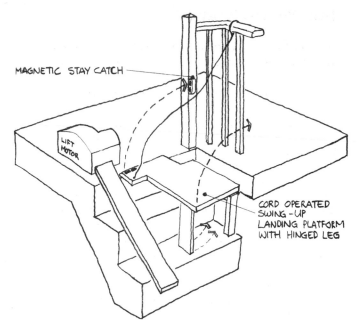

The landing platform.

The platform and lift in use.

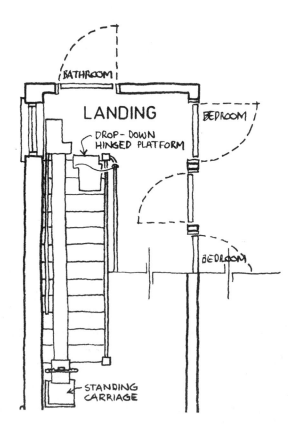

Plan of the stairway. 1:50.

203

Stairlifts and Hoists (4)

PLATFORM LIFT GIVING WHEELCHAIR ACCESS TO THE UPPER FLOOR VIA A RECONSTRUCTED STRAIGHT STAIRWAY

* Wheelchair Stairlift by Gimson and Company (Leicester) Limited.

The requirement for wheelchair access to the upper floor, and the unsuitability of the house layout for a through ceiling lift, led to consideration of stairway reconstruction to allow installation of a wheelchair stairlift as the only alternative.

The partition wall between the hall and the lounge was moved back to allow construction of a new stairway and sufficient circulation space to be preserved in the hall.

A 1200 x 790 x 70mm deep well was made in the floor at the base of the stair way to allow the lift platform to rest level with the surrounding floor.

In its upper position, the lift was made to rest level with the landing so that the safety barrier/drop down ramp could bridge the point of abutment, with no space lost for turning from the lift in either direction.

The wheelchair stairlift arriving at the upper landing level. As it makes no difference which way the wheelchair sits on the platform, the user can always face the direction of travel.

The controls positioned mid way along the side panel of the lift facilitate access for operation from a wheelchair, and a battery powered alarm bell strip on the adjacent wall gives an added sense of security.

When not in use the lift platform is stored at the base of the stairway, with the safety rail in its folded position against the wall, to allow free access to the stairway and the full opening of the front door to the house.

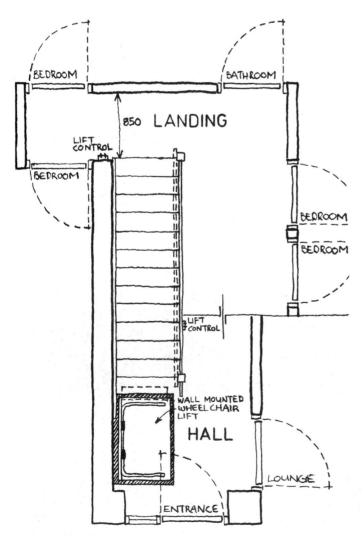

Plan of the stairway. 1:50.

204

Stairlifts and Hoists (5)

A STAIRLIFT AND HOIST COMBINATION GIVING ASSISTED MOBILITY UP THE STAIRS AND ACROSS WINDERS INTO A MEZZANINE LEVEL BEDROOM

* Slimliner stairlift and Travelmaster hoist by Wessex Medical Equipment Limited.

Varying floor levels and juxtaposition of rooms precluded installation of a through ceiling lift for a child whose parents were having increasing difficulty in carrying him up the stairs. A stairlift was considered the most suitable solution, if the problem of transfer to the bedroom over the stair winders could be overcome.

The stairlift rail was extended beyond the travel of the stairs to bring the seat in line with overhead tracked hoisting above the winders.

The bedroom door was stopped short of full height to allow the hoist track to pass above. The differences in ceiling heights were overcome by suspension of the track from a 445mm long vertical steel tie braced with a steel strap fixed to the wall to prevent lateral movement.

Extension of the stairlift track at the top allows the seat to rest level with a helper standing on the stair above that of the bedroom door threshold. Slings, already positioned in the stairlift seat prior to transfer, are easily hooked onto the overhead tracked hoist for onward travel into the bedroom.

Hazard of assisted transfer over the stairs is eliminated and the combination of stairlift and hoist works efficiently, although the gap over the door transmits some noise and draught to the bedroom from the stairway.

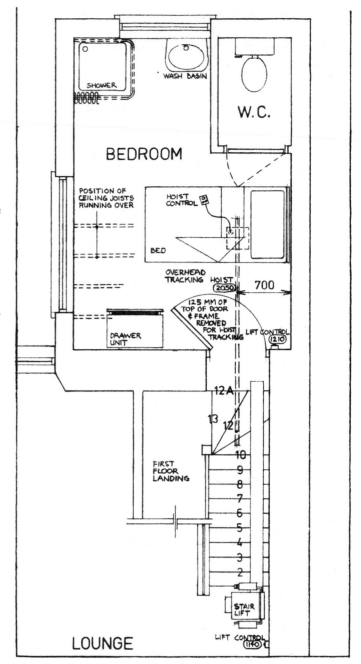

Plan of the stairlift and hoist run. 1:50.

The three main stages in lifting from the hall to the bedroom.

Stairlifts and Hoists (6)

OVERHEAD HOIST TRACKING ACROSS A LOW TRANSVERSE STRUCTURAL BEAM

* Commodore hoist by SML Ltd.

The requirement to use lifting aids, to assist those caring for a person dependent on help for all aspects of daily living, was not adequately met by mobile hoisting and led to the consideration of overhead tracked electric hoisting. However, the position of a structural beam across the bathroom appeared to preclude a straight run from bed to bath. Separate tracking in the bathroom was not considered to be desirable, as the bath would have needed to be moved to ensure transferring space. A means to allow single tracking to pass underneath was therefore considered to be the preferred option to lift from bed to bath, the wc not being required in this instance.

40 x 40mm tubular steel struts were suspended from a 150 x 50mm timber plate fixed to the ceiling to carry the overhead tracking 955mm down from the ceiling and under the downstand beam in the bathroom. Alternate struts were tied back to the adjoining wall by 40mm steel angle brackets to prevent lateral movement.

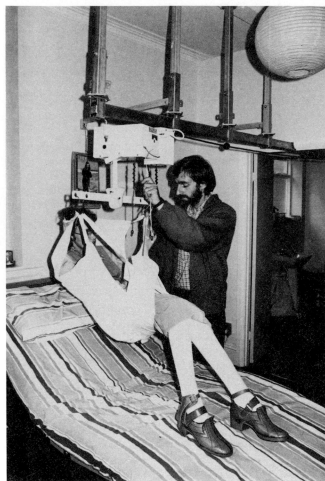

The hoist in use.

A double pole pull switch fused flex outlet was used to supply the cable recoil drum and avoid snagging on the low beam.

The purpose of providing continuous tracking is achieved, but the brackets are unsightly, and there is some jolting and noise as the hoist passes over each joint.

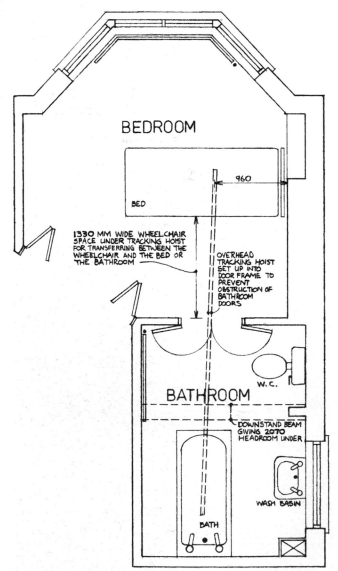

BEDROOM

960

BED

1330 MM WIDE WHEELCHAIR SPACE UNDER TRACKING HOIST FOR TRANSFERRING BETWEEN THE WHEELCHAIR AND THE BED OR THE BATHROOM

OVERHEAD TRACKING HOIST SET UP INTO DOOR FRAME TO PREVENT OBSTRUCTION OF BATHROOM DOORS

W.C.

BATHROOM

DOWNSTAND BEAM GIVING 2070 HEADROOM UNDER

WASH BASIN

BATH

Plan of hoist tracking under transverse beam. 1:50.

206

Stairlifts and Hoists (7)

TO LIFT FROM THE GROUND FLOOR TO THE BEDROOM ABOVE AND INTO THE BATHROOM ADJACENT

* Commodore hoist and switchplate by SML Ltd.

A means to transport three dependent children between the ground floor and their bedroom and bathroom on the first floor of a three storey house was sought. The narrow and curving staircase was not suitable for a stairlift. Insufficient height could be gained, in an appropriate place, for installation of a through ceiling lift because of the steep pitch of the roof that extended over part of the two upper floors on one side of the house. Hoisting was seen as the only viable alternative.

A 1150 x 780mm hatchway was formed between the living room and the children's bedroom above, and a 950mm high guard rail was installed around this on the upper floor. T shaped overhead tracking, linked via a switchplate, was installed for lifting between floors and for traversing between the bedroom and bathroom. The direction of the switchplate is changed by pull cords when the hoist is directly underneath. Small semi circular safety rails on the turntable prevent the hoist from rolling off the track as turns are made. As the hoist is pushed along the track manually, care had to be taken to ensure that the track was level.

A hatchway with two 375 wide x 1570mm high doors was formed in the bathroom wall starting at 780mm from the floor. The top of the hatchway was notched to accommodate the track.

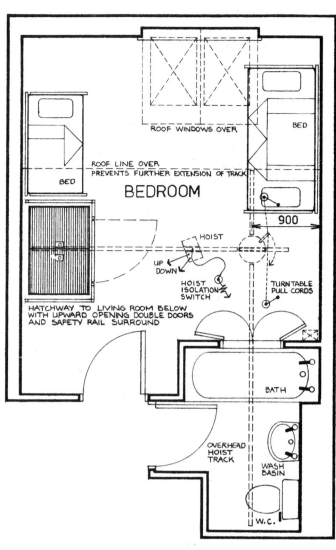

Plan of the turntable hoist arrangement. 1:50.

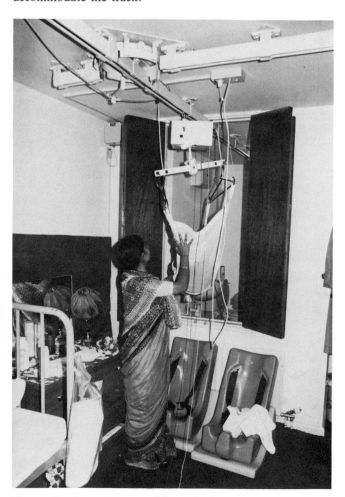

Traversing from the turntable to the bathroom.

Hoisting from the ground floor through the hatchway.

207

P

Kitchens (1)

A STORAGE AND FOOD PREPARATION AREA FOR USE FROM A WHEELCHAIR

* Kitchen units by Hygena.

The principal aim in the design of this kitchen was to provide specific task related areas to promote efficiency and reduce the need for continual wheelchair alignment in moving around the comparatively small room.

A storage and food preparation area was formed along one side of the room, consisting of a corner carousel, deep drawers, low level wall cabinets and work surfaces.

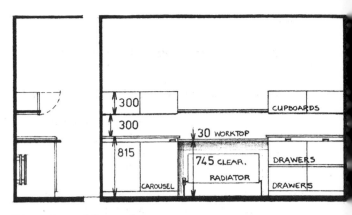

Dimensions of the work area.

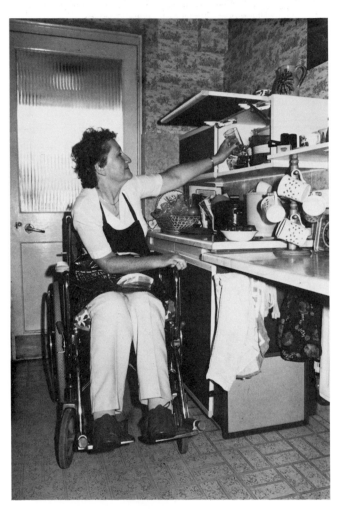

The low level wall cabinets are easily accessible.

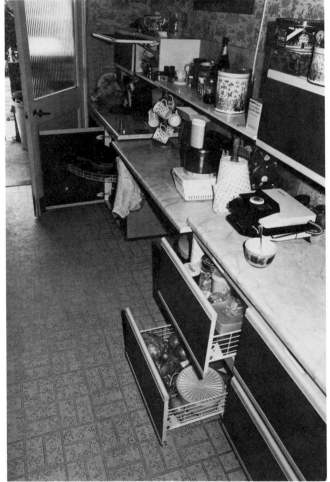

Labour saving appliances and frequently used items are stored on the shelf or the worktops, where they are easily reached from sitting at the 775mm high central work area that has knee room under.

Kitchens (2)

A KITCHEN LAYOUT SUITABLE FOR AMBULANT AND WHEELCHAIR DEPENDENT USERS

* Kitchen layout and units by Optima Benchcraft Limited.

The family required a kitchen that was efficient for the wheelchair user, who had the day to day responsibility for cooking, but which could also comfortably accommodate other members who worked from standing.

A U shaped work area with worktops set at height 820mm was made for the wheelchair user, incorporating pull out worktop and storage baskets, a double oven, hob and sink. All storage units are easy to use, with a variety of drawer depths provided.

A 900mm high worktop with freezer, tumble drier, washing machine and drawers under was fitted to the fourth side of the room for use from standing.

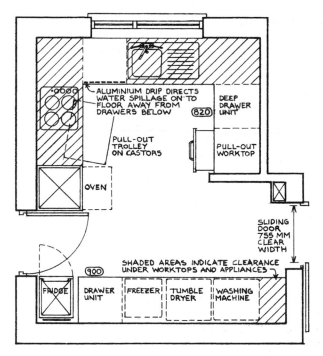

Plan of the kitchen. 1:50.

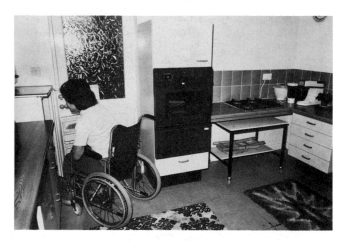

Positioning of the refrigerator is such that the right hinged opening door does not impede access to it. The oven door drops down to the same height as the trolley that also has a recessed lower shelf to give knee room.

Kitchens (3)

AN ADDITIONAL AND OCCASIONAL WORK SURFACE WITHOUT PERMANENT INTERRUPTION OF WHEELCHAIR CIRCULATION IN A SMALL KITCHEN

* Spaceaidor wall table by Panilet Tables.

Insufficient storage was possible in the small kitchen, if knee space was provided under wall mounted work surfaces for access by the wheelchair user.

Floor standing storage was provided at the walls and a 460mm wide x 1170mm long, wall mounted folding table was used to give an accessible work area that opened into the room.

The material used, and the balancing of its own weight, makes the table very light and easy to operate. The top, supported on a drop down, adjustable height leg, is secured by tightening of a wing nut.

The narrow leg does not impede access to or use of the table from a wheelchair and sufficient knee room can be given by adjustment of the table top from 686mm to 762mm, at installation.

When not in use the table folds back leaving the laminated surface to the outside and proud of the wall by 50mm, which neither interferes with wheelchair circulation nor leaves the folding mechanism exposed to risk of catching.

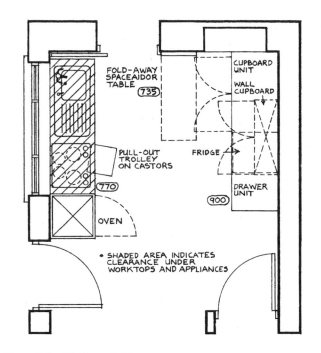

Plan of the kitchen. 1:50.

The three stages in erecting the table.

Kitchens (4)

A KITCHEN FOR THE VISUALLY HANDICAPPED AT THE DISABLED LIVING FOUNDATION

A demonstration centre of kitchen and household layout and equipment where there is opportunity for experimentation and experience of ideas and methods for people with limited or no sight.

Features of the kitchen are:

* Cupboard units with good contrast of colour and texture. Distinct drawer line emphasis of the perimeter. Removal of wall cabinet doors or use of sliding and roller doors remove hazard of bumping into those left half open.

* Areas of kitchen designated for specific tasks to avoid confusion. Use of colour contrasts helps locate utensils on work surfaces.

* Combinations of lighting type, direction and intensity.

* Methods of kitchen organization, identification, labelling and measuring. Storage and anchorage ideas to avoid spillage or loss. Adaptation to and choice of hob, cooker, microwave oven and ways to promote efficiency, safety and correct identification.

* Natural coloured cork tiles with darker coloured border floor covering.

There is opportunity to experiment with various pieces of equipment and layout.

Directional lighting over work areas.

Bathrooms (1)

A ROLL IN SHOWER BASE ON THE FIRST FLOOR

The opportunity to replace a step over shower base with the required roll in type was taken at the time of installation of a replacement through ceiling lift.

Floor boards were removed and the joists notched to give a fall of 20mm to the shower grating in the 1240mm x 1200mm shower area. The floorboards were replaced and the entire floor area covered in 6mm marine plywood. Angled timber fillet pieces were shaped to negotiate the drop into the shower area, and the whole floor was covered in Altro safety flooring taken 120mm up the walls to form waterproof skirting.

A general fall on the floor, caused by inadequate trimming of an earlier aperture for a lift, determined the positioning of the waste outlet in the centre of the floor, thereby utilizing the existing slope. This necessitated a ridge at the main access point to the shower area, which was not as ideal as the corner siting originally planned. It is not, however, a problem to the user and effectively contains water within the area.

The first floor shower.

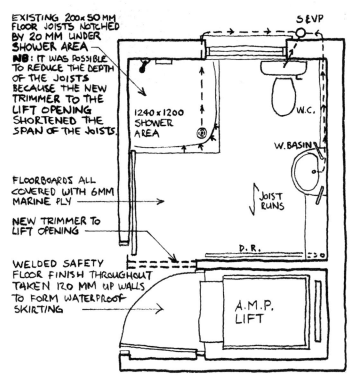

Plan of the shower room. 1:50.

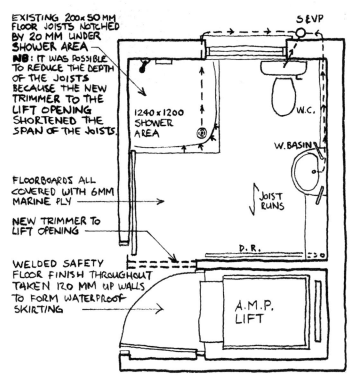212

Bathrooms (2)

A GROUND FLOOR SHOWER WITHIN EXISTING SPACE

Conversion of one reception room to a bedroom, and enlargement of the ground floor cloakroom to allow installation of a shower, enabled use of the stairs to be eliminated.

The side wall to the understairs pantry was removed to open it into the adjacent cloakroom and the door to the pantry from the hall was blocked up.

The concrete floor to the cloakroom was extended and dished to give a level access, walk in shower cubicle.

The width and headroom allowed by the steeply rising stairway gave sufficent space for a stand in shower that met building regulation requirements.

The understairs shower.

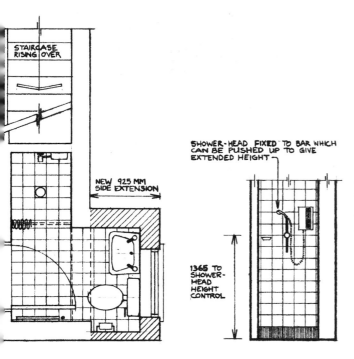

The understairs shower room. 1:50.

213

Bathrooms (3)

INSTALLATION OF A ROLL IN SHOWER WITHIN EXISTING SPACE AND OVERVOMING PROBLEMS OF SPACE AND DRAIN DEPTH LIMITATIONS

* Adaptation of a Chiltern shower base by Andrisa Design and Construction Limited.

Owing to the lack of space, the lack of depth of the existing drain and the high cost of relaying new drainage under an existing solid floor, no satisfactory provision of a dished floor could be made. A Chiltern 100 shower base fitted with an anti flood device was installed as a solution to provide the access required.

There was insufficient space for the waste water to be pumped through the anti flood device into a washing machine type waste outlet, as usually used with this base. Instead the outlet was plumbed into the 100mm soil pipe by means of a 19mm trapped copper waste pipe in place of the rubber pipe. The copper waste pipe was made up on site by the plumber to fit into the very limited space at the rear of the shower base.

The shower area.

The soil/vent pipe was totally encased and the sides of the shower were formed in plasterboard with a ceramic tile finish. The tiles at the base were sealed with bathroom type sealant to ensure that water did not penetrate the plasterboard.

There is no access to the soil/vent pipe from the shower room, but the likelihood of blockages occurring is reduced as the anti flood valve also acts as a filter that can be easily cleaned.

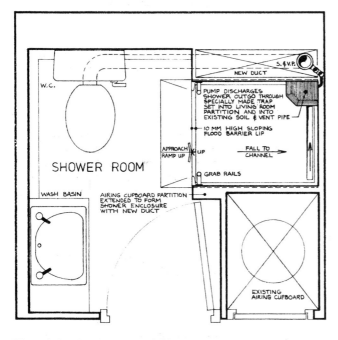

Plan of the shower room. 1:20.

GLOSSARY OF MEDICAL TERMS

Angina pectoris

A pain in the chest, usually arising in connection with diseases of the blood vessels to the heart. An attack occurs when there is unusual demand for blood in the heart muscle, commonly as a result of strenuous activity or excitement.

Arthritis

Inflammation of one or more joints.

Osteoarthritis

'Wear and tear' to the tissue at the ends of bones, causing pain and stiffness of the joint in use. It is most commonly a problem in the large weight bearing joints of the hips and knees, occuring in older age.

Rheumatoid arthritis

A constitutional disease of unknown cause, in which the joint becomes painful and swollen due to inflammation of the joint lining. Eventually, if the disease is uncontained, gross deformity and limitation of joint movement may occur.

Spinal arthritis

Inflammation of joints of the spinal column, usually resulting in stiffness and pain.

Arthrodesis

Surgical fixation of the joint.

Biopsy

Removal and examination of tissue from the body for diagnostic purposes.

Brain damage

Areas of the brain may be damaged before or at birth, or later by injury, disease, infection or impairment of circulation of the brain fluids. As different areas of the brain have distinct functions, symptoms vary greatly according to the extent and level of damage incurred and may affect physical and mental functioning.
See hemiplegia, cerebral palsy.

Cardiac failure

Failure of the heart to properly carry out its task of pumping blood to the organs of the body, because of disease or damage. Symptoms include a build up of fluid in the legs and lower half of the body, and acute breathlessness.

Cataracts

A slow clouding of the lens of the eye, which becomes unable to focus light onto the retina. As the retina transmits the image to the brain, cataracts eventually cause vision to be totally obscured.

Continuous ambulatory peritoneal dialysis

See renal failure.

Cerebral haemorrhage

An escape of blood into the brain. One of the causes of cerebrovascular accident and brain damage.

Cerebral palsy

Damage to the developing brain, usually at birth. Consequential disabilities include poor muscular coordination, weakness and involuntary muscular spasms.

Cerebrovascular accident

Interruption or cessation of blood flow to the brain causing the areas which are starved of blood to become damaged or die. The degree of damage, the areas affected and the amount of recovery which takes place affects the resulting level of disability.
See hemiplegia, brain damage, cerebral haemorrhage.

Chronic bronchitis

Recurrent inflammation of the air passages in the lungs caused by infection. Presents as a persistent, sputum producing cough with difficulty in breathing, usually aggravated by environmental factors such as a cold damp atmosphere and exposure to irritant dust, smoke or fumes.

Disc problems

A disc of cartilage that separates each vertebra of the spinal column, acting as a shock absorber, may become ruptured or displaced and press on the spinal cord or nerve causing pain, loss of sensation or paralysis.

Dystonia muscularum deformans

A rare disease of adolescence, causing grave incapacity and deformity from involuntary muscular contractions, particularly involving the trunk.

Emphysema

A chronic condition in which the air sacs of the lungs become enlarged as they lose their elasticity. As they can no longer effectively expel waste products, blood tends to become overloaded with carbon dioxide causing shortness of breath, wheezy respiration and a susceptability to attacks of bronchitis.

Expressive dysphasia

Difficulty in expressing oneself in speech. It is often a result of a cerebrovascular accident affecting the speech centre of the brain.

Frog plaster

A plaster cast used to temporarily restrain the lower limbs after surgery on hip joints.

Glaucoma

A disease of the eye in which pressure within the eye rises and destroys the visual nerve fibres. In chronic cases, there is gradual loss of vision to blindness.

Haemodialysis

See renal failure.

Hemiplegia/hemiparesis

Paralysis or partial paralysis in which only one side of the body is affected, usually caused by cerebro vascular accident.

Hiatus hernia

A displacement of a portion of the stomach through an opening in the diaphragm.

Incontinence

Emptying of the bladder or bowels at an inappropriate time or in an inappropriate place.

Laminectomy

Surgical operation to remove the arch of a spinal vertebra to expose a portion of the spinal cord for relief of pressure, removal of a growth or similar.

Multiple sclerosis

A disease of the brain and spinal cord, in which scattered patches of the sheaths surrounding nerve fibres are attacked and damaged. Symptoms vary according to the parts affected and progress of the disease is unpredictable, sometimes with recurrent remissions from symptoms. Progression may involve paralysis and rigidity in the limbs, impairment of speech and eyesight, incontinence and uncontrollable muscular spasms.

Myositis ossificans progressiva

A disabling condition due to the formation of bony bars within the muscles. Progress of the disease and consequent disability is variable depending on the muscles affected and the extent of bony tissue present. More muscles become affected with increasing age but life span is not directly affected.

Osteoarthritis

See arthritis.

Parkinsons disease

A slowly progressive disease affecting the part of the brain which controls voluntary movement. Muscles become increasingly rigid with a distinctive gait, mask like facial expression, difficulty initiating functional movement and muscular tremors, which may affect the whole body.

Peripheral neuritis

Inflammation of the nerves in the outlying parts of the body.

Phocomelia

A congenital deformity in which the long bones of the limbs are minimal or absent.

Pneumonia

Acute inflammation of the lungs in which the air sacs become filled with fluid and breathing is affected.

Poliomyelitis

An acute infection involving the brain and spinal cord, sometimes resulting in permanent paralysis of muscles served by those parts of the central nervous system which are affected. Wasting of the paralysed muscles occurs, often seen as a withered limb.

Quadraplegia

When a condition affects all four limbs. See tetraplegia.

Renal failure

The failure of the kidneys to perform their main functions of purifying the blood, by filtering of waste products, and controlling the volume of liquid in the body.

Haemodialysis by use of an artificial kidney provides a medical substitute for the faulty kidneys. In this procedure the patient's blood is circulated through a dialysing membrane into a specially prepared dialysing fluid which restores the normal biochemical balance of the blood. Dialysis takes an average of five hours and must be carried out approximately three times a week, when the patient must sit or lie connected to the dialysis machine. Preparation of the machine for dialysis and cleansing afterwards must be carried out with scrupulous care and attention to detail. Setting up and taking down the machine can add a further two hours to the process.

CAPD: continuous ambulatory peritoneal dialysis is a daily drainage of fluid into and out of the abdomen to achieve the results of dialysis. The body fluids in the peritoneal cavity are removed and replaced, usually four times a day, with two litres of dialysate fluid through a permanently inserted tube. The patient must sit in a comfortable chair for fifteen to twenty minutes of the procedure and use an elevated stand to support the drainage bag, but no machinery is involved and CAPD can be performed anywhere with the appropriate equipment.

Retinitis pigmentosa

An hereditary degenerative disease of the retina, the light sensitive surface on the inside of the eyeball which transmits the image to the brain.

Rheumatoid arthritis

See arthritis.

Scoliosis

Abnormal curvature of the spine.

Senile dementia

Serious impairment or loss of mental capacity, usually accompanied by disturbances in emotion and behaviour.

Spasm

Involuntary contraction of a muscle.

Spasticity

A tendency to spasm; a term usually associated with some condition affecting the parts of the central nervous system influencing movement.
See cerebral palsy, multiple sclerosis, spasm.

Spinal arthritis

See arthritis.

Spinal muscular atrophy

An hereditary condition of varying severity in which wasting of certain muscles occurs; often of the lower limbs and trunk with sparing of the upper limbs. Contraction of joints and other deformities related to posture are likely to develop.

Splenectomy

Surgical removal of the spleen.

Tenodesis grip

Use of the normal mechanics of the action of tendons in the wrist and fingers, to produce flexion of the fingers in a cylindrical grip when the wrist is extended.

Tetraplegia

Paralysis or partial paralysis of all four limbs, usually as a result of damage to the spinal cord. The site of damage determines the exact muscle groups which are inactivated by loss of their nerve supply, the position of the lesion being identified by numbering of individual bones of the spinal column. Hence C5/6 denotes a lesion between the fifth and sixth cervical vertebrae. Some movement and/or feeling in the affected part may be retained if the lesion is incomplete.

Thrombosis

Formation of a blood clot within the heart or blood vessels. This is particularly dangerous if the clot forms within the heart or brain, or if pieces of the clot break away and are circulated in the blood stream to sites where they may become lodged and prevent the further flow of blood. See cerebrovascular accident.

Legislation and regulations

In England and Wales both local social services authorities (London borough councils, metropolitan district councils and county councils) and housing authorities (London borough councils, metropolitan district councils and shire district councils) have powers to assist with house adaptations for disabled people.

Social services authority powers

Social services authorities have a general duty to make arrangements for a house adaptation to be undertaken for a disabled person where a need is established. The relevant powers are in section 29 of the National Assistance Act 1948 and section 2 of the Chronically Sick and Disabled Persons Act 1970.

For the purposes of determining eligibility for assistance, the definition of "disabled person" used by both social services and housing authorities is that contained in section 29(1) of the 1948 Act (as amended) which reads:

> A local authority may, with the approval of the Secretary of State, and to such extent as he may direct in relation to persons ordinarily resident in the area of the local authority make arrangements for promoting the welfare of persons to whom this section applies, that is to say persons who are blind, deaf or dumb, or who suffer from mental disorder of any description and other persons who are substantially and permanently handicapped by illness, injury or congenital deformity or such other disabilities as may be prescribed by the Secretary of State.

With regard to house adaptations, section 2(1) of the 1970 Act makes explicit the duties of social services authorities under the 1948 Act. It reads:

> 2(1) Where a local authority having functions under section 29 of the National Assistance Act 1948 are satisfied in the case of any persons to whom that section applies who is ordinarily resident in their area that it is necessary in order to meet the needs of that person for that authority to make arrangements for all or any of the following matters, namely–
>
> (e) the provision of assistance for that person in arranging for the carrying out of any works of adaptation in his home or the provision of any additional facilities designed to secure his greater safety, comfort or convenience.

Advice is given in the Joint Circular *The Chronically Sick and Disabled Persons Act 1970* (DHSS Circular 12/70, MHLG Circular 65/70) on how a social services authority should assess the need for provision under section 2. Paragraph 7 of the circular reads:

> The duty requires the authority to assess the requirements of individuals determined by them to be substantially and permanently handicapped as to their needs in these matters. If they are satisfied that an individual is in need in any (or all) of these matters, they are to make arrangements that are appropriate to his or her case. The task of assessment should be undertaken as a normal part of the authority's social work service, ie it should be an occasion for considering all relevant needs and not merely those to which the Section refers; and a judgement whether these needs or others are of prior importance should be drawn from a complete and not a partial picture of the situation.

The assessment duties of social services authorities under section 2 of the 1970 Act will be amplified and made more specific when section 3 of the Disabled Persons (Services, Consultation and Representation) Act 1986 is brought into effect; this is dependent on a commencement order, no date for which has at July 1987 been fixed.

Where a social services authority identifies a need under the 1970 Act for a house adaptation, they may arrange to undertake the provision directly, or arrange for it to be undertaken by an appropriate agency acting in co-operation with them and the client concerned. Where the authority assists with funding, the financial status of the client and members of his household may be taken into account. Section 17 of the Health and Social Services and Social Security Adjudication Act 1983 concerns charges for local authority services provided under Section 29 of the 1948 Act among other powers; section 17(3) reads:

If a person:

(a) avails himself of a service to which this section applies and,

(b) satisfies the authority providing the service that his means are insufficient for it to be reasonably practicable for him to pay for the service which he would otherwise be obliged to pay for it, the authority shall not require him to pay more for it than it appears to them that it is reasonably practicable for him to pay.

Housing authority powers

The powers that local housing authorities have to assist with house adaptations for disabled people derive principally from the Housing Acts of 1957, 1974 and 1980. These and other pieces of housing legislation have been consolidated in the Housing Act 1985.

The powers are of two distinct kinds. First, there are those to award improvement grants, which are in Part XV of the 1985 Act. Second, by virtue of sections 8–10 in Part II of the 1985 Act (the main powers and duties of local housing authorities) council house adaptations can be directly funded.

In respect of council house adaptations the powers of social services authorities and housing authorities overlap. With a view to clarifying responsibilities and advising on the procedures that might best assist disabled people, a joint circular *Adaptations of housing for people who are physically handicapped* (DOE 59/78, DHSS LAC (78) 14, Welsh Office 104/78) was issued in 1978. Relevant extracts are from paragraphs 5 and 6:

> Responsibility for identifying, assessing and advising on the housing needs of individual disabled people, including the need for adaption of their homes, should

remain with social services authorities, in collaboration with health authorities.

The Secretaries of State accordingly now ask that . . . . all housing authorities accept responsibility for work involving structural modification of the dwellings owned or managed by them and that responsibility for non-structural features, and the provision of aids and equipment, should rest with social services authorities (or as appropriate health authorities).

Annex 1 to the Circular presents a comprehensive list of items that can be regarded as "structural" features and which, when provided for a disabled person in council housing, are admissible for funding by the housing authority.

Housing associations

Registered housing associations may fund adaptations for disabled people living in dwellings that the association owns. Powers are vested in the Housing Corporation acting as agent for the Secretary of State for the Environment; the Corporation makes grants to housing associations (HAG) for approved projects. The governing legislation derives principally from the Housing Act 1974 and is in Part III (section 75) and Part II (sections 41-53) of the Housing Associations Act 1985.

As with housing authorities, the powers to assist with adaptations for disabled people overlap with those of social services authorities and the position is similar. Paragraph 12 of DOE Circular 59/78 says "The general provisions of this circular relating to the adaptation of existing local authority housing are equally applicable to housing associatitons". Under Housing Corporation procedures housing associations are required to seek the advice of social services authorities on the type of adaptation needed. Housing Corporation Circular 16/86 *Adaptations to dwellings for physically handicapped people* introduced a streamlined procedure for project approval.

Grants for house adaptations

Improvement or intermediate grants may be available under the home improvement grant system for adaptation works required to a dwelling occupied by a disabled person. The legislation relating to these grants is in Part XV of the Housing Act 1985 which consolidated the provisions mainly in Part VII of the Housing Act 1974 and Schedule 12 to the Housing Act 1980. A dwelling for a disabled occupant is defined in Section 518 of the 1985 Act as a dwelling which is the occupant's only or main residence or will become so following completion of the works.

Improvement and intermediate grants

By virtue of Section 518 of the 1985 Act improvement grants are available at the discretion of the local authority for work required to adapt a house for the accommodation, welfare or employment of a disabled occupant.

Under section 474(1)(b) of the 1985 Act intermediate grants may be given towards the cost of works required for the improvement of a dwelling by the provision of a standard amenity where that amenity is missing or where, in the case of a dwelling for a disabled occupant, an existing amenity of the same description is not readily accessible to him by reason of his disability. The standard amenities are: (i) fixed bath or shower, (ii) washbasin, (iii) sink, (iv) hot and cold water supply, and (v) wc.

A local authority may only entertain a grant application provided the following conditions are met:

(i) The applicant has the necessary title to the dwelling, ie has a freehold or leasehold interest with at least five years unexpired, or is a tenant as defined in section 463(3) of the 1985 Act.

(ii) The applicant must provide a certificate of future occupation. An owner occupier would have to certify that the dwelling would be occupied for a period of five years by him and members of his household or a member of his family. A landlord would have to certify that for a period of five years the dwelling would be let or available for letting as a residence and not for a holiday, to a person other than a member of his family.

Intermediate grants are mandatory provided that all the normal qualifying conditions are met. They are available at 75 per cent of the eligible expense or 90 per cent if the local authority considers that the applicant could not meet his share of the work without undue hardship. The eligible expense is the cost of work required for the provision of a standard amenity or the relevant eligible expense limit whichever is the lower. The eligible expense limits are from time to time raised by the Department of Environment; at present (July 1987) they are

	Outside London	In Greater London
	£	£
A fixed bath or shower	340	450
The water supply to a bath or shower	430	570
A wash hand basin	130	175
The water supply to a basin	230	300
A sink in the kitchen	340	450
The water supply to the sink	290	380
A wc	515	680

The local authority must award an intermediate grant if the application fulfils the conditions. Where an application is made for an intermediate grant, the grant may also be given for works of repair or replacement needed to put the dwelling into a state of reasonable repair. It may be more advantageous for a disabled person to apply for an improvement grant, however, because the eligible expense limits are higher in relation to such grants.

Improvement grants are discretionary and local authorities can approve grant in such circumstances as they see fit. They are able to approve grant up to a maximum of 75 per cent (or 90 per cent for those in hardship) of the eligible expense. The current eligible expense limits for improvement grants are £13,800 in Greater London and £10,200 elsewhere. Thus larger sums are available by way of improvement grant than inter-mediate grant, but only at the discretion of the local authority.

Hardship addition

The Department of the Environment advised local authorities on the enhanced rate of grant for those in hardship in paragraph 10 of Appendix B of Circular 21/80 *Housing Acts 1974 and 1980: Improvement of older Housing*:

> The appropriate percentage may be increased from 75 per cent to 90 per cent where it appears to the local authority that the applicant would not be able to pay his share of the cost of the works without undue hardship. It is for the local authority to determine what constitutes undue hardship, but some guidance may be helpful. The onus usually rests with applicants to show why exceptional help towards the cost of the work is necessary to avoid undue hardship, and a statement of the financial resources of any such applicants should, therefore, normally be expected.

> Many people, especially the elderly, are reluctant to divulge their financial resources. Local authorities are advised, therefore, to emphasise that any information they receive will be treated in the strictest confidence— and so to treat it. Favourable consideration should generally be given to applicants whose financial resources would qualify them for supplementary benefit or family income supplement, even if such benefit has not been claimed; and, although criteria related to income, upon which eligibility for rate rebate is assessed, are not necessarily a true reflection of ability to meet capital expenditure, many of those qualifying for rate rebate are unlikely to have adequate savings to meet their normal share of the cost or have sufficient income to bear without stress the loan charges that would arise if they resorted to borrowing. Finally, very sympathetic consideration should be given to any applicant whose principal source of income consists of a state retirement or disability pension.

Paragraph 5 of DOE Circular 36/81 *Housing Act 1974: House Renovation Grants for the Disabled* advises that the higher appropriate percentage and "category A" eligible expense limits for grants for disabled people apply not only to works specifically needed by a disabled occupant, but also for any other eligible work of improvement and/or repair included in the grant application. The advice is that local authorities may wish to exercise their discretion to approve grant at less than the prescribed percentage where a significant proportion of the eligible work is not directly related to the needs of the disabled occupant.

Second or subsequent grants

Paragraph 7 or Circular 36/81 advises that where a second or subsequent grant is sought for the adaptation of a dwelling for a disabled occupant, authorities should treat such applications as though no previous grant had been made for the dwelling when calculating the amount of grant to be approved.

Central government funding

The local authority will normally receive 90 per cent of the loan charges incurred in making the grant from central government. The capital expenditure, however, still has to be met within the authority's total resources.

Dwellings under construction

With regard to dwellings under construction, paragraph 21 of DOE Circular 26/85 *Housing Acts 1974 and 1980: Home Improvement Grants* advises:

> Under Part XV of the 1985 Act, works qualify for grants only if they are works required for the improvement, repair or conversion of an existing building. Improvement grants are therefore not available to enable works of adaptation to be carried out to dwellings under construction.

Grants for flats and common parts

Paragraphs 11–16 of Circular 26/85 advise on grants for flats and common parts. Section 15 of and Schedule 3 to the Housing and Planning Act 1986 contain provision for a new common parts grant that may be given to make the common parts suitable for the use of a disabled occupant of a dwelling in the building.

Grants for Council tenants

Home improvement grants are available for secure tenants under Section 463 of the 1985 Act. In the case of a council tenant a local authority cannot be a party to the contracting of grant-aided adaptation works, but may arrange for some other person or body to act as agent on behalf of a disabled person. Where a council tenant receives a grant, the social services authority may, at its discretion, meet all or part of the applicant's share of the cost under its powers under Section 2 of the 1970 Act. The circular letter *Housing Acts 1974, 1980 and 1985 Home Improvement Grants* issued to local authorities by the Department of the Environment on 26 March 1986 advised that if housing authorities similarly contribute to the applicant's share, they may claim Exchequer contribution towards the cost incurred in making the grant; this was an exception to the advice regarding Exchequer contribution in paragraphs 27–29 of Circular 26/85.

Housing associations

As secure tenants under Section 463 of the 1985 Act housing association tenants may also apply for improvement grants, but the normal route for funding housing association adaptations is HAG, as noted above.

Dialysis Adaptations

District health authorities are responsible for any necessary adaptations directly related to the installation of home dialysis equipment, as advised in paragraph 21 of DOE Circular 59/78. In exceptional circumstances a local authority may use their discretion to approve an improvement grant for work required to adapt or provide a room housing home dialysis equipment where they consider that such an adaptation is needed to make the house suitable for the accommodation or welfare of a disabled person.

Building regulations approval

Where in the course of adapting a house for a disabled person modifications are made to the structure of the dwelling, the works undertaken must comply with the requirements of the Building Regulations 1985. As a rule approval will not be required for the ramping of a dwelling entrance, the replacement of kitchen or bathroom fixtures or fittings or the installation of a stairlift, but might need to be obtained for the relocation of kitchen or bathroom fixtures or the installation of a vertical home lift. In cases of doubt advice should be sought from the building control officer of the local housing authority.

Planning permission

So long as the overall use of the house is not changed planning permission is not required for internal modifications designed to assist disabled people. Adaptations or extensions affecting the external appearance of a house will mostly amount to development requiring planning permission, but the Town and Country Planning General Development Order 1977 (as amended) grants a general permission for a wide range of such works and these can therefore be undertaken without the need to make a planning application. A free booklet prepared by the Department of the Environment: *Planning Permission, A guide for Householders** sets out the "permitted development" tolerances. It will very often be possible to build an extension to provide ground floor sleeping accommodation, to install a hardstanding for a car and a porch or carport to provide protection from the weather, or to erect a shed or outhouse in the garden to accommodate essential medical equipment without the specific permission of the local planning authority. Permitted development rights are occasionally withdrawn however, and it is therefore worth checking the position with the planning officer of the local district council before starting work.

Listed buildings and conservation areas

If a building is on the statutory list of buildings of special architectural or historic interest (usually called "listed buildings"), listed building consent is needed before it is demolished (whether totally or partially), altered or extended in any way which affects its character as a listed building. This control applies to planning permission. As it is a criminal offence to carry out work without getting consent, the local authority (district council or London borough council) should be consulted before any adaptation work is undertaken.

In conservation areas, consent is needed before an unlisted building is totally or partially demolished. Consent is not, however, required for alterations and extensions.

The right to buy

Where a local authority dwelling is to be adapted for a disabled tenant and where the housing authority contracts the works (rather than awarding an improvement grant) there may be circumstances where the right of the tenant to buy his house is affected. Paragraph 8 of Schedule 5 of the Housing Act 1985 says:

The right to buy does not arise if the landlord or a predecessor of the landlord has carried out, for the purpose of making the dwelling-house suitable for

occupation by physically disabled persons, one or more of the following alterations—

(a) the provision of not less than 7.5 square metres of additional floor space;

(b) the provision of an additional bathroom or shower-room;

(c) the installation of a vertical lift.

Where one of these conditions may occur, the tenant should seek advice from his local housing authority.

---

*Obtainable from local planning authorities or direct from the Department's Distribution Section, Building 3, Victoria Road, South Ruislip HA4 ON2.

Printed by HMSO, Edinburgh Press
Dd 024003 C30 4/88 (244787)